eBook and Digital
Course Materials for

e-  als

T0043777

Hard Road to Freedom

The Story of
Black America
Volume One: to 1896

Lois E. Horton
James Oliver Horton

**This code can be used only
once and cannot be shared!**

Carefully scratch off the silver
coating to see your personal
redemption code.

If the code has been scratched
off when you receive it, the
code may not be valid. Once
the code has been scratched
off, this access card cannot be
returned to the publisher. You
may buy access at
www.oup.com/he/horton1e.

The code on this card is valid for
2 years from the date of first
purchase. Complete terms
and conditions are available at
learninglink.oup.com.

Access length: 6 months from
redemption of the code.

OXFORD
UNIVERSITY PRESS

VIA ☺ learning link

Visit **www.oup.com/he/horton1e**

▼

Select the edition you are using and
the student resources for that edition.

▼

Click the link to upgrade your access
to the student resources.

▼

Follow the on-screen instructions.

▼

Enter your personal
redemption code when prompted.

VIA YOUR SCHOOL'S LEARNING MANAGEMENT SYSTEM

Log in to your instructor's course.

▼

When you click a link to a protected resource,
you will be prompted to register for access.

▼

Follow the on-screen instructions.

▼

Enter your personal
redemption code when prompted.

For assistance with code redemption
or registration, please contact customer
support at **learninglink.support@oup.com.**

About the Cover

Theodor Kaufmann, *On to Liberty* (1867), Metropolitan Museum of Art

A German artist, Kaufmann emigrated to the United States after participating in the failed popular 1848 revolution in Germany. He became a U.S. soldier and correspondent artist during the Civil War. This painting depicts a group setting off from plantation slavery along a dirt road during the war in hope of gaining freedom. The women's brightly colored clothing, beads, and the bundles carried on their heads reflect their African cultural heritage. Such escapes were particularly arduous and dangerous for families with children.

HARD ROAD TO
FREEDOM

HARD ROAD TO
FREEDOM

THE STORY OF BLACK AMERICA

**VOLUME 1
TO 1896**

Lois E. Horton
James Oliver Horton

New York   Oxford
Oxford University Press

Oxford University Press is a department of the University of Oxford.
It furthers the University's objective of excellence in research, scholarship,
and education by publishing worldwide. Oxford is a registered trade mark of
Oxford University Press in the UK and certain other countries.

Published in the United States of America by Oxford University Press
198 Madison Avenue, New York, NY 10016, United States of America.

For titles covered by Section 112 of the US Higher Education Opportunity
Act, please visit www.oup.com/us/he for the latest information about
pricing and alternate formats.

Library of Congress Cataloging-in-Publication Data

Names: Horton, Lois E., author. | Horton, James Oliver, author.
Title: Hard road to freedom : the story of Black America / Lois E. Horton,
    James Oliver Horton.
Description: New York : Oxford University Press, [2022] | Include
bibliographical references and index. | Contents: Volume one. To 1896 |
    Summary: "A higher education history textbook on the story of Black
    Americans in the United States"—Provided by publisher.
Identifiers: LCCN 2020057932 (print) | LCCN 2020057933 (ebook) | ISBN
    9780197564806 (v. 1 ; paperback) | ISBN 9780197564813 (v. 1 ; looseleaf) |
    ISBN 9780197564844 (v. 2 ; paperback) | ISBN 9780197564851
    (v. 2 ; looseleaf) | ISBN 9780197564837 (v. 1 ; epub) | ISBN 9780197564875
    (v. 2; epub) | ISBN 9780197567326 (epub ; combined ebook) | ISBN
    9780197567319 | ISBN 9780197564820 | ISBN 9780197564868
Subjects: LCSH: African Americans—History—Textbooks.
Classification: LCC E185 .H6446 2022 (print) | LCC E185 (ebook) | DDC
    973/.0496073—dc23
LC record available at https://lccn.loc.gov/2020057932
LC ebook record available at https://lccn.loc.gov/2020057933

Printing number: 9 8 7 6 5 4 3 2 1
Printed by LSC Communications, United States of America

Brief Contents

Contents

List of Maps

Profile

Documenting Black America

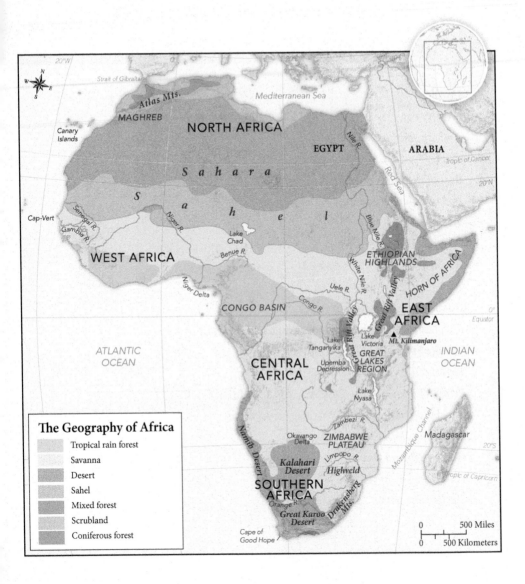

The Geography of Africa

- Tropical rain forest
- Savanna
- Desert
- Sahel
- Mixed forest
- Scrubland
- Coniferous forest

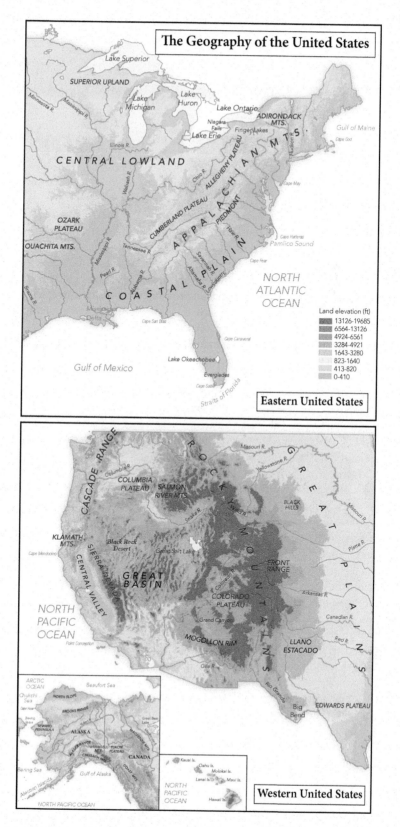

The Geography of the United States

Eastern United States

Lake Superior

SUPERIOR UPLAND

Minnesota R.

Mississippi R.

Lake Michigan

Lake Huron

Lake Ontario

Niagara Falls

Finger Lakes

ADIRONDACK MTS.

Gulf of Maine

Cape Cod

Illinois R.

CENTRAL LOWLAND

Ohio R.

ALLEGHENY PLATEAU

Wabash R.

Hudson R.

APPALACHIAN MTS.

CUMBERLAND PLATEAU

PIEDMONT

Cape May

OZARK PLATEAU

OUACHITA MTS.

Tennessee R.

Mississippi R.

Alabama R.

Savannah R.

Tennessee R.

Cape Hatteras

Pamlico Sound

Pearl R.

COASTAL PLAIN

Altamaha R.

Lowcountry

Cape Fear

NORTH ATLANTIC OCEAN

Brazos R.

Mississippi Delta

Cape San Blas

Cape Canaveral

Gulf of Mexico

Lake Okeechobee

Everglades

Cape Sable

Straits of Florida

Land elevation (ft)

- 13126-19685
- 6564-13126
- 4924-6561
- 3284-4921
- 1643-3280
- 823-1640
- 413-820
- 0-410

Western United States

CASCADE RANGE

Columbia R.

COLUMBIA PLATEAU

SALMON RIVER MTS.

Missouri R.

Yellowstone R.

ROCKY MOUNTAINS

GREAT PLAINS

BLACK HILLS

Snake R.

Missouri R.

KLAMATH MTS.

Cape Mendocino

SIERRA NEVADA

Black Rock Desert

Great Salt Lake

Platte R.

Snake R.

FRONT RANGE

CENTRAL VALLEY

GREAT BASIN

Colorado R.

COLORADO PLATEAU

Arkansas R.

NORTH PACIFIC OCEAN

Point Conception

Grand Canyon

MOGOLLON RIM

LLANO ESTACADO

Canadian R.

Red R.

Gila R.

Rio Grande

Big Bend

EDWARDS PLATEAU

ARCTIC OCEAN

Beaufort Sea

Chukchi Sea

Cape Hope

NORTH SLOPE

BROOKS RANGE

Great Bear Lake

Bering Strait

SEWARD PENINSULA

ALASKA

MACKENZIE MTS.

ALASKA RANGE

WRANGELL MTS.

YUKON PLATEAU

CANADA

CHUGACH MTS.

COAST MTS.

Bering Sea

Gulf of Alaska

Aleutian Islands

NORTH PACIFIC OCEAN

Kauai Is.

Oahu Is.

Molokai Is.

Lanai Is.

Maui Is.

NORTH PACIFIC OCEAN

Hawaii Is.

Hard Road to Freedom

Telling the Story of Black America

Hard Road to Freedom tells the story of Black people in America as an expression of one of the nation's fundamental principles, the pursuit of freedom. It fashions a narrative from an African American perspective and brings together stories formerly told separately. This interweaving depicts African Americans' part in the creation of American history and culture. It is a social and cultural history, as well as a political history, incorporating the story of music from spirituals to jazz and hip hop and literature from slave narratives to poets and contemporary novelists.

People are often surprised, fascinated, even shocked, when they first learn about the history of African Americans. Sometimes outraged, they demand to know why they haven't heard this story before. Why did their textbooks ignore the dramatic tales of the Black experience—the ways Gabriel Prosser or Nat Turner rebelled against slavery; the inventive and heroic escapes of William and Ellen Craft or Harriet Tubman; the accomplishments of Fredrick Douglass or Madame C.J. Walker; the bravery of such Freedom Riders as John Lewis; or the sacrifice and determination of Fannie Lou Hamer? Why has no one told this story? It is true that for most of the country's history, general American history textbooks and courses paid little attention to this aspect of American history, save for a few references to slavery, usually discussed in connection with the period just before the Civil War. But it is not true that the story of Black America has not been told.

Black people told their own stories again and again during their time in America. Over more than four hundred years, they told it in stories to the next generation; they told it in oral testimony, in written petitions to the government, in autobiographical narratives, in poetry and song, in dance and religious ceremonies. In an autobiography published in 1760, Briton Hammon told of his enslavement in New England, his shipwreck in Florida, his imprisonment by the Spaniards, and his service aboard a British warship. In the many autobiographies that followed, Africans and African Americans recounted their lives in West Africa, and they remembered African history and culture. They described the horrors of capture and enslavement, and the restrictions on those who gained a limited freedom. Published at the end of the eighteenth century, the influential autobiography by the African Olaudah Equiano related how he had been captured and brought to America when he was only eleven years old.[1]

A flood of slave narratives telling the stories of African Americans who had experienced the inhumanity of slavery was published in the early and mid-nineteenth century, becoming a powerful weapon in the fight against slavery during the decades before the Civil War. Some formerly enslaved people—Frederick Douglass, Nat Turner, Harriet Jacobs, William Wells Brown, and Jarena Lee among them—wrote or dictated widely read autobiographies that countered proslavery propaganda. James W.C. Pennington, an enslaved blacksmith and carpenter who taught himself to read and write, wrote two books after he escaped from slavery in 1827. The first, a general African American history called *A Textbook of the Origin and History of Colored People*, was used in the Free African School in Hartford, Connecticut. Since he was still a fugitive from slavery, he had to flee to Britain after his 1849 autobiography, *The Fugitive Blacksmith*, revealed his identity and location. In the 1850s William Cooper Nell, a free Black man and community activist in Boston, published two histories detailing the role of African Americans in the Revolution: *The Services of Colored Americans in the Wars of 1776 and 1812* (1851) and *Colored Patriots of the American Revolution* (1855). Nell hoped to counter charges that Black people had no history worth recording and to establish Black entitlement to American freedom and citizenship.[2]

Other African American histories followed. Formerly enslaved autobiographer William Wells Brown published *The Black Man: His Antecedents, His Genius, and His Achievements* in 1863. He followed this with several works of fiction and a play dealing with race during the Civil War. George Washington Williams's landmark *History of the Negro Race in America*, published in 1882, influenced most of the important chroniclers of the African American experience who came afterward. Williams carefully documented his work with extensive footnotes, hoping to prevent his account of the role and accomplishments of African Americans from being dismissed as propaganda or wishful thinking. More than a half century later, when John Hope Franklin was preparing his classic study, *From Slavery to Freedom*, he was so impressed with Williams's scholarship that he would one day write his biography.[3]

Scholarly African American histories, biographies, and autobiographies continued to flourish in the early decades of the twentieth century. W.E.B. Du Bois published his Harvard University doctoral dissertation, *The Suppression of the African Slave-Trade*, in 1896 and went on to produce a host of important historical and sociological studies. DuBois's work ranged from a landmark analysis of the Reconstruction period after the Civil War to a study of the Black community in Philadelphia that anticipated the mid-twentieth century social history movement. Carter G. Woodson, born in West Virginia one generation from slavery, earned a Ph.D. from Harvard University in 1912. Determined to raise popular awareness of the contributions of Black people to America, he organized the Association for the Study of Negro Life and History in 1915 and established the *Journal of Negro History*. Historians Charles H. Wesley, Luther Porter Jackson, Lorenzo J. Greene, and

L.D. Reddick were among the first Black scholars to publish articles in this journal. The journal also made many important historical documents available for study.

Meanwhile, such Black institutions of higher learning as Howard University, Fisk University, and Morehouse College began offering courses in Negro History, and in 1926 Woodson and his organization established Negro History Week, an observance which eventually became Black History Month. Celebrated at first almost exclusively in Black schools and churches, this one-week observance introduced Black history into school curricula, encouraged the publication of work dealing with African Americans, and stimulated the Black press and a few white newspapers to run related stories. By the 1930s the federal government aided this work with the Federal Writers Project of the Works Progress Administration, gathering the recollections of elderly people who had lived in slavery before 1865. Until World War II there were few Black Ph.D.s in the field of history—by 1940 only eighteen, more than half of whom had earned their degrees at Harvard University and the University of Chicago. Among the recipients were Rufus Clement, Benjamin Quarles, and John Hope Franklin. Along with those still active from the earlier years, these scholars set the stage for a major breakthrough in the study of African American history. Their advances in the field were capped by the publication of Franklin's *From Slavery to Freedom* in 1948.[4]

Black scholars played a critical role in the Supreme Court's *Brown* decision, which struck down the concept of "separate but equal" in 1954, fueling the postwar drive for civil rights. Their work, which laid the foundation for arguments for racial equality by challenging the segregationist assumptions that dismissed the importance of Black people to the nation, presented historical evidence placing Black people squarely in the center of the American experience. White scholars, too, contributed to this work during the 1950s. Kenneth Stampp and Stanley Elkins corrected earlier contentions that slavery was a benign institution. Likewise, studies focused on the history of slavery were especially relevant to policy discussions during the civil rights era, and by the late 1960s, federal social policy advisors debated whether the destructive effects of slavery served as an explanation for twentieth-century African American poverty. Some scholars argued that slavery had robbed Black people of their African heritage, disturbed Black family and community values, and left them without a culture. The debates inspired a new generation of historians to undertake social historical studies to examine the validity of such claims. Young scholars called for a "history from the bottom up" that broadened the vision of America to include those at the lower socioeconomic levels of society.

During the 1970s studies of slavery established the existence of a slave community, a social and cultural space that allowed enslaved people to resist much of slavery's destructive intent. Studies by such historians as John Blassingame, Herbert Gutman, and Eugene Genovesse provided convincing evidence of the resilience of African American families and culture. Lawrence Levine's study of Black folklore and culture proved conclusively that Black people had shaped a remarkably rich social and cultural life and had preserved a considerable African heritage. By the 1980s African American history had moved beyond demonstrating the significance of Black contributions and celebrating the first

Black achievers. Newer works took up DuBois's task—the study and analysis of Black communities and culture—with modern research techniques and technologies. Important studies of Boston, Cleveland, Detroit, Philadelphia, Providence, New York, and many other Black communities began to illuminate the often-obscured interior world of Black urban America, and a few investigated Black rural life. Works of political history drew on social data to describe and analyze race in America in new and valuable ways.

The decades of the late-twentieth and early-twenty-first centuries brought a profusion of works that extended the breadth and depth of African American history. Much research focused on the experiences of Black people, from people enslaved in particular times and places, through periods of racial progress and during setbacks, to social and political movements organized for Black advancement. Other works examined Black experiences as part of an analysis of the creation and maintenance of such institutions as slavery, work, healthcare, immigration, family, and gender roles. This scholarship has given us a fuller, more useful understanding of the historical experience of African Americans. In our 1997 book, *In Hope of Liberty*, we attempted to add to this scholarship by investigating the lives and relationships of northern Black people during the eighteenth and early nineteenth centuries and also by showing that African American culture helped create the general American culture developing during that time. Our aim in that book was to link the historical experience of Black people to that of other Americans, making the point that no American history happened in isolation from other American experiences. We have tried to continue that theme in this book.

The Hard Road to Freedom: Briefly Told

Hard Road to Freedom begins with African cultures and the slave trade in which countless Africans lost their freedom. Those speaking out against the trade that dominated New World development and created so much wealth were voices crying out in a wilderness of greed and economic windfall. The evolution of American slavery is the recapitulation of the development and codification of the American system of racial slavery and the story of cultural resistance to the hardening system.

The age of the Revolution brought the promise of African American freedom, raised along with the colonists' cries of liberty. Whether Black men fought for the British or for the independence of the new American nation, they were fighting for their own freedom. For them the Revolution was an antislavery struggle, which freed more African Americans than did any other act before the Civil War. In its aftermath the nation was regionally divided by the issue of slavery or freedom. In newly formed northern Black communities, African Americans called on the country to live up to its founding principles, while in the South, slavery expanded its territory, tightened its grip, and increasingly stifled dissent.

Enslaved people resisted a hardening bondage, forming communities of support that sustained the hope of freedom in desolate times. They found encouragement in the increasing strength of antislavery voices. Slavery's opponents saw the Civil War as a second American Revolution, a blow for freedom that would complete the first. Though the sacrifice and anguish of war did end slavery, they brought an ambiguous freedom. The promise of Reconstruction faded into southern sharecropping and segregation, policed by organized terrorism.

At the turn of the twentieth century, reformers focused on economic freedom. Progressive movements struggled to create interracial alliances among farmers and industrial workers, and Black people pursued strategies for the internal development of economic and political institutions. As expanding industries drew more African Americans north, a cultural renaissance in northern cities gave voice to sophisticated and varied forms of self-expression that broadened arguments for Black freedom. The Great Depression of the 1930s was especially devastating for Black communities, but it also created the opportunity for new alliances between the growing numbers of poor displaced laborers.

World War II made the dangers of racism abroad clear, and America's domestic racial policy became an international embarrassment in the context of a Cold War competition with Communism for the loyalty of the world's people of color. African American soldiers had fought for a double victory, to bring freedom to the world and equality at home. Their demands and expectations helped spawn a massive modern civil rights movement that gathered force during the post–World War II period, seeking freedom first through the courts and then through nonviolent protest. Martin Luther King, Jr., became the best-known spokesman for the movement, marshaling the moral power of the nation's principles, but masses of Black and white people raised their voices together, speaking truth to power.

Southern resistance to civil rights demands, the federal government's equivocal support, its distraction by the Vietnam War, and the assassinations of progressive leaders, including Martin Luther King, Jr., deepened the anger and widened divisions in the movement by the late 1960s. Voices of rage demanded "freedom now." With the war abroad and riots and upheaval at home, a political backlash brought into power racial and economic conservatives who advocated the strategy of a "colorblind" emphasis on individual rights in their acrimonious debates with those pleading for a continued focus on racial equality.

A long period of politically conservative power brought tax and budget policies that exacerbated economic inequality under presidents of both parties, even while opportunities resulting from the gains of the civil rights movement increased the numbers and standing of the Black middle class. As conservatives carried on the long tradition of blaming crime and poverty on poor Black people, progress, including the increased visibility and prominence of African Americans in popular culture, seemed to fuel white racial resentments and prompt charges of "reverse discrimination."

By the twenty-first century, more Americans were aware of the nation's racial and cultural diversity and its multiracial past. Greater awareness in Black society also supported demands for economic equity and racial justice in legal policies and treatment by police. A devastating attack in New York City by Middle Eastern terrorists briefly brought Americans together but also drew the nation into controversial wars in Iraq and Afghanistan that, along with an economic crisis threatening world-wide depression, ultimately exposed the nation's longstanding racial and economic fault lines.

Out of this maelstrom was elected the nation's first African American president. Barack Obama, a man of mixed race born in Hawaii, campaigned on the theme of hope and promised to bring people together. His decisive victory was hailed by many as the harbinger of a new racial renaissance. Obama's young First Family did bring a new style and an awareness of Black history and culture to the White House, but it soon became clear that his proposals would face solid Republican opposition. The fact of his presidency also fueled white resentment that brought a backlash in the next election.

Centuries of scholarship and activism have made it clear to many Americans that African American history is a critical part of American history and that African Americans have figured prominently in the creation of American culture. Indeed, African American history is American history, made in America by Americans. Throughout that history, Black Americans have called the nation to live up to its founding principles. Awareness of the quest for racial justice and equality can help advance African Americans, all Americans, and the nation itself along the hard road to freedom.

Digital Resources that Enhance the Learning Experience with *Hard Road to Freedom*

Oxford University Press offers a complete package of digital resources for students and teachers:

Enhanced eBook

Every new copy of *Hard Road to Freedom*, print or electronic, comes with a code that provides access to digital resources designed to enhance student engagement with the Black American experience, including an eBook enhanced with these features:
- Interactive timelines
- Matching activities
- Flashcards
- Quizzes
- Notetaking guides
- Links to videos, primary sources, and interactive maps

Oxford Learning Link

https://learninglink.oup.com/

Adopters of *Hard Road to Freedom* have access to the Oxford Learning Link, where they can download a computerized test-item file, primary sources, videos from the OUP US History Video Library, and PowerPoint slides of all the images and maps in the text, as well as additional slide decks from the OUP Image Library.

Oxford Learning Link Direct

For those instructors who wish to integrate Oxford's instructor and student learning resources directly into their campus's learning management system (LMS), an interoperable course cartridge can be installed. Contact your local OUP sales representative for details.

Volumes and Formats

To accommodate a wide range of teaching calendars, course sequences, and reading preferences: *Hard Road to Freedom* is available in different volumes and formats:

- **Combined Volume**—Chapters 1–17
  Enhanced eBook: ISBN 9780197567326
- **Volume One**—Chapters 1–8
  Paperback: ISBN 9780197564806
  Looseleaf: ISBN 9780197564813
  Enhanced eBook: ISBN 9780197564837
- **Volume Two**—Chapters 8–17
  Paperback: ISBN 9780197564844
  Looseleaf: ISBN 9780197564851
  Enhanced eBook: ISBN 9780197564875

The enhanced eBook can be purchased from VitalSouce, RedShelf, Chegg, and other vendors.

---

[1] William L. Andrews, *To Tell A Free Story: The First Century of Afro-American Autobiography, 1760-1865* (Urbana, IL: University of Illinois University Press, 1986).

[2] R.J.M. Blackett, *Beating Against the Barriers: Biographical Essays in Nineteenth-Century Afro-American History* (Baton Rouge, LA: Louisiana State University Press, 1986); James Oliver Horton and Lois E. Horton, *Black Bostonians: Family Life and Community Struggle in the Antebellum North* (1979; New York: Holmes and Meier Publishers Inc., 1999).

[3] John Hope Franklin, *George Washington Williams: A Biography* (Chicago: University of Chicago Press, 1985).

[4] Northwestern University awarded the Ph.D. in history to Rufus Clement in 1930; Benjamin Quarles received his doctorate from the University of Wisconsin in 1940; and John Hope Franklin received his Ph.D. in history from Harvard University in 1941.

Acknowledgements

In the course of first researching and writing this book, a host of friends and colleagues provided support and assistance. It began with a project we undertook with Norbert Finzsch—a book on African American history for German readers. John Vlach, Allen Isaacman, Laurence Glasco, William Chafe, James Grossman, Denise Meringolo, Stephanie Batiste, Michele Gates-Morese, and Paul Gardullo read manuscript chapters and offered valuable suggestions. Rod Paolini shared his personal experience and knowledge of Chicago politics. Batiste and Candice Hewitt also assisted us with the seemingly unending picture research. Many archivists and librarians around the country provided invaluable assistance. Students in classes at George Mason University reacted to early chapters, and faculty and students at the George Washington University's American Studies Department provided useful insights into history and American culture. Thanks to the George Washington University and the National Museum of American History at the Smithsonian Institution for partial funding of this project.

This edition owes much to the enthusiasm and work of Charles Cavaliere, Executive Editor at Oxford University Press, his assistant, Danica Donovan, and their staff. Special thanks goes to the readers for Oxford University Press for their thoughtful reading and invaluable suggestions based on the first edition of this work. Sadly, James Oliver Horton was not available for the preparation of the revised edition, which remains true to the original vision. I am greatly indebted to discussions over the years with many talented colleagues, including Raymond Arsenault, David Blight, Lonnie Bunch, James Grossman, Andrea Mosterman, Carla Peterson, Dwight Pitcaithley, Richard Rabinowitz, Suzanne Smith, Britta Waldschmidt-Nelson, and Michelle Zacks. I am also thankful to Manuela Thurner, for her informal long time research assistance. On the new chapters, I am especially grateful to Michael Horton for his keen editorial eye and to Nancy Weiss Hanrahan for her encouragement and astute sociological analysis. Finally, my gratitude goes to Danielle Horton-Geer, a superb and knowledgeable research assistant, reader, and commenter, and to Alex Horton-Geer, an avid student of African American history. By this edition, they have grown up to understand their place in this story.

REVIEWERS

Kibibi V. Mack-Shelton, *University of Massachusetts—Boston*
Laurie Lahey, *University of South Florida*
Bianka Stumpf, *Central Carolina Community College*
Dann J. Broyld, *Central Connecticut State University*
Angela Flounory, *University of Michigan—Dearborn*

HARD ROAD TO
FREEDOM

Africa and the Atlantic Slave Trade

This 1643 portrait by the Dutch painter Jasper Becx shows Don Miguel de Castro of Soyo. Don Miguel was sent by Soyo as an envoy to the Dutch Republic to ask for mediation in a conflict the small principality had with the much bigger Kingdom of Kongo.

1

CHAPTER OUTLINE

West Africa

1.1 Place African American history in the context of African history. Identify the empires and states of West Africa and the customs and beliefs that characterized them.

Europeans and the African Slave Trade

1.2 Understand how European traders fit into the existing politics of African nations.

The Middle Passage

1.3 Summarize the conditions of enslaved Africans in the Middle Passage.

Growth of the African Slave Trade

1.4 Understand the reasons for the increase of the slave trade from the sixteenth through the eighteenth centuries. Analyze the impact of the slave trade on the Atlantic economy.

★ **OLAUDAH, WHOSE NAME** meant "the fortunate one," was born in 1745 to an elder among the Ibo (also called Igbo) people living in Benin, the eastern area of present day Nigeria, in West Africa. **Olaudah Equiano** was his full name, although later in his life he would also be called Gustavus Vassa. His first few years were fortunate indeed. Indulged as his mother's favorite, he was the youngest son in a large family of comfortable means in a warm, productive land in "almost a nation of dancers, musicians, and poets." Trade with neighboring settlements linked Equiano's people to a far-flung commercial network, but most daily contacts were local, and most disputes were decided by the village elders. Living more than a hundred miles from the coast, the young boy had no contact with European traders and knew nothing of their society. Through local oral histories, however, Equiano probably had heard stories of his own people, the kingdom of Benin, and the ancient empires and great civilizations to which he was tied. Beginning in ancient times, African storytellers memorized proverbs and tales from their peoples' history, and could recite them to educate and entertain the villagers. As the archivists of their people, these talented and specially trained men, were often trusted government advisors respected for their skill.[1]

Equiano lived in a small corner of a vast continent. Second only to Asia in size, Africa has a land area of 11,700,000 square miles, stretching from the Mediterranean to the Cape of Good Hope, almost six times the size of Europe. Its geographical characteristics vary from the dry Sahara Desert in the north, an area the size of the United States, or the Kalahari Desert in the south to the grasslands of the Sudan to some of the most beautiful tropical rain forests in the world, situated in the central regions of the continent. It is a land infinitely diverse in climate, terrain, wildlife, and human culture (see map on page xiv). Between 6000 and 2500 BCE, a desert gradually emerged in Africa where once a green belt had existed. Equiano knew that his home was but a small part of this vast expanse—that his nation and its people were rooted in an ancient civilization, indirectly descended from those who migrated south from the fertile Sahara as that region became too dry to sustain agriculture.

Long before, in the fourteenth century BCE, the Egyptians had retaken much of northern Africa from the darker-skinned peoples of Kush who retreated southward. Archeological records reveal that the people of Kush established a strong kingdom based on agriculture, commerce, and iron manufacturing. They built urban centers and massive stone structures and dominated the trade routes to the Red Sea and the ivory markets of northern Africa for many centuries. In the third century CE their power was challenged by another emerging nation, occupying the region of present-day Ethiopia centered in the commercial city of Axum. Finally, around 350 CE, the commercial conflict between these two nations became open warfare that ultimately destroyed Kush, scattering its people among other national groups to the east and to the west toward the Atlantic coast.[2]

The contentions creating critical changes in northeastern Africa during this period included religious conflicts. Christianity was taking root in Egypt and spreading to the south and west, challenging traditional religions in those regions. After Rome became Catholic most African Christians broke away from the Roman Church and formed the Coptic Church. ("Coptic" comes from a Greek word meaning "Egyptian church.") Over many centuries, as it spread, Christianity faced stiff competition from the many traditional local religions and from Islam, which was

Timeline

Chapter 1

c. 300–1076
Kingdom of Ghana

c. 1170–1900
Kingdom of Benin

c. 1200–1500
Kingdom of Mali

1464–1591
Songhay Empire

1482
Portugal establishes trading post of Elmina on the Gold Coast.

1492
Columbus lands in the West Indies.

c. 1500–1539
Life of Estevanico, first African explorer of North America

after 1500
Portugal increasingly becomes involved in slave trade to supply labor for its Atlantic sugar plantations.

particularly influential in the region of the Sudan. In regions where Islam was accepted, oral historians added the Koran to their other recitations; in Christian areas, they incorporated the Bible.

West Africa

In the fourth and fifth centuries, a powerful trading nation arose to the southwest of Egypt. It took the name **Ghana** from the title given to its ruler, and by the eighth century it dominated West Africa. It controlled the trade routes across the Sahara that connected Africa with Mediterranean Europe, its people acting as middlemen between the people of West Africa and the northern Arab people, and imposing tariffs on salt, gold, rubber, ivory, brass, and the small numbers of enslaved people that flowed north from the grasslands of central Africa. The tariff collected on this trade increased Ghana's wealth, and the wealth made it militarily strong. By the eleventh century Ghana's rulers commanded an army estimated at two hundred thousand warriors. From the north Ghana received the influence of Muslim merchants, Arabic as a written language and the Islamic faith. The Muslim influence was apparent in its capital city of Kumbi-Saleh, which not only had a national palace and other opulent state buildings but also had a Muslim quarter with twelve mosques and guest accommodations for Muslim visitors; Kumbi-Saleh was a center for education as well.

Ghana's wealth was enhanced still further by the gold brought from the mines of the Senegal River region and by the craftsmanship of its ironworkers, who were skilled at making weapons for warfare. This empire too was constantly challenged by its neighbors, who sought to acquire its wealth. Muslim warlords chipped away at the territory and trade that were the sources of Ghana's power, and in 1076 they captured the capital, executing all who refused to convert to Islam. As the result of military losses and successive droughts, Ghana finally ceased dominating its region in the late twelfth century.

The successor state to Ghana was the kingdom of **Mali**, which became extraordinarily wealthy and powerful during the thirteenth century. Travelers from the Middle East and Southern Europe came in caravans to trade in Gao, Kangaba, Jenne, and other commercial cities of the empire. In the fourteenth

1565
St. Augustine founded by Spanish, first European settlement in present-day United States.

1621
Dutch West India Company founded.

1650-1800
Height of the Atlantic Slave Trade

1655
Britain establishes plantations in Jamaica.

1672
Royal African Company formed.

c. **1745-1795**
Life of Olaudah Equiano

c. **1780**
Over eighty thousand enslaved Africans forcibly brought to the Americas annually.

and fifteenth centuries scholars came to Timbuktu to study Koranic theology, diplomacy, and law at the University of Sankore. The city and its university became a major center of Islamic learning offering special education in geography and mathematics. European visitors were impressed with the grandeur of Mali and the grace and adroitness of its rulers. Under Mansa Kango Musa, a devout Muslim who made regular pilgrimages to the holy city of Mecca, Mali reached the zenith of its power between 1312 and 1332. With these pilgrimages **Mansa Musa** made a mighty impression on rival states. In 1324 five hundred enslaved people wielding heavy golden staffs heralded his arrival at the gates of Mecca. His camel caravan escorted by many thousands of his servants, carried thirty thousand pounds of gold. In terms of wealth, governmental organization, and military power, fourteenth-century Mali dominated its region and rivaled any nation in Europe. Centuries later British historian E.W. Bovill wrote that Mansa Musa ruled over a nation as "remarkable for its size as for its wealth, and which provided a striking example of the capacity of the Negro for political organization." J.C. DeGraft-Johnson believed that Mansa Musa "came nearest to building a united West Africa. Whether you lived in the Gambia, Sierra Leone, the Ivory Coast, the Gold Coast, Togoland, Dahomey, or Nigeria," DeGraft-Johnson asserted, "you could not help but feel the power and strength of the Mali Empire, the empire which sought to fuse all of West Africa into one whole." Thus Mali and its glory were directly connected to Benin's history. Through his ancestors, Equiano was linked to all West Africans who were dominated by and shared in the ancient kingdom's power.[3]

In the late fifteenth century Mali's power waned, and **Songhay** (Songhai), a nation in the Western Sudan that had been converted to Islam in the beginning of the eleventh century, rose to power. Songhay, with its capital city of Gao on the banks of the Niger River, became a mighty trading nation. Under its control Timbuktu and Jenne flourished, their markets and schools drawing an ever-increasing economic and intellectual traffic from North Africa, the Middle East, Asia, and southern Europe, especially Spain and Portugal. At the height of Songhay's power, Timbuktu alone had 180 schools, and white and Black scholars at the University of Sankore studied grammar, literature, geography, science, law, surgery, and diplomacy. African scholars from Songhay carried their learning to the educational centers of southern Europe. Its government was a complex structure, comprising elected and appointed officials. Its military was a professional corps distributed throughout the provinces of the nation under the command of provincial governors. Its economy revolved around trade, agriculture, and herding, and its economic success attracted the attention of rival states in North Africa. In 1591 the Sultan of Morocco dispatched troops, many of whom were Spanish mercenaries, to attack Songhay. The resulting war was a costly one for both sides. Despite their superior weaponry, which included firearms previously unknown in the region, twenty thousand Moroccan troops fell. However, the warfare weakened Songhay's ability to withstand internal conflicts and pressures from neighboring states, and the empire disintegrated by the early seventeenth century.[4]

Equiano's nation of **Benin** had gained importance in the fifteenth century, growing from a walled city to a nation state as a result of its conquest of states

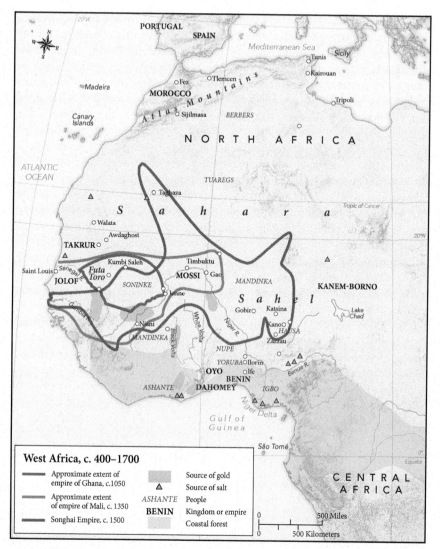

Map 1.1 West Africa, c. 400–1700

west of the Niger River. The religion and science of his people reflected the long history of diverse influences in the region. They were not Muslim, although there were strong Islamic influences. Equiano reported that his people had no public places of worship but were attended by "priests and magicians, or wise men." There were strict religious rules governing funerals, food preparation, and cleanliness. The people believed in only one "Creator of all things," but also believed that spirits could affect the world. There was a close link between religion and science. Religious "magicians" also practiced the art of bleeding, much like Europeans at the time (and Americans well into the nineteenth century).

Although religious practices varied widely in West Africa, the importance of ceremonial music and dance was universal. Special dances, songs, or poems marked any significant event, victory in battle, marriage, birth, death, or an agricultural festival. Public dances were highly stylized, with special positions occupied by married men, married women, young single men, and "maidens," representing battle, domestic life, sports, and courtship. Later in his life, after he left Africa, Equiano saw Greeks dancing in ways that reminded him of the dances done by his people.

Benin was an agricultural nation and a land of traders. By the end of the fifteenth century its cloth was popular with European traders, and its bronze and ivory art could be found in Europe. The farmers of Benin were famous for their pepper, and in 1482 the Portuguese established a trading post—**Elmina** ("the mine")—to deal largely in this one coveted spice. Africans received copper, coral beads, umbrellas, and guns in exchange for pepper and some enslaved people taken from the interior as prisoners of war. Increasingly after 1500 the Portuguese became more interested in the slave trade to supply labor for their sugar plantations on the island of São Tomé in the Gulf of Guinea, in southern Portugal, on Madeira, and later on Cape Verde and in Brazil. Their plantation system drew on the earlier experience of Mediterranean sugar plantations in Cyprus, Crete, and Sicily, which used Muslim war prisoners and Slavic forced labor from the port towns of the Black Sea. In fact, so closely were Eastern Europeans identified with this forced labor, through many centuries of bondage,

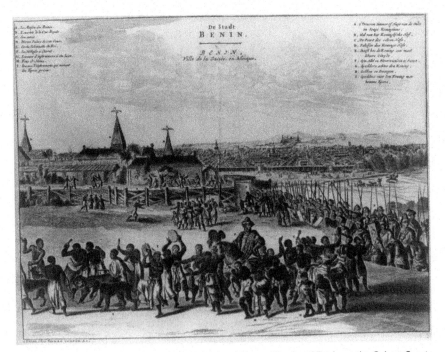

Seventeenth-century engraving depicting a celebration near the city of Benin on the Guinea Coast of West Africa.

that the word "slave" originated in the ethnic designation of Slav, only gradually coming to denote bound laborers of African origin. As Islam spread in the Mediterranean world, Muslim conquerors considered "infidels" suitable for slavery and by the 700s had added millions of sub-Saharan Africans to the enslaved populations. After Europeans established themselves in the New World in the sixteenth century, they spent the next three centuries competing for control of the massive Atlantic slave trade, which provided much of the labor for their colonization of the Americas.[5]

Slavery was already well established in Benin and other areas in North and West Africa before European involvement. Those held in bondage were generally taken in war, the losers of some battle who might have been killed but for their capture. Traditionally, enslaved peoples' value increased with the distance from their homes. Before the fifth century, Romans were willing to pay higher prices for North African enslaved people because their remoteness from their homeland made them a more secure investment. In the Muslim world, the enslaved at a distance from their homes were valued as "strangers" who might be provided with trusted positions because they were thought to have no local loyalties other than to their owner. These men were often used as special military guards in their owner's household or harem. As a logical consequence of this reasoning, as enslaved people became more familiar with the social customs and

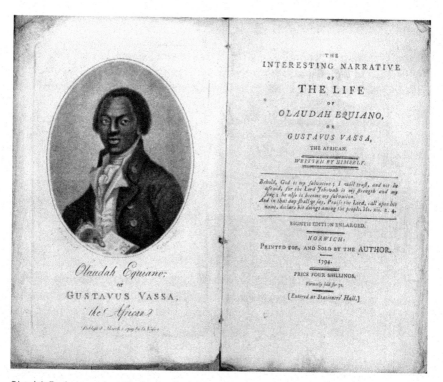

Olaudah Equiano, as shown in the frontispiece to *The Interesting Narrative of the Life of Olaudah Equiano; or Gustavus Vassa, the African.*

the politics of a region, they also became less suitable for slavery in that region. This might have critical implications for their children, whose familiarity with the local society might brand them as unfit for slavery.[6]

In Benin enslaved people became servants, tenders of the livestock, domestic workers, and agricultural field laborers. They were denied the freedoms accorded to others in the society and were subject to harsh punishment for infractions of the rules which governed owner/enslaved relationships. They endured harsh, restricted lives, but they had hope for a better future. Among Equiano's people an enslaved person might rise from that lowly position to become a full citizen, equal in rights and status to any others in the society. Equiano had witnessed many sales as a child, as well-armed traders with large sacks traversed his region offering to buy or sell enslaved people. Before travelers were allowed to transport the enslaved through Benin lands, however, they were required to certify the lawfulness of their acquisition. Kidnappers were themselves enslaved as punishment for their violations of the rules. Equiano claimed that only war prisoners and criminals were held by his people or sold to passing traders. This was the expectation with which Benin's traders initially participated in the slave traffic with the Portuguese. Their understanding eventually changed, but by that time their principles had been compromised by the allure of the guns that came in the trade and greatly magnified the military might of Benin.[7]

Europeans and the African Slave Trade

Equiano explained the process. "When a trader wants slaves, he applies to a chief for them, and tempts him with his wares. It is not extraordinary," he observed, "if on this occasion [the chief] yields to the temptation with as little firmness, and accepts the price of his fellow creature's liberty, with as little reluctance as the enlightened [European] merchant's." Benin was among the first nations in its region to be supplied with substantial numbers of firearms and horses, which facilitated the expansion of its empire beyond the Niger Delta to Lagos and from the Atlantic coast into Yorubaland.[8]

As with other powerful nations Benin was constantly challenged by rivals, and as the pressure to maintain a strong military presence was unrelenting, trading enslaved people for weapons of war increased. Eventually during the eighteenth century, Benin's power waned so that by the time Equiano was born its military might was overshadowed by competitor nations who controlled more of the area's trade. The Yoruba empire of Oyo largely supplanted Benin in the Portuguese trade during much of the eighteenth century. Oyo and Ashante became two of the most powerful nations of the region, controlling much of the slave trade and defending their commerce against the military incursions of Muslim traders. Their power allowed them to require tributes and taxes from Europeans in return for the privilege of trading in the region. Access to the coast was important for participation in the European trade. Along the coast from the Senegal River in the northwest to Angola in central Africa, European nations established trading posts that grew with the slave trade into over fifty forts dotting three hundred miles of coastline. The greatest concentration of forts was along the **Gold Coast**, reflecting the original impetus for European involvement in African trade. The largest of these forts were called castles, elaborate walled settlements providing accommodations and offices for European traders, storage facilities for supplies, and holding pens for over a thousand enslaved people. In 1482 the Portuguese built Elmina, one of the first of the large castles, on the Gold Coast in present-day Ghana. From coastal garrisons like these, European nations contended for control of the slave trade, as African nations contended for internal control of the trade. Elmina fell to the Dutch in 1637; the Cape Coast Castle built by the Swedes in 1653 had been held successively by West Africans, the Dutch, and the English by 1665.[9]

Dahomey, a non-Muslim inland nation, broke through to the coast and replaced the coastal traders who had served as go-betweens selling Dahomey goods and enslaved people to the European coastal traders. Among the people of Dahomey, enslaved people often filled out the ranks of military forces used to capture more people, who were then sold to further strengthen Dahomey military power. Perhaps it was a group from Dahomey who came to Equiano's village while the adults were away in the fields. But it was no military unit that found the eleven-year-old Equiano and his sister alone in their compound. This was a small slave-raiding party of two men and a woman, who seized the pair and took them off into the woods, where they were bound and placed in large sacks. They were taken first to a neighboring state where their own language was spoken and were sold to a chieftain. Equiano's owner was a blacksmith, and the boy was employed working the bellows at the forge. The children remained in this "very pleasant country" for only a short time before they were sold again and separated. Equiano was eventually taken to the Atlantic coast, where he was shocked by his first encounter with Europeans. "Their complexions . . . differing so much from ours, their long hair, and the language they spoke (which was very different from any I had ever heard) . . ." confirmed his fear that he would be killed by these "white men with horrible looks, red faces and long hair" whom he considered "bad spirits." He was also surprised by the ethnic and linguistic diversity of the Africans he met, and astonished by his first sight of the ocean and the great ships lying at anchor.[10]

Although Equiano had never seen Europeans before, contact between southern Europeans and African people was already centuries old. The North African conquest and occupation of the Iberian Peninsula beginning in 711, lasted for hundreds of years. For more than seven centuries Africans and Europeans shared this region, with the Africans wielding power. There was regular interaction between the races until the Spanish pushed these African "Moors," as they were called, back across the Mediterranean in the eleventh century and finally retook control of the entire peninsula in 1492 with the conquest of the kingdom of Grenada. By that time the region had become what historian Ronald Sanders called "the most racially varied society in western Europe."[11]

Yet, Iberians were ambivalent on the question of color. Muslim slavery had long carried negative, dehumanizing stereotypes for enslaved people, white or Black, but the lowest position was reserved for the darkest of the enslaved. The number of Black people in the society encouraged both racial tolerance and racial restriction. Although the Black population was eventually absorbed into the society, legal prohibitions, like those that separated burials by race, relegated Africans to common graves ("*pocos dos Negros*"); narrowed interracial associations; limited Black movement; and lowered African social and political status in the society. Still, it is likely that the historical experience of the region made the Spanish and the Portuguese more aware than the English of the nuances of ethnicity, culture, and skin color among the Africans they encountered in West Africa. Mid-sixteenth-century Spanish traders' and travelers' impressions of Africa evidenced an awareness and an appreciation of the human variety they encountered. As the English observed, many Spaniards considered differences in skin color to be "[o]ne of the marveylous thynges that god [*sic*] useth in the composition of man." They were conscious of white and black as the extremes of human skin shades, "utterlye contrary," but they also recognized yellow, tan, brown, and other colors as well. Other Europeans tended to simplify or even ignore cultural differences between Africans and to call them all "black." The English especially, who came to West Africa in the fifteenth and sixteenth centuries, were much more likely to see an indistinguishable African **blackness**. As the English became increasingly important in the growing Atlantic slave trade, "blackness" gradually imputed to African people the negative characteristics associated with the term in the English language. According to the fifteenth-century *Oxford English Dictionary* blackness was evil, sinful, ugly, and unclean, and the English identification of Africans as black marked the African character with these connotations in the English mind. Slavery was certainly not limited to Africans. (From the 1500s to the early 1800s Muslims had enslaved more than a million western and southern Europeans, for example.) Yet, as historian David Brion Davis observed, for Europeans and others, who had "struggled for centuries to find markers that would help justify class polarities and also help to identify, at some distance, people who could be classified as 'natural slaves,'" the physical distinctions of Africans were "made to order."[12]

Contrary to British stereotypes, Africans were ethnically, linguistically, religiously, and culturally varied peoples. In fact, the wide variety of African cultures and histories makes it difficult to tell their story except in the broadest terms. The family was central to African social, economic, and political life. Family lineage was traced through the father in West Africa and through the mother in west central and central Africa. In most regions the lands of the nation were controlled by large extended families. Three families generally collaborated in selecting national leaders. The royal family supplied eligible male candidates, another family selected the leader from among those who were eligible, and still another family invested the ruler with the power of office. As in other traditional societies, individuals were connected to their history through their family. Africans removed from family, from their ancestors and their land, were separated from an important part of their identity and were truly lost and alone. In the months and years after his enslavement, Equiano preserved the memory of his family and traditions as best he could; writing and publishing his autobiography decades later, in 1789, helped him preserve a part of his identity.

The Middle Passage

During the days that Equiano was held on the coast, he and his fellow African prisoners learned much about their white captors, and after he found an African with whom he could communicate, he began to understand his situation. He was to be taken far away to the white man's country in one of the great ships. He was relieved once he was convinced that these strange men were not going to eat him, a common fear among those who had never before seen Europeans, and he began to believe that life might be no worse for him than for enslaved people in his land. Still, what he saw worried him—"the white people looked and acted . . . in so savage a manner, for I had never seen among any people such instances of brutal cruelty." He was terrified not only by the way white men treated the Africans but also—especially—by the way white people treated one another. "One white man in particular I saw . . . flogged so unmercifully with a large rope . . . that he died." The man's body was tossed overboard in a manner unthinkable to an African socialized in a society that held funeral ceremonies sacred.[13]

After several days the ship came that was to carry the Africans from their homeland. They marveled at the ship's arrival under full sail and wondered at the magic that brought this machine and these men to this place. In the next days and weeks, life for these Africans became almost unbearable as they endured what has come to be called the **Middle Passage**. A cargo of "black people of every description chained together" below decks in the hold of the ship for six to eight weeks. As Equiano remembered,

> The stench of the hold while we were on the coast was so intolerably loathsome that it was dangerous to remain there for any time, and some of us had been permitted to stay on the deck for the fresh air; but now that the whole ship's cargo were confined together, and the heat of the climate, added to the number in the ship, which was so crowded that each had scarcely room to turn himself, almost suffocated us.[14]

The passage from the west coast of Africa to America was one of the most agonizing and dangerous parts of the enslavement process for the Africans. As if to testify to Equiano's description, hearings on the slave trade were held by the English Parliament in the 1780s. In these hearings a diagram of a slave vessel, the *Brookes*, sailing out of Liverpool, depicted the unbelievably crowded conditions aboard one slave ship. Resulting legislation prescribed the space to be provided to each enslaved person aboard. Even had these rules of space allocation been enforced—and they seldom were—enslaved people would have had half the room allowed to European immigrants brought during the seventeenth century to America as indentured servants, or even to prisoners transported to colonies such as British colonial Georgia or Australia. On the slave ships shelves were added to increase the capacity of the hold, dividing the area into two sections. A space six feet by one foot four inches was allotted for each adult man, five feet ten inches by one foot for each adult woman, five feet by one foot two inches for each boy and four feet six inches by one foot for each girl. Using these calculations, British lawmakers estimated that a ship of the *Brookes*'s size could reasonably transport up to 451 enslaved people, albeit in the most cramped conditions. The full horror of the Middle Passage is barely suggested by the impersonality of reducing human beings to deck space dimensions. The full story was even more grotesque, and many in Parliament were shocked to learn from a former crew member's testimony that the *Brookes* had completed the trip several years earlier carrying a slave cargo of nearly 600 people, and they had lost many during the voyage.[15]

Alexander Falconbridge, a British surgeon, made the voyage from West Africa to the West Indies thirty years after Equiano's journey. Dr. Falconbridge's description of the hardships of the trip and the crowded conditions in the hold, reveals little improvement. When the doctor ventured below decks in an attempt to attend the sick, he was forced to step on chained bodies that covered the entire floor. He reported that each person was locked in irons attached to a long chain fixed to the lower deck, binding fifty or sixty men to the ship and to one another. Twice a day, at about eight in the morning and at four in the afternoon, weather permitting, these men were allowed abovedecks for food and exercise. As Falconbridge described it, their food consisted "chiefly of horsebeans, boiled to the consistence of a pulp; of boiled yams and rice, and sometimes of a small quantity of beef and pork."[16]

Conditions on-board ship made death from disease, malnutrition, mistreatment, or lack of fresh air frequent. Those who resisted bondage by refusing nourishment were force fed by the application of special jawscrews to force their mouths open. The whip was liberally employed to discourage protest of any kind. Equiano told of a group of Africans on his ship who elected suicide over slavery, making their way through the deck netting and flinging themselves into the ocean to drown. The crew "rescued" several of them and pulled them back aboard. Those who survived were severely and brutally punished as an object lesson to others who contemplated such action.

While some Africans sought freedom through suicide, others watched for opportunities to escape or to rebel. Slavery's defenders often argued that the dangers of ocean crossings in general accounted for the high death rate among the enslaved people. In reality slave ships were floating prisons that held men and women for weeks under the most inhumane circumstances. The ship's crew members were essentially prison guards, and there was great incentive for these guards to take their work seriously, since all knew the danger of slave rebellions at sea. Captain Philip Drake, an experienced slave trader, explained to those seeking to enter the business that "The Negroes [fight] like wild beasts" and warned that "slavery is a dangerous business at sea as well as ashore."[17]

Slave ships generally carried more crew members than other vessels, partly because of their special security needs. Many felt it essential to have at least one crewman for every ten enslaved people, and although this was not always the case, a ratio of one to twelve or fifteen was not uncommon. Some slave ship captains increased the security aboard their vessels by keeping enslaved men chained below decks for the entire trip. This may have helped protect the crew, but it devastated the health of the men, killing many more than died during the average voyage.

Life on a slave ship was dangerous and uncomfortable even for the captain and crew. The crew's diet was almost as meager as the captives', except that they received regular and larger portions of meat and a ration of rum. Disease was far more dangerous below decks, but the crew was not immune to the deadly

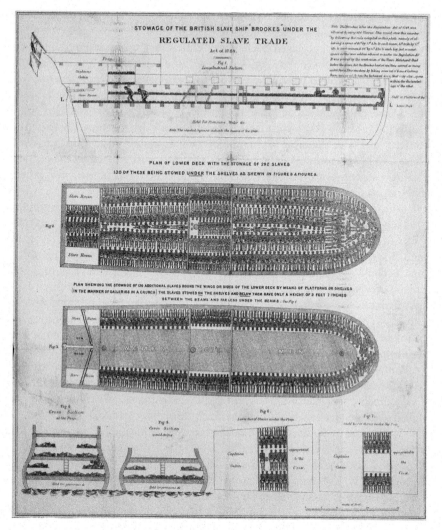

Schematic drawing of the slave ship *Brookes*, used to illustrate British regulations for the number of humans to be loaded aboard during the Middle Passage from Africa to the Americas. British law required no more than 451 enslaved people to be carried by a ship of that size. Abolitionist member of Parliament William Wilberforce produced records to show, however, that this ship had transported as many as 609 enslaved people on some of its voyages to North America.

plagues that were common on slave ships. Under these conditions the mortality rate was very high, twenty-five percent, sometimes reaching one third for the enslaved and almost that for the crew. Slave ships attracted a steady escort of sharks because the dead were tossed over the side each morning. Most captains endured the hardships in return for a share in the profit from the sale of the captives. While profits fluctuated, returns from 10 percent to 150 percent on investments per voyage were usual. Some crew members were paid; others were impressed into service or were convicts offered duty aboard a slave ship as the only alternative to prison. Yet, even under the worst of circumstances, the voyage abovedecks could not be compared to the voyage in the hold. Enslaved people, of course, had no choice and profited not at all.

African women received somewhat different treatment aboard ship than did the men. They were sometimes confined to a separate section of the hold and were often allowed to remain abovedecks for longer periods of time because they were believed to be less dangerous. Thus, they were somewhat less likely to suffer the health hazards and extreme physical hardships of the crowded quarters in the hold. However, because they were abovedecks, the women were at the constant mercy of the crew. Although all women were at risk, young enslaved women were especially likely to be raped and otherwise abused by the captain and crew while they were at sea. Often the captain depended on the crew's access to the women to quiet dissatisfaction during long difficult voyages.

Although captains generally allowed women and children to remain untethered above deck, many knew better than to underestimate their female captives. As one captain was cautioned, "putt not too much confidence in the Women nor Children lest they happen to be Instrumental to your being surprised which may be fatal." Women too were responsible for deadly shipboard rebellions. An unnamed woman played a key role in an abortive escape attempt by three captives being transported aboard the English ship *Robert* in 1721. Because she was allowed to move about the ship more freely, she was able to carry information from one captive to another and coordinate the attack. The strike killed two of the crew, but it ultimately failed and the men involved were executed. Adding a gruesome touch to the deadly business, the captain forced the three insurgents to eat the heart and liver of one of the dead white crewmen before he killed them. As if to make a special example of the woman, the captain had her hanged by her thumbs, whipped, slashed with knives, and allowed to bleed to death.[18]

Horrifying as these events were, they were not unique. The slave trade was one of the bloodiest, most brutal aspects of African, European, and American history. After Europeans established settlements in America, their labor needs increased greatly. The Spanish in Latin America used Native American people at first, but they died in such large numbers and at such a rapid rate that they provided an inadequate supply. King Charles II of Spain had prohibited the use of African labor in New Spain, but he was persuaded to lift the ban by those who, like Bishop Bartolomeo de Las Casas, advocated the importation of African labor as a "humanitarian effort" to keep the Native American populations from total destruction. Later, after witnessing the brutality of African enslavement, Las Casas reconsidered and opposed the importation of Africans, but by the mid-sixteenth century Africans had become the favored substitute for Native American labor.

Growth of the African Slave Trade

The African slave trade, which had progressed at a trickle during the fourteenth and fifteenth centuries, became a torrent during the next four hundred years, as it was redirected from southern Europe to South America, the Caribbean, and to a lesser extent North America. The first slave ships, mainly Spanish, to come directly from Africa to the western hemisphere traded in the West Indies as early as 1532, while the Portuguese brought Africans to supply their sugar plantations in

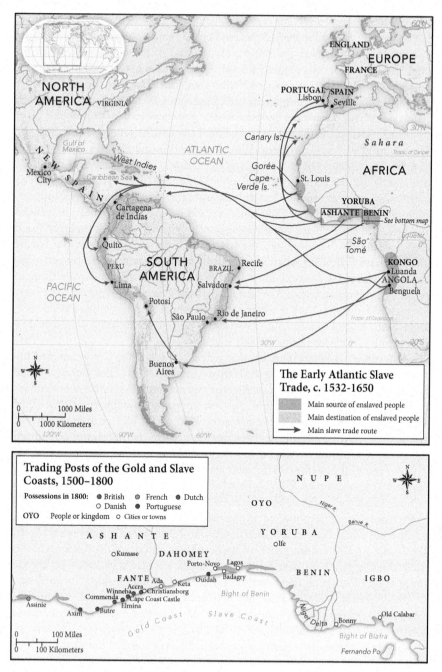

Map 1.2 The Early Atlantic Slave Trade, c. 1532–1650

Brazil after the mid-sixteenth century. The wealth extracted from the Americas by the Spanish and the Portuguese was directly connected to the increased demand for sugar, which outpaced the supply from southern Europe. As the number of Europeans who could afford to indulge a taste for sweets grew, the value of sugar increased and the demand for enslaved people to cultivate this extremely labor-intensive crop climbed sharply. By the end of the century sugar production in the Caribbean and Brazil was absorbing two thousand Africans a year. The Africans imported to the Spanish colonies of South America were not all used in sugar production immediately. They replaced Native American laborers in the gold mines of New Spain and suffered comparably high death rates. By the end of the eighteenth century, however, sugar cane had become the Americas' major slave crop.

Other Africans came not as enslaved captives but as sailors or as part of the Spanish military forces. Ancient cultural artifacts found in Latin America suggest to some scholars that Africans may have traveled to the Americas hundreds of years before the arrival of Christopher Columbus, although this hypothesis is not universally accepted. Certainly, many came during the age of European exploration. At least one of Columbus's crew is believed to have been of African ancestry, and thirty Black individuals traveled with the Spanish explorer Vasco Núñez de Balboa when he became the first European to discover the Pacific Ocean in 1513. In 1519 when Hernándo Cortes defeated the Aztecs in what is now modern-day Mexico, more than three hundred Africans were there to position his cannon. Other Africans entered the American West with the early Spanish expeditions. They produced the first wheat crop harvested in America, and in 1565 helped to build St. Augustine in Florida, the first city established by Europeans in the present-day United States.[19]

Estevanico, a Black Spaniard who acted as a guide for Cortes, excited the Spanish imagination by relating the Native American tales of the "Seven Cities of Gold." In 1539, with Estevanico guiding the way and acting as Native American interpreter, Father Marcos de Niza led Spanish troops through the American Southwest (in the areas that are the present-day states of New Mexico and Arizona) in search of the mythic treasure site. Posing as a medicine man, Estevanico enlisted the aid of several Native American villages in the search. The Spanish hoped to discover these cities with their limitless supply of gold, but their dream was never realized. Estevanico was killed by Native American forces, and the expedition retreated to the main Spanish settlement in Mexico. Yet the journey had fueled the Spaniards' fantasies of great wealth, and the story of Estevanico encouraged many other expeditions to continue the search. Centuries after Estevanico's death the Zuni Native American people of the Southwest still tell of the Black man who died searching for the golden city. Although Africans played various roles among the Spanish in America, they were most likely, by far, to be enslaved in South and Central America. It is fair to say that Spain's ascension to economic and military dominance during the fifteenth and sixteenth centuries rested on African and Native American slave labor.[20]

The Portuguese also produced great quantities of sugar in Brazil, using labor supplied from its slave trading posts in the Congo (Kongo) and Angola. Although they gained an early lead through their involvement in the slave trade, the government did not officially sponsor the activity until the late seventeenth century, and Portugal was overshadowed by other European traders who rose to power with the full support of their government. After Holland emerged from Spain's control at the end of the sixteenth century, it established a government-assisted slave

King Nzinga Mbemba Affonso (1460–1542)

A Kongolese crucifix from the eighteenth century. Kongolese leaders like King Nzinga Mbemba Affonso who adopted Christianity used devotional objects like crucifixes to demonstrate their political and religious authority. In the middle of the crucifix is the figure of Saint Anthony, who became popular in the Kongo when Italian missionaries spread his cult in the 1600s.

NZINGA MBEMBA, RULER of the vast Kingdom of Kongo in the mid-sixteenth century, attempted to appease Portugal and prevent the devastation caused by European merchants and the slave trade.

Manikongo [title for the ruler of Kongo] Nzinga Mbemba Affonso ruled over Kongo during a tumultuous time in the kingdom's history from 1509 to 1542. Nzinga was born in the mid-fifteenth century, and when the Portuguese first arrived in Mbanza, Kongo's capital, he was a provincial chief in his early thirties. Knowing that for more than seventy years, the Portuguese had been making claims to large swaths of Africa and had expanded their trade for gold and enslaved people farther and farther down the coast, Nzinga likely understood the danger to his future kingdom.

In the decade before taking the throne, Nzinga devoted himself to acquiring European knowledge, goods, and weapons. He converted to Christianity, took the Portuguese name Affonso, and learned to speak Portuguese eloquently enough to maintain a lengthy correspondence with two of Portugal's kings during his rule. He walked a thin line, keeping the Portuguese close enough to protect himself and his people from their greed and expansionism, but not so close as to be subsumed by the European nation. Affonso resisted European prospectors, knowing that if the Portuguese found the silver or gold that they coveted within his land, Kongo would be quickly overrun, and when the king's envoy urged him to adopt Portuguese law and court protocol, he refused.

It became clear, however, that no matter what language the Africans spoke or what religion they practiced, European rulers would never see them as equals or even

(Continued)

truly as allies. In 1526 Affonso wrote to King João III begging him to cease the abduction of his people for the slave trade, arguing it was depopulating his nation, and insisting he stop his merchants from flooding Kongo markets with European goods that were destabilizing the kingdom and its economy. He asked for teachers and priests rather than traders, but the Portuguese continued to ignore restrictive laws he had set on the buying and selling of enslaved people and his embargoes on certain European goods. At several points, he even attempted to appeal directly to the pope in Rome to end the slave trade, but Portugal detained his emissaries whenever they arrived in Lisbon.

King João III's replies showed little respect and even less sympathy: "You . . . tell me that you want no slave-trading in your domains, because this trade is depopulating your country," he said, "The Portuguese there, on the contrary, tell me how vast the Congo is, and how it is so thickly populated that it seems as if no slave has ever left." Affonso's sorrows came to a head when in 1539, near the end of his life, a ship carrying ten of his nephews, grandsons, and other relatives to Portugal for religious schooling was diverted to Brazil, and his family members were enslaved.

Following King Affonso's death, Kongo declined—its population diminished, and its provincial and village chiefs grew rich on the very slave trade that was decimating its people. In 1665 Portugal defeated the kingdom in battle and its manikongo was beheaded. By the late 1800s the entire territory of the former kingdom was ruled by European powers.

Source: Hochschild, A. *King Leopold's Ghost: A Story of Greed, Terror, and Heroism in Colonial Africa* (Boston: Houghton Mifflin, 1998), 11–15.

trading effort that resulted in the formation of the Dutch West India Company in 1621. This company held a monopoly on all slave trading between Africa and the Dutch New World, and produced spectacular profits for the nation and company stock holders. Holland translated its economic power into a strong naval force and managed to push Portugal out of its Gold Coast trading posts. Rivalries with neighboring France and, later, England eventually weakened Holland's hold on the slave trade and allowed other Europeans to participate in the profits, but Holland continued to trade enslaved people for at least another one hundred years.

As Europeans realized the economic potential of the African trade, more nations established slave trading centers in West Africa. During the seventeenth century Sweden, Denmark, and Brandenburg took part in the lucrative trade. Thus, by the eighteenth century the continent of Africa was supplying great wealth and power to Europe and to Europe's emerging American settlements. Meanwhile, Africa was being drained of one of its greatest assets—many of its young, strong, healthy people.[21]

England entered the slave trade later than most of its competitors, but it quickly eclipsed the field. The English had traded for gold and ivory in Africa for more than a century before Sir John Hawkins became one of the first English traders to bring enslaved Africans, in a ship called *Jesus*, to be sold in New Spain. Initially there was resistance at home to British participation. Queen Elizabeth I was afraid that God would punish her nation for selling human beings, but her fears of a catastrophic event were calmed when Hawkins demonstrated the vast profit to be made. Subsequently she encouraged him to undertake another slave-trading voyage and invested her own money in the enterprise. Thus, long before England established colonies in America it profited from the New World through its participation in the slave trade.

Three times during the 1560s Hawkins sailed between Africa and America, and each time the returns were considerable, so much so that several English merchants followed his example. British colonists in America entered the slave trade in 1644 when Boston merchants sponsored their first commercial voyage to Africa. Their ship, the *Rainbow*, brought enslaved people and other merchandise to British colonies in the Caribbean. In 1655 Britain established plantations in Jamaica and imported Africans to grow sugar cane. The growing profit from sugar encouraged increased enslaved labor importation so that by 1673 there were ten thousand Africans and only eight thousand English settlers in Jamaica. Within fifty years Africans accounted for almost 70 percent of the island's population.

In 1672 the **Royal African Company** was formed to coordinate the slave trade, by then partly underwritten by the Crown. The company entered the trade just at the point of its most rapid expansion. Clashing with Holland over its move into Dutch-controlled West African areas, England expanded its participation. The trade became so lucrative that even though the Royal African Company secured a grant of monopoly from the Crown in 1673, it could not prevent other English dealers from infringing on its trade. Finally in response to mounting pressure, the British Parliament rescinded the company's monopoly in 1711 and opened slave trading to all Englishmen. By that time Britain had established colonies in North America and was supplying them with enslaved Africans.

The economic rivalries underway in Europe bore striking similarities to those hundreds of years earlier in western and northern Africa. Both centered around the African and European intercontinental trade. On both continents powerful nations had risen to preeminence based on their ability to control and profit from that trade, only to be supplanted by competing nations. Whether Ghana or Portugal, Songhay or Spain, each owed its economic and consequent military power to the profit from that trade. Old World dominance was constructed on traditional commodities which included gold and enslaved people. From the eighth to the sixteenth century most of the Western world's gold came from the Sudan, controlled there by African merchant powers. Much of the struggle in the fifteenth and sixteenth centuries focused on Europe's attempt to circumvent that control. Europe's incursion into the Americas was a part of this effort. There, too, gold, and the Africans to extract it, became central to increasing wealth and power. By the mid-sixteenth century, sugar grown in America became ever more significant, overshadowing production in southern Europe. The wealth generated by trade in these commodities underlay the political and military power of Europe as it had for Africa.

Figures are disputed, and estimates have ranged from eleven to fifteen million, but recent analysis has estimated the total number of enslaved people who departed from Africa bound for the Americas between 1450 and 1900 at nearly twelve million. The vast majority of those taken in slavery were males, a fact only marginally affected by economics. Generally males brought higher prices as labor for the early American sugar plantations and gold mines, but after the late

King Nzinga Mbemba Affonso, Letters to King João III of Portugal

(July 6, 1526)

Sir, Your Highness should know how our Kingdom is being lost in so many ways that it is convenient to provide for the necessary remedy, since this is caused by the excessive freedom given by your agents and officials to the men and merchants who are allowed to come to this Kingdom to set up shops with goods and many things which have been prohibited by us, and which they spread throughout our Kingdoms and Domains in such an abundance that many of our vassals, whom we had in obedience, do not comply because they have the things in greater abundance than we ourselves; and it was with these things that we had them content and subjected under our vassalage and jurisdiction, so it is doing a great harm not only to the service of God, but the security and peace of our Kingdoms and State as well.

And we cannot reckon how great the damage is, since the mentioned merchants are taking every day our natives, sons of the land and the sons of our noblemen and vassals and our relatives, because the thieves and men of bad conscience grab them wishing to have the things and wares of this Kingdom which they are ambitious of; they grab them and get them to be sold; and so great, Sir, is the corruption and licentiousness that our country is being completely depopulated, and Your Highness should not agree with this nor accept it as in your service. And to avoid it we need from those (your) Kingdoms no more than some priests and a few people to teach in schools, and no other goods except wine and flour for the holy sacrament. That is why we beg of Your Highness to help and assist us in this matter, commanding your factors that

seventeenth century, women were in demand and brought prices comparable to males. African merchants, however, were less willing to sell African women. Women were valued at home as the bearers of children and, in most African societies, as the chief agricultural producers. There were also fewer females available to African coastal traders because people were likely to be taken in battle, making men most likely to be captured. Very few children were taken because they brought prices too low to make their trade profitable. Only about 10 percent of those who made the Middle Passage were under the age of ten.[22]

Economics did substantially determine enslaved people's destination, however, and since the return on slave labor used in sugarcane fields was great, African laborers brought the highest prices in the sugar-producing regions south of the present-day United States. Ninety percent of all the enslaved Africans brought to the Americas were sold to those regions. During the first 350 years of the slave trade to the West (1502–1860) more than 50 percent of the Africans they should not send here either merchants or wares, because it is our will that in these Kingdoms there should not be any trade of slaves nor outlet for them. Concerning what is referred [to] above, again we beg of Your Highness to agree with it, since otherwise we cannot remedy such an obvious damage. Pray Our Lord in His mercy to have Your Highness under His guard and let you do forever the things of His service. I kiss your hands many times. . . .

(October 18, 1526)

Moreover, Sir, in our Kingdoms there is another great inconvenience which is of little service to God, and this is that many of our people, keenly desirous as they are of the wares and things of your Kingdoms, which are brought here by your people, and in order to satisfy their voracious appetite, seize many of our people, freed and exempt men, and very often it happens that they kidnap even noblemen and the sons of noblemen, and our relatives, and take them to be sold to the white men who are in our Kingdoms; and for this purpose they have concealed them; and others are brought during the night so that they might not be recognized.

And as soon as they are taken by the white men they are immediately ironed and branded with fire, and when they are carried to be embarked, if they are caught by our guards' men the whites allege that they have bought them but they cannot say from whom, so that it is our duty to do justice and to restore to the freemen their freedom, but it cannot be done if your subjects feel offended, as they claim to be.

Source: Mbemba Affonso, Nzinga, Letters of Nzinga Mbemba (Afonso I) of Kongo to the King of Portugal, *July 6, 1526 and October 18, 1526. From Oxford First Source, https://www.oxfordfirstsource .com/view/10.1093/acref/9780199399680.013.0089/acref-9780199399680-e-89.*

were enslaved in the West Indies by Spanish, French, Dutch, Danish, Swedish, and English sugar planters. Slightly less than 40 percent were bound to the Portuguese in Brazil; only 6 percent of Africans brought to the western hemisphere were enslaved in the British colonies of North America. Most Africans brought to North America in the early years were sold from the large slave markets and plantations in the West Indies. After 1700, however, North American officials, slave importers, and their customers became convinced that West Indian traders sold the strongest and healthiest Africans to the more lucrative Caribbean market and shipped the less able, or sometimes the most rebellious, workers northward. Joseph Dudley, colonial governor of Massachusetts, complained that Africans imported from the West Indies were "usually the worst Servants they have." Many suspected that they were "Criminalls or otherwise of Little worth." By the mid-eighteenth century, traders were bringing an increasing majority of those enslaved in North America directly from Africa.[23]

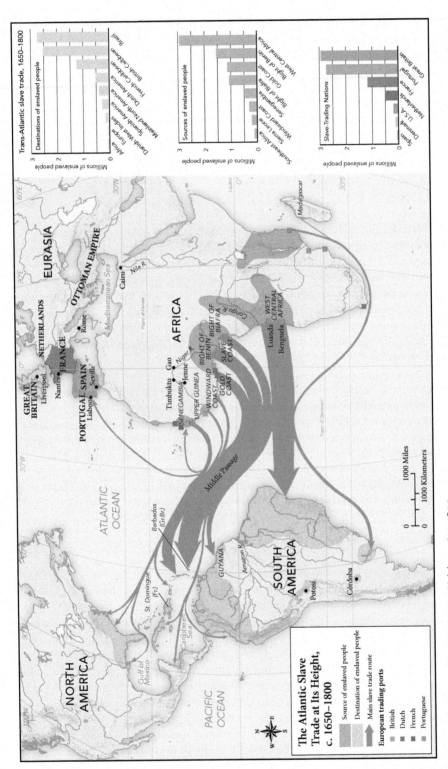

Map 1.3 The Atlantic Slave Trade at Its Height, c. 1650–1800

From 1700 to 1710, about fifty years before Equiano was enslaved, fewer than seven thousand enslaved Africans were exported to the Americas, and importations increased so rapidly that by the 1780s they stood at more than sixty thousand annually. Perhaps it was this staggering increase in the Atlantic slave trade that fueled the stories about the white men's cannibalism that Equiano heard—stories that provided one possible explanation for the Europeans' voracious appetite for enslaved Africans. Equiano was landed in the West Indies in the 1750s and eventually was taken to the colony of Virginia. He spent more than a decade struggling to regain the freedom he had lost. Once free, he raised his voice on behalf of the millions kidnapped from their homelands in Africa and cast into the wilderness of American slavery.[24]

Who, What, Where

Atlantic Slave Trade p. 9	Gold Coast p. 11
Benin p. 6	Mali p. 5
Blackness p. 12	Mansa Musa p. 6
Dahomey p. 11	Middle Passage p. 13
Elmina p. 8	Olaudah Equiano p. 3
Estevanico p. 18	Royal African Company p. 21
Ghana p. 5	Songhay p. 6

Review Questions

1.1 Describe the major empires and states of West Africa before the expansion of the Atlantic slave trade. What were the distinguishing features of these societies?

1.2 How did European traders fit into the existing politics of African nations, and how did this contribute to the growth of the slave trade? How did British views on race differ from other Europeans?

1.3 What were the conditions of enslaved Africans in the Middle Passage? Why is Equiano's autobiography an important source for studying the Middle Passage?

1.4 What are the reasons for the increase of the Atlantic slave trade from the sixteenth through the eighteenth centuries? What impact did the slave trade have on the Atlantic economy?

For additional digital learning resources please go to **https://www.oup.com/he/horton1e**

The Evolution of Slavery in British North America

Two enslaved women working in a tobacco field near Fredericksburg, Virginia, overseen by a white man smoking a cigar in March 1798. This watercolor was sketched from life by Benjamin Henry Latrobe, the English-born architect best known for designing the U.S. Capitol.

CHAPTER OUTLINE

Slavery in the Chesapeake

2.1 Understand the role that slavery played in making Virginia economically viable. Analyze the differences in the development of slavery in Virginia and Maryland.

Slavery Farther South

2.2 Understand the role of slavery in the economy of the Carolina colony. Explain why Georgia failed to remain slave-free.

Slavery in the Middle Colonies

2.3 Compare and contrast the economies of the southern and Middle Colonies and the role slavery played in the Middle Colonies. Understand the development of an antislavery stance among the Quakers.

Slavery in New England

2.4 Analyze the similarities and differences between slavery in New England and in the other colonies.

Enslaved and Free Black People

2.5 Understand the developments that led to decreasing freedoms for both enslaved and free Black people over the course of the seventeenth and eighteenth centuries.

Black and Native American People

2.6 Understand the complex relationships between Black and Native Americans in the early colonies.

Colonial Black Culture

2.7 Understand the development of colonial Black society. Analyze the role that Africans played in the development of American culture.

⭐ **IN VIRGINIA, OLAUDAH** Equiano became one of the tens of thousands of Africans and African descendants who tended the tobacco fields, maintained the households of planter families, and provided the skilled labor to build their homes and establish their settlements. By the time of Equiano's arrival, colonial law in British North America had transformed a loose system of African long-term labor into codified, perpetual, and inherited racial slavery. Virginia was a corporate venture financed by the sale of stock in the **Virginia Company** of London. The company employees who settled Jamestown in 1607 had not intended to build a society based on African slave labor. Drawing their lessons from Spain's extraction of gold from America, they hoped for riches from a similar enterprise employing Native American labor. Despite a desperate first decade during which many Native Americans and many colonists died, the English settlers soon recognized that Virginia held a different sort of promise. With some instruction from the Native American population, farmers hoped to take advantage of the mild climate and fertile soil to supply both food and cash crops to sustain the colony. Tobacco, not gold, was to become the source of Virginia's wealth, and the unexpected arrival of more than twenty Africans aboard a British privateer in **1619** presented Virginia's British settlers with another potential source of labor to harvest this wealth.[1]

Slavery in the Chesapeake

Britain saw great potential for the **Chesapeake** colony of Virginia. It might provide produce that could not be grown at home and offer a place to transplant the growing numbers of unemployed people who crowded English cities and threatened the peace and stability of British society. Taxes on goods traded from the colony brought needed revenue to the national treasury, and merchants and stockholders looked forward to reaping great profits. This lucrative potential could not be realized, however, without a stable, reliable labor force. Attempts to force Native Americans to labor were unsuccessful, as most escaped back to their own people, rebelled against British demands, or died of European diseases. When Native American labor proved infeasible, the Virginia Company turned to Britain's poor,

Timeline

Chapter 2

1607
Founding of Jamestown, Virginia, first permanent English settlement in North America.

1619
First Africans brought to British North American colonies land in Jamestown, Virginia. Established the

Virginia General Assembly, which became the House of Burgesses, the first representative government in British North America.

1620
Pilgrims arrive on the *Mayflower* at New Plymouth, Massachusetts.

1635
African Anthony Johnson freed.

1651
Anthony Johnson receives land grant of 250 acres in Northampton, Virginia.

1670
Repeal of Virginia law that had allowed free Black individuals and indentured servants to vote.

launching a campaign enticing them with promises of a new start in a place with virtually limitless land and great potential wealth. The land was strewn with gold, they were told, and a man could get rich quickly with little work. Those unable to pay their own passage were allowed to sign indentures, pledging five to seven years of work in return for the cost of the trip. Many believed the company's promises, and these **indentured servants** provided much of Virginia's work force during the early seventeenth century. But as the British birthrate fell and wages and the prospects for employment in Britain rose after the 1630s, they became a less reliable labor source. As fewer of the English poor were willing to become indentured servants in Virginia, the company turned to African laborers, and the number of Black servants in the colony began to increase steadily.

At the same time British holdings in the West Indies were turning to the cultivation of sugarcane for a reliably profitable crop and importing growing numbers of enslaved Africans to supply the labor. Many slave traders believed that Africans' resistance to enslavement could be broken by the harsh system of gang labor in these sugar **plantations**. Accordingly, until well into the eighteenth century, many enslaved people bound for the mainland were taken first to the West Indies for a process called **seasoning**. In his short stay in the West Indies, the young Equiano was horrified by the brutality of the life people enslaved on sugar plantations were forced to endure. It was under these conditions that the British developed the customs and laws governing the operation of their slave system, providing the precedents in English law that were applied to mainland colonies. Gradually, over the next hundred years, the British colonies established a uniquely American form of racially based slavery.

North American slavery emerged slowly and unevenly, simultaneously manifesting different stages of development in different locations. The conditions for early Black laborers in Virginia were ill-defined, and they were sometimes allowed their freedom after a set period of time, almost always serving longer than white indentured servants. There is evidence that some Black men and women were already serving for life by the middle of the seventeenth century. This implication can be drawn from the fact that when owners recovered

1676
Bacon's Rebellion in Virginia, participants include enslaved people and white indentured servants.

1688
"Germantown Protest": Quakers in Germantown, Pennsylvania, denounce slavery and the slave trade.

1696
South Carolina establishes first comprehensive slave code in British North America, modeled on that of Barbados.

1712
Enslaved Africans and Native American allies burn sections of New York City.

Nine white people killed and twenty-one enslaved people executed.

1750
Enslaved persons are 61 percent of the population of South Carolina but only 2 percent of the population of Pennsylvania.

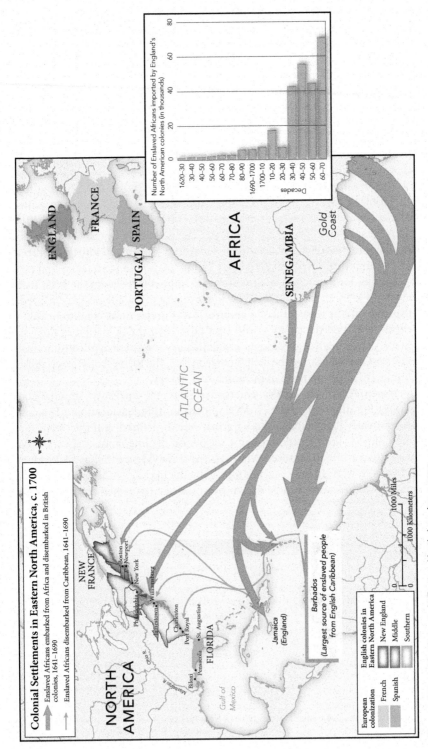

Map 2.1 Colonial Settlements in Eastern North America, c. 1700

seven escaped servants in Virginia in 1640, all were whipped, branded, and put in chains for a year, but only the white servants' terms of service were extended as punishment. No such adjustment was necessary for the African, Emanuel, whose original service was apparently not limited by time. In the same year, three other Virginia servants ran away from their owner. When they were caught, two of them, a Dutchman and a Scot, received four additional years in servitude, but the third, a Black servant named John Punch, was ordered to serve for the rest of his life. In some instances, Black and white individuals of similar circumstance seemed to be treated similarly. When a white man and a Black woman were found guilty of fornication in 1650, the church required them both to stand in shame before the congregation, clad only in white sheets, following a customary form of church-administered justice.[2]

By mid-century it was becoming clear, however, that Africans would not be treated like other colonials. In 1652 Virginian John Pott's purchase of ten-year-old Jowan included "her Issue and produce duringe her (or either of them) for their Life tyme. And their Successors forever." African slavery was thereby hereditary and perpetual, a condition recognized in law in 1660 in Virginia and 1663 in Maryland. In 1662 the Virginia assembly reversed the English common-law tradition whereby a child took its father's status by declaring that bondage passed to a child if the child's mother was bound. In this way Virginia assured that the offspring of Englishmen and African women remained in service and provided a larger supply of perpetual servants. During the same decade another potential avenue to Black freedom was closed when the question of whether an African convert to Christianity could be held in slavery was resolved by a General Assembly ruling that baptism did not protect an African from perpetual bondage. As more Africans served for life, the punitive value of lengthening the time of service was lost, and owners demanded that they be allowed to use corporal punishment against enslaved people who resisted their control. Virginia authorities agreed, and in 1669 they ruled that owners would not be held liable for such punishment even if the enslaved were killed, since it was presumed that no person would intentionally destroy his own property.[3]

In Maryland, the Chesapeake colony established by Cecilius Calvert in 1634 as a haven for Catholics, indentured servitude played a greater role in the labor system for a longer period, and British convict labor was imported when voluntary servants became more difficult to find. Many Africans served terms much like white indentured servants and their similar situations increased the likelihood of interracial cooperation in such ventures as running away. In 1664, in an attempt to help protect slaveholders from the loss of people they held in slavery, Maryland passed legislation aimed at discouraging the most intimate form of interracial association. The law declared that any white woman marrying an enslaved African could be forced to serve her husband's owner for as long as her husband lived. By 1700 heavy penalties were imposed for interracial marriage, Africans commonly served for a lifetime, and enslaved people's children were automatically enslaved. Eighteenth-century advertisements for runaways demonstrate that legislation could not entirely prevent such liaisons. Isaac Cromwell, a forty-year-old enslaved **mixed-race person** escaped from northern Maryland with Ann Greene, an Englishwoman who was an indentured servant in the same

Anthony Johnson

IN THE EARLY 1620S, slave traders captured a man in Angola, gave him the name Antonio, and brought him to the Americas, where he was sold to a colonist in Virginia. During these early days in British North America, before the system of slavery was strictly codified, some bound Africans were treated much like indentured servants. Although, unlike European servants, they had no contracts, some Africans were freed after a period of servitude. Perhaps this was how Antonio and his wife Mary, also African, gained their freedom. Antonio may also have been granted a tract of land as the customary freedom dues for an indentured servant. By 1641 Antonio, a free man known as Anthony Johnson, was the owner of a small farm with livestock on Virginia's eastern shore. By mid-century, the Johnsons' farm had grown to about 250 acres, and the family held servants of their own.

During the formation of slavery, although race was a factor, color did not yet define life chances as comprehensively as it would by the nineteenth century. The Johnsons suffered a setback in 1653 when fire burned many of the buildings on their farm. The colonial court, noting that Johnson and his family were respected members of the community, granted them tax relief. A few years later, however, the Johnsons' white neighbor, Edmund Scarburgh, forged a letter in which Anthony Johnson appeared to acknowledge a debt. Though Johnson clearly was illiterate, the court granted Scarburgh a substantial portion of his land on the strength of that letter. The family purchased more land in Maryland and continued to live on their Virginia land. But when Anthony died in 1670, an ominous court ruling foreshadowed a more precarious future for free Black people. A white planter was allowed to seize the Virginia land because, the court said, as a Black man, Anthony Johnson was not a citizen of the colony. His children maintained their hold on enough land to remain independent farmers, but they faced greater racial restrictions. By the turn of the eighteenth century, slavery was defined by laws, laws that restricted the lives of all Black people, both free and enslaved.

area. They fled on two of Isaac's owner's horses and his owner believed they were living together in Philadelphia as husband and wife. When Peggy, an enslaved woman who spoke with a Welsh accent, escaped, she left with her Portuguese lover who was an indentured servant.[4]

The status of some Black individuals in both Chesapeake colonies remained ambiguous until the end of the seventeenth century. There were exceptional experiences like that of Anthony Johnson, who was brought to Virginia in 1622, gained his freedom and eventually prospered as a middling planter. Freed after a term of service, he married and acquired substantial acreage and a herd of cattle. Johnson became a slaveholder, turned a reasonable profit from his land,

and even used the colonial court system to protect his right to the labor of those he enslaved against a claim by a white neighbor. He was one of a few free Black men who moved to the ranks of small planters before 1700. By the eighteenth century Africans constituted 80 percent of the unfree workers in the region, largely replacing the Chesapeake's white indentured servants, and slavery had evolved from ambiguity to a permanent, inherited status. Increasingly white people came to assume that any Black person was enslaved unless there was explicit evidence to the contrary.[5]

Slavery Farther South

To the south of the Chesapeake the British established the colony of **Carolina** in 1663. The initial settlers in the southern part of the colony that later became South Carolina produced timber and livestock for the British colonies in the West Indies, but within a generation rice became the chief money crop. Carolina settlers came mainly from the British West Indian colony of **Barbados**, where enslaved Africans worked in the sugarcane fields. Unlike the Chesapeake, Carolina relied on slavery from its beginning, with the enslaved first herding livestock and felling the timber to be shipped to Barbados, then cultivating rice. Since Africans had grown rice for hundreds of years in the region south of the Gambia River in West Africa, many were brought to South Carolina to teach rice culture to their English owners and to grow rice in the lowlands along the Atlantic coast where tidewater flooded the fields and West African techniques were most successful. Black people were the vast majority of the population in this region, especially during the summer months, when the danger from malaria drove white people farther inland. They were 90 percent of the population by the mid-eighteenth century in the wealthiest, most established plantation areas near the capital city of Charleston and more than 60 percent in the entire region. The largest plantations in the British North American colonies were located in tidewater Carolina, where the subtropical heat and humidity in the summer was much like those in the areas from which these Africans had been taken. Those who had spent their childhood in these regions had generally developed some resistance to such diseases as malaria, giving them an advantage over the British, who had a high mortality rate from tropical diseases.[6]

Carolina's demand for slave labor was so great that Charleston became the major port of entry for Africans brought to the American mainland from Africa and the Caribbean. By the time of the American Revolution almost one hundred thousand enslaved people had entered through Charleston harbor, most of them bound for the rice growing regions of the colony. Its majority African population made it more like the Caribbean than other parts of North America. The great number of Black enslaved people in Carolina enabled Africans there to retain more of their languages and cultural practices for longer than perhaps anywhere else in North America. The plantations of Carolina became the home of large African enslaved communities, with internal social and political structures based on West African models. Especially in the **Low Country** of southern Carolina, an amalgam of African cultures shaped an American African culture. In Africa traditional rivalries might have made many of these people deadly enemies, but in Carolina their suffering and shared disadvantage brought them together.

The large number and high proportion of Africans in Carolina created other similarities with slavery in the West Indies—heightened white fears of slave rebellion and harsh measures to control the enslaved population. Rumors of slave unrest in Charleston in 1711 and 1720 led to death by burning for suspected rebels. White slaveholders' insecurity undoubtedly helps to explain the extremely harsh **slave codes** enacted in South Carolina in 1696, even harsher than the Barbadian codes on which they were modeled. These codes were so restrictive that some owners complained that they infringed on slaveholders' property rights. Enslaved people without written permission were restricted to their owner's property, and any white person who discovered an enslaved person violating this rule could whip them, although the punishment could not exceed twenty lashes. Fines were imposed on any white overseer who discovered an unknown enslaved laborer on his plantation and did not report and whip them. No owner could allow his enslaved worker to hunt except with a special license, renewed monthly. Owners were required to inspect all slave quarters regularly to ensure that no weapons were available. Volumes of regulations detailed punishments ranging from whipping for lesser offenses, branding for petty theft, cutting off the right ear for the first offense of striking a white person, castration for a fourth escape attempt, and death for rape, attempted murder, or murder of a white person. Those who administered punishment were not held liable if death resulted inadvertently. These sanctions were among the most draconian anywhere in the Americas.[7]

Yet even in South Carolina there was occasional evidence of surprising tolerance during the colonial era. One striking example of this was the establishment of a school in Charleston for area enslaved people. The plan, sponsored by the Society for the Propagation of the Gospel in Foreign Parts, an auxiliary of the Anglican Church, was to train the enslaved in the Christian religion and to have them instructed by another enslaved person specially educated to be the schoolmaster. In 1743 the school opened under the direction of Harry, considered a "genius" by some local white residents, and the student body quickly rose to sixty. Although some white people were concerned about the experiment, the school continued for more than twenty years until Harry died in 1764. The coexistence of this school with South Carolina's harsh slave codes illustrates the contradictory nature of American slavery.[8]

On the southern border of South Carolina lay the colony of Georgia. Granted by the Crown to James Edward Oglethorpe in 1732, this colony was intended to serve an important military function as a strategic outpost separating British North America from Spanish Florida to its south, standing against the expansionist ambitions of one of England's most powerful rivals. Among its earliest British settlers were the abject poor of English society, many drawn from the nation's debtors' prisons. British liberal reformers saw this new land

Table 2.1   Selected Key Legal Developments Concerning Slavery and Race in British America, 1635–1696

YEAR	COLONY	KEY PROVISIONS
1635	Barbados	Governor declares that all Africans and Native Americans brought to the island are to be considered enslaved unless they have a contract that says otherwise.
1641	Massachusetts Bay	Defines legal slavery within the colony.
1643	Virginia	Women of African descent and all men to be counted for the tithe to support Church of England.
1661	Barbados	First comprehensive slave code in English America, setting model for South Carolina to follow.
1661	Virginia	Indentured servants who run away with enslaved people must serve time that the enslaved person missed as well as time that they missed.
1662	Virginia	Child's legal status to follow that of the mother rather than the father.
1664	Maryland	The court recognizes slavery as a lifelong legal condition.
1665	New York	New English Assembly, composed largely of migrants from New England, recognizes slavery as lifelong condition.
1667	Virginia	Denies that baptism provides legal grounds to sue for freedom.
1670	Virginia	Native Americans taken captive outside colony and imported to serve for life; those captured within colony to serve twelve years (if children) or until age thirty.
1679	New York	Enslavement of Native Americans prohibited.
1680	Virginia	Enslaved Black people barred from carrying arms, gathering (particularly for feasts and burials), or leaving plantations without a pass from their owner.
1691	Virginia	White people barred from marrying Black, mixed-race, or Native American people; children born of unions between Englishwomen and Black men to become servants; mothers to pay fine, become servants, or have their servitude extended. Owners owed compensation if their runaway enslaved men and women are killed while being captured. Freed people ordered to leave colony.
1692	Virginia	Special courts created for trying enslaved people accused of crimes.
1696	South Carolina	First comprehensive slave code in English North America established, modeled after that of Barbados.

as an asylum in which these unfortunates of society might be rehabilitated. Their dream was to establish Georgia as a utopian community of independent small farmers. No one person could own more than five hundred acres, and the inheritance of land was restricted. To encourage hard work and civility among the settlers, alcoholic drink was outlawed, and in the interest of public tranquility slavery was forbidden. Further, since white Georgians feared that Africans might join with the Native Americans and the Spanish in military action against them, both enslaved and free Black people were prohibited from entering the colony.

This commitment to a slave-free colony was not universally accepted among the colonials, and many bent on rapid economic development argued for the necessity of slave labor. These "malcontents," as other Georgians called them, claimed that white laborers could not grow rice as profitably as enslaved laborers did in South Carolina. Opponents of slavery, motivated as much by anti-Black prejudice as humanitarian sentiment, countered by citing the example of German planters from Salzburg who were successfully growing rice in the small community of Ebenezer, near Savannah. After a decade of debate, it became clear that the original vision of Georgia as a utopian community would not be sustained. In 1742 the ban on alcohol was lifted, and eight years later restrictions on slavery and large landholdings were repealed. Thereafter Georgia moved rapidly in the direction of other southern colonies, establishing large plantations where great numbers of enslaved people supplied the labor on which the wealth of a powerful planter class was based.[9]

Slavery in the Middle Colonies

North of the Chesapeake, there were a few large plantations, but most slaveholdings were much smaller, and Black persons accounted for a tiny proportion of the population, especially in New England. Whereas in 1750 enslaved Black people constituted 61 percent of the colonial population in South Carolina, 31 percent in Maryland, and 46 percent in Virginia, they were only 2 percent in Pennsylvania, 7 percent in New Jersey, and 14 percent in New York. In New England, except for Rhode Island's 10 percent, no colony's enslaved population exceeded 3 percent of the total. Although slavery was not the major enterprise in the northern colonies that it was in the South, it was still economically and socially important. Slavery became an issue for debate early in the life of Pennsylvania, a colony established by English **Quakers** on Maryland's northern border in 1661. In 1682 its founder and governor, William Penn, who had envisioned a refuge for Quakers persecuted in England, proposed to limit slavery in the colony. Two years later, 150 Africans were imported to help clear the land. Penn preferred to have Pennsylvanians rely on indentured labor, with African indentures for fourteen years of service, and many Black men received land as their customary freedom dues. But demand for labor in the colony was too great to be satisfied by the supply of indentured servants. Within three years of his original proposal, Penn decided that perpetual slavery was more economical than temporary service, abandoned his plan, and became a slaveholder himself. As the number of white servants declined, Pennsylvania came more and more to rely on African slave labor, and its capital city of Philadelphia became a major slave-trading center.[10]

By 1760 almost 8 percent of the inhabitants of Philadelphia were of African descent. Estimates of the Black population in Pennsylvania vary widely, ranging from 2,500 to 5,000 in 1721 and 2,900 to 11,000 by mid-century. After that time, a large and relatively sudden influx of German and Irish indentured servants reduced the demand for enslaved Africans and curbed the growth of the colony's Black population. Whenever the supply of white servants was disrupted, however, Pennsylvania slaveholders imported more Africans. Some Pennsylvanians expressed concern about the colony's growing number of enslaved people. In fact, as early as 1707 and 1722 white laborers complained of competition from slave labor. Others expressed fears that the increasing number of Africans would bring a greater danger of slave rebellion. Acting partly on these fears and partly on a desire to generate revenue for the colony, the Pennsylvania Assembly imposed a tax on the importation of enslaved people. Still, the continuing demand for slave labor made it difficult to effectively control the number of importations. Pennsylvania's taxes were easily circumvented by landing slave cargos in neighboring New Jersey and smuggling them overland into the colony; smuggling became so common that New Jersey seaside towns such as Perth Amboy and Cape May became major slave ports.[11]

Yet, Pennsylvania's Quakers had always been uneasy about slavery, and their discomfort grew with the increasing enslaved population, while their disquiet moderated the institution. In fact many visitors reported that slavery in Penn's colony was milder by far than in colonies farther south. Many Quakers favored providing opportunities for the colony's Black men and women, and in the 1750s, Israel Acrelius, a visiting minister, was impressed by the better treatment of Pennsylvania's enslaved people. In 1758 Philadelphia Quaker educator, Anthony Benezet, established a school for Black people and used the educational achievement of his students as the basis for his arguments against the notion of African intellectual inferiority, calling it "a vulgar prejudice founded on ... pride and ignorance."[12]

Sometimes the tolerance extended to the enslaved individuals provided them with opportunities that approached independence. Many were allowed to "hire out" their time, providing most of their earnings to their owners but keeping a portion for themselves. Although marriages of enslaved people were not legal, there were apparently some efforts to prevent the separation of families when they were sold. So long as they did not seem dangerous, few restrictions were imposed on their movements, and during their nonwork hours they associated freely with family and friends among other enslaved people, free Black persons, and even white servants. The lax enforcement of slave codes angered some colonists, but by the mid-eighteenth century sentiment against slavery had gained strength in Pennsylvania, and the annual Quaker Meetings debated ways to discourage the importation of more enslaved Africans and encourage the **manumission** of enslaved people already there. Despite an increase in antislavery sentiment, slave codes still restricted enslaved people in Pennsylvania. They were clearly distinguished from free people in colonial law and were not guaranteed legal protection. Curfews, restrictions on gatherings of enslaved people, pass systems, and harsh penalties including whipping, castration (for attempted rape), and death (for burglary, murder, or rape) were used to control Pennsylvania's enslaved population, as they were in the southern plantation colonies.

Discussions among the Quakers continued, and by 1693 the Yearly Philadelphia Meeting asserted that no Quaker should buy enslaved people except as a means of freeing them. More radical Quakers called on all slaveholding members to free people they held in slavery. During the 1730s Benjamin Lay, a Quaker from Barbados who had witnessed large-scale slavery, testified at one meeting after another about the horrors of the institution and once even abducted a slaveholder's child to dramatize the pain slavery caused to families. He was expelled from the meeting for this action and for the publication of *All Slave-Keepers That Keep the Innocent in Bondage*, in which he roundly condemned all Quakers who participated in or condoned slavery. Other influential Quakers opposed to slavery included John Woolman from New Jersey, whose antislavery writings were widely read among Quakers, and educator Anthony Benezet. By 1758 the work of the Quaker antislavery activists bore fruit—Penn's Yearly Meeting declared that Quakers who imported, bought, or sold people after that year should be expelled from the congregation. Further, it strongly suggested that slaveholding members free their enslaved people and provide them with Christian training. These were tentative steps, but they marked the start of a conviction among Quakers that spread from Pennsylvania throughout the **Middle Colonies** into New England and even into the South, where Quaker settlements became centers of antislavery philosophy.[13]

The Middle Colonies continued to import white servants throughout the pre-Revolutionary period. Interracial relationships developed as enslaved Black men and women often worked with white laborers and indentured servants in ways not common on the larger southern plantations. These workers associated with each other in iron manufacturing in New Jersey and Pennsylvania, as dock laborers in New York City, and even in the skilled trades of the urban centers. Consequently, Africans in the Middle Colonies were more likely to learn about English culture and to learn the English language faster and better than Africans in the large, insular African communities on southern plantations. Whereas most enslaved people in the South were required to know only enough English to be able to carry out the work-related orders of owners and overseers, in the Middle Colonies they often lived in the owner's household and spent much of the day with European Americans.

Differences in background and experience help to explain the differences in linguistic abilities reflected in newspaper advertisements for runaways. Black people brought from the West Indies often spoke French and Spanish. One man named John, who was born in Dominica and ran away soon after coming to Philadelphia in 1745, was described as speaking French well but only a little English. Another fugitive, it was said, spoke Spanish but no English, while a third was fluent in English, French, and Spanish. One runaway from Pennsylvania spoke both English and "Swede," and a New Jersey runaway, Claus, spoke "Dutch and good English." Black enslaved people in the region that had been controlled by the Dutch frequently spoke both English and Dutch. When Toney left his owner in Philadelphia, he was well-dressed in a "Striped Linsey Woolsy

Jacket," a "Tow shirt," matching pants, and a felt hat. His distinguishing characteristics included his being "a likely lusty" twenty-four-year-old who spoke English and "High Dutch" (actually, proper German).[14]

Because the British colony of New York began as the Dutch corporate colony of New Netherland, slavery there had a slightly different foundation. Although the first eleven captive Africans were landed in New Netherland in 1626, slave labor was never an important part of the colony's economy. Enslaved Africans worked the Dutch West India Company's great Hudson River Valley estates as they did the plantations of the South, but most were employed on smaller farms or were a part of the Dutch military forces that defended the colony against Native Americans during the early 1640s. The Dutch intended their reliance on slave labor to be temporary, but white workers moved quickly from agricultural work to trades, leaving the colony with too few farm hands and an unstable labor supply. By the 1640s the Dutch regularly imported enslaved Africans to fill their labor needs.

The Dutch West India Company employed a flexible style of bondage called **half freedom**. Africans were allowed to live independently in exchange for their agreement to pay a yearly tax and provide labor to the company when needed. Under these circumstances they lived daily lives much like free persons. Married people supported their own families and lived in family units. Despite the fact that the children of people bound under the half-free system owed their labor to the company for life, this was still one of the mildest forms of slavery practiced in North America. If they were freed, Black people were accorded the same rights as white locals in the colony. They could own property, pursue trades, and even intermarry with white people. Race was a factor in that being Black carried with it the probability of being enslaved, but Black individuals were treated as free people so long as their white neighbors knew that they were free.[15]

In the 1660s England went to war against The Netherlands, attempting to eliminate Dutch trade competition and to gain control of the Hudson River fur-trading region. When the British took over the colony in 1664, they gradually made slavery there conform to the system in their other American colonies, and enslaved people lost the advantages of the half-freedom arrangement. As the number of enslaved people increased, rising colonial anxieties encouraged harsh restrictions. In 1682 flogging was prescribed for any four or more enslaved people meeting together without white supervision. A sunset curfew was imposed on all enslaved adults in New York City, but when that arrangement proved inconvenient for owners, the provision was changed and enslaved people were required to carry lighted lanterns when they moved about the city after dark. A slave regulating act was passed in 1702, in 1708 whipping became mandatory for minor infractions, and after 1710 colonial courts rejected several cases brought against owners by enslaved laborers claiming unpaid wages. By the early eighteenth century virtually all that remained of New York's Dutch past were a few large estates in the Hudson Valley, Dutch cultural festivals and traditions, and the Dutch language spoken by many Black and white people in the colony.[16]

Under the British during the first half of the eighteenth century, New York became the major slaveholding colony north of Maryland, with more than ten thousand enslaved people, constituting about 15 percent of the population by 1750. With continued growth, there were more than nineteen thousand enslaved persons in New York on the eve of the Revolution. Enslaved people were provided with virtually no legal protection, and none could testify against a free person in a court. As in other northern colonies, slavery was not the basis of New York's economy, but enslaved people did provide an important part of the labor supply, and there were many slaveholders in the colony. In the rural areas outside of New York City, enslaved people accounted for between one fifth and one third of the population. The estates on Long Island and in the Hudson River Valley, as well as those in the tobacco-growing areas of the Narragansett region of Rhode Island, continued to use large numbers of enslaved workers throughout the eighteenth century, functioning more like the plantations of South Carolina than did most other regions in the North. New York City was the major urban slaveholding center. Only Charleston surpassed it in slave ownership, and although the proportion of slaveholders in the population declined as the century progressed, the actual number of enslaved people in the city increased, so that by the mid-eighteenth century they were a common sight. In the early 1770s one foreign visitor to New York was surprised by slavery's visibility, remarking, "It rather hurts the European eye to see so many negro slaves upon the streets."[17]

Slavery in New England

There were fewer Black people in **New England** than in the Middle Colonies, but even there slavery was a familiar aspect of colonial life. From 1624 when Samuel Maverick became the region's first slaveholder, New Englanders imported small numbers of Africans, mainly from the British West Indies. The enslaved population increased slowly—only a few enslaved people arrived each year before 1700, and only a few dozen each year during the first part of the eighteenth century. By 1700 there were barely one thousand Africans in all of New England; about half of those were in Massachusetts.

The **Puritans** of New England seem to have struggled more with the morality of slavery than did the planters of the Chesapeake or Carolina, though somewhat more legalistically than the Quakers in Pennsylvania. In the Massachusetts Body of Liberties of 1641 colonial authorities justified slavery only for those who sold themselves or were captured in "just wars." Previously, in 1637, the colony's need for labor had encouraged a tortured interpretation of this principle, allowing several hundred Native American men captured during the Pequot wars to be taken to the West Indies and traded there for enslaved Africans who were then brought to New England. Pequot women and children captured during the wars remained in Massachusetts and were treated as servants. This interpretation hardly satisfied the spirit of Massachusetts's principles, but it provided justification enough given the rising expense of white labor. The Massachusetts General Court clarified this issue with a ruling in 1645 that the importation of enslaved Africans was legal so long as the purchase was made from "legitimate" slave traders. By 1670 the question of the status of children born to enslaved women and white men was resolved by following the precedent set in Virginia that such offspring took the status of their mother. Massachusetts set the example for other New England colonies, and by the early 1700s slavery was legal and well established in the region. Economic pressures had overcome theological and philosophical reservations to allow slaveholding in the region, but the number of enslaved people remained very small. Massachusetts was the largest slaveholding colony in New England, but even in Boston where the enslaved were concentrated, there were only 150 Africans by 1690 and fewer than 500 in 1710. The average slaveholder held only two people, and only about 12 percent of Boston's white population owned even one.[18]

With such small slaveholdings, enslaved Africans were as integrated into the colonial household and society in New England as they were in the Middle Colonies. This situation not only facilitated their learning English but often provided them with other advantages. The experiences of enslaved people in the household of a physician in Plymouth, Massachusetts, provide examples of the potential benefits from this form of slavery. Four enslaved people—Pompey, his wife Phyllis, Quasho, and Prince, the household cook—lived in two rooms above the kitchen in the home of Dr. LeBaron, a widower with many children. LeBaron exercised authority over them, but he also allowed them privileges not generally granted to people enslaved in the South. Phyllis controlled her own money and successfully invested in business ventures available in the busy commercial port. With part of the profit she made for her share in the trade of a schooner, she bought a set of "Guinea-gold beads" that she wore along with her "portentous turban" to express her own African sense of beauty and style.[19]

When disagreements arose between a northern owner and the enslaved people who lived in his household, compromises were likely to be reached, or the enslaved people might even be able to impose their own wills. When Dr. LeBaron decided to extend the classical allusions in his household by adding "Julius Caesar" to the Pompey already there, he suggested that Quasho accept that name. Quasho refused, saying that his mother in Africa had called him by the name of Quasho Quando, and he did not intend to take another.

Newport, July 6, 1764.
Juſt imported in the Sloop *Elizabeth,* from *Africa*, and to be ſold, by

John Miller,

At his Houſe, or Store ;

A Number of healthy

Negro Boys and Girls.
Likewiſe to be ſold,—*Tillock's* and *Kippen's* Snuff, by the Caſk or Dozen.

A notice in a newspaper advertising enslaved Africans for sale: "Just imported in the Sloop *Elizabeth*, from *Africa*," *Providence Gazette*, July 6, 1764.

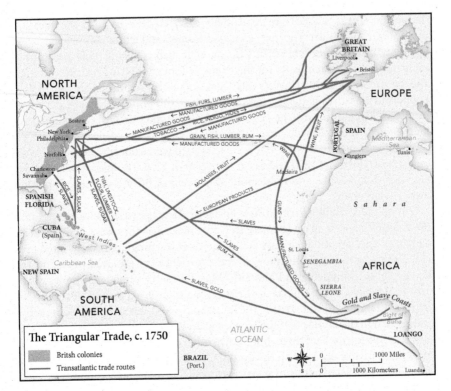

Map 2.2 The Triangular Trade, c. 1750

LeBaron attempted unsuccessfully to change Quasho's mind with punishments ranging from the deprivation of food to whipping. He then tried bribery but finally dropped the matter.[20]

Although colonies in New England had fewer enslaved people, and they were less likely to be strictly controlled than in the South, enslaved Africans were an integral part of New England's labor system. They worked mainly on small farms or as domestic servants, unskilled workers, or even skilled artisans in the cities. Most white residents in Massachusetts agreed with colonial Governor John Winthrop that the colony could not survive without "a stock of slaves sufficient to dow [sic] all our business." Except perhaps in the areas with large estates, the economic importance of slavery in New England and New York was more a matter of slave trading than of slaveholding. New England sea captains often commanded the slave trading vessels, merchants from New England and New York often financed the ventures, goods produced in these regions served as items traded for enslaved Africans, and vessels built in New England moved the trade across the ocean. Slaveholding was an important part of this **Triangular Trade**, since African workers in New England provided labor for the distilling industry that turned West Indian sugar into rum. The New England ships that brought sugar to North America, finished goods and rum to Africa, and Africans to American slavery were built with enslaved labor.[21]

Enslaved and Free Black People

Although much of the colonial economy rested on slave labor, and many white people believed that slavery was the only suitable institution for controlling Africans, not all Africans were enslaved. As slavery evolved and the number of enslaved people increased, especially in the plantation South, and legal measures for the protection of slaveholders' property rights were established, free Black men and women were increasingly seen as a threat to those rights. It became more difficult for people to gain their freedom, as a few had before the mid-seventeenth century. Thus, the development of slavery was closely tied to a deterioration of the rights of free Black persons, and such prosperous freed people as the Anthony Johnson family of seventeenth century Virginia became increasingly rare. In 1691 Virginia's General Court declared that no enslaved person might be set free unless that freedom was accompanied by enough money for transportation out of the colony within six months of emancipation. In 1723 the judgment was strengthened by a declaration that manumission could only be given for some "meritorious service" certified by colonial officials. Those Black individuals who did acquire their freedom were not truly free; their rights were severely restricted by special regulations devised to control them. In Virginia free Black men had no right to vote or to a jury trial, and they could be sold into slavery for minor infractions.

Since the free Black population in Maryland was smaller than in Virginia, it was less threatening, and there were fewer restrictions on manumission. An attempt to prohibit emancipation failed to pass the colonial legislature in 1715, but by mid-century the requirement of special written freedom forms issued by the colonial authorities made freeing someone more difficult. Concerns that freed people might become public charges prompted other regulations requiring that a manumitted person be healthy, capable of self-support, and not over fifty years of age. As in Virginia, many of the restrictions placed on the movement of enslaved people also applied to free Black persons, and these restrictions made it extremely difficult for them to find employment outside of indentured servitude.

A series of slave rebellions in Barbados from 1639 to the 1690s made South Carolina planters, many of whom came from Barbados, uneasy about their growing Black population. They were especially concerned about the potentially disruptive influence of free Black people on their enslaved people and took measures to discourage the growth of the free Black population. In 1715 the colony passed a regulation preventing the emancipation of any runaway or rebellious enslaved person, although a master could free someone for loyal and faithful service. Once freed, however, just as in Virginia, a Black person was required to leave the colony within six months. In what might seem an unnecessary addition, a 1721 colonial statute limited the right to vote to "free white men." Planters' apprehension intensified after a major slave uprising at the Stono River in South Carolina in 1739 and with the expanding number of African arrivals in the colony. Between 1735 and 1740, slave traders brought twelve thousand Africans to work the South Carolina rice fields. This prompted colonial officials' futile effort to control the size of the colony's

DOCUMENTING BLACK AMERICA

Venture Smith

Venture Smith, an African, tells of his capture and enslavement.

I was born at Dukandarra, in Guinea, about the year 1729. My father's name was Saungm Furro, Prince of the tribe of Dukandarra. My father had three wives. Polygamy was not uncommon in that country, especially among the rich, as every man was allowed to keep as many wives as he could maintain. . . . I descended from a very large, tall and stout race of beings, much larger than the generality of people in other parts of the globe, being commonly considerable above six feet in height, and every way well proportioned. . . .

[At word of a planned attack by an army supplied and incited by white people] my father and his family set off about the break of day. The king and his two younger wives went in one company, and my mother and her children in another. We left our dwellings in succession, and my father's company went on first. We directed our course for a large shrub plain, some distance off, where we intended to conceal ourselves from the approaching enemy, until we could refresh ourselves a little. But we presently found that our retreat was not secure. For having struck up a little fire for the purpose of cooking victuals, the enemy, who happened to be encamped a little distance off, had sent out a scouting party who discovered us by the smoke of the fire, just as we were extinguishing it and about to eat. As soon as we had finished eating, my father discovered the party and immediately began to discharge arrows at them. This was what I first saw, and it alarmed both me and the women, who, being unable to make any resistance immediately betook ourselves to the tall, thick reeds not far off, and left the old king to fight alone. For some time I beheld him from the reeds defending himself with great courage and firmness, till at last he was obliged to surrender himself into their hands.

They then came to us in the reeds, and the very first salute I had from them was a violent blow on the head with the fore part of a gun, and at the same time a grasp around the neck. I then had a rope put about my neck, as all the women in the thicket with me, and were immediately led to my father, who was likewise pinioned and haltered for leading . . . my father was closely interrogated respecting his money. . . . But as he gave them no account of it, he was instantly cut and pounded on his body with great inhumanity. . . . All this availed not in the least to make him give up his money . . . until the continued exercise and increase of torment obliged him to sink and expire. . . . I saw him while he was thus tortured to death. The shocking scene is to this day fresh in my memory. . . .

The army of the enemy was large, I should suppose consisting of about six thousand men. . . . After destroying the old prince, they decamped and immediately marched

Black population in 1741 by levying a tariff on further importations. Although the number of free Black men and women remained relatively small, the enslaved population soared. Within a decade, Africans and their descendants accounted for almost two thirds of South Carolina's population. Controls on towards the sea, lying to the west, taking with them myself and the women prisoners. . . . The enemy had remarkable success in destroying the country wherever they went. For as far as they had penetrated they laid the habitations waste and captured the people. The distance they had now brought me was about four hundred miles. All the march I had very hard tasks imposed on me, which I must perform on pain of punishment, I was obliged to carry on my head a large flat stone used for grinding our corn, weighing, as I should suppose, as much as twenty-five pounds; besides victuals, mat and cooking utensils. Though I was pretty large and stout of my age, yet these burdens were very grievous to me, being only six years and a half old. . . .

[At the end of the long march and more slave-raiding battles, in a coastal settlement called Anamaboo,] the enemy's provisions were then almost spent, as well as their strength. The inhabitants, knowing what conduct they had pursued, and what were their present intentions, improved the favorable opportunity, attacked them, and took enemy, prisoners, flocks and all their effects. I was then taken a second time. All of us were then put into the castle and kept for market. On a certain time, I and other prisoners were put on board a canoe, under our master, and rowed away to a vessel belonging to Rhode Island, commanded by Captain Collingwood, and the mate, Thomas Mumford. While we were going to the vessel, our master told us to appear to the best possible advantage for sale. I was bought on board by one Robertson Mumford, a steward of said vessel, for four gallons of rum and a piece of calico, and called VENTURE on account of his having purchased me with his own private venture. Thus I came by my name. All the slaves that were bought for that vessel's cargo were two hundred and sixty.

After all the business was ended on the coast of Africa, the ship sailed from thence to Barbadoes. After an ordinary passage, except great mortality by the small pox, which broke out on board, we arrived at the island of Barbadoes; but when we reached it, there were found, out of the two hundred and sixty that sailed from Africa, not more than two hundred alive. These were all sold, except myself and three more, to the planters there.

The vessel then sailed for Rhode Island, and arrived there after a comfortable passage. Here my master sent me to live with one of his sisters until he could carry me to Fisher's Island, the place of his residence. I had then completed my eighth year. After staying with his sister some time, I was taken to my master's place to live.

Source: Venture Smith, A Narrative of the Life and Adventures of Venture, A Native of Africa, But Resident Above Sixty Years in the United States of America. Related by Himself. (Middletown, CN: J. S. Stewart, Printer and Bookbinder, 1897 [1798]), 4–10.

enslaved and free Black people were tightened, and a new law prohibited freeing anyone except for some exceptionally honorable service and with official approval. Even so, freed Black individuals could remain in the colony only for six months.[22]

Despite the restrictions, the number of free Black men and women increased all over the South, and a few even prospered. Some free Black men became landowners, a few grew wealthy, and a small number became slaveholders. In North Carolina those few who could meet the property requirement became eligible to vote after 1737, when the king lifted the colony's prohibition against Black and Native American people voting. It is surprising that Carolina slaveholders tolerated even their small free Black population in the eighteenth century, but some were tied by blood to the most powerful planters, who saw them as trusted allies, a protective buffer against slave rebellion. This trust was sometimes misplaced, as when free Black individuals were implicated in slave conspiracies, but free Black people could often use it to their advantage. Still, their lives and freedom were precarious, and restrictive and exclusionary laws could be enforced whenever the white minority felt threatened.[23]

There were more free Black persons south of Maryland and Virginia, but a larger percentage of the total Black population was free in the Middle Colonies and in New England. Many factors encouraged the growth of a free Black population in these areas—many Black people gained their freedom after serving their terms as indentured servants; Quaker opposition to and Puritan reservations about slavery led to fewer restrictions on manumissions. Philosophical and moral reservations also seemed more persuasive in regions where slavery was not the dominant labor system and where there were relatively few Africans.

Especially where there were small slaveholdings, the lives of free and enslaved Black people were intertwined, and often they were members of the same family. Marriages involving enslaved people were not generally recognized in the colonies, and even under the best circumstances, they were maintained only at the owner's convenience. The tenuous existence of enslaved families is illustrated by the advertisement in a New England newspaper offering for sale a "likely negro woman about 19 years and a child of about six months of age to be sold together or apart." One way for free Black people to protect enslaved members of their families was to secure their freedom, and free Black individuals often spent years working and saving to purchase the freedom of family members. Laws restricting free Black persons often made it more difficult to gain the freedom of family members in the southern colonies. On occasion, because newly freed Black people could not legally remain in a colony, it was more efficient for a free Black person to purchase a family member and hold that person in slavery. Such ownership would be a legal convenience allowing the newly purchased family member to remain. Many of the people listed as the property of free Black persons in South Carolina, Virginia, and elsewhere in the South were "owned" under these circumstances.[24]

Dealing with the problem of enslaved family members was only one of many problems faced by free Black men and women. Even the most fortunate were not truly free to take advantage of opportunities open to white people. In New England, Lucy and Abijah Prince were well off by the standards of the day, though both had been enslaved in Deerfield, Massachusetts. Lucy had been kidnapped into slavery at the age of five in her native Africa. She was known in Deerfield for her narrative poem describing the attack she witnessed by Native Americans on the village in 1746. Abijah Prince gained his freedom through his owner's will that also gave him a sizable plot of land. This land provided the funds to buy Lucy's freedom and to give the couple a comfortable start when they married in 1756. The Princes acquired additional land in nearby Vermont, where they raised their six children and settled into a life as respectable community members. Despite their exemplary lives, when their oldest son, Caesar, reached college age he was refused permission to enroll at Williams College in western Massachusetts. Not easily discouraged, Lucy set their case before the college trustees, presenting a three-hour argument drawing upon the law and the Bible, but to no avail. The college held fast to its policy that no Black person, no matter how qualified, could attend Williams.[25]

If the financially stable, determined Prince family faced obstacles to their advancement in New England, one of the most tolerant regions in the colonies, it is not surprising that less well-situated free Black individuals in less tolerant surroundings fared poorly. North or South, they were discriminated against, restricted, and generally despised. Free Black men and women were often limited to the least desirable sections of a town for their residences or to the least productive land in the countryside for their farms. In most public places they were segregated, and regardless of the weather they were relegated to the outside of carriages, the outside decks of ships, and the unsheltered decks of ferries. If they were allowed to attend white churches at all, they were often limited to seats in the rear or in out-of-the-way areas, and they were barred from or segregated in places of public entertainment. More important economically, free Black people also faced occupational restrictions and were often unable even to take up the trades they had practiced in slavery. As early as 1717 the Connecticut colony required that Black persons get special permission from colonial officials before they could open any business. Under such conditions, it is not surprising that most free Black people were poor, and they faced all the hardships of poor people as well as some problems peculiar to being Black. Many New England towns, for example, could simply order transient poor white people deemed undesirable and any free Black people presumed to be undesirable out of town.

The sea offered one of the few areas of employment open to free Black men, and a great many worked as sailors throughout the eighteenth century. Unlike life ashore, life at sea was generally unsegregated, partly because of the limitations of the ships' quarters and partly because conditions for everyone were so harsh that any attempt at fine differentiation would have been futile. The sea offered some of the best opportunities for Black men during the period, even though they were generally relegated to the lower ranks and the least desirable, most dangerous jobs and often got a smaller share of the profits from the voyage. For free Black women, there were few desirable alternatives to domestic service, and Black women provided the domestic labor for many rural and urban colonial households. In the South almost all of these women were enslaved, but in the North both enslaved and free women were in the domestic

Report of Rebellion Plans in Virginia

Petersburgh, (Virginia) May 17. Several alarming accounts have been received in this town, of a very dangerous insurrection among the negroes on the eastern shore of Virginia; the particulars of which we have not been able to obtain:—reports state, that about two weeks ago, the negroes in that part of the state, to the amount of about 900, assembled in different parties, armed with muskets, spears, clubs, &c. and committed several outrages upon the inhabitants.—A favourite servant of colonel Savage's, who had joined them, met his master on the road, took his horse and some money from him, and treated him in a very insolent manner. Caleb, a negro, the property of mr. Simpkins, was to command this banditti; he was also a favourite servant of his master's, and had long lived with him in the capacity of an overseer. A barrel of musket balls, about 300 spears, some guns, powder, provisions, &c. have already been discovered and taken; the spears, it is said, were made by a negro blacksmith, on the eastern shore. A considerable number of the negroes have been taken, and, it is expected, will be hanged. The militia have turned out, and are obliged to keep constant guard.

It appears, by a letter which has been lately discovered in Norfolk, from one of the negroes on the eastern shore, that they had concerted a plan with the negroes about

work force. On occasion, a skilled Black woman might be employed as a seamstress or a weaver, among the most desirable jobs available to Black people in any region.

Black and Native American People

There was no clear place for free Black men and women in the society of the colonies. Yet they were not the only marginalized peoples in British North America—they shared this position with Native Americans. Most of the Native Americans who had survived the wars with the English and exposure to European diseases lived on the fringes of colonial society, trading and occasionally working for the colonists, their presence on the frontier a constant source of conflict and concern. Frontier settlers who continually demanded that colonial authorities protect them from Native Americans were sometimes willing to take matters into their own hands when officials were slow to act. Often the informal colonial forces that defended frontier settlements or attacked Native American neighbors included Black people as well as white.

In 1676 Nathaniel Bacon, a white frontier planter, led an interracial army of poor white residents, servants, and enslaved people on a massacre of the

Norfolk and Portsmouth, to commit some violent outrages in and about those two towns—the letter states, that 600 of them were to cross over the bay, at a certain time in the night; and, when they arrived at those towns, they were to be joined by the negroes in that neighbourhood. They then meant to blow up the magazine in Norfolk, and massacre the inhabitants. Since the discovery of this letter, a guard of fifty men in each of the towns of Norfolk and Portsmouth, has been regularly kept up; several negroes have been taken up on suspicion, and lodged in jail, and a number of guns have been discovered, concealed under houses and other secret places, all loaded, most of which were English muskets, with fixed bayonets. It is hoped, that a timely check will be given to this alarming outrage.

The present unguarded situation of our country, renders the above circumstances more particularly interesting: and it is hoped will be a means of urging our rulers to make some speedy and effectual provision for arming and organizing the militia, which for three years past has been most shamefully neglected, and has left us almost destitute of every means of defence.

Source: Daily Advertiser *(New York), May 28, 1792.*

Occaneechee tribe of Native Americans. Incensed when colonial authorities condemned his actions, Bacon turned his interracial force against the governing elites. The colonial governor declared Bacon and his men outlaws and moved against them with a substantial force. Bacon was killed and his army defeated, but among those who held out longest were eighty Black resisters and twenty white. This incident alerted Virginia's elites to the dangers of interracial alliances among the lower classes. In fact many laws were designed to control the perceived threat to the public order and to slavery represented by such relationships. In Virginia the first racially based laws prohibited interracial marriages. In 1705 Massachusetts also prohibited such relationships, providing that Black men and women in interracial relationships be whipped and sold into slavery outside the colony. White men would be whipped, fined, and held responsible for any children resulting from the relationship, and white women would be whipped and bound into a period of indenture. A 1726 Pennsylvania law declared that any free Black person who married a white person could be sold into slavery.[26]

Bacon's Rebellion also illustrates the complex, shifting interracial alliances that emerged during the eighteenth century. British colonials found both enemies and allies against rival Europeans among Native Americans. Black people often found common cause with Native Americans against white colonists, but even in the areas of greatest slaveholding, they sometimes helped defend the colonies against European or Native American enemies. In 1747, for example, South Carolina expressed formal appreciation to the Black militiamen who "in times of war, behaved themselves with great faithfulness and courage, in repelling the attacks of his Majesty's enemies." Both free Black and Native American people, however, were generally viewed with suspicion by white settlers. Indeed, occupying similar statuses sometimes brought Black and Native American people together in political and personal alliances. On occasion they were allied in military action, as in 1657 when a force of Black and Native American people attacked and burned part of Hartford, Connecticut, or in 1727 when Black and Native American people terrorized Virginia settlements. Fearful white authorities responded to such incidents with restrictive regulations. In 1690 several Connecticut settlements set a 9 p.m. curfew for both Native American and Black people. Boston officials prohibited Black and Native American people from carrying canes or sticks that might be used as weapons. New Yorkers enacted harsh laws calling for the execution of any enslaved person caught traveling forty miles north of Albany in order to discourage enslaved people's attempts to escape to Native American allies or to the French in Canada.[27]

Black and Native American people frequently developed close personal relationships as well. Large numbers of Native American men had been killed or exiled from New England in the wars in the seventeenth century, leaving a Native American society with a gender imbalance heavily favoring women. The preference for importing male slave labor, on the other hand, resulted in a higher proportion of men in the area's Black population during the late seventeenth and

Indigenous and African people in Louisiana, c. 1735. An enslaved African boy stands to the left of an Atakapa hunter, who holds a calumet (peace pipe) used in Indigenous diplomatic rituals throughout the Southeast.

early eighteenth century. Colonial records document the significant number of Native American–African marriages that resulted partly from these complementary imbalances. The customary practice of treating the offspring of these marriages as Black was made official in 1719 in South Carolina by the colonial governor's proclamation that all those "not entirely Indian" would be counted as Black. The records of colonial New Jersey indicate that that colony also listed those of combined Native American and African parentage as Black. Under this provision Cyrus Bustill Jr., the son of a Black baker and a Delaware Native American woman, was listed on official documents as "negro." As an adult, Bustill was a successful Quaker businessman, an advocate of antislavery and a powerful spokesman for the Black community.[28]

Some people of Native American and African heritage functioned as a member of both groups. Paul Cuffe of Massachusetts was born to a Native American mother and an African father. Although Cuffe spent most of his life outside Native American society, he claimed his Native American heritage and signed separate political petitions representing both Native American and African interests. Several of his siblings lived alternately in Native American and non–Native American settlements in Massachusetts. His older brother John married a Native American woman and remained in a Native American community. Intermarriage between Black and Native American people was so common that treaties struck between colonial authorities and several Native American nations to prevent their sheltering fugitive enslaved people commonly threatened to separate families. Such treaties were generally ineffective, and cooperation between Africans and Native Americans was always a potential source of instability for colonial slaveholding societies.[29]

Colonial Black Culture

By the middle of the eighteenth century, colonial British America had developed the beginnings of a distinctly American culture, a culture shaped by the influence of Africans and Native Americans and by the limitations and possibilities of the "new world." Black celebrations through the eighteenth and well into the nineteenth centuries illustrate one aspect of this cultural evolution. Negro elections or Black coronation festivals were popular seasonal celebrations generally held in the spring or early summer. Especially in northern colonies, but also in the Chesapeake region, enslaved people selected a ceremonial king or governor and celebrated with several days of merrymaking. In New Amsterdam, Africans participated in a two-day observance of Paas (or Easter), vying for the honor of having baked the best Paas cake and competing in traditional Paas cake-throwing. The Dutch celebration of Pinkster, or Pentecost, celebrated in New Amsterdam and New York (and New Jersey), was eventually dominated by Africans and their traditions. Black people celebrated all these festivals in similar ways, often electing "kings" from among families known to be from the ruling class in Africa. Celebrations combining African and European traditions and resembling those in the West Indies and Latin America featured parades with high stepping and baton twirling, athletic competitions, great feasts, and

This drum is one of the oldest surviving African-American objects. Made in Ghana, in West Africa, it would have been played during religious ceremonies and on social occasions and most likely traveled across the Atlantic on a slave ship.

abundant music and dancing. White residents were often fascinated by the performances of African celebrants. One white observer in Albany, New York, reported that at one festival the enslaved king, a "Guinea man" dressed in an elaborate costume and wearing a yellow lace hat, led a long parade sitting astride one of the finest horses in the region provided for the occasion by his owner. Later he led the "Guinea dance," an "original Congo dance as danced in [their] native Africa." Dancers were accompanied by music provided by musicians playing traditional African instruments, including banjos, violins, and drums.[30]

What was less apparent to European observers of these celebrations was their connection to Western African theology and religious practice and their function as a form of cultural resistance. Equiano observed the centrality of dance and music among his people not only for secular purposes but as sacred ritual. Singing, drumming, and dancing were part of the worship of African ancestors and gods. These were ancient expressions of spirituality. "So essential [were] music and dance to West African religious expression," historian Albert J. Raboteau noted, "that it is no exaggeration to call them 'danced religions.'" These rituals helped form the connection between worlds. For the African, enslaved in a foreign place, the music and dance of these African American celebrations provided outward expression of the African cultural traditions, and familiar practices of worship passed down over generations of American slavery. Preserving these traditions provided links with African cultural homelands, helping African Americans resist slavery's attempt to define their identity. During the seventeenth and eighteenth centuries, African religions were more important than Christianity in the spiritual lives of the vast majority of American Black men and women. African religions were especially strong among the large African American populations of the lower South, where traditional African religious beliefs and forms of worship remained well into the nineteenth century.[31]

In America religion was just one aspect of many of these multi-layered Black celebrations. Some white people, especially indentured servants, attended and even participated in these celebrations, as a poem composed in

1760 made clear. According to the poet, the merrymakers were "Of black and white, and every sort." Colonial officials were not comfortable with the association of white and Black servants at these celebrations. According to a white observer from Lynn, Massachusetts, "Black celebrations" included so many of "the lower class of ... our own complexion" that it alarmed the elite who feared they might lead to dangerous political alliances among the "mean" classes against the "better" classes of the colonies. The eighteenth-century poet echoed these apprehensions, describing the revelers as "a motley crew of Whites and Blacks and Indians too." Colonial elites also attended the festivals, perhaps to oversee such associations but also to enjoy the merriment—merriment undoubtedly made especially attractive by what these staid white European Americans perceived as African abandon. Children of the upper class were sometimes taken to the celebrations by Black servants. Years later James Eights remembered a Pinkster celebration he attended as a boy with a household servant and his wonderment at the music, the baskets and other wares being sold by Native American families, and the exotic animals, including a lion and tiger, on display.[32]

Each group in the colonies contributed to the amalgam shaping American culture. Africans provided their knowledge of agriculture to make the rice culture of South Carolina profitable, and African techniques for inland river navigation greatly enhanced the ability of planters to move their goods to market. Both African and Native American medicine, though sometimes discounted by Europeans as superstition, were widely used and incorporated into eighteenth- and nineteenth-century American medical practice, especially in the southern colonies. Planters called upon African doctors to treat their enslaved men and women and their own families. In South Carolina an enslaved man named Caesar was granted freedom and a cash reward for developing antidotes for several poisons based on African herbal cures. In Massachusetts, Puritan minister Cotton Mather learned the principle of inoculation as a defense against smallpox from his Black servant. Mather reported interviewing several Africans

Enslaved people's cabins in Savannah, Georgia, reflecting a traditional West African design.

who explained that the practice of inserting a small amount of material from an active smallpox pustule into a small cut on the arm of a healthy person was used with great success to prevent death from the disease in West Africa. Although the patients did become mildly ill, they never developed smallpox. Africans used this rudimentary inoculation technique for protection against several diseases in other colonies in North America and in the West Indies. African medical knowledge, including the use of barks and herbs to treat everything from headaches to syphilis, eventually blended with European medical practices and a host of Native American medicines to form early American medical practice.[33]

Americans of European origin probably owed the greatest part of their culture to their European roots, but much of what they came to consider American had African roots. Before the end of the eighteenth century African music changed white Americans' musical sense. African foods like okra, collard greens, and yams became the foundation of American southern style cooking, and the American greeting "Howdy" was blended from the English "How do ye" and the African American "How de" or the Afro–West Indian "Hodi."[34] An emergent multiracial and multicultural America was apparent in the British colonies. This culture developed in the context of the important political and social changes facilitated by America's colonization. The lines of social status among white people that were so fundamental in England underwent a gradual erosion, a process already noticeable by the eve of the Revolution. The availability of cheap land dampened Europeans' willingness to accept extended indentures or to work for wages for any longer than was necessary to become landholders. This propensity for personal independence encouraged a political commitment to individuality that by the late eighteenth century came to be known as the republican ideal. Ironically this passion for personal independence grew simultaneously with a reliance on a system of racially defined enslaved labor that became the very antithesis of freedom. The presence of an enslaved African people provided the contrast by which white Americans defined liberty. Black Americans, however, refused to accept a definition of liberty that excluded them and remained determined to claim freedom for themselves.

Who, What, Where

Review Questions

2.1 What role did slavery play in making Virginia economically viable? Describe the differences in the development of slavery in Virginia and Maryland.

2.2 What was the position of slavery in the economy of the Carolina colony? Why did Georgia fail to prevent the spread of slavery?

2.3 What were the similarities and differences between the economies of the southern and Middle Colonies? What was the position of slavery in the Middle Colonies? How did an antislavery stance develop among Quakers?

2.4 What were the similarities and differences between slavery in New England and the other colonies?

2.5 Which developments led to decreasing freedoms for both enslaved and free Black people over the course of the seventeenth and eighteenth centuries?

2.6 Why did complex relationships form between Black and Native Americans in the early colonies?

2.7 Which influences shaped colonial Black society? How did Africans influence the development of American culture?

For additional digital learning resources please go to **https://www.oup.com/he/horton1e**

Slavery and Freedom in the Age of Revolution

This watercolor, painted by a French officer who participated in the Siege of Yorktown (1781), shows the variety of soldiers who fought for American independence, including, from left to right, a Black soldier of the First Rhode Island Regiment, a New England militiaman, a frontier rifleman, and a French officer.

3

CHAPTER OUTLINE

Social Disruption and the First Great Awakening

3.1 Understand the impact of First Great Awakening on Black–white relations in the colonies.

Interracial Relationships and Discontent

3.2 Identify the ways that race impacted growing class divisions in colonial American society.

Crispus Attucks and the Boston Massacre

3.3 Describe how Crispus Attucks' role in the Boston Massacre provides insight into race relations in colonial Massachusetts.

Revolution and the Fight for American Freedom

3.4 Contrast the ways that Black participation in the Revolution was encouraged and discouraged.

Black Soldiers

3.5 Discuss the reasons that Black men served as soldiers in both the British and Continental armies.

The Post-Revolutionary Question of Black Freedom

3.6 Discuss how the success of the American Revolution impacted the antislavery movement.

JUST BEFORE 10 a.m. on a Sunday morning in September 1739, William Bull, the lieutenant governor of South Carolina, and his four companions confronted their worst nightmare on the road near Charles Town (later called Charleston). Suddenly, the horrified party faced an army of enslaved men, hesitated for a moment, and then wheeled their horses around and rode for their lives. The men's military action had begun in the early morning hours, when twenty Black captives from the Kingdom of Kongo met at the Stono River about twenty miles west of Charles Town. Led by an African named Jemmy, these former warriors hoped to take advantage of the distraction provided by the war being waged between Spain and Britain to fight their way to freedom.[1]

Colonial Spanish Florida, bordering Georgia, was barely 150 miles south of South Carolina. Hoping to disrupt the British plantation economy, in 1693 the Spanish crown granted freedom to enslaved people who ran away from the British colonies. Thereafter many South Carolina fugitives escaped to Fort Mose, near St. Augustine; and in 1738, the Spanish governor of Florida granted these Black men and women homesteading lands where they founded Gracia Real de Santa Teresa de Mose. Fiercely loyal to the Spanish Crown, this first free Black settlement in colonial North America became an asylum for fugitives, who formed a sizable military force to man its garrison. The Spanish Fort Mose discouraged the British raids that endangered settlements in the St. Augustine area throughout the early eighteenth century.[2]

Hoping ultimately to make their way to Florida and the protection of the Spaniards, the South Carolina rebels near the Stono first broke into a store to acquire guns and ammunition and killed two shopkeepers in the process. As they marched south they stopped at plantations, and other enslaved men joined them. By midmorning at least fifty boldly marched down the road "with Colours displayed, and two Drums beating." Their banners were "like the unit flags that African armies flew in their campaigns." By afternoon they numbered more than a hundred. Those of the original rebels who had been soldiers in their Kongo homeland provided the battle strategy. They were skilled with firearms and conversant with Kongolese military rituals, and they joined in the traditional battle dance that in Africa served as a military drill in preparation for meeting the colonial militia that had formed during the day. Most of the large Black army that engaged the militia, however, were agricultural workers without military training. The initial battle took place in an open area, leaving the Kongo men, who traditionally fought in brief encounters without cover against a force of superior arms. Forty Black rebels fell in the initial engagement. As they were driven from the field, military men withdrew to regroup, but many untrained fighters fell away, hoping to return to their owners with their rebellion undiscovered. The military men marched thirty miles toward Florida before they were overtaken by the militia. Most of the rebels were killed, but some escaped to the swamp and the woods. A year later, colonial authorities were still pursuing members of the fugitive band, and one rebel eluded capture for more than three years.[3]

Timeline

Chapter 3

1739
Slave rebellion in Stono, South Carolina.

1741
Suspicious fires in New York City result in execution of thirty-one Black and five

white people convicted of slave conspiracy.

1758
Pennsylvania Quakers demand that their members not import, buy, or sell enslaved people.

1765
British Parliament passes the Stamp Act. Black resistance groups participate in anti–Stamp Act protests.

1770
African American population of British North America is 459,822—more than

The **rebellion at the Stono River** reinforced fears among planters of both the possibility of slave rebellion and the threat of Spanish invasion. Within a year, James Oglethorpe led the South Carolina and Georgia militia in a land and sea attack on Fort Mose and drove the Black forces out of the settlement to the safety of nearby St Augustine. Spanish Black men rebuilt the fort, but British raids continued intermittently throughout the next two decades. In 1742 South Carolina was again shaken by word that a Spanish force, with at least one Black battalion, threatened an invasion. These uncertain times prompted colonial authorities to place greater restrictions on enslaved and free Black people. Instability may also have prompted some efforts to forestall rebellion, perhaps explaining the 1740 regulation that provided fines for slaveholders who failed to give enslaved laborers sufficient food or clothing or to allow them the customary Sundays off from work.[4]

Social Disruption and the First Great Awakening

The threat of slave uprising and the growing size of the colony's Black majority made most South Carolina slaveowners intolerant of any perceived challenge to their control. When, during this period, evangelical missionaries moved into the colony seeking to convert not only white but also Black residents, planter reaction was decidedly cool. Hugh and Jonathan Bryan were at first persuaded by Methodist preacher George Whitefield that the people they enslaved ought to be brought to Christianity. When planters in the vicinity suspected that the enslaved people were drawn mainly by what they took to be an evangelical anti-slavery message, however, the experiment was brought to an abrupt conclusion. Still, elsewhere in the colonies evangelical missionaries were successful in converting thousands of white and many Black people.[5]

A religious fervor called the **First Great Awakening** emerged in England during the 1720s and brought a new spirit of equality and democracy to America in the 1740s and 1750s. Revivals swept into America with plainspoken, emotion-laden preaching, a contempt for formal church hierarchy, and a greater emphasis on believers' ability to communicate directly with God. The new sects formed under this movement, the Methodists and the extremely decentralized Baptists,

21 percent of the total population; 89 percent of Black Americans live in the southern colonies.

Boston Massacre: five men killed, including Crispus Attacks, an escaped fugitive from slavery.

1775

First Atlantic world antislavery society established in Philadelphia: the Society for the Relief of Free Negroes Unlawfully Held in Bondage.

1775–1783

American Revolution: More than five thousand

African Americans serve in Continental Army.

1777

Vermont abolishes slavery.

1783

Slavery abolished in Massachusetts.

converted thousands in the British North American colonies. Their appeal was especially strong for ordinary white people, and they even made converts among less isolated African Americans in northern colonies and in the Chesapeake region. The strength of African cultures in the large slave communities of the lower South, however, hampered conversions there. Evangelical revival services of prayer, song, and testimonials, often held in tent encampments, created a far different atmosphere from the more staid services of established churches. Some of the difference was attributable to the democratic nature of participation; congregations included Black and Native American as well as white people; enslaved as well as free people; and men, women, and children. Some of the difference was due to the influence of African music and styles of worship. Much as white

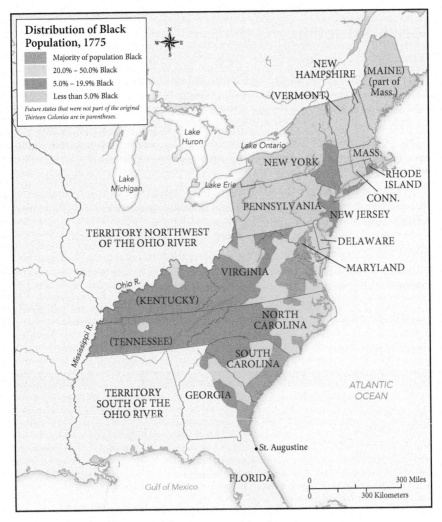

Map 3.1 Distribution of Black Population, 1775

people were drawn to African performances in the celebrations of Pinkster and governors' elections, evangelicals found that the style of worship practiced by Africans and African Americans was a great attraction to white yeoman farmers, servants, and the nonelites. Some preachers relied on the participation of Black parishioners to help "bring down the spirit," allowing white congregants to throw off their inhibitions, commit themselves fully to the religious spirit, and accept the call to God's salvation.[6]

Informal evangelical worship practices allowed interracial gatherings to incorporate many aspects of African spirituality and worship styles, such as call-and-response singing, and this form and context gave the message of Christianity greater appeal to the enslaved people. Particularly in the **Upper South**, evangelical religion became a mixture of African and European practices, providing another arena for interracial interaction. Massive numbers of white people were attracted to the simple, more democratic theology and the more emotional worship style, which might include both music and dancing. Fearing such associations and disapproving of such practices, many of the church-going colonial elite vehemently objected to this brand of worship.

An especially dangerous aspect of evangelical religions in the eyes of the elites was that virtually anyone seemed to be able to assume a position of leadership. One Boston reporter was upset by the fact that "there are among the exhorters . . . young persons, sometimes lads, or rather boys; nay women and girls; yea, Negroes, have taken upon them to do the business of preachers." From the perspective of the established clergy and other colonial authorities, this was the unmistakable sign of their diminishing control over potentially dangerous elements of society, as "private persons of no education and but low attainments in knowledge" were allowed to preach the gospel. The stand that many evangelical preachers took against slavery, even in the South, provided sure proof of the dangers. For those already uncomfortable with the work of educating enslaved children and adults being conducted by the Anglican Church's Society for the Propagation of the Gospel in Foreign Parts, the antislavery language of the evangelicals was especially disconcerting.[7]

The interaction of Black and white individuals, especially poor servants and enslaved people, in religious gatherings, festivals, and cooperative political actions was so prevalent in the North during the colonial period that authorities passed legislation to block such alliances, much as they had done to curb Black and Native American interaction. An ordinance adopted in Rhode Island in 1708 forbade any free person, white or Black, from entertaining an enslaved person except in the presence of their owner, but such regulations did not keep evangelical reformers from their ministry among servants and enslaved people. Sarah Osborn of Newport, Rhode Island, was one who opened her home to the poor of all stations and conditions. She conducted a school during the week and held educational religious services on Sunday evenings. An average of seventy African Americans attended her Sunday evening gatherings by the 1760s. From these meetings sprang a small religious community of free and enslaved Black people, many of whom became prominent in the religious life and the antislavery struggle of the Revolutionary period. Newport Gardner, who later gained his freedom and opened a music school for Black and white students, regularly attended Osborn's religious meetings. Also a part of this group was a young African-born woman named Obour Tanner, who occasionally held her own services. Tanner's preaching deeply affected Phillis Wheatley, an enslaved Bostonian who was also a well-known poet, and the evangelical message often appeared in her poetry. This evangelicalism brought Black and white Americans together in religious worship in a manner that allowed them near equality in their participation. The potential social disruption of evangelical practice was exacerbated by the nature of the evangelical message itself: a theological equality which became part of the foundation of early antislavery thought.

Interracial Relationships and Discontent

There is little doubt that colonial authorities feared the potential disruptiveness of interracial associations, although moralistic arguments often obscured their political concerns. In New York, officials claimed that such socializing was "destructive to the morals of servants and slaves." The influential editors of the *New York Weekly Journal* described these associations as "the principle [*sic*] bane and pest of the city." Elite concerns were well founded, since there were many occasions when interracial actions challenged colonial authority. In New York City two white saloon keepers, John Romme and John Hughson, operated theft rings that included a number of enslaved and free Black persons. Romme and Hughson made arrangements to sell the stolen goods supplied to them by their associates. By the 1740s each man's tavern served as a criminal headquarters catering to an interracial clientele that included street gangs. Hughson's pub was especially popular with New York enslaved people, and on their Sundays off many spent the afternoon after church services enjoying the special dinner served there. Black and white diners partook of goose and mutton served with fresh baked bread, rum, cider, and punch. There was music, dancing, and conversations about unjust owners and inconsiderate bosses, all reinforcing the commonalities of their social and economic status.[8]

These commonalities were said to have shaped the discussions at Hughson's tavern into a major "slave plot" to burn New York City and kill many of its white inhabitants in 1741. Mary Burton, who lived at the tavern, informed the authorities of the plot, which she insisted she had overheard being discussed by three Black Spanish sailors. A major investigation concluded that this plot was indeed being planned, and 150 Black and 25 white individuals were prosecuted for their alleged roles in the conspiracy. Although the evidence presented at the trial was circumstantial at best, 32 Black and 4 white accused (including Hughson and his wife) were executed. Historians disagree about whether there was actually a plot or whether it was an exaggeration of a scheme to cover criminal activity and made believable by the general fear of such plots. There may well have been some New Yorkers old enough to remember the attack on the city in 1712, when enslaved and Native American people set fires, killing nine white residents and wounding several others. The proven existence of the 1712 slave plot lent credibility to testimony about the 1741 plot. Real or not, anxiety about interracial

A LIST of NEGROES committed on Account of the Conspiracy.

Negroes.	Masters or Owners.	Committed	Arraigned	Convicted.	Confessed.	Burnt.	Hanged.	Transported to	Discharged
Antonio, } Spaniards	Peter De Lancey,	6 April,	13 June,	17 June,				Spanish W. Indies.	
Augustine, }	Macmullen,	1 April,	13 June,	17 June,					
Antonio,	Sarah Maynard,	1 April,	13 June,	17 June,					
Albany,	Mrs. Carpenter,	12 May,	8 June,	10 June,				Madeira.	
5 Abraham, a free Negro		1 June,					12 June,		
Adam,	Joseph Murray, Esq;	26 June,			27 June,			Madeira.	
Draso,	Peter Jay,	9 May,	25 June,		25 June,			Madeira.	
Bastian, a'ias Tom Peal,	Jacobus Vaarck,	12 May,	8 June,	10 June,	11 June,			Hispaniola.	
Ben,	Capt. Marshall,	9 June,	12 June,	13 June,			16 June,		
10 Bill, alias Will,	Coenradt Ten Eyck.	12 June,	3 July,		30 June,			Madeira.	
Bridgewater,	Abraham Van Horne,	22 June,	5 July,		27 June,			Hispaniola.	
Billy,	Mrs. Ellison,	25 June,	1 July,						
Braveboy,	Mrs. Kierstede,	27 June,	10 July,		30 June,			Madeira.	
Burlington,	Joseph Haines.	3 July,							15 July.
15 Caesar,	Vaarck,	1 March,	24 April,	1 May,			11 May,		
Cuffee,	Adolph Philipse, Esq;	6 April,	28 May,	29 May,		30 May,			
Cuba, a Wench,	Mrs. Constance Lynch,	4 April,						-	
Curacoa Dick,	Cornelius Tiebout,	9 May,	8 June,	10 June,		12 June,			5 July.
Cato,	Alderman Moore,	9 May,	15 July,		22 June,				
20 Caesar,	Alderman Pintard,	9 May,	3 July,		22 June,			Madeira.	
Cuffee,	Lewis Gomez,	24 May,	5 June,	8 June,		9 June,			
Caesar,	Benjamin Peck,	25 May,	6 June,	9 June,		9 June,			
Cato,	Joseph Cowley,	25 May,	12 June,	13 June,			16 June,		
Cook,	Gerardus Comfort,	26 May,	6 June,	8 June,		9 June,			

A page from "A Journal of the Proceedings in the Detection of the Conspiracy formed by some White People in conjunction with Negro and other Slaves, for burning the City of New-York in America, and murdering the Inhabitants," published in 1744 by Daniel Horsmanden, who presided over the trial of the accused conspirators. Black and white men and women who were found guilty suffered burning, hanging, and deportation.

joint action was strong enough to create near panic among the white citizens of New York: strong enough to lead to the execution of thirty-six people.[9]

Attacks by the resentful poor became an increasing threat to authorities during the mid-eighteenth century as wealth and power became more concentrated in the hands of those at the top of colonial society, a trend reflected in tax rolls and an increasing display of wealth. The economic disparity was most apparent in the South, but after midcentury it was clear everywhere that the poor were less likely to rise above poverty than they had been before. In the cities growing relief roles testified to the relative permanence of poverty—three times as many people received relief in Philadelphia in 1765 as had in 1750. The consolidation of wealth was accompanied by a concentration of power, and economic and political advantages were reflected in the application of the law, as colonial courts were likely to favor those of higher rank over those of lesser status. In 1767, for example, the court refused to render a judgment against a military officer and governor designate on behalf of a "yeoman." The court justified its refusal on the grounds that a "[g]entleman by office" might "abate [such a] writ." Gentlemen also seem to have been immune from certain punishments routinely prescribed for crimes. Although whipping was a common sentence for those found guilty of even petty offenses in New York, and gentlemen were occasionally found guilty of such offenses, no gentleman was ever whipped in colonial New York City.[10]

The increasing distance between rich and poor did not go unnoticed by those at the bottom of colonial society, and officials were concerned about a "general murmuring against the government and the rich people." The problem was evident as early as the 1730s, when unemployment and inflation worked a special hardship on the poor in some cities, while yeomen farmers in the surrounding countryside received decreasing prices for their produce from urban merchants. Poor people from Boston tried to solve this problem by bypassing local merchants, traveling into the farm areas, and buying directly from producers, but by the end of the decade evidence of the merchants' continued price manipulation provoked them to mob action. Like those who gathered in Romme's tavern in New York, according to contemporary accounts, these poor urbanites who eventually forced price reforms were "young People, Servants and Negroes."[11]

Another important issue that prompted interracial action was British **impressment**, the practice of drafting young men into British naval service in a summary fashion that was virtually kidnapping. British "press gangs" roamed rural areas and towns, taking young men whenever naval personnel needs required it. Men were taken immediately and without warning, fathers forced to leave their work in the fields, sons forced from their dinner tables. Taverns and other places where the common people gathered were the favored sources of manpower, and poor people of all races were vulnerable. Public reaction to impressment was strong and often violent. In the 1740s Bostonians battled press gangs in the streets in what one inquiry called a "riotous, tumultuous assembly of foreign seamen, servants, Negroes and other persons of mean and vile condition." At one point in the melee several thousand people attacked the governor's house. Local authorities expressed sympathy for those unfairly impressed, but they vigorously condemned this interracial, lower-class mob violence. In the 1760s impressment attempts provoked riots in Maine, New York, Maryland, and Virginia. Five hundred "seamen, boys and Negroes" resisted the press gangs in Newport, Rhode Island, in the summer of 1765. Clearly this was an issue that galvanized popular opinion into concerted action. While the revolutionary cry of "No taxation without representation!" might have rallied those in the middle and upper ranks of colonial society in the 1770s, in the eyes of the poor, impressment was the most serious sign of English disregard for American freedom. For the poor impressment was at least as devastating as the taxes imposed by Britain.[12]

Developments in the colonies by the 1770s had created some divergence of interests between groups of colonists, according to their place in the economy. Poor people reacted most strongly to colonial policies that inflated prices, threatened jobs, and deprived them of their liberty. All colonials were concerned with these issues, but the elites were not generally sympathetic to the freedom demanded by enslaved people and servants. They were determined to wrest additional political power from England and to establish control over trade policies. In the years after the mid-eighteenth century the growing numbers of middling Americans, not at the bottom but below the elite, were less likely to protest impressment than they were to react when the crown tightened controls on the American economy and threatened what they saw as the "rights of Englishmen." Nevertheless they often joined the poor in mass action, especially on economic issues.

In 1765, when Parliament enacted the **Stamp Act** in an attempt to force the colonies to reimburse the Crown for expenses incurred during the French and Indian War (1754–1763), colonials claimed that Britain had no right to levy a tax designed to raise revenue rather than to regulate trade. The regulation required that fees be collected in the colonies, as they were in Britain, for stamps to be affixed to newspapers, wills, contracts, marriage licenses, and other legal documents. This had the effect of raising the cost of doing business and was especially burdensome for merchants and lawyers. Although poor people were seldom involved in such transactions, colonial leaders fostered their opposition by drawing a parallel between the Stamp Act and impressment, arguing that in both cases Britain ignored the rights of Americans. The resulting mob actions that erupted all over the colonies included a far more diverse group of protesters than many earlier actions, bringing together Black and white, poor and non-poor. In New York City mob leaders, who were beginning to be thought of as revolutionaries, gathered at the Queen's Head Tavern to lay plans and discuss strategy. Owned and operated by "Black Sam" Fraunces, a West Indian man of mixed-race, the tavern became notorious as the revolutionaries' headquarters during the 1760s and 1770s. From the Queen's Head, New Yorkers launched their equivalent of the Boston Tea party in 1774.[13]

Crispus Attucks and the Boston Massacre

As the political debate between the colonies and the mother country over economic control continued, colonial leaders called on the mobs with increasing frequency. Mob actions supported the cause of well-to-do colonials, but mob participants often had their own interests, and mobs always presented the troubling prospect of uncontrolled popular excess. Samuel Adams and other members of the "better" classes who had ties to the lower ranks attempted to direct the mob but occasionally lost control, as in 1770 when sailors, dock workers, and the unemployed attacked British soldiers in Boston. This particular revolutionary mob was reacting to the specific grievances of its members, and its leader was not controlled or trusted by the colonial elites. He was **Crispus Attucks**, formerly enslaved, in his late forties who had escaped from his owner outside Boston in 1750 and had remained free for twenty years. In an ad placed by his owner in the *Boston Gazette and Weekly Journal* the year he escaped, he was described as a "well set" mixed-race man, twenty-seven years old, six feet two inches tall, with short curly hair and "knees nearer together than common." Attucks was part African and part Native American and during the years of his freedom he worked as a seaman on whalers sailing out of Boston and in a rope factory in the city's North End.[14]

As a seaman Crispus Attucks faced the danger of impressment, the economic pain of inflation at the end of the French and Indian War in 1763, and the uncertainty of irregular employment. When Britain redoubled its efforts to regulate colonial trade under the navigation acts and other tax legislation, it dispatched soldiers to American ports. In Boston, as elsewhere, British troops were a constant reminder of the authority of the Crown and the power of the Parliament over daily life in the colonies. For ordinary working people the soldiers were also competitors in the job market. With full-time employment to satisfy most of their needs, soldiers could afford to accept part-time work below the customary wages. This competition for jobs lowered the wages that employers were willing to pay and imposed great hardships on the colonial work force. This was an important aspect of workers' resentment of British soldiers and contributed greatly to the tensions between the two groups. In Boston during the winter of 1770, seamen and laborers instigated sporadic attacks on the British troops.

These were the issues that dominated the conversation of the seamen and laborers who gathered to drink in a Boston pub on the afternoon of March 5, 1770. Tempers flared when an unsuspecting newly-arrived British soldier entered the pub, ordered a drink, and inquired about part-time employment in the city. The crowd became hostile; one seaman suggested that the soldier clean his outhouse, another made similarly insulting propositions. Confronted by such anger, the young soldier left the pub. For the rest of the afternoon and into the early evening, the men continued drinking, and their talk became bolder. Finally the club-wielding crowd of twenty or thirty "saucy boys, negroes and mulattoes, Irish teagues and outlandish jack-tarrs," led by Crispus Attucks, spilled into the street and snaked its way to the Customs House on King Street. There they confronted the British soldiers standing guard. Attucks took the lead in harassing the sentries, poking one of them with a stick and calling him a "lobster," an allusion to the British soldiers' red coats. Some threw snowballs, then chunks of ice, and finally stones. The situation escalated rapidly— "the multitude shouting and huzzaing, threatening life, the bell ringing, the mob whistling and screaming like an Indian yell, the people from all quarters

Crispus Attucks, the First Martyr of the American Revolution, King (now State) Street, Boston.
March 5th, 1770. Page 16.

Nineteenth-century romanticized sketch of the Boston Massacre of 1770.

throwing every species of rubbish they could pick up in the street." "The way to get rid of these soldiers is to attack the main-guard," Attucks shouted. "[S]trike at the root: this is the nest."[15]

Deadly violence swiftly followed. As word of the Customs House confrontation spread, crowds gathered in other parts of the city to challenge British soldiers, and in one skirmish a soldier stabbed a young boy with his bayonet. At the Customs House Attucks and his compatriots grew still bolder until finally a British officer, fearing the mounting danger to his troops, gave the order to fire into the crowd. When the order was ignored it was given again, but once more the soldiers failed to react. The people in the crowd assumed the troops would retreat, not fire, but they were wrong. A third order rang out: "Damn you, fire, be the consequence what it will." This time soldiers responded with a volley; three in the crowd were killed, and two others were wounded. Attucks was hit twice and died instantly, the first to die in what became the revolutionary cause of American independence.[16]

The events of March 5, 1770, became known as the **Boston Massacre**, mythologized not as the reckless actions of a few intoxicated seamen and laborers, but as the symbol of American colonists' willingness to stand up to armed troops to oppose British tyranny. Attucks's role was central to the event and is crucial for understanding social and political relations in the late eighteenth century. When Massachusetts held a trial, the British soldiers were defended by Boston attorney John Adams, a future revolutionary leader. Adams was troubled by the Crown's disregard for the rights of the colonials as English citizens, but he was even more disturbed by the increasingly frequent "mob violence." He denounced the mob's taunts and rock throwing, and condemned Attucks for having "undertaken to be the hero of the night," but he expressed no surprise that the mob was interracial or that its leader was an African American. Nor were racial distinctions made during the funeral services held for those who died at the Boston Massacre. Despite Adams's condemnation the fallen were treated as patriots. Their funeral procession was a "vast multitude of people, walking, six deep, and a long train of carriages belonging to the principal gentry of the town." Their bodies were given a place of honor in one of the city's most prestigious cemeteries. The ceremony, it was said, attracted "the greatest concourse which had then ever assembled upon one occasion in America." Crispus Attucks was buried along with the three other fallen patriots.[17]

John Adams later acknowledged that the Boston Massacre opened the rift with England that became American independence. The presence of the British army continued to be an irritant; as Sam Adams put it, a standing army was "always dangerous to the liberties of the people." During the 1770s even those who feared the excesses of the mob came to accept them as useful to building the revolution. In his diary, John Adams recorded a letter to the royal governor of Massachusetts, Thomas Hutchinson, signed with the name Crispus Attucks. The letter held Hutchinson responsible for the troops under his authority and argued that his crimes against "the people in general" were "chargeable before

God and man, with our blood." In the diary this letter was dated 1773, three years after Attucks was killed. Thus, it is likely that Adams wrote the letter and signed Attucks's name, thus recognizing the formerly enslaved man as a revolutionary symbol and acknowledging the important role Black people played in the cause of American freedom.[18]

Revolution and the Fight for American Freedom

As the rhetoric of revolution escalated, white people concerned about the loss of their freedom used the word "slavery" to describe the relationship with Britain they wished to avoid. African Americans pointed out the hypocrisy inherent in the use by slaveholders of the rhetoric of slavery and freedom. In 1773 and 1774 Massachusetts enslaved men confronted colonial authorities with the question of their freedom. "We expect great things from men who have made such a noble stand against the designs of their fellow men to enslave them," they declared. Their demands were not revolutionary, simply that enslaved people be allowed one day a week to labor for their own benefit so they might accumulate funds to purchase their own freedom. This petition was refused, but others followed, each carefully worded to highlight the parallels between their cause and the colonists' desire for a "free and Christian country."[19]

Colonials organized Committees of Correspondence to protest Britain's denial of their rights as Englishmen, while Africans in Massachusetts called on the Enlightenment ideal of the natural rights of man to petition for an end to their enslavement. Some colonial leaders had made the connection between their desire for freedom from English tyranny and the enslaved people's longing for liberty. When James Otis asserted in 1765 that all those born in the colonies were "British subjects" entitled to civil rights, he concluded that all Black as well as white people were "by the law of nature free born" and argued therefore that slavery must be ended. Abigail Adams pointed forcefully to the incongruity in a letter to her husband in 1774: "It always seemed a most iniquitous scheme to me to fight ourselves for what we are daily robbing and plundering from those who have as good a right to freedom as we have."[20]

African Americans found themselves in a complex situation at the start of the Revolution. They had grievances against both the British and the Americans. When Parliament closed down the Port of Boston as a punishment for the Boston Tea Party, Black seamen and dock laborers suffered the consequences just as their white counterparts did. Both Black and white workers were endangered by impressment and angered by the passage of the punitive "Intolerable Acts" forced on the colonies in 1774. Despite their shared circumstances, however, most American patriots seemed willing to pursue freedom from England without acting against slavery at home. Black protests created fears among some southern patriots. After "some Negroes had mimicked their betters in crying Liberty," as Henry Laurens of South Carolina put it, their focus shifted from the threat of British tyranny to the more pressing prospect of slave insurrection at home.[21]

The ambivalence many Black individuals felt toward the American cause continued as political protest became a war for independence. Africans and African descendants took up arms along with their fellow Americans when the British marched through Lexington, Massachusetts, on their way to capture American arms in the nearby town of Concord. Some were Minutemen who served with the special militia, while others volunteered as the British army approached. Massachusetts Black men like Peter Salem of Framingham, Samuel Craft of Newton, and Cato Wood and Cuff Whittemore of Arlington stood their ground in Lexington and Concord with their white compatriots when the "shot heard around the world" was fired, signaling the beginning of the Revolutionary War. "Prince the Negro" was wounded in the battle that followed. Titus Coburn, Salem Poor, Grant Cooper, and Peter Salem, who eventually served seven years in the Continental Army, were among those who held out against the British at the battle of Bunker Hill near Boston. Several Black men who participated in the battle were commended for bravery, and Peter Salem's hometown later erected a monument to his courage as a Revolutionary soldier.[22]

Despite Black participation in the initial Revolutionary military actions, their presence in the Continental forces was questioned. On July 9, 1775, just five days after he was appointed commander of the American troops, George Washington, a slaveholder from Virginia, ordered that although those already on active duty might remain, no new Black recruits should be enlisted. Black participation was heatedly debated by the Continental Congress. Representatives from southern areas struggling to control their large population of enslaved people were keenly aware of the danger of arming Black men. At the same time they contended that Black men were too servile and timid by nature to make good soldiers and asserted that white southern military men could not be induced to serve beside Black soldiers. Edward Rutledge, the delegate from South Carolina, led southerners in demanding that all enslaved and free Black men be removed from the army. Northerners, less fearful of slave revolt, were more likely to see the benefits of Black enlistment and argued that Black soldiers had proven their worth in early battles. The attempt to remove Black men failed, and Washington's compromise stood as a recognition of the courage of the African Americans who had already served. The strength of southern fears is apparent in light of the fact that Black Americans had already served in all the colonial wars, including King William's War (1690–1697), Queen Ann's War (1702–1713), King George's War (1744–1748), and the French and Indian War (1755–1763). In 1747 South Carolina had officially thanked Black troops for helping defend the colony. Further, Africans had formed the major body of the Spanish army in the American Southwest as early as the sixteenth century, had served with the Dutch in New Netherland before British occupation, and fought for the British in Barbados. Given this evidence it seems likely that it was the fear of arming slaves, not skepticism over their fitness for military service, that was at issue.

White southerners had good reason to be concerned about arming enslaved men and to fear the specter of interracial uprisings. There were many rumors

PROFILE

Phillis Wheatley

Frontispiece from a book of poems written by Phillis Wheatley in 1773.

IN THE SUMMER OF 1761, a young African girl no more than seven or eight years old arrived in Boston on the ship *Phillis*. Slave traders had captured her in the Gambia River region of West Africa in the Fulani nation. In Boston, John and Susanna Wheatley bought her and called her by the name of the ship that brought her to the colonies. Phillis was extraordinarily bright, and the Wheatleys allowed her to learn to read and write. Within sixteen months she was proficient in English, and within three years was literate in Latin. In 1767 Phillis published a poem in Rhode Island's *Newport Mercury*, and by the mid-1770s published several others, many about freedom. She joined Boston's Old South Church, where the Wheatleys were members. The church served as a forum for patriotic meetings during the 1770s, although John and Susanna Wheatley remained loyal to Britain. In 1772 Phillis accompanied her owners to England, where she met the British abolitionist Granville Sharp and Benjamin Franklin, who was in London at the time. Franklin was impressed by her talent, and the Londoners helped her publish a book, *Poems on Various Subjects, Religious and Moral*, in 1773. Phillis returned to Boston as America's first Black published author, and that fall, the Wheatleys granted her freedom.

Then in her early twenties, Phillis Wheatley strongly supported the American Revolution. Her poem dedicated to George Washington drew an enthusiastic reception from the commander of the Continental forces and an invitation to visit him at his headquarters. Her views on freedom may have influenced Washington's personal struggle over slavery. In 1778 Phillis Wheatley married John Peters, a free Black man. The couple struggled financially while Phillis worked on an ambitious three-hundred-page manuscript, a project she did not live to publish. She died in childbirth in Boston in 1784. One of her last poems, written in honor of the Treaty of Paris, ending the Revolution, was entitled "Liberty and Peace." As manumission societies were formed at the end of the eighteenth century, Phillis Wheatley came to symbolize the Africans' longing for freedom and became a reminder of talents to which the slave system generally denied expression.

about servant and slave conspiracies planning to provide military service to the British and to strike against southern plantations. According to one southerner many believed that the "malicious and imprudent speeches of some among the lower class whites . . . induced [the enslaved] to believe that their freedom depended on the success of the King's troops." In South Carolina, newspapers reported that large bands of "the most infamous banditti and horse thieves [which included] a corps of Indians, with negro and white savages disguised like them" were raiding settlements and "stealing slaves" throughout the region. These **banditti** were groups of fugitives from slavery, indentured servants, Cherokees, poor farmers, and "backcountry Tories" who worked independently and with British forces and were commanded by Black men like "Captain" Jones, "Colored Power Man," or the mixed-race William Hunt. These guerrilla bands burned and looted plantations, stole horses, and attacked continental forces in many regions. In New Jersey, a band under the leadership of Tye, "a Negro who [bore] the title of colonel," attacked American fortifications and a number of large slaveholding estates, freeing enslaved people and indentured servants. Guerrilla fighters continued to operate even after the end of the war. For more than half a century, bands of Black men calling themselves the King of England Soldiers harassed southern plantations and freed enslaved people when possible. Ironically the persistence of these bands bore testimony to the power of the Revolutionary message of liberty.[23]

Many patriots argued that the only way to discourage Black participation in **loyalist** groups like the banditti was to enroll them in the American cause. It was the colonial governor of Virginia, Lord Dunmore, however, whose actions quickly forced the Americans to reconsider their policy on Black enlistment. In November he struck at the heart of the colonials' contradiction with a strategy designed to infuriate and humiliate them, especially the slaveholders. Dunmore promised freedom to all enslaved people and indentured servants who escaped from their rebellious owners and fought on the side of the British. In light of the ruling in the *Somerset* case a few years before, enslaved people were inclined to believe the British offer of freedom. James Somerset was an enslaved man who had run away from his owner in England in the early 1770s. When he was recaptured and his owner threatened to ship him to Jamaica to be sold, abolitionist Granville Sharp persuaded the court to take up his case. In a carefully worded decision the British court ruled that no enslaved person could be forcibly taken from England. Some enslaved Americans acted on the promise of the Somerset ruling directly, as their owners attested when they advertised for their return. One enslaved Virginian, an owner speculated, would probably "board a vessel for Great Britain . . . from the knowledge he has of the late Determination of the Somerset Case." Another owner believed his runaway enslaved couple was on the way to Britain, "where they imagine they will be free," he said, adding, "a Notion now too prevalent among the Negroes." Drawing the implication from the court ruling that slavery was incompatible with the rights granted by English common law gave the hope of freedom to enslaved people in England and in the colonies and gave credence to Dunmore's promise of freedom for military service.[24]

DOCUMENTING BLACK AMERICA

Petition for Freedom by Enslaved People in Massachusetts

Boston, April 20th, 1773

Sir, The efforts made by the legislative of this province in their last sessions to free themselves from slavery, gave us, who are in that deplorable state, a high degree of satisfaction. We expect great things from men who have made such a noble stand against the designs of their *felllow-men* to enslave them. We cannot but wish and hope, Sir, that you will have the same grand object, we mean civil and religious liberty, in view in your next session. The divine spirit of *freedom*, seems to fire every humane breast on this continent, except such as are bribed to assist in executing the execrable plan.

We are very sensible that it would be highly detrimental to our present masters, if we were allowed to demand all that of *right* belongs to us for past services; this we disclaim. Even the *Spaniards*, who have not those sublime ideas of freedom that English men have, are conscious that they have no right to all the services of their fellow-men, we mean the *Africans*, who they have purchased with their money; therefore they allow them one day in a week to work for themselves, to enable them to earn money to purchase the residue of their time, which they have a right to demand in such portions as they are able to pay for (a due appraizement of their services being first made, which always stands at the purchase money). We do not pretend to dictate to you Sir, or to the Honorable Assembly, of which you are a member. We acknowledge our obligations to you for what you have already done, but as the people of this province seem to be

Black Soldiers

The promise of "liberty to slaves," as the insignia on the uniforms of Dunmore's Ethiopian Regiment proclaimed, was wildly successful. In a few months three hundred Black men served in the regiment, and by the end of the war eight hundred Black men had served, constituting more than half of Dunmore's troops. Other effects of the proclamation were to provide the British with support troops and to deprive many slaveholders of their labor supply. Wherever the British went, nearby enslaved Black people sought sanctuary with them, though only the approximately one thousand formerly enslaved men who fought in the army were promised freedom. Estimates are that the Americans lost as many as one hundred thousand of their approximately five hundred thousand enslaved people to the British during the war. The disruption of wartime itself, of actuated by the principles of equity and justice, we cannot but expect your house will again take our deplorable case into serious consideration, and give us that ample relief which, *as men*, we have a natural right to.

But since the wise and righteous governor of the universe has permitted our fellow men to make us slaves, we bow in submission to him, and determine to behave in such a manner as that we may have reason to expect the divine approbation of, and assistance in, our peaceable and lawful attempts to gain our freedom.

We are willing to submit to such regulations and laws, as may be made relative to us, until we leave the province, which we determine to do as soon as we can, from our joynt labours procure money to transport ourselves to some part of the Coast of *Africa,* where we propose a settlement. We are very desirous that you should have instructions relative to us, from your town, therefore we pray you to communicate this letter to them, and ask favor for us.

In behalf of our fellow slaves in this province, and by order of their Committee.

> Peter Bestes,
> Sambo Freeman,
> Felix Holbrook,
> Chester Joie.

For the Representative of the town of Thompson

Source: Herbert Aptheker, ed., *A Documentary History of the Negro People in the United* States, vol. 1 (New York: Citadel Press, 1951), 7–8.

course, also provided opportunities for those who did not need the motivation of British promises to escape from bondage. By 1778 Thomas Jefferson reported that thirty thousand enslaved Virginians had run away to the British; others have estimated that South Carolina lost at least twenty-five thousand and that Georgia lost more than twelve thousand of its fifteen thousand enslaved people before the war's end.[25]

Lord Dunmore's strategy forced the patriots to compete for the loyalties of African Americans and reconsider their policy against enlisting Black men. The threat of conspiracies and guerrilla actions by allied white loyalists and enslaved Black men became reality in many communities and was rumored in many others. In a letter to one of his officers, Washington worried that Dunmore's Black troops would draw more and more of the enslaved people to the British lines. Indeed Washington predicted that the use of Black troops would make

Dunmore "the most dangerous man in America," and that ultimately "success [would] depend on who [could] arm the Negroes the faster." Under these circumstances he saw little recourse but to reverse his policy on Black recruitment. Recruiting Black men into the Continental forces would also help address the problem of a growing troop shortage. White soldiers were reluctant to serve for longer than short three-month enlistments or to serve great distances from their homes, and the availability of Black troops might ease this situation. On January 6, 1776, Congress acted on Washington's recommendation and set into motion a series of orders that eventually opened the Continental ranks to African Americans. The dwindling white enlistments as the war continued created economic hardships and reinforced the argument for recruiting Black men. Most states matched Dunmore's promise of freedom for enslaved men who served in the army, and in the end, all the states except South Carolina and Georgia enlisted Black soldiers.[26]

Some states allowed the enlistment of enslaved Black men as replacements for white men unwilling or unable to serve the American cause. This proved a boon to many slaveowners, who sent their enslaved men to service in their stead. Nathan Dibble and his son Eli, both of Connecticut, avoided military service by sending their enslaved man, Jack Anthony, to serve in their places. After a term of service which lasted until the end of the war Anthony was granted his freedom. London Hazard, enslaved in Rhode Island, served for several members of his owner's family in order to secure his freedom, and Cezar Negro, who had been born at sea during his mother's crossing from Africa, won his freedom after serving in place of his owner's son. James Armistead, who served as a spy for General Lafayette, was granted his freedom by the Virginia legislature in 1786. Black men served with Francis Marion, "the Swamp Fox," and his guerrilla band in South Carolina. Thousands of enslaved men gained their freedom by helping to win freedom for the United States, many serving in place of their owners or members of their owners' families. In doing so, these Black soldiers generally served for long periods, often two to three years longer than white soldiers. Prince Hazeltine served in the Second Massachusetts Regiment for six years and was not discharged until the end of the war. He received two badges of merit for his heroism at Worcester, where he rescued several of his fellows from an explosion and fire that cost many lives. He was so badly injured in the process that for the rest of his life he was unable to work regularly.[27]

Not all who fought were enslaved men fighting for their own freedom; free Black men also served in the Continental Army. Since few free Black men could afford to pay for a substitute, and because most believed that their lives might be better in an independent United States, a great many served. Abijah Prince served with the Green Mountain Boys of Vermont under the command of Ethan Allen. As a part of the French allied contingent, five hundred freemen from Haiti also took their places among the American forces. Henri Christophe, who later became the King of Haiti, was one of them. The official count of Black Revolutionary soldiers and seamen was five thousand, but many more served as spies, guides, laborers, and musicians. Unknown numbers of Black women served the Continental forces as nurses and cooks, and a few disguised themselves as men and served as regular soldiers. Many Black individuals served as merchant seamen and military sailors in both the American and the British navies. Even white men who objected to arming enslaved people on land were generally willing to allow enslaved and free Black men to serve on warships. Black men either served in integrated units or in a few all-Black regiments.[28]

James Armistead, shown above was an enslaved African American man whose Virginian owner allowed him to enlist under Lafayette. He was the General's valet and a spy for the revolutionary forces. During the Battle of Yorktown he gathered critical intelligence for the Americans. In reward, he was granted his freedom and took the name James Lafayette.

After the British took the capital city of Newport, destroyed many farms, and occupied two-thirds of the state, Rhode Island raised its own Black unit, some free and some enslaved promised their freedom in return for fighting. The majority of members of the regiment were Africans and African Americans, but it also included men from sovereign Narragansett groups, other Native Americans, and men of mixed race. Most of its recruits came from the Narragansett region, an area with some of the few large slaveholding estates in the North. As in the South, the large planters in Rhode Island objected to arming enslaved men and were successful in ending their enlistments but were too late to stop the members of this unit, all of whom became known as "black," from going into action. This First Rhode Island Regiment was commanded by Col. Christopher Greene, a white Quaker who violated the pacifist tenets of his religion to join the war effort. The regiment served in its home state and in Virginia and New York. Greene had led a unit of four hundred Black troops in Delaware before taking charge of the Rhode Island unit, and other Black units were formed in Connecticut and Massachusetts. New York, New Jersey, and New Hampshire enlisted Black men in the ranks of its general military units. In Maryland the state legislature rejected the idea of raising an all-Black regiment and integrated enslaved and free Black men into its regular state militia. Virginia allowed free Black men to join its militia but refused to arm enslaved men, although some slaveholders enrolled enslaved men in their stead by claiming that they were free. No amount of persuasion could break the resolve of Georgians and South Carolinians not to allow Black troops to be raised within their borders, however. Several plans were proposed, one supported by Alexander Hamilton of New York that would have provided three thousand Black men to assist Georgia and South Carolina in filling their quota of troops, but they were soundly rejected. As one South Carolinian wrote, "We are much disgusted here at the Congress recommending us to arm our Slaves, it was received with great resentment, as a very dangerous and impolitic step." A counterargument was advanced that by enlisting enslaved men in common cause with slaveowners, slave uprisings might actually be averted, but it was to no avail, even when it appeared South Carolina and Georgia would fall to British forces. White Georgians tolerated having Black troops from the French West Indies defend the port city of Savannah, but fear of the consequences of arming enslaved men prevented them from making any further concessions. Georgia fell to the British in early 1779, and Charleston, South Carolina, was taken in the summer of 1780, but still no Black troops were enlisted.[29]

Yet Black soldiers fought in every theater of the war, even in the South. They saw action in the Green Mountains of Vermont and in the Blue Ridge Mountains of North Carolina. They endured the snow and freezing temperatures alongside the white troops at places like Valley Forge, Pennsylvania. Cato Cuff was frostbitten so badly there that he could never work outdoors in cold weather again. At the Battle of Lake Champlain in New York, Samuel Coombs, though wounded himself, tended the wounds of other injured men. Prince Whipple and Oliver Cromwell were among those who manned the oars of the boat carrying George Washington across the Delaware River to the battle at Trenton, and Black men like African-born Prince Bent of the Rhode Island regiment were serving with Washington when Cornwallis surrendered.[30]

The Post-Revolutionary Question of Black Freedom

The Revolution brought independence to the new American nation and freedom to thousands of African American enslaved people, but not all Black men and women promised freedom were freed even after they had completed military service. Many substitution agreements between owners and enslaved men consisted only of a verbal promise, which owners easily denied at war's end. Some enslaved men successfully brought suit against these owners, but the national government did little to ensure that owners abided by state legislation freeing men who served. Although many were properly freed and some freed themselves by simply walking away from slavery during the postwar disruption, many others remained in slavery.[31]

The last British contingent which surrendered New York in November, 1783, took four thousand Black men with them. More than fourteen thousand Black soldiers departed that fall, and most of those who had not served with the British forces but had simply escaped to British lines remained in slavery. Some went to Canada with Loyalists or to England with the troops. Others ended up on sugar plantations in Jamaica or some other British West Indian colony where life for enslaved people was unspeakably harsh. The British granted some people a choice of destination; Phyllis Thomas, "a free black woman," was granted passage to the West Indies or "elsewhere at her option." Other free Black individuals traveled to Britain, Europe, Canada, or parts of Latin America. Some found opportunities abroad that they would probably not have had in the United States. Bill Richmond, held in slavery by the Duke of Northumberland on New York's Staten Island, went to London with his owner when the Duke withdrew from America. There Richmond was educated, became a boxer, and by 1800 was billed as "the Black Terror," a bare-knuckle contender for the national championship. Although he lost to champion Tom Cribb in a brutal one-and-one-half-hour contest for the title, Richmond's fame enabled him to retire from the ring and establish the Horse and Dolphin Inn and his own boxing academy at the Royal Tennis Court; he trained many well-known British personalities, including Lord Byron, who attended regularly.[32]

Hundreds of Black men and women who went to Canada settled in Nova Scotia, accounting for at least 10 percent of those who settled the Halifax area during the early 1780s. Many were families like Charles and Dolly and their five children, who had been enslaved in New York and settled in Port Roseway, Nova Scotia. There Charles found work as a carpenter with the British army engineers, they survived the harsh winters, and the family built a life in freedom. Others who settled in Canada were not as fortunate, and with increasing urgency the new Black Canadians reported that land and employment were difficult to secure, racial intolerance was increasing as the Black population grew, and life was generally hard. Even though these people valued their new freedom, neither Canada nor England offered most Black people the opportunities they sought for progress and self-determination, and many migrated elsewhere. A few went to other countries in Europe, but by 1790 many American-born Black people were among the settlers of the British West African colony of Sierra Leone.[33]

In the new United States, antislavery forces continued their agitation during the war, arguing that slavery was inconsistent with both Christianity and the values of the Revolution. Many colonies—even including Virginia, North Carolina, and Georgia—had temporarily outlawed the slave trade during 1774 and 1775. In 1775 the first antislavery society in the Atlantic world was established in Philadelphia, called the **Society for the Relief of Free Negroes Unlawfully Held in Bondage**. Two years later Vermont became the first state in the nation to abolish slavery within its borders, adopting a state constitutional provision that declared, "All men are born equally free and independent." Local abolitionists attacked slavery everywhere but in the Deep South. In 1779 a group of enslaved men petitioned the legislature in New Hampshire for their freedom. They argued that their being kidnapped from their native Africa and held in the United States against their will was plainly against all natural law, since the "God of nature gave them life and freedom, upon the terms of most perfect equality with other men." But New Hampshire officials were deaf to their plea, though the 1783 state constitution seemed to deny slavery's legitimacy. Although slavery waned in the state, and the number of enslaved people dwindled to practically zero before the nineteenth century (eight enslaved people were recorded in the state in 1800), the institution was not officially abolished there until 1857.[34]

The antislavery arguments of the enslaved and their abolitionist allies were more directly successful in other northern states. Most of these states abolished slavery through strategies of **gradual emancipation** that were less economically and socially disruptive than **immediate emancipation**, at least from the perspective of the white society. They freed only people born after the passage of the state law. In Connecticut a combination of economic depression and antislavery pressure encouraged the legislature to institute a plan that freed the children born to an enslaved mother when they reached their twenty-fifth birthday. In Pennsylvania, any born to an enslaved mother after 1780 were to be set free at twenty-eight years of age, being treated as an indentured servant until that time. New York and New Jersey enacted gradual emancipation plans in 1799 and 1804. Massachusetts answered the revolutionary rhetoric in a petition for immediate emancipation, after the state Supreme Court ruled in 1783

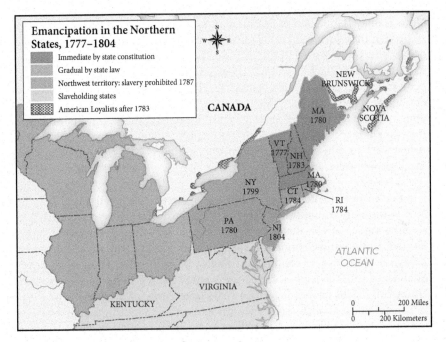

Map 3.2 Emancipation in the Northern States, 1777–1804

that slavery was incompatible with the state constitution of 1780. By 1800 slavery was abolished or in the process of being gradually abolished throughout the North.[35]

The ideals and the rhetoric of the Revolution made arguments for emancipation difficult to ignore, but other factors also contributed to the demise of slavery in the North. Urban white workers, wanting to limit both employment competition and the number of Black people in the local population, pressured officials to abolish slavery. Northern employers found free labor sufficient for their needs and thus a financially viable alternative to slavery. The relatively small number of enslaved people in most northern states, and the fact that northern economies were generally not built on slavery meant that there were few powerful voices in favor of the institution. All these circumstances created the conditions under which the arguments of those working for emancipation could be successful.

In the **Lower South**, where planters held the political and economic power, the impact of Revolutionary idealism was negligible. As South Carolina and Georgia resisted enlisting enslaved men in their militia during the war, they stood fast against the winds of abolition drifting across the northern states. Maryland, Virginia, and North Carolina retained slavery too, but far less adamantly. There, for a generation or more, state regulations allowed and even encouraged the voluntary manumission of enslaved people. As a result the free Black population in those Upper South states grew substantially during the late eighteenth century and the first two decades of the nineteenth. By 1810 more than 107,000 free Black men and women, almost 58 percent of the nation's total free Black population of 186,000, lived in the southern states. The rate of growth of the southern free Black population declined after the 1820s as fewer southern enslaved people were freed. The numbers in slavery grew substantially to 1.5 million by 1820 and to more than double that number by mid-century. Thus slavery became more significant in the South as it was gradually abolished in the North, and the social and political distance steadily increased between North and South.[36]

The divergence between the North and the South regarding slavery created new dangers for people in slavery in the North. When it seemed clear that slavery would be abolished in the North, many slaveholders rushed to sell their enslaved men and women farther south before freedom prevented them from doing so. Even after the passage of emancipation laws, children and young adults particularly faced this risk. Under gradual emancipation, enslaved young people might be held as servants only until they reached their mid-twenties. Although the practice was illegal, handsome prices for them in the plantation South provided an incentive for northern slave owners to sell their enslaved youth to the South before they reached the age of manumission. In Connecticut in 1792, one slaveholder was charged with attempting to circumvent state law by "exporting" two enslaved children. The closer the enslaved lived to the South, the greater the danger of being transferred into southern slavery, and many traveling slave traders roamed the southern regions of the North in search of good buys.

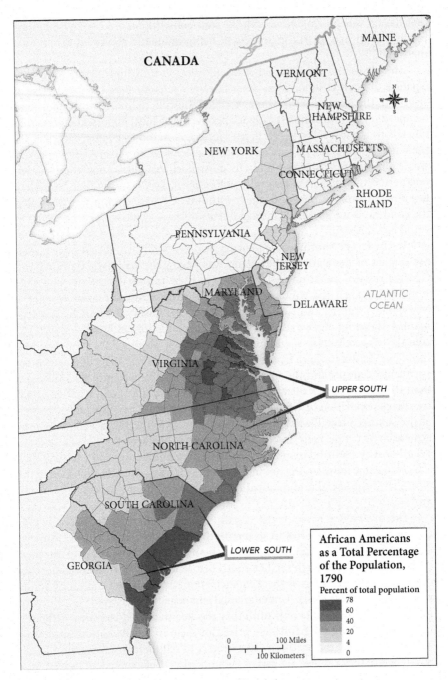

Map 3.3 African Americans as a Total Percentage of Population, 1790

Some owners tricked the people they owned, sending them into the South for temporary employment and selling them once they were there. Eighteen-year-old Harvey had only a few more years to serve when he was persuaded to travel from Middlesex County, New Jersey, to Louisiana to work "temporarily." He was enslaved there for the rest of his life. In this way, many young people never gained their promised freedom, and the tragedies of slavery continued for them long after official emancipation in the North. Isabella, an enslaved woman with a strong Dutch accent who lived in New York State, understood the dangers as well as anyone. She looked forward to freedom for herself and her children under New York's emancipation law, but before freedom came her youngest son was given as a wedding present to her owner's daughter who was leaving New York for Alabama. When a distraught Isabella confronted her owner, the white woman refused to take her concerns seriously. "A fine fuss to make about a little nigger! Why, haven't you as many of 'em left as you can see to?" Many parents carried such painful memories into freedom as slavery came to an end in the North. Isabella was eventually able to recover her son, but the incident contributed to her determination to fight against slavery and for the rights of women. In that fight she took the name Sojourner Truth.[37]

With the prolonged process of gradual emancipation in most of the North, many African Americans throughout the country continued to suffer the hardships of slavery after the Revolution. Even those who were freed faced hard times in the postwar period, as all Americans were confronted by economic uncertainty and an unstable currency. The situation was especially difficult for the poor, including formerly enslaved people and indentured servants, and those who had gained their freedom by fighting in the war often carried additional burdens. Cato Howe was freed from bondage in return for his years of service for Massachusetts, returned to his wife and farmwork. The Howes settled in a section of Plymouth, Massachusetts, known as New Guinea or Parting Ways with the families of three other Black war veterans—Plato Turner, Quamony Quash, and Prince Goodwin. The depression of 1784 meant that the farmers received

LEMUEL HAYNES

Portrait of Lemuel Haynes, former Revolutionary War soldier and African American minister to a white congregation in eighteenth-century Vermont.

Elizabeth Freeman (c.1744–1829), also known Mum Bett, was the first enslaved African American to file and win a freedom suit in Massachusetts, in 1781.

low prices for their produce. When Howe developed rheumatism from his war wounds he had trouble working around the farm, and his life became even harder. Recognizing the hardships suffered by these veterans, in 1792 the town of Plymouth granted the men the rights to 106 acres of the land where they were living in return for the labor it would take to clear it. Despite this aid, the support and friendship of his comrades, and the pension to which his wartime service entitled him, Cato Howe was forced to rely on public assistance in his old age.[38]

For African Americans the Revolution brought an incomplete freedom and a precarious status in the United States. In Georgia and South Carolina, nearly all of the enslaved people who did not escape to the British lines remained in slavery. In the Chesapeake region, slavery remained as an institution, but the conditions under which owners could free people were liberalized so that the number of free Black men and women increased. In the North, slavery was ending, but freedom brought limited benefits to the formerly enslaved people. The lingering revolutionary spirit held promise, but the future of Black people in America was even more uncertain than the future of the new nation.

Who, What, Where

Review Questions

3.1 What impact did the First Great Awakening have on relations between white and Black people in the colonies?

3.2 In what ways did race impact growing class divisions in colonial American society?

3.3 How was Crispus Attucks's role in the Boston Massacre emblematic of race relations in colonial Massachusetts?

3.4 Why was Black participation in the Revolution both encouraged and discouraged by the patriots?

3.5 Why did Black men serve as soldiers in both the British and Continental armies?

3.6 How did the success of the American Revolution impact the antislavery movement?

For additional digital learning resources please go to **https://www.oup.com/he/horton1e**

The Early Republic and the Rise of the Cotton Kingdom

Captain Absalom Boston.

CHAPTER OUTLINE

⭐ **JAMES FORTEN RETURNED** from the Revolution to a Philadelphia that was the new nation's largest city and its financial, intellectual, and scientific center. This commercial hub had over thirty-two thousand residents and a rapidly growing Black population of over eleven hundred, which would double in the next decade. The fourteen-year-old Forten, born free in Philadelphia, had served aboard the colonial ship *Royal Louis* and had been captured by the British and held for seven months on a prison ship before finally returning to his family in his home city. Forten learned the trade of sailmaking and was so talented at the work that by the age of twenty he was foreman of a shop owned by white sailmaker Robert Bridges. He became a prominent member of the city's free Black community, which by the mid-1780s accounted for almost 90 percent of the African Americans in Philadelphia. The small enslaved population continued to dwindle in the city and in the state, but the nation remained largely committed to the institution, no matter how it contradicted the national purpose.[1]

The United States was beginning to work out the meaning of citizenship for its people; and African Americans, having sacrificed to make independence possible, were determined to gain both liberty and full citizenship. Especially in urban areas the establishment or expansion of free Black communities provided crucial economic and social support. The willingness of reformers to aid the newly free with services like education was a hopeful sign, as was the emergence of antislavery organizations. The debate over slavery was critical to the future of the United States as the new nation contemplated the construction of its government. The documents of the Revolution were filled with the language of equality, arguing for the right to liberty and self-determination. These sentiments had contributed to the decisions to abolish slavery in nearly all the northern states, and African Americans now called upon the nation to live up to its principles. Indeed historian Gary Nash has called the 1770s and 1780s the "opportune time for abolishing slavery" in the country. According to Nash the new nation could have outlawed slavery at that time because antislavery sentiment was strong; the Lower South, where slavery was dominant, was too weak to stand alone; a belief in innate Black inferiority was not yet widespread; and western lands might have been used to compensate slaveholders for freeing their enslaved people or for Black

Timeline

Chapter 4

1787
Adoption of the United States Constitution.
Northwest Ordinance outlaws slavery in the territory northwest of the Ohio River.
British found Sierra Leone as West African colony for freed enslaved people.

1789
George Washington inaugurated as the first president of the United States.

Olaudah Equiano publishes his *Narrative*.

1790
The first United States Census is conducted, recording nearly four million residents, over 750,000 (19 percent) of whom are Black.

1791
Benjamin Banneker assists in surveying the area that would become the District of Columbia.

Enslaved people revolt in French colony of St. Domingue (Haiti).

1793
Eli Whitney invents the cotton gin.
Congress passes the first federal Fugitive Slave Law.

1800
U.S. population 5,308,483. Black population 1,002,037 (19 percent).
Gabriel's massive slave revolt in Virginia is betrayed.

colonization. Post-Revolutionary leaders, however, having rebelled against a strong colonial power, were acutely aware of the dangers of governmental centralization, and wartime disagreements had exposed the divergent interests of the new states. Thus they limited the power of the federal government to impose its will on the states by establishing a relatively weak, decentralized system of government under the Articles of Confederation, leaving the issue of slavery to the separate states.[2]

The Question of Slavery in the New Nation

The turbulent decade of the 1780s exposed the vulnerability of a limited federal government. In the years after the Revolution, economic pressure increased as returning soldiers faced deteriorating conditions. The Continental script with which they were paid was practically worthless, their debts had accumulated, and the prospects for financial improvement seemed remote. Britain had been the major market for colonial goods before the war, and the loss of that market, combined with England's restrictions on American trade with the British West Indies, fueled a depression, further demoralizing urban workers and small farmers. In western Massachusetts debt-ridden farmers led by Daniel Shays, a Revolutionary War hero and prominent landholder, revolted against the increasing number of farm foreclosures. From August 1786 to March 1787, under Shays's leadership, thousands of armed farmers closed the local courts and prevented authorities from foreclosing on their property. One of Shays's inner circle was Moses Sash, a free Black laborer from Massachusetts who had also served in the war. Sash had received land as part of the payment for his service—land he too was struggling to retain. For those in authority concerned with political and economic stability, **Shays's Rebellion** was especially distressing. Congress had neither the funds nor the authority to raise troops to put down the revolt.

Thomas Jefferson elected president and is the first president to reside in Washington, D.C.

1803
Louisiana Purchase more than doubles the land area of the United States.

1804
Haiti achieves independence from France.

1808
United States prohibits the African slave trade.

1809
Thomas Paul organizes the Abyssinian Baptist Church in New York City.

1812–1814 War between the United States and Great Britain

January 1815 Andrew Jackson commands–U.S. troops, including a large force of African Americans, in the Battle of New Orleans.

1816
American Colonization Society established.

1819
Florida purchased by U.S. from Spain.

1820
West African colony of Liberia founded by colonization society for settlement of freed enslaved people.

Missouri Compromise maintains balance of slave and free states.

Black war veteran Prince Hall offered to take a force of seven hundred Boston area African American volunteers to quell the rebellion, but Massachusetts preferred to raise a force of white troops paid by wealthy Boston merchants. By the spring of 1787 the privately financed militia had routed Shays and his followers, many of whom then turned to state politics to redress their grievances. Boston Black men were greatly offended by the rejection of their offer of service to the new republic. Three months after Shays's Rebellion ended, Prince Hall and more than seventy others petitioned the Massachusetts General Court for funds to transport all Black Americans who wanted to go to Africa.[3]

At the same time, representatives were meeting in Philadelphia in a constitutional convention to consider broad new powers for the federal government. As the founding fathers sat in hot, humid, summertime Philadelphia arguing, compromising, and finally composing the Constitution, slavery was a major point of contention, a point on which the Lower South especially resisted compromise. Northern states were already moving toward the abolition of slavery, and delegates like Pennsylvania's Benjamin Franklin and New York's Alexander Hamilton had expressed the expectation that the new nation would follow their example. Virginia delegates, George Washington, Thomas Jefferson, Patrick Henry, and others had assumed that an end to slavery would have to be negotiated at the **Constitutional Convention**. Yet northern delegates did not press the South, especially resistant South Carolina and Georgia. Perhaps feeling their weakness as a fledgling nation faced with continuing European designs on its territory and resources, the framers of the Constitution avoided a confrontation on the contentious issue. The harmony purchased at the cost of leaving the slavery question unresolved allowed the convention to construct a Constitution that provided a strong tripartite central government with access to financial resources and increased control over a military that might be called on to meet foreign threats or contain popular unrest. As it was finally written the Constitution never referred to slavery directly but did accommodate slavery in three respects. First it protected property rights in enslaved people by providing slaveholders with the assurance that runaways would be returned even if they crossed state lines. Second it allowed the African slave trade to continue for a period of twenty years (and to reopen in places like South Carolina where it had been closed), protecting it until 1808. Finally it provided additional representation, and thereby greater political power, in the federal House of Representatives to slave states by allowing three-fifths of the enslaved to be counted in determining the basis for a state's representation. The Constitutional Convention did not define the requirements for citizenship, in effect reaffirming the traditional political system giving citizenship rights to propertied white males. Although the **Bill of Rights**, the first ten amendments to the Constitution, seemed to offer the possibility of some legal protection for African Americans, the position of free Black people remained unclear. The general term "person," occasionally with the qualifier "free," was used to refer to American citizens, while the term "other" delineated enslaved people, to whom no constitutional rights were guaranteed.

Although the silence of the Constitution on slavery left the existence and regulation of this institution to each state, the new Congress did concern itself with slavery in the territories directly under federal control. In 1787 Congress passed the **Northwest Ordinance** governing territories north of the Ohio River that were not yet ready to gain admission to the Union as states. This ordinance outlawed slavery in these northwestern territories, but by not mentioning the southwestern territories gave tacit approval for the introduction of slavery there. As a concession to slave owners, enslaved people already in the

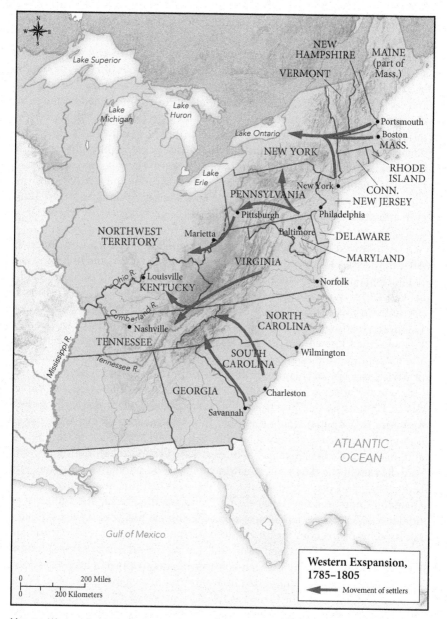

Map 4.1 Western Expansion, 1785–1805

northwest territories, including those brought in by the French before British settlement, could remain in slavery. Strong proslavery feeling in the portion of the territory that later became the states of Indiana and Illinois led to continual attempts by officials to circumvent the ordinance. As each new state was admitted to the union, the issue of Black status was debated by state constitutional conventions. During the next two generations, western and southern territories applying for admission either protected slavery or outlawed slavery and restricted Black migration. In Kentucky in 1792, antislavery elements raised religious and philosophical objections, but strong proslavery forces made Kentucky the first new slave state admitted to the Union. Four years later Tennessee, with more than ten thousand enslaved people, applied and was admitted as another slave state. In areas covered by the Northwest Ordinance, new states tried to limit the size of their Black population. Indiana, Michigan, Wisconsin, and Iowa prohibited Black immigration, and Illinois threatened bondage for Black Americans who attempted to settle there permanently. Ohio passed a series of "Black laws" requiring that free Black individuals post a five-hundred-dollar bond of good conduct, and denying Black persons the right to vote in most areas, to hold public office, or to testify against a white person in court. Free Black people were prevented from serving on juries and testifying against white people in many states. Restrictive laws were irregularly enforced, however, and the free Black population continued to grow, especially in areas bordering the South.[4]

Discouraged about their prospects for equality in America, members of African societies in Newport and Providence, Rhode Island, and in Boston and Philadelphia expressed cautious interest in the British colony of **Sierra Leone** in West Africa during the late 1700s. Finding hope for freedom and greater opportunity in this African colony, they were especially encouraged for a time in 1787 when the English committee for Sierra Leone hired the African Olaudah Equiano, then known as Gustavus Vassa, as the clerk in charge of outfitting and loading the ship bound for the colony. In his long route from his capture in Africa as a boy to this responsible position, Equiano had indeed been fortunate under adverse circumstances. He had spent only a few weeks in Barbados in 1756; as no one purchased him for plantation work there, the traders took him to Virginia, where they sold him to a tobacco planter who named him Jacob. He spent a month of terrible isolation. He could not speak English, and no one spoke his language. While working around the owner's house and yard, he caught the eye of a visiting sea captain, who purchased him, took him to England, and named him Gustavus Vassa. When this new owner received an appointment as a naval officer in 1756 during the French and Indian War, Equiano embarked on a dangerous life. During his five years at sea, he had a fair amount of freedom for an enslaved person, learning to read; accumulating some clothing, books, and cash; and sharing the perils and camaraderie of ships at war. At the end of the war, however, he was stripped of his possessions, sold to the West Indies, and resold in Montserrat to a Quaker man from Philadelphia. Equiano's fortune turned again as his new owner allowed him to work for wages and to purchase his freedom in the summer of 1766. For the next two

Freetown, Sierra Leone, as it appeared in the early nineteenth century.

decades the free African sailed the Caribbean and traveled in various parts of Europe, returning to London several times and working there for extended periods. In 1785 he visited America, spending time in Philadelphia. By this time Equiano had become a part of the antislavery movement, and within a year he was a major figure, appointed by Britain to supervise efforts to supply the Sierra Leone colony.[5]

In 1789 readers of English in Britain, America, and Europe were captivated by an extraordinary new autobiography. Published in London, this two-volume account was the work of an African of indisputable intelligence, imagination, talent, and humanity. *The Interesting Narrative of the Life of Olaudah Equiano or Gustavus Vassa* was Equiano's powerful first-hand account of his life in Africa, his capture and enslavement, and his life under the British-American slave system. It was so popular that at least eight editions were sold in the first five years of its printing. Equiano's writing provided a glimpse of what Europeans and Americans saw as the exotic society in his African home, but it was also a morality tale that condemned Christians' complicity in slavery's destruction of African lives and African families and unequivocally blamed the avarice of Christian slaveowners and their accomplices for the horrors of the slave trade. Equiano's literary skill created a powerful argument for antislavery forces, which used it to refute notions of African inferiority.[6]

Southern Fears of Black Freedom

In the face of post-Revolutionary antislavery sentiments in much of the United States, and the growing international interest in abolition, slavery became more firmly entrenched in the American South during the last decade of the eighteenth century. Thomas Jefferson had published his suspicions of Black inferiority in his *Notes on Virginia* in 1787. Although he was troubled by slavery, his reflections later formed the core of a powerful proslavery argument. In his writing, Jefferson ignored the accomplishments of such prominent Black men as Equiano, the impressive poetry of Boston enslaved woman Phillis Wheatley,

PROFILE

Benjamin Banneker

Benjamin Banneker, astronomer and mathematician who assisted in the surveying of Washington D.C.

THE SCIENTIST, MATHEMATICIAN, and astronomer Benjamin Banneker was born free near Baltimore, Maryland, in 1731. His father came to North America from Guinea, West Africa, in slavery and was later freed. His mother was also free, the child of an English indentured servant and an African who had gained his freedom before she was born. Benjamin's white grandmother taught him to read, and he became an avid reader with a natural aptitude for mathematics. He once constructed a mechanical clock on mathematical principles alone, having never seen one. Banneker farmed until rheumatism made it impossible, but retirement at middle age allowed him to take up mathematics and astronomy in earnest. In 1791 the presidentially appointed surveyor, Andrew Ellicott, asked Banneker to help him survey the area for the new national capital of Washington, D.C. For three months Banneker made the astronomic calculations each night that Ellicott used for his surveying the following day. Returning to Baltimore, Banneker organized his calculations and, in 1792, published them as the first of several almanacs.

Banneker was more than a man of science. He was also a man of keen political understanding, who used his learning and accomplishments to argue for racial equality. Ellicott and other scientists familiar with his work were impressed, but some were unwilling to acknowledge his obvious talent. Learning of Thomas Jefferson's doubt about the intelligence of African Americans, Banneker sent Jefferson copies of his calculations. Jefferson returned a polite reply but privately expressed doubts that a Black man could have produced such intricate work. Curiously Jefferson, one of the most intellectually inquisitive men in America, never tested his doubts and never invited Banneker to demonstrate his skill.

Banneker's almanac sold widely in the United States and Great Britain, and at least twenty-eight editions were published before his death in 1806. Benjamin Banneker died in his sleep at his home in Baltimore, just one month short of seventy-five years of age. In 1980 the U.S. Postal Service issued a postage stamp in his honor.

or Benjamin Banneker's sophisticated mathematical computations and observations in his scientific almanac. Jefferson was anxious that his reflections not be taken by his fellow slaveholders as an attack on slavery. Southern slave states were deeply affected by events on the French-held island of **St. Domingue** in the Caribbean. The spirit of revolution spread from France in 1789 to St. Domingue as enslaved people there determined to secure freedom for themselves. In the late summer of 1791, they rebelled against their owners with such fury that the French government sent troops to the colony to subdue them. By the time the French forces arrived, Black rebels had organized themselves under the leadership of a formerly enslaved carriage driver named **Toussaint L'Ouverture**. In 1793 enslaved and free Black fighters defeated the French army stationed in the capital and captured the city. White residents fled in ships bound for the United States, and on their arrival American newspapers were filled with their accounts of the horrors of the rebellion, stories that terrified southern slaveholders.[7]

Meanwhile, in St. Domingue, full-scale war frustrated Napoleon's plans for expansion of the French Empire in North America. Finally, in 1800, he resolved to end the resistance and sent a force of twenty-five thousand men. The French offered to negotiate a peace with the rebels, but when L'Ouverture arrived for the talks, he was captured, shackled, and taken to Paris. Nevertheless, the revolt continued, and on the first day of January 1804 Jean-Jacques Dessalines, its new leader, proclaimed Haiti's independence, the first independent Black nation in the Western Hemisphere. France's defeat ended Napoleon's dreams of a New World empire and encouraged him to dispose of his American lands while some profit could still be derived from them. In 1803, in exchange for fifteen million dollars, approximately four cents an acre, France sold the United States a huge tract of land. The **Louisiana Purchase**, as it was called, amounted to 828,000 square miles, stretching from the Gulf of Mexico northward to the Canadian border, and from the Mississippi River on the eastern boundary to the Rocky Mountains in the west. President Thomas Jefferson's acquisition of this new territory doubled the size of the United States, and slaveholders saw the promise of a vast new area open to slavery.

Although most of the estimated ten thousand French slaveholders who fled the **Haitian Revolution** for the United States settled in the South, some brought their enslaved people to northern cities such as Philadelphia and New York. In 1792 they petitioned Pennsylvania for the right to keep them, noting that Congressmen who brought their own enslaved people to the national capital at Philadelphia when Congress was in session were exempt from the abolition laws. In answer to their petition, authorities reaffirmed Pennsylvania's constitutional commitment to freedom and recommended that the legislature immediately and totally abolish slavery in the state. Between 1787 and 1810, of the 508 French-speaking enslaved

DOCUMENTING BLACK AMERICA

Benjamin Banneker's Letter to Thomas Jefferson

Maryland, Baltimore County
Near Ellicott's Lower Mills August 19th, 1791

Thomas Jefferson Secretary of State

Sir, I am fully sensible of the greatness of that freedom, which I take with you on the present occasion; a liberty which Seemed to me Scarcely allowable, when I reflected on that distinguished, and dignified station in which you Stand, and the almost general prejudice and prepossession which is so previlent [sic] in the world against those of my complexion.

I suppose it is a truth too well attested to you, to need a proof here, that we are a race of Beings who have long laboured under the abuse and censure of the world, that we have long been looked upon with an eye of contempt, and that we have long been considered rather as brutish than human, and Scarcely capable of mental endowments.

Sir, I hope I may Safely admit, in consequence of that report which hath reached me, that you are a man less inflexible in Sentiments of this nature, than many others, that you are measurably friendly, and well disposed towards us, and that you are willing and ready to Lend your aid and assistance to our relief from those many distresses and numberous calamities to which we are reduced.

Now, Sir, if this is founded in truth, I apprehend you will embrace every opportunity to eradicate that train of absurd and false ideas and oppinions [sic] which so generally prevails with respect to us, and that your Sentiments are concurrent with mine, which are, that one universal Father hath given being to us all, and that he hath not only made us all of one flesh, but that he hath also without partiality afforded us all the Same Sensations, and endued [sic] us all with the same faculties, and that however variable we may be in Society or religion, however diversified in Situation or color, we are all of the Same Family, and Stand in the Same relation to him. . . .

Sir, Suffer me to recall to your mind that time in which the Arms and tyranny of the British Crown were exerted with every powerful effort, in order to reduce you to a State of Servitude; look back I entreat you on the variety of dangers to which you were exposed. . . .

people freed in Pennsylvania, 45 were granted immediate freedom, 2 purchased their own freedom, and the rest were indentured in accordance with the gradual emancipation law. The association of the enslaved French speakers with the Haitian Revolution, their extreme poverty, their tendency to settle together in the least desirable part of the city, and their practice of **vodou** aroused white fears of disorder. These fears were confirmed in New York City in 1801, when twenty people tried to prevent a white Haitian immigrant from selling her enslaved people

This, Sir, was a time when you clearly saw into the injustice of a State of Slavery, and in which you had Just apprehensions of the horror of its condition, it was now Sir, that your abhorrence thereof was so excited, that you publickly held forth this true and invaluable doctrine, which is worthy to be recorded and remembered in all Succeeding ages. "We hold these truths to be Self evident, that all men are created equal, and that they are endowed by their creator with certain inalienable rights, that amongst these are life, liberty, and the persuit [sic] of happiness."

Here, Sir, was a time, in which your tender feelings for your selves had engaged you thus to declare, you were then impressed with proper ideals of the great valuation of liberty, and the free possession of those blessings to which you were entitled by nature; but Sir how pitiable is it to reflect, that altho you were so fully convinced of the benevolence of the Father of mankind, and of his equal and impartial distribution of those rights and privileges which he had conferred upon them, that you should at the Same time counteract his mercies, in detaining by fraud and violence so numerous a part of my brethren under groaning captivity and cruel oppression, that you should at the Same time be found guilty of that most criminal act, which you professedly detested in others, with respect to yourselves. . . .

This calculation [his almanac sent as a present], Sir, is the production of my arduous study. . . . altho you may have the opportunity of perusing it after its publication, yet I chose to send it to you in manuscript previous thereto, that thereby you might not only have an earlier inspection, but that you might also view it in my own hand writing.

And now Sir, I Shall conclude and Subscribe my Self with the most profound respect,

Your most Obedient humble Servant

Benjamin Banneker

Source: Sidney Kaplan, *The Black Presence in the Era of the American Revolution, 1770–1800* (Greenwich, CT: New York Graphic Society Ltd./Smithsonian Institution Press, 1971), 118–21.

out of the state, threatening to "burn the house, murder all the white people in it and take away a number of the black slaves." The incendiary potential became even clearer when hundreds of Black men congregated at the house that evening and clashed with fifty watchmen attempting to keep order. The authorities prevailed, the enslaved were not freed, and twenty-three rioters were jailed.[8]

The Haitian Revolution itself aroused the fears of southern Americans. White nightmares of the spread of slave revolts seemed to be coming true in

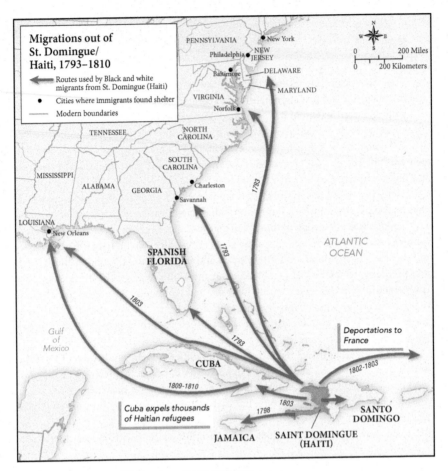

Map 4.2 Migration out of St. Domingue/Haiti, 1793–1810

1800 when a slave plot was unearthed just outside of Richmond, Virginia. As was typical in the Upper South, Richmond area enslaved people enjoyed a good deal of geographic mobility. They were often able to hire out their time to planters who needed extra help. Most of their pay was claimed by their owners, but they were generally able to retain a portion of it. Some saved to purchase their freedom or that of family members. While working on William Young's plantation just a few miles northeast of Richmond, Ben Woolfolk, an enslaved man hired during the summer of 1800, was approached by one of the men Young owned and asked to take part in an uprising. As the details of the plan became known over the next few months, it became clear that only enslaved people on the Young plantation and several from Richmond were involved. Three brothers—Martin, Solomon, and Gabriel—all skilled blacksmiths who were enslaved on a plantation in Henrico County, near Richmond, belonging to Thomas Prosser, were involved at the beginning of the plot, and **Gabriel** eventually became the leader. The number of recruits grew as Black boatmen and other "traveling" enslaved men carried the word from plantation to plantation and into the cities of the region. The plan was to attack Richmond, take Governor (and future President of the United States) James Monroe prisoner, and use the victory to encourage a general slave revolution in Virginia. These plans took shape in the context of a bitter dispute between the two major political parties in the United States, the Federalists and the Democratic-Republicans, during the election year of 1800, and growing tensions between the United States and France. There were general fears that the election of 1800 would result in armed hostilities between Federalist and Democratic-Republicans, and Gabriel and his followers planned to take advantage of any disruption that might occur. Gabriel attempted to enlist the cooperation of local white men, apparently believing his attack on slavery could become the foundation for a larger interracial class-based revolt against the privileged. He sought the cooperation of a Frenchman who might aid in devising military strategy and hoped that white artisans in Richmond, angered by the merchants' use of skilled enslaved workers to curb wages, might join as the revolt progressed or at least might not take up arms against it.[9]

The initial strike was planned for August 30, but it was postponed because of a fierce rainstorm. The delay proved fatal to the revolt's success, as enslaved informants revealed the plan to unsympathetic white people. Word soon reached the governor, state forces were assembled, and within a few days scores of enslaved people were arrested. A white seaman's efforts to help Gabriel escape failed when two enslaved seamen informed officials of his hiding place. At the trial, testimony revealed the extent of the conspiracy—apparently thousands of enslaved people were ready to join the revolt once it began. Gabriel was one of at least twenty-seven men convicted and hanged for their participation. For years after Gabriel's defeat, other enslaved people in other parts of Virginia remained ready to revolt, and authorities uncovered a number of conspiracies, one reportedly involving hundreds of people in at least eight counties in southern Virginia and northeastern North Carolina. Other plots were uncovered in South Carolina, though it is unclear how many of these were genuine attempts at revolt, as opposed to slaveholders overreacting to the Haitian Revolution and Gabriel's plot. Real or not, fears of slave uprisings led to the execution of twenty-five more Black men in Virginia in 1802 and to the passage of laws in Virginia, North Carolina, and South Carolina regulating enslaved and free Black people. Laws established slave patrols, restricted the movements of free and enslaved Black persons, limited emancipations, and mandated the removal of free Black men and women from the state of their manumission. By the middle of the first decade of the nineteenth century, the South had tightened its grip on slavery, reversing the trend toward a more flexible system of bondage and a less restrictive policy of manumission that had been most prominent in the Upper South.[10]

Southerners urged Congress to bar Black people from Haiti or elsewhere in the French West Indies from entering the United States lest they infect American enslaved people with a rebellious spirit. Congress responded in 1803 with regulations restricting West Indian immigration. It had also restricted mail carrying positions to white people in 1802, since Black post riders had helped to spread the word of rebellion among enslaved people in Virginia. The government also feared that, as U.S. Postmaster General Gideon Granger said, carrying the mail allowed Black men to learn of their human rights and disseminate that knowledge. As a further safeguard some in the South called for the removal of all free Black and troublesome enslaved people from the country. At James Monroe's suggestion, President Thomas Jefferson considered the American West as a place to establish a colony for this purpose, but Jefferson decided eventual American expansion into the West should not be blocked by a Black colony. He considered the West Indies, particularly Haiti, as a place where unwanted Black Americans might be shipped. The South, however, feared any arrangement that might enlarge the population of the Black West Indian revolutionary forces. There was a brief flirtation with a plan to ship unruly enslaved people to the British African colony of Sierra Leone, but as many were concerned that this would reward rebels with freedom, the idea was at least temporarily abandoned. Finally, the purchase of Louisiana from France and the opening of the southern regions of that area to slavery partially solved the problem of the disposal of unwanted bound laborers. In 1812, Louisiana was admitted to the United States as the first slave state carved from the new territory. Of the thirteen states formed in the territory, four—Louisiana, Alabama, Missouri, and Arkansas—allowed slavery.

Growing Demand for Enslaved Labor in the Western South

Initially, the heart of Louisiana's economy was sugar. Cane could not be grown as easily as in the West Indies, and yields were not as great, but profitable cultivation of the crop, investors and growers believed, required enslaved laborers, and rising prices encouraged owners in the Upper South to sell any extra hands into the new western South. Since the gang labor of sugar plantations called for a largely male workforce, Louisiana quickly acquired an enslaved population of relatively young males who outnumbered white residents in many of the large plantation areas.

A shift to cotton production in the western South dramatically increased the demand for slave labor in that region. Cotton had been grown in limited quantities in a few coastal areas of the eastern South since the seventeenth century, but South Carolina planters generally preferred to concentrate on rice cultivation. A few small planters grew cotton, and enslaved workers made their clothing from cotton they grew in small gardens. During the Revolution, a boycott of English cloth encouraged home production, but the most desirable long-staple cotton could be grown only near the coast. The short-staple cotton could be grown inland, but the tedium involved in removing the seeds from the fiber of this type of cotton made its production difficult and costly. The invention of a simple device called the **cotton gin** in 1793 by Eli Whitney, a Yale-educated teacher who traveled to South Carolina to tutor planters' children, made it economically feasible to expand the production of this crop. Using this new machine, essentially a box containing a rotating cylinder with protruding nails, a worker could remove seeds fifty times faster than by hand. The Louisiana Purchase provided fertile land; treaties and skirmishes subdued the Creek, Chickasaw, Choctaw, and Cherokee Native American people who lived there; and Whitney's new technology made it possible to create a new **Cotton Kingdom**, in the western area known as the **Deep South**. The new states of Mississippi, Alabama, and Arkansas joined western Georgia to become the prime cotton-growing region of the nation. Its rich black soil (hence the area's designation as the **Black Belt**) produced the crop that became the foundation of the nineteenth-century southern economy and plantation culture. The Black Belt's demand for enslaved laborers increased just after Congress ended the African slave trade in 1808, and this reduction in the supply increased the value of enslaved people in the Upper South who might be sold to the Deep South. The average price of a prime field hand grew fitfully during the first half of the nineteenth century from about six hundred dollars in 1802 to as much as eighteen hundred dollars by 1860. Over the same period the number of enslaved people in the nation increased dramatically from about seven hundred thousand to nearly four million. Although cotton prices fluctuated, they generally increased during the early decades of the century, and production rose dramatically in response. By 1815 cotton, the chief slave crop in the United States, was also fast becoming the country's single most valuable export, supplying the raw material for the textile mills of Britain and France. It continued its growth throughout the antebellum years, representing one-third of the value of all American exports by 1820, more than half by 1840, and almost 60 percent by the time of the Civil War. Mississippi alone produced ten million pounds of cotton in 1821, thirty million pounds in 1826, and eighty million pounds by 1834.[11]

In Louisiana sugar was also an important slave crop, and like cotton its cultivation exacted a terrible toll. In 1830 a New Orleans newspaper estimated that there was a death rate of at least 25 percent among enslaved laborers transported

Enslaved men, women, and children picking cotton in a field.

from the Upper South to work in the cane fields, and one contemporary observer speculated that the life expectancy of an enslaved worker in the cane fields was no more than seven years. Historian Charles Duncan Rice described sugar-producing Louisiana's reputation as "the most terrifying of all the various hells of the Deep South to which blacks from the older slave economies of the tidewater states could be sold." Sugar profits generally grew throughout the antebellum years and soared after mid-century, as the demands of this crop absorbed the labor and the lives of thousands of enslaved people. Yet cotton remained king even in Louisiana, and the steady increase in its economic value ensured its political power. Whatever the crop, especially after 1830, slavery was the dominant labor system in the South. Its centrality to the economy of that region, and thereby to the nation, made its abolition unlikely, especially in areas where it was most concentrated.[12]

Expanding the Internal Slave Trade

The development of the Deep South expanded the **internal slave trade**, and as the trade became more profitable, the major cities of the eastern and upper South became primary trading centers supplying the burgeoning labor needs farther south. During the late summer and early fall, traders in Washington, D.C., and Alexandria and Richmond, Virginia, bid on likely workers to be sold in New Orleans, Louisiana, and Mobile, Alabama, in December and January, when planters had marketed their summer crop and could afford cash payment. It was also in winter that planters returned to the Deep South from their retreats to more healthful climates where they routinely sought escape from summer's malaria and yellow fever. Then too, newly arrived workers had time to become acclimatized before the onset of summer heat and humidity. Traders generally auctioned enslaved people in large urban slave markets, but they traveled around to local plantations selling individuals when market sales were slow.

In the Black Belt, enslaved laborers generally found the work harder, the hours longer, the climate nearly unbearable, and the treatment more brutal. Since many planters were absentee owners during the heavy growing season, overseers with no personal financial investment in enslaved people to safeguard were left to handle the day-to-day operation of the large plantations. An enslaved person's life expectancy was diminished by severe conditions in the Deep South. The hot, humid climate so good for growing sugar cane in Louisiana was also ideal for breeding malaria-carrying mosquitoes. Cane cultivation in Louisiana was more intense and physically demanding than in the West Indies, where the growing season was slightly longer. Even after the worst summer heat was over, the work was hard. During the sixteen- to eighteen-hour days between mid-October and late December, when the crop was harvested, enslaved laborers worked at an exhausting pace, and owners increased the amount of cane each worker was expected to harvest as brutal, industrial-type agricultural techniques were employed and new varieties of sugar cane increased the yield per acre.

On the expansive cotton plantations of Mississippi and Alabama, established during the first three decades of the nineteenth century, large gangs of enslaved labor cleared the land during the early years of settlement. They also endured the "factory-like modes of regimentation" that modernized the work of cultivation and harvesting described by historian Edward E. Baptist as the "system of measurement, accounting and torture" that forced ever greater production. Each enslaved field laborer was assigned a daily quota, adjusted upward according to his or her previous day's accomplishment. Under this rationalized system each squad, led by the fastest worker and overseen by a "pushing" man with a whip, was goaded into faster and more efficient picking. Failure to meet the individual quota at the end of the day meant a brutal whipping adjusted according to the deficiency. Under this system an increase of 4,000 percent in the number of enslaved people from fifty thousand to two million, in the cotton-producing regions of the United States between 1805 to 1860 resulted in a 10,000 percent increase in the cotton produced, from twenty million pounds to two billion pounds. This slave-produced cotton became the engine of American economic development, undergirded the industrial development of the North, was the foundation of a vast network of development involving banks, insurance companies, and investment houses, and produced unsurpassed wealth for the slaveholders of the Cotton Kingdom.[13]

Lewis Clarke, an enslaved man from Kentucky, reported that workers knew that being taken to the Deep South was a horrible fate because they were "driven very hard there, and worked to death in a few years." Even the threat of being "put

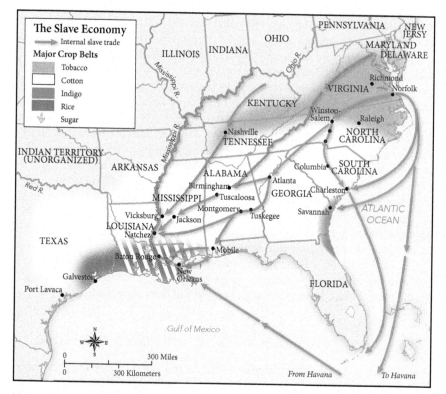

Map 4.3 The Slave Economy of the South

in the master's pocket" (that is, traded South for money the owner could put in his pocket) was enough to cause rebellion, flight, or even suicide. James Williams, enslaved in Alabama, knew of some people who, when they learned that they were to be sold South, "[died] of grief, and others [who committed] suicide on account of it." One made himself unfit to be sold South by cutting off the fingers of his left hand with an ax. Another drowned herself, and a third cut her own throat with a razor. All were terrified of labor in the Deep South, a fate some regarded as worse than death. Owners often used this fear to control their enslaved workers.[14]

The burgeoning internal slave trade increased the splintering of enslaved families in the Upper South and disrupted relatively settled enslaved communities that had been established on the Eastern Seaboard for many generations. Prior to 1820 a southern planter or his son was likely to move west, as Native Americans were driven from the land, with many of the enslaved workers from his eastern plantation. The opening of the Deep South, however, changed this pattern. By 1820, 70 percent of those taken South were moved by traders who realized great profits from the relatively high prices brought by young males in the markets of the Black Belt. Between 1820 and 1830 a quarter of a million enslaved people were traded south, with a devastating impact on their families and communities. In New Orleans, Natchez, Montgomery, and elsewhere in the western South, males between the ages of ten and thirty were considered "prime hands," bringing the best prices. About 10 percent of all Upper South enslaved workers in their teens and 9 percent of enslaved workers in their twenties were sold south during the 1820s. One study has estimated that after 1815, about one-third of all adults were sold south before they were forty years old. High transportation costs discouraged conveying very small children or other family members so that generally only the most valuable were taken. A major route for transporting enslaved people was the Mississippi River, and so great was the likelihood that a family might lose a member, especially a son or a young father, to this internal slave trade that a new phrase, being "sold down the river," was added to the American lexicon and came to describe the disastrous consequences of these sales. Statistics on enslaved families tell the story of the trade's impact and the harsh conditions in the Deep South. Ann Patton Malone found that only just over half (57 percent) of enslaved people in the rural Louisiana parishes she studied were able to establish two-parent or couple households. Most of the young enslaved men brought from Kentucky to work on Walter Bashear's plantation in Louisiana, for example, never married. Messages exchanged with their families in Kentucky made clear that old relationships were not ended by this forced migration. "If you see Daddy," "poor little Hannah" instructed her mistress, "give my love to him." The opening of the Deep South may have brought great economic opportunity for the planter class, but it increased the misery of their slave laborers.[15]

Establishing Free Black Communities in the North

During this same period, as slavery ended in the North, Black families there were reunited or established. Expanding trade with Europe and economic prosperity attracted many free African Americans to the eastern port cities in search

TABLE 4.1   Free African American Population

City	1790	1800	% Increase 1790–1800	1830	% Increase 1790–1830
Boston	761	1,174	54	1,875	146
New York	1,078	3,499	225	13,960	1,195
Philadelphia	1,420	4,210	197	9,795	590

Source: *Negro Population in the U.S., 1790–1915 (Washington, D.C.: Government Printing Office, 1918; New York: Arno Press, 1968), 55; Leonard P. Curry, The Free Black in Urban America, 1800–1850 (Chicago: University of Chicago Press, 1981), 250.*

of work and the relative security provided by a Black community. Even during the colonial era, free Black men and women had been largely city dwellers, and most had congregated in the Atlantic seaport towns and cities where work was available and new Black communities were beginning to take shape. This trend continued during the late eighteenth and early nineteenth centuries with the Black population of the major northeastern coast cities growing in actual numbers and as a proportion of the cities' populations. Free Black people were, in fact, the most urban group in America (see Table 4.1).[16]

Paul Cuffe, living in coastal Massachusetts, was one of the free Black men who profited from the growing post–Revolutionary War trade. By the time the Revolution was over, Cuffe was a mature man of twenty-five with many years of experience as a sailor fishing the waters around Nantucket and in the North Atlantic and whaling off Mexico and the West Indies. He had grown up in relative security, with close ties to his many siblings and his mother's people in the Native American community at Chilmark on Martha's Vineyard. When his father, the African freedman Cuffe Slocum, died before the war, he left Paul's mother, Ruth, and her ten children settled on their 116-acre farm in Dartmouth, Massachusetts. After the war Paul Cuffe married a Native American woman, Alice Pequit, and established a partnership with his brother-in-law Michael Wainer. By the early 1790s Cuffe and Wainer had two schooners fishing and

Paul Cuffe, sea captain, shipbuilder, and merchant, with an engraving of his ship, *Traveller*, 1812.

whaling off the coast of Newfoundland, the beginning of a successful, lifelong business partnership.[17]

As the urban free Black population increased, Black families formed the basis for more stable, expanded, and diverse community institutions. Among the first institutions were mutual aid societies, cooperative organizations formed to provide funds for burials and aid to members' widows, the sick, and the unemployed. Racial prejudice and often, ironically, their desperate poverty frequently disqualified Black Americans from the sources of aid available to most of their white counterparts. Early charitable institutions were loath to aid those they did not consider to be a local responsibility or those whose extreme poverty, or supposed poor character and bad habits they believed did not make them good candidates for reform. Thus African Americans were likely to be forced to rely on the resources of their own communities. This necessity, a traditional African communal ethic, and the African religious significance of a proper burial all contributed to a proliferation of mutual aid societies among free Black people. There was a general increase in associations in American society after the Revolution, but their growth among Black men and women also drew on the African traditions still vivid in the memories of thousands of African-born Americans. In many African societies an individual's identity was derived from the family, an individual's primary responsibility was to the family, and the community was simply an extension of the family. This **communalism** became the basis for social organization in the Black communities established in the West Indies and North America. "What is mine goes," instructed one African proverb, but "what is ours abides." One of the earliest mutual aid groups, the African Union Society, was organized in Newport, Rhode Island, in 1780. The Free African Society was formed in Philadelphia in 1787 by free Black people in cooperation with white antislavery Quakers, and Black communities in Boston organized the African Society in 1796. Through these organizations, people contributed to the support of the spouses and orphans of deceased members and to disabled, unemployed, or destitute members and their families. The Philadelphia organization, with two prominent community leaders, Richard Allen and Absalom Jones, among its founders, also provided aid to formerly enslaved people. Both Allen and Jones had been enslaved, and each had bought his own freedom shortly before establishing the Free African Society.[18]

Another early African American community organization was the **Masons**. Even before the Revolution, **Prince Hall**, a native of Barbados and the son of a free mixed-race mother and a British father, organized a small Black Masonic group in Boston. After he arrived in Massachusetts, Hall had become a soapmaker and eventually a Methodist lay preacher. Under his leadership, a group of Black men applied to the white Masonic order in Boston for an official license as a lodge, but the Boston Masons refused to recognize an organization of Black Masons. Hall then turned to the British order, through an Irish military regiment stationed in Boston, and they accepted his application. In 1775, just before the British troops were expelled from the city by American forces, fifteen African Americans were initiated into the British lodge, and they continued to meet during the Revolution. After the war, Hall, who had served six years with the American troops, again applied to the American Masonic order for recognition, and again was refused. Finally, he turned to the Grand Lodge of England, which officially granted permission in 1784 for the formation of the African Lodge Number One of Boston. Formally established in 1787 and renumbered Lodge 459, it was the first Black Masonic lodge in the United States. It became a center for community mutual aid, political action, and a catalyst for other Black Masonic organizations in Providence and Philadelphia. By the turn of the nineteenth century, there were several Black Masonic lodges, some initiated with the support of the Boston group. Philadelphia was rapidly becoming an important center of masonic activity; one of its lodges was established by Black sailors with the aid of the Grand Lodge of Germany in 1798. The proliferation of lodges throughout the North established regular lines of communication among many Black communities, facilitating political organization in the nineteenth century. Like other African American associations, Masonic organizations were multipurpose mutual aid, religious, and political action groups.

By the turn of the nineteenth century, African Americans had formed hundreds of mutual aid societies, fraternal organizations, and community service groups boasting thousands of members throughout the North. Often these groups included both males and females, although some—like the African Masonic lodges or the Female Benevolent Society of St. Thomas in Philadelphia—were restricted. Membership dues provided the funds for the operation of these groups and the benefits they provided. Membership in the African Benevolent Society of Newport, Rhode Island, required a fifty-cent initiation fee, and the African Marine Fund in New York City required an initiation fee of one dollar. Additional monthly dues ranged from twelve and a half to fifty cents. Boston's African Society, for example, charged twenty-five cents to enter the society and another twenty-five cents for monthly dues. These were considerable fees for a generally poor

Portrait of Prince Hall, founder of the Colored Fraternity of Free and Accepted Masons, Boston, Massachusetts.

people, but these organizations provided essential services in a manner congruent with African Americans' values, and attracted a great many members. Various contemporaneous studies of the benevolent societies in Philadelphia provide some measure of the growth and importance of such organizations. In 1830 there were almost fifty societies, sixty by 1836, and one hundred by 1838, paying out approximately six, nine, and fourteen thousand dollars in annual benefits, respectively. Though there was undoubtedly an overlapping membership, the nearly 7,500 members in 1838 represented a remarkable level of organization in the city's Black community of 10,507 people.[19]

Early Black organizations concerned themselves not only with the financial and social needs of community members but also with their spiritual and political needs. Free African Societies often provided religious services, and some were the forerunners of African American churches. Philadelphia's Bethel Church, founded by Richard Allen, and the African Church (later called the African Episcopal Church of St. Thomas), founded by Absalom Jones, both grew from the membership of the Free African Society. In Boston the African Baptist church grew out of the African Society of that city and drew its original membership from that organization. As in traditional African life, there were never great distinctions between secular and sacred institutions in African American

First African Baptist Church, Savannah, Georgia.

society. Black churches—the communities' most important public institutions—served as social centers where community drama groups, bands, youth organizations, men's and women's clubs, and debating societies met. They often hosted community educational facilities and served as political forums and convention halls. The first Black school in Boston met originally in the basement of the African Meeting House, the home of the African Baptist Church. The building also provided space for William Bassett's music classes for Black children, for community band concerts, and for the rehearsals of the Social Harmonic Society, a popular local choir. Similar activities found rooms in the churches of Philadelphia and New York City. In almost all African American communities across the North, whenever community meetings were held, most were held in the Black churches.[20]

As the political center of most Black communities, the church was also a training ground for Black leaders. In white society a young man aspiring to political prominence might enter law, run for minor local office, or work for a politician. In Black society the most common route to community leadership was through the church. Black ministers were both the guardians of the spiritual life of the community and its political leaders. Their activities might range from leading worship services, ministering to the sick, and feeding the hungry to hiding fugitives escaping from bondage.[21]

Free Black Americans in the South

It was much more difficult for free Black men and women to establish organizations in the South, since southern slaveholders were greatly suspicious of free Black people who were not under their direct control. Laws prohibiting Black gatherings without white supervision limited the movements of all African Americans. Restrictions grew stronger and were enforced more rigorously during periods when rumored or actual slave revolt made slaveholders more apprehensive. Still, southern free Black people formed societies to meet the spiritual and practical needs of their communities. Although some societies managed to meet secretly, public gatherings required white sponsorship. Typically a white clergyman was responsible for the oversight of a Black church and its many related organizations. Despite white obstructions African American communities in major southern cities with sizable Black populations, such as Charleston, Richmond, Baltimore, and Washington, D.C., were nearly as well organized as those in the North. By 1836, the Baltimore Black community, for example, had about forty fraternal, literary, religious, and temperance associations, many attached to churches. White southerners often saw Black organizations as a threat, but the Brown Fellowship Society, the oldest Black organization in the South founded in 1790 in Charleston, South Carolina, seemed to represent a type of Black organization that white southerners could use. Some of the membership was drawn from mixed-race people who fled the Haitian Revolution after siding with the French colonials against the Black revolutionaries.

The color consciousness of these light-skinned Haitians found expression in groups like the Brown Fellowship, groups of economically and socially privileged African Americans whom white people judged less threatening to white supremacy. Members were often related to prominent local white families, and many slaveholders hoped they would provide information about the enslaved population, warning of unrest and conspiracies.[22]

The position of southern free Black Americans was complex. Unable to depend on southern law for protection, patronage from powerful southern white people was the only buffer between them and the systemic injustice they were liable to suffer in the slave South. Indeed, some slave conspiracies were betrayed by other African Americans, both enslaved and free. But even elite Black groups were involved in the common political issues of central concern to all African Americans, the opposition to slavery and the protection of fugitive enslaved people. Northern groups were the most visible proponents of Black freedom, since even the limited white southern tolerance for antislavery expression had disappeared by 1830. The abolition of slavery, the most serious and immediate problem, was but one of many political concerns for Black individuals in America. As the new nation defined the rights of citizens through the passage of state constitutions, the rights of free Black Americans were increasingly limited.[23]

African Americans in the War of 1812

Discrimination and an uncertain future in America continued to spark interest in emigration, especially among African-born Black men and women. Massachusetts Captain Paul Cuffe, with an African father and a Native American mother, was one of those interested in African colonization. In 1810 he set sail in his ship, *Traveller*, with his nephew Thomas Wainer as first mate and an all-Black crew, to explore the prospects for settlement in and trade with Sierra Leone. Cuffe was impressed by the settlement he found and hopeful that he could eventually demonstrate that a profitable trade not including enslaved people could be established between Africa and the United States. Among the 3,500 settlers were formerly enslaved Americans who had come to the British colony by way of England or Canada, where they had gone with withdrawing British forces after the Revolution. There were also local Africans, Black individuals from the British West Indies, and people rescued from slave trading ships off the African coast. A handful of Europeans, approximately 1 percent of the colony's population, controlled almost two-thirds of the property in Sierra Leone. Recognizing that initial support for any trading venture would have to come from the British merchants who financed the European property holders, Cuffe sailed for England.

By April 1812, when Cuffe and Wainer returned to the United States, continuing tensions with Britain had escalated, and the United States had instituted a trade embargo. Since the *Traveller* had been in England, U.S. customs authorities confiscated Cuffe's cargo when he entered port in Rhode Island, an inauspicious beginning to his African trading venture. Through his connections with wealthy Quaker merchants, Cuffe was able to meet with President James Madison and Secretary of the Treasury Albert Gallatin, who helped him gain the release of his ship and cargo. But his standing in the business community did not protect him from the indignities of discrimination in public lodging and on public transportation, discrimination that increased his commitment to African settlement. In New York, Philadelphia, and Baltimore, Cuffe met with Black leaders, reporting on the promise of Sierra Leone and encouraging them to establish organizations to promote Sierra Leone and organize potential settlers.

The trading ventures of merchants and captains like Paul Cuffe were deferred by the growing hostility between Britain and the United States. Many common sailors suffered more directly, losing work and wages as trade diminished. Americans complained that Britain acted with intolerable arrogance, not respecting the new nation's shipping rights, violating its territory, and impressing its citizens. Contrary to the peace agreements ending the Revolutionary War, British troops remained in western forts, and Britain seized neutral American ships to prevent them from trading with its enemy, France. English impressment gangs roamed European ports and boarded American ships at sea, forcibly taking likely-looking sailors to serve aboard British vessels. Many Black men were among the American sailors British naval authorities abducted.[24]

During the spring of 1812 relations between England and the United States deteriorated further, and in June, President James Madison issued a formal declaration of war. Despite the Revolutionary War service of African American men, American authorities again heatedly debated the question of Black participation in the military. For southerners the prospect of arming their enormous, generally enslaved Black population again evoked the terrifying specter of the Haitian Revolution. Meanwhile the British once again promised freedom to American enslaved men who joined their forces. Thousands of enslaved people escaped to the British army lines, some volunteering for military service. One alarmed southerner reported that Black men were "flocking to the enemy from all quarters." African Americans served aboard British vessels in battles in the Great Lakes and Chesapeake Bay, and when British troops attacked Baltimore and invaded and burned the capital city of Washington in 1814, newly freed men were among them. When the United States offered to free enslaved men in return for military service, many volunteered, even when the terms were unattractive and discriminatory. New Yorkers had to serve for three years before they were freed, and the cash payment normally provided to soldiers was generally paid instead to their owners. As in the Revolution, enslaved men fought for both Britain and the United States, often joining whichever force promised liberty.[25]

Many free Black Americans, motivated by patriotism or local loyalties, served with American forces on sea and land. They formed separate units in New York, Philadelphia, and other cities along the Atlantic coast. One New York "Citizen of Color" argued that it was the "duty of every colored man resident in this city to volunteer" when British forces threatened the coast, believing that white Americans would see this as a "test of patriotism." The spirit and unity of the builders of New York's fortifications were reflected in a popular song called "The Patriotic Diggers." "To Protect our rights / Gainst your flints and triggers," the singers challenged, "See on Brooklyn Heights / Our patriotic diggers," claiming, "Men of every age, / Color, rank, profession."[26]

In New England, strong antiwar sentiment discouraged residents from participating in the war, and African Americans there were also less likely to join the American army. Black sailors from New England, however, were prominent participants. Commander Isaac Chauncey, who engaged the British on the Great Lakes, counted the fifty Black sailors under his command as "among [his] best men." At first Captain Oliver H. Perry was uncomfortable with his integrated crew, one quarter of whom were Black, but after defeating the British fleet in 1813, he praised the action of his Black sailors and singled out several for special commendation. Likewise Captain Nathan Shaler lauded his Black sailors, telling of one who after "a twenty-four pound shot struck him in the hip, and took away all the lower part of his body," urged his shipmates on saying, "Fire away boys! —No haul a color down." Captain Shaler asserted that "while America has such tars, she has little to fear from the tyrants of Europe."[27]

Many American sailors were captured and spent time as prisoners of war in British jails, and some Black sailors who had been impressed into British service chose to go to prison rather than fight for England when the war broke out. As many as eleven hundred Black and five thousand white Americans were confined in England's Dartmoor prison by 1814. At first the British housed the Americans together, but as the population grew, they eventually segregated the prison barracks by race. Still, visiting between barracks and continual interaction among the prisoners gave Dartmoor an interracial cultural life. The Black barracks became an important center of prison life, where interracial casts performed Shakespearian plays, interracial audiences enjoyed African music and dance, and regular church services were held by a Black minister. Boxing classes were conducted by Richard Seaver, a Black sailor from Salem, Massachusetts. Classes in reading and writing were taught by inmates of the Black barracks. Dartmoor was no interracial utopia—it was a prison filled with sailors where racial tensions occasionally erupted into conflict, but it also had a lively interracial political, economic, and social life. Although the prison was segregated, shipboard habits, identifications, and friendships carried over to prison life. One Black prisoner from Newburyport, Massachusetts, for example, made a point of sharing his card-game winnings of "a two penny loaf and a pint of coffee" with his white mates from his hometown.[28]

In December 1814 Britain and the United States negotiated an end to their hostilities with the Treaty of Ghent. Napoleon had abdicated as emperor of France, ending the war in Europe and removing the issue of neutrality rights for American shipping. The issue of impressment was not resolved, but the war's end reduced England's need for sailors. Britain did drop its demands for territorial concessions and for American recognition of an independent Native American state and finally withdrew from the western boundaries of the United States. Ironically, the battle of New Orleans, the best-known battle of the war, was actually fought after the war was over, and it involved Black men as combatants on both sides. In New Orleans, General Andrew Jackson, future president of the United States, faced a British invasion. Jackson commanded a force of frontier militiamen that included at least six hundred mixed-race and free Black men. He was uncertain of Black soldiers' willingness to engage the English in battle

Drum played by Black 14-year-old drummer Jordan B. Noble in the Battle of New Orleans.

and so made plans to move them to the rear rather than risk their joining the British troops. In a desperate effort to secure the loyalty of the city's people of color as British forces approached, Jackson promised Black troops the same pay, equipment, food, and 160-acre land grants as white troops. Years later Jackson confided to President James Monroe that he had been uncomfortable recruiting Black troops but had employed them largely to prevent the British from using them against the city.[29]

Contrary to Jackson's fears Black and white Americans together successfully defended New Orleans, inflicting heavy casualties on the invaders and providing the United States with an important victory. Jackson kept his promise to the free Black men and rewarded them for their service, but the enslaved men who fought with him were not so fortunate. James Roberts, born in slavery on the Eastern Shore of Maryland, was twice unlucky. He had earned his freedom for service in the Continental forces during the Revolutionary War, but his owner sold him to a slaveholder in New Orleans for fifteen hundred dollars instead. Decades later, when the call went out for enslaved men to defend the city against the British invasion, Roberts volunteered, hoping to gain his freedom. After the battle, Jackson extolled the bravery and skill of the Black soldiers who had stood with him but insisted he was powerless to interfere with owners' rights over their enslaved property. Roberts returned to slavery a bitter man, feeling he had once again been "duped by the white man." Many of the enslaved who escaped to the British fared little better and were sold to the West Indies by British officers who made considerable profit from this illegal trade. In response to persistent complaints by New Orleans slaveholders, England finally agreed to pay over one million dollars in 1826 to compensate them for the loss of enslaved people who escaped during the battle.[30]

The Issue of African Colonization

Winning the war reinforced the developing American identity and heightened nationalism especially for white Americans, but some Black men and women continued to contemplate emigration to Africa. Less than a year after the peace had been signed, Paul Cuffe set sail for Sierra Leone on the *Traveller*, carrying goods for trading and fifty-eight African American passengers. Cuffe settled his people on the land he purchased in the colony and by the spring of 1817 returned to the United States to promote colonization. He soon found powerful allies among a number of white men who had formed a group in 1816 to promote the colonization of Black people in West Africa. Hoping for Congressional financing, and calling their organization the **American Colonization Society**, they included some of the era's most prominent men. Virginian Charles Fenton Mercer, New Jersey minister Robert Finley, and Francis Scott Key, composer of the present-day national anthem, "The Star-Spangled Banner," were among the society's founders. Members included powerful political figures such as Henry Clay, the U.S. representative from Tennessee; Daniel Webster, U.S. senator from Massachusetts; future president John Tyler; Supreme Court Justice Bushrod Washington; and General Andrew Jackson. The fact that this distinguished group was composed mainly of slaveholders aroused Black suspicions, but Paul Cuffe's commitment to promoting African settlement and trade led him to an association with some of the society's members. Cuffe's knowledge of shipping, of West Africa, and of Sierra Leone were extremely useful to the colonizationists. He was able to convince several Black leaders in New York and Philadelphia to consider the organization's project, but most rank-and-file Black community members in northern cities rejected any association with the American Colonization Society. The Black masses of Philadelphia remained unconvinced even though many of the city's important leaders, James Forten and Richard Allen among them, originally supported colonization. Cuffe's African Institutions provided organizational support, prominent white leaders addressed large crowds promoting the society, and Cuffe himself spoke in Black churches extolling the wonders of Africa and the opportunities opened by colonization.

In 1820, with financial help from the federal government, the society founded its own colony and called it **Liberia**. Daniel Coker, one of the country's most prominent Black ministers, led eighty-six African American settlers who set sail on the *Mayflower of Liberia* for a new life in the West African colony. There was significant Black support for the American Colonization Society in the states of Virginia and Maryland in the Upper South. There opportunities for free Black people were extremely limited, and some owners were willing to free people who agreed to emigrate. Several Black Americans from Richmond, Virginia, were members of another group, which set off in 1821. Lott Cary, a formerly enslaved man who bought his own freedom, was one of them. His emigration was sponsored by Richmond's First Baptist Church, an interracial congregation who sent him as a missionary to the African people. Like many settlers Cary had many reasons for emigrating. "I am an African," he declared, explaining that he wanted to regain his heritage and hoped to develop his talents without the restrictions burdening Black people in America. For Black Americans born in Africa, colonization offered the opportunity to rejoin the friends and family they had been forced to leave behind many years before. African-born Boston Crummel, originally from the region of Sierra Leone and enslaved in New York for many years, was anxious to go home, but Crummel's wife, who had been born on Long Island in New York, was far more skeptical about emigration and about the colonization society. During the years before the Civil

War the colony of Liberia survived, but it drew only small numbers of emigrants from the United States.

The establishment of the colonization society was directly connected to the growing importance of cotton, slavery, and the planter class. Even though slavery became increasingly isolated in the South as northern states abolished the institution during the early years of the nineteenth century, the national power of slaveholders grew. Slaveholders such as James Monroe, Andrew Jackson, Henry Clay, and John C. Calhoun held the highest political offices in the nation. New York bankers financed southern cotton production, and Massachusetts textile mills depended on a steady supply of raw cotton. The American Colonization Society provided a convenient vehicle for white people uneasy with slavery but unwilling to confront the power of cotton and its slave system directly. The society allowed the discomfited to subscribe to somewhat contradictory aims. They could advocate removing free Black men and women to Africa, thereby placating slaveholders seeking a more secure slave system without the danger posed by free Black Americans; they could reassure the northern white workers who were becoming increasingly concerned about competition from Black labor; and they could use the language of freedom and opportunity in campaigns to recruit Black people for colonization. The multiplicity of goals accommodated by the American Colonization Society's program help to explain both its popularity with white people and its failure to attract most northern Black Americans. Remembering Black men who had participated in the Revolutionary struggles and defended the new nation in the War of 1812, many African Americans were insulted and offended by colonization schemes sponsored by slaveholders.

As Black people struggled to define their place in the United States after the war, there were confusing signals from white authorities. Northern states abolished slavery, but many restricted African Americans' civil rights. Colonization seemed to provide incentives for slaveholders to free their enslaved people and allow them to emigrate, but the increasing power of the Cotton Kingdom promised an entrenched slave system in the South. As regional tensions between slave and nonslave states grew, Congress became the arena for the struggle to maintain their balance of power. When the territory of Missouri applied for admittance to the Union early in 1819, northern congressmen tried to exact the gradual release of its ten thousand enslaved laborers and a restriction on the further introduction of enslaved people in return for Missouri's becoming a state. The southern congressmen argued that this was unconstitutional, but a crisis was avoided by a compromise providing for the simultaneous admission of Missouri as a slave state and Maine as a free state, and an agreement that Missouri's southern border would be the northern limit of slavery. The **Missouri Compromise of 1820**, as it was called, was one of a succession of confrontations between the slaveholding and nonslaveholding states, increasing in seriousness and marking the country's widening sectional rift. Years later Black abolitionist Frederick Douglass identified the Missouri Compromise as the first of those "shocking development[s] of that moral weakness in high places which [attended] the conflict between the spirit of liberty and the spirit of slavery."[31]

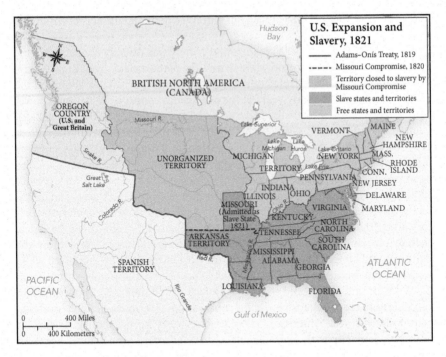

Map 4.4 U.S. Expansion and Slavery, 1821

Who, What, Where?

American Colonization
   Society p. 112

Bill of Rights p. 88

Black Belt p. 99

Communalism p. 104

Constitutional Convention p. 88

Cotton gin p. 98

Cotton Kingdom p. 98

Deep South p. 99

Gabriel p. 96

Haitian Revolution p. 93

Internal slave trade p. 100

Liberia p. 112

Louisiana Purchase p. 93

Masons p. 104

Missouri Compromise p. 113

Northwest Ordinance p. 89

Paul Cuffe p. 103

Prince Hall p. 104

Shays's Rebellion p. 87

Sierra Leone p. 90

St. Domingue p. 93

Toussaint L'Ouverture p. 93

Vodou p. 94

Review Questions

4.1 What factors contributed to the rise of an antislavery movement in the Early Republic?

4.2 What are the origins of southern fears of free Black people?

4.3 Why did cotton cultivation and slavery expand across the Deep South?

4.4 How did the economy of the Deep South impact the internal slave trade?

4.5 What were the characteristics of free Black urban communities in the North?

4.6 What were the main differences between northern and southern free Black communities?

4.7 What motivated African Americans to serve in the military?

4.8 Why was emigration to Africa an attractive option for some Black Americans?

For additional digital learning resources please go to **https://www.oup.com/he/horton1e**

Slavery and the Slave Community

Plantation Burial. Painted around 1860, this image offers an unusually intimate view of African American spirituality. Mourners—men, women, and children—express their grief during an evening burial service.

5

CHAPTER OUTLINE

Violent Resistance

5.1 Understand the consequences of violent resistance, both spontaneous and planned.

Community among the Enslaved Workers

5.2 Contrast the community that revolved around the slaveholder with the one that existed among the enslaved people.

Religion and Resistance

5.3 Understand the ways that African Americans adapted Christian beliefs to their circumstances.

Surviving Slavery

5.4 Analyze the ways that community relationships aided the survival of the enslaved people.

Women in Slavery

5.5 Analyze the ways that slavery was different for Black women.

Brutal Labor and Resistance

5.6 Understand how the brutality of plantation life fueled resistance.

⭐ **DURING THE EIGHTEENTH** century, when Equiano was captured and enslaved, slavery was a profitable but still relatively small institution in British North America. By the nineteenth century slavery had grown, filling a large part of the labor needs of the new nation and following the westward expansion of the plantation South. The number of enslaved people had increased from fewer than seven hundred thousand in 1790 to more than one million by 1810. Even after the constitutional ban on the African slave trade went into effect in 1808, the institution of slavery continued to grow. Illegal imports combined with natural increases to result in a population of nearly four million enslaved people by 1860. As the northern states completed their abolition of slavery during the first decades of the nineteenth century, nearly all of slavery's growth occurred in the southern states, especially in the western South. These developments increased sectional differences and exacerbated tensions growing from the diverging interests of North and South. The great increase in the enslaved population was especially notable in light of the fact that the number imported directly from Africa had actually declined during the last half of the eighteenth century. Many enslaved people's experience in the nineteenth century differed from Equiano's in the previous one, when all Africans had been separated from their families and homelands. With the opening of the western South, however, those born into slavery in America also faced the danger of being separated from their families as members were sold to the large plantations in places such as Mississippi and Louisiana. The voracious appetite of this labor system for new workers increased the danger for free Black Americans even in northern states. In the 1840s musician Solomon Northup, a freeborn man in his early thirties, lived in New York State with his wife and three children. One day while his wife was out of town, he was enticed by the promise of a job playing his fiddle and traveled first to New York City and then to Washington, D.C., where he was kidnapped into slavery. He was taken through Virginia to the auction block in New Orleans. On the way, he encountered two other free men who had also been kidnapped, one from Cincinnati, Ohio, and the other from Norfolk, Virginia. Northup was an enslaved laborer for twelve years on the sugarcane and cotton plantations of Louisiana before he could get word to his family in New York and gain his freedom.[1]

During the nineteenth century, an increasing proportion of enslaved people in North America had been born in the United States, and the changing character of the enslaved population had important consequences. Enslaved people born in Africa suffered the torment of lost liberty and forced labor and the anguish of separation from their cultural homes and extended families. The many languages people from West and Central Africa spoke were often so distinct that communication between Africans was initially difficult. Over time, however, multiple tongues mingled on the plantations in British North America and combined to form a language not native to any but which made communication between Africans of different backgrounds possible. The longer Africans lived in the United States, the more familiar they became with the English language and with the society of their captors. African linguistic styles continued to influence the English spoken by even those Africans who had lived in America for an extended period or those born there, and in areas with many Black Americans they influenced white speech as well. Following African speech patterns, African Americans

Timeline

Chapter 5	**1820**	**1828**
	Missouri Compromise	Andrew Jackson elected
1788		president.
Abd Al-Rahman Ibrahima	**1822**	
captured in West Africa and	Denmark Vesey's slave revolt	
sold to slave traders.	thwarted in South Carolina.	

sometimes dropped the unstressed syllables of English words or eliminated the verb in an English sentence, as in "Henry, he in field." African- and American-born enslaved people suffered equally under the slave labor system, but the African Americans' greater knowledge of European ways, more sophisticated understanding of the slave structure, and wider support system better equipped them to cope with their situation. The greater facility with English and the **Creole languages** developed by American-born Black men and women made it possible for them to communicate with white people beyond simple work-related matters. This also allowed them greater access to information, an important tool in their struggle to deal with the power of slaveholders and white society.[2]

Violent Resistance

African-born enslaved people—reputedly more difficult to control, more likely to run away, and more likely to risk their lives in resistance or escape—were also more likely to fail in their attempts and to be recaptured or killed. They lacked experience dealing with owners and overseers, and were unfamiliar with the countryside. The defiant stance or bold action of proud Africans that has provided material for heroic historical drama, could mean death for the enslaved. In the early nineteenth century, when a night patrol accompanied by yapping dogs galloped about the Virginia countryside to discover Black people lingering in revelry past their curfew, most enslaved people could have been expected to disappear safely into the darkness. Instead, Robert, "an athletic, powerful slave, who had been but a short time from his 'father land' [and] whose spirit the cowardly overseer had labored in vain to quell" sent the women to a nearby cabin and rallied the men to stand their ground. He stationed two men just inside the door of a darkened cabin with orders to rush out and chase off the patrol's horses when they broke in. In the violent encounter that ensued, two white men and six Black men were killed, and several on both sides were injured. Three Black men, including the African, left widows and children, and all enslaved people in the area suffered the consequences of their resistance. "[White] people flocked from every quarter, armed to the teeth, swearing vengeance on the defenseless slaves." The most experienced understood that all would suffer for the defiant acts of a few.[3]

1829
After forty years in slavery, Abd Al-Rahman Ibrahima returns to Africa.

1831
Nat Turner's rebellion in Virginia

1841
Solomon Northrup kidnapped and sold into slavery.

1860
Harriet Jacobs publishes *Incidents in the Life of a Slave Girl, Written by Herself.*

PROFILE

Abd al-Rahman Ibrahima

Abduhl Rahaman (Abd al-Rahman Ibrahima), West African prince, son of the King of Timbo, enslaved in America for almost forty years.

(1762–1829) ABD AL-RAHMAN IBRAHIMA was a son of the ruler of the Muslim Fulbe people from the West African interior, who traded ivory, livestock, gold, and enslaved people to coastal settlements. Ibrahima received a traditional Islamic education and pursued advanced studies in Macina and Timbuktu, more than a thousand miles from home. At seventeen he returned home and joined the army; by the time he was twenty-six, he was a husband, father, experienced horseman, and army commander. After a battle in 1788, he was ambushed, taken prisoner, and sold to slave traders, along with fifty warriors.

Eight months, six thousand miles, and a series of sales brought Abd al-Rahman, or Abduhl Rahahman, to Natchez in Spanish-controlled territory. Tobacco planter Thomas Foster, a man of little learning, bought him and another African on credit for $930. The striking, six-foot-tall al-Rahman, with shoulder-length hair and a dignified bearing explained to his owner, probably through a Mandinka translator, that his father would pay a king's ransom in gold for his return. Foster responded by naming him Prince.

Six years later Foster bought Isabella, an American-born Christian woman, and soon Ibrahima and Isabella were married. Al-Rahman endured the rigors of slavery while maintaining his religion and some Arabic literacy. His integrity gained his owner's trust, and on weekends he was able to take produce to the Natchez market, where occasionally newly imported Africans gave him news from home. In 1807 he encountered John Cox, a man who had known him and his father in Africa. Cox tried to arrange al-Rahman's freedom, but Foster refused to sell him. Cox publicized the story, and Al-Rahman became a celebrity, eventually gaining enough recognition that

Secretary of State Henry Clay and President John Quincy Adams became his advocates. Foster agreed to sell him, but only if he agreed to go to Africa. Aided by the African Colonization Society and a one-year fundraising tour, Ibrahima and Isabella sailed for Africa in 1829. During forty years of slavery al-Rahman had continued to hope for freedom and to return home, but he died in Africa before he could get home. Two of his nine children and five of his grandchildren joined Isabella in freedom in Liberia the following year.

The violent retaliation against slavery that slaveholders and their allies feared was a realistic and ever-present danger. Overseers were most vulnerable to such attacks because they worked more closely with enslaved workers than other white people, because their job was to force compliance with the work routine and plantation discipline, and because they were the ones most likely to administer punishment. It was during the administration of punishment that overseers were particularly susceptible to angry reprisals, as when an overseer punished a young enslaved man in Marksville, Louisiana, for failure to complete assigned work. The man explained that he had been unable to complete his work because the overseer had sent him on an errand that had taken much more time than either of them had anticipated. The overseer was unmoved by this argument and forced him to kneel for a severe whipping. After the first few blows, the man, smarting from both the whip and the particular injustice, leaped to his feet, grabbed an ax, and hacked the overseer to pieces.[4]

While an angry reaction to some specific injustice or brutal treatment may have triggered violence, rarely was the enslaved person reacting to a single act.

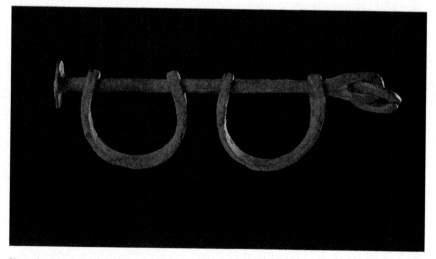

Slave shackles.

More often a long line of such abuses culminated in violent retaliation. Some workers created detailed plans and organized their movements carefully, as when a group came together on one South Carolina plantation to plan a strategy for doing away with their abusive overseer. Understanding southern class antagonisms, they planned to take advantage of their owner's prejudice against working-class overseers. The enslaved workers surprised the well-armed overseer when he was alone, beat him to death, and carried his body to a nearby swamp and burned it. When the overseer did not arrive for work, his planter employer assumed that he was irresponsible and had simply walked off the job.[5]

The most radical kinds of resistance were those that struck not simply at the injustice of an individual slaveholder or overseer but more consciously against the institution itself. There were fewer of these full-blown slave revolts, but they were extremely important for what they symbolized for both owner and enslaved. The Stono rebellion in mid-eighteenth-century South Carolina, the Haitian Revolution at the end of the eighteenth century, and Gabriel's rebellion in early-nineteenth-century Virginia all created fear in white communities. In an effort to guard against revolt, governments sometimes placed severe restrictions on the movements and activities of enslaved people. Fear drove planters to constant vigilance. Some owners sat up all night, armed and on guard against expected violence, and both owners and the enslaved understood why. "How can men, who know they are abusing others all day," one enslaved man asked rhetorically, "lie down and sleep quietly at night . . . when they know that men feel revengeful, and might burn their property, or even kill them?"[6]

Such was the fear in the early 1820s when the word was passed in Charleston, South Carolina, that carpenter **Denmark Vesey**, a formerly enslaved man who had won his freedom in a lottery, was planning a revolt. In one of the most extensive slave plots in American history, potentially involving up to nine thousand enslaved people, Vesey and his aides worked for over a year, drawing up plans, fashioning weapons, and participating in West African war rituals under the supervision of enslaved conjurer Gullah Jack. Their plan to attack Charleston, capture guns and ammunition from the city armory, and march into the countryside liberating people from slavery as they went was discovered. South Carolina's governor, whose enslaved man had been part of the plot, called out troops to crush the rebellion before it could get underway. The conspirators were captured, thirty-seven were banished from the region, and thirty-five, including Vesey, were executed. The Vesey conspiracy caused near panic in South Carolina as rumors circulated that it had been inspired by northern opponents of slavery and free Black Americans outside the state. There were theories that educated Black people were the main conspirators. Throughout the region new restrictions were imposed on enslaved and free Black Americans, and old regulations that had languished were rigidly enforced. During such times free Black southerners were especially vulnerable, and most kept out of public view until white fears had subsided.

The most successful slave revolt during the antebellum period took place in Southampton County, Virginia, in the summer of 1831. Under the leadership of enslaved preacher **Nat Turner**, an army of seventy or more attacked and killed fifty-seven white locals, driving others into the swamps and creating hysteria in the entire region. It took a superior force of some three thousand, including militia from surrounding areas and neighboring states, three days to end the slave revolt. In a frenzy of retribution, white slaveholders killed hundreds of enslaved people, many of whom had played no role in the rebellion. By early

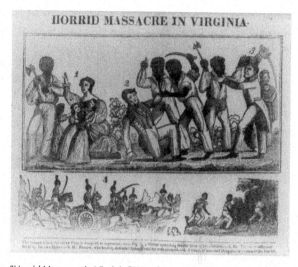

"Horrid Massacre in Virginia." Woodcut, of Nat Turner's rebellion, depicting white southern fear of slave revolts and romanticizing white bravery.

winter, Turner was arrested, tried, and convicted of insurrection and murder, and on November 11, he was hanged in Jerusalem, Virginia. Turner's rebellion was the embodiment of white southern nightmares, swift and deadly, involving more and more enslaved people as the revolt progressed. Such open violence, however, was the exception in the antebellum South. Slaveholders were protected by a broad array of military forces from other communities, surrounding states, and ultimately the national government. This realization tempered revolutionary actions among most enslaved people, but some were willing to resort to violence despite the nearly inevitable deadly consequences.[7]

In order to control its enslaved population in the face of continuous resistance and periodic unrest, the South became a police state. Both slaveholding and non-slaveholding white people were charged with manning the slave patrols that watched transportation routes and gathering places to ensure that enslaved people were not off plantations without permission and did not meet in unauthorized groups. This martial atmosphere helped encourage a southern attitude of militarism, as historian John Hope Franklin argued in his classic study, *The Militant South*. In order to enslave millions of Black people and to maintain them in bondage, southern society was forced to tolerate and came to honor a military social climate that accepted violence as a necessity, brutalizing and dehumanizing all those involved.[8]

Slavery's brutality helped define a general climate of sanctioned violence in southern society and also spawned violence among white citizens. The historian Bertram Wyatt-Brown, studying pre–Civil War southern culture, argued that the concept of honor was the centerpiece of southern relationships, especially among white males. Presumably honorless Black Americans were the defining "others" against whom even poor white men could measure their own status.

Violence against Black people was a display of white power and a defense of white honor. Insults by Black people to white men could also lead to the violent defense of a man's honor. To be without honor was to be lower than a white person, to be more nearly Black, and graphic accounts of heroic violence among southern white men became part of the regional folklore. "Honor in the Old South applied to all White classes, though with manifestations appropriate to each ranking." Among the southern elites, dueling was the classic means of defending honor; savage fist fights were common among lower-class men, and both were tolerated by authorities. Murder and assault rates in the slaveholding South were at least ten times higher than in New England. The South was equal in its rates of violence to the West, which had less organized legal authority and a much higher proportion of the young single men who were most likely to be violent. "Violence in the South," as Wyatt-Brown has argued, "had its unique source in slavery and the structures of black subordination."[9]

In the face of the formidable power exercised by slaveholders, most enslaved people wisely limited their protests to covert actions. It was widely believed that the most effective and practical protest was action that could not be traced to its perpetrator. Most enslaved individuals asserted themselves in ways less likely to result in severe punishment. Many resisted the slaveowners' authority by actions slaveowners viewed as deceitful and dishonest, including such tactics as breaking tools, setting barns afire, or lying to and tricking the owner. Stealing was another way enslaved people could exert control while also obtaining necessities or small luxuries. They frequently justified it with the argument that taking something belonging to the owner was simply redistributing the owner's property, since they themselves were also the owner's property. Although, for them, stealing from their owner was generally acceptable or even admirable, stealing from fellow enslaved people was not.

Slavery was more than the absence of freedom, it was the denial of enslaved people's humanity. Theirs was a constant contention for human dignity and for some measure of autonomy within the plantation society. Owners held the great advantage, of course. Backed by local and national laws, they could punish with impunity or even kill enslaved people who threatened their authority. Resisting slavery was a complex matter involving many kinds of action and inaction. It was not always a confrontational refusal to submit to the authority of owners or overseers. Resistance was also a matter of surviving, trying to protect loved ones, and remaining loyal to friends and fellows.

Community among the Enslaved Workers

Some earlier historians believed that the owner's influence was absolute. It is true that enslaved people were required to adapt to the culture of the slaveholders, but more recent scholars have uncovered other influences. They have noted a wide variety of "significant others"—people other than the owner—who played important roles in an enslaved person's life, and have described the two separate interlocked communities that developed on the plantation. One community revolved around the "big house," where the owner and his family had the greatest control and where the enslaved people were most likely to apparently acquiesce to white authority. This was where most white people gained their impressions of slavery and of southern Black people, and this was the plantation community that formed the popular image of the genteel courtly South in the American imagination. There was another very different plantation community in the slave quarters, however, where white people held far less direct power and the expressions of the enslaved were less guarded. It was in this community that they could maintain some degree of dignity and control. In view of owners' attempts to be the only significant influence on enslaved people, the maintenance of a community was a form of resistance to slavery.

By the nineteenth century, most enslaved people lived on large plantations. Although three-quarters of southerners held no bond laborers, and most slaveholders owned fewer than five, three-quarters of the enslaved people lived in groups of ten or more, and half lived in slave communities of twenty or more. The growth of the institution, the development of the western South, and more equal numbers of men and women resulted in living arrangements that ranged from small households or extended "families" to complex enslaved communities. **Solomon Northup**'s experience of being kidnapped into the Lower South in the 1840s illustrates many of these possibilities. His autobiography gives a remarkable firsthand account of the unpredictable life and degradation of enslaved men and women and provides an unusually detailed picture of their lives in the Lower South during this period.[10]

When first sold in New Orleans, Northup was taken several hundred miles north up the Mississippi River and the Red River to a lumber camp maintained by his owner William Ford. There Northup lived near the Ford family with ten other enslaved people. Working in or around the house were Rose, from Washington, D.C., who had been there five years; Sally, the mother of two toddlers; John, a sixteen-year-old who worked as the cook; and Eliza, who had been purchased by Ford along with Northup. Eliza had been the enslaved mistress of a wealthy man near Washington, D.C., living for years as his wife and bearing his child. She had the bad fortune, however, to be part of her owner's property, which fell to his lawful wife in their divorce settlement, and she was sold. Rose and Eliza became immediate friends on the basis of their both having come from Washington, but the Fords were dissatisfied with Eliza's work, and she was soon sent to the fields. According to Northup's account, she was disconsolate and never recovered from being separated from her two young children when they were all sold separately into slavery. In addition to two men who worked at the mill—Sam, also from Washington, D.C., and Anthony, a blacksmith from Kentucky who had been with Ford for ten years—there were three enslaved lumbermen—Northup; Walton, Rose's husband, who had been born in slavery on Ford's plantation; and Harry, who was also purchased with Northup. These eleven people—some related by birth and some by common background; some who had spent many years with the same owner, and others newcomers—were all united by their status and lived and worked together in a kind of extended family.[11]

Yet unpredictable change was the awful norm of an enslaved person's life. Northup lived with these people a relatively short time, though he did remain in the same area for his entire time in slavery and so maintained contact with them. After a few years working there, and on Ford's large plantation farther south, he was hired out and eventually sold. He continued to be hired out periodically during slack times on his home plantation or busy times for others, and so worked and lived in different situations. He was employed as a carpenter, hired out to assist a white carpenter or to work on his own; was a fiddler for local plantation parties; and worked as part of the gang labor cutting cane on large sugar plantations. For most of his remaining ten years in the South, Northup worked on a small cotton plantation as the property of Edwin Epps, an uneducated and harsh man who had worked as a slave driver and overseer before renting and then purchasing his own plantation. On the plantation where he spent the last eight years, Northup joined an established group of eight other enslaved people who had been together for many years.

The laborers' fortunes were directly linked to their owner's financial stability, and the consequences of an owner's insolvency were often dire for them. All but the youngest of Epps's enslaved workers had belonged to a county sheriff in South Carolina named James Buford. When Buford fell on hard times, these seven people were put in chains and marched the long distance across the Mississippi River to the plantation of Archy B. Williams, who used them to pay his overseer Edwin Epps. Five of Epps's nine enslaved people belonged to the same family. Phebe, her husband Wiley, Phebe's two grown sons by a former husband, and Edward, born to Phebe and Wiley after their purchase by Epps. In addition to this family the small community in the slave quarters included Susan, the elderly Abram, and a young woman named Patsey. Abram was a storyteller and philosopher who had been born in Tennessee and lived there until the 1830s, when a slave trader sold him to Buford in South Carolina. He regaled his fellows with tales of Tennessee's General Andrew Jackson and the exploits of his Black soldiers in the War of 1812. Such resourceful enslaved people could sometimes carve personal space from the largely inflexible world of the plantation.[12]

Religion and Resistance

Special talents or abilities, like Abram's storytelling or Solomon's fiddling, gained people respect and authority among their enslaved fellows. Enslaved conjurers and preachers who ministered to the spiritual needs of the community were influential, although the preacher's role was especially complex. Some slaveowners insisted that their bondsmen convert to Christianity, and large numbers of them had professed the Christian faith by the mid-nineteenth century. Yet even converts did not simply adopt European religious beliefs. Many Africans and African Americans never adopted Christian beliefs, and those who did generally adapted them to their own African cultural and spiritual traditions, using them for their own practical purposes. The planters encouraged the acceptance of a religion emphasizing obedience, sin, and gentleness, but enslaved people were drawn to the Old Testament stories from Exodus, featuring themes of escape from bondage and freedom from oppression. Enslaved preachers who supported the people's longing for freedom were sure to find favor within the slave community. Many planters eventually came to see religion as a vehicle for reinforcing their power, arguing that God commanded the enslaved to obey their owners and to be loyal, leaving any relief from bondage for the next life. Enslaved people privately rejected arguments that slavery was the will of God visited upon Africans as punishment for an ancient sin. "I was not very long in finding out," recalled Frederick Douglass, that "it was not color, but crime, not God, but man, that afforded the true explanation of the existence of slavery."[13]

African Americans not only adapted Christian beliefs to their previous belief systems and their present condition, they also incorporated African styles of worship into their Christian services. Far less staid and solemn than Europeans in their worship, Africans celebrated their religion with rhythmic song and dance. The **ring shout**, a ritual circle dance done by the Dahomey, the Kongo, and other societies of West Africa, symbolized a oneness with nature and with ancestors and the solidarity of community. It linked the sacred and the secular worlds and was an important display of religious emotion. As Europeans and Africans met in America, some American religious customs took on African characteristics. This was especially true in the South, for both Black and white Americans but was most obvious among African American enslaved people. As one enslaved Virginian recalled, "The way in which we worshiped is almost indescribable. The singing was accompanied by a certain ecstasy of motion, clapping of hands, tossing of heads, which could continue without cessation about half an hour; one would lead off in a kind of recitative style, others joining in the chorus. The old house partook of the ecstasy; it rang with their jubilant shouts, and shook in all its joints."[14]

White people had different reactions to African American forms of Christian worship. vSome were repulsed by what they called its primitive heathenish display. Owners sometimes found it threatening and unnecessary, and a few refused to allow their enslaved people to openly practice any form of religion. One slaveholder discouraged their

This drawing captures the expressive and emotional quality of African American Christianity.

religious interests, saying, "You niggers have no souls, you are just like those cattle, when you die there is an end of you, there is [nothing] more for you to think about than living."[15]

Efforts to curb religious worship among the enslaved were generally unsuccessful. A particular brand of African American Christianity remained a central part of Black Americans' activity and identity throughout the pre–Civil War period, and the enslaved preacher remained an important actor in the community. The preacher's job was neither comfortable nor safe. Planters who tolerated such preachers were especially watchful for any hint of their subversion of plantation authority. Thus, most enslaved preachers were forced to either provide the owner's message of obedience or to speak only indirectly about the worldly concerns of their congregations. Some preachers became expert in a kind of theological doublespeak, or what historian Charles Joyner refers to as the African tradition of "indirection," which allowed strong criticism of authority without direct confrontation. The preacher might appear to be in compliance with the owner's wishes but instead provided theological reassurance and expressed the grievances of their enslaved fellows. The enslaved people generally dismissed preachers who appeared to believe the owner's message. Frederick Douglass commented, "I could entertain no such nonsense as this [affirmation of the owner's beliefs]; and I almost lost my patience when I found any colored man weak enough to believe such stuff." John White, like most enslaved people, assumed that when a preacher spoke in support of slavery's rules, "the old preacher was more worried about the bullwhip than the Bible." Those who provided support or access to power had standing in the enslaved community, but those perceived as working for the owner were generally dismissed.[16]

Surviving Slavery

While the role of enslaved preachers gave them distinction in the community, others commanded respect for their strength or skill or their influence with the owner or other white people. Some planters took great pride in individual enslaved athletes who represented the plantation in competitive races and boxing matches. Skilled blacksmiths and carpenters were especially important to plantation maintenance and often had particular leverage with owners. Enslaved musicians who entertained at plantation functions could often use their prestige to influence the owner and benefit the community. The same might be said for favored servants or the skilled cooks important to the success of the owner's dinner parties. In the fields, slave drivers, often enslaved themselves, were also important. They worked under the direction of white overseers, and the whips they carried symbolized their power and their responsibility for enforcing plantation rules. They turned enslaved laborers out to the fields in the morning, ensured continuous work during the day, and enforced the curfew at night. Drivers might have some privileges, but they also had to do a share of the work. Theirs was a difficult position because they often lived among those they were expected to discipline. Thus, they often worked out informal agreements with the other enslaved people, making them and their position useful to the community. Solomon Northup recalled that he developed such skill with the whip that he was able to simulate a whipping by snapping the whip close to but not quite touching the skin, "throwing the lash within a hair's breath of the back, the ear, the nose, without, however, touching either of them." From a distance he could make a light touch seem like brutal punishment. The victims must play their roles convincingly lest the driver be found out, and all would be punished. "I would commence plying the lash vigorously, when according to arrangement, they would squirm and screech as if in agony." Unfortunately, enslaved people could not depend on this level of skill or the driver's willingness to risk punishment to spare their fellows, but compromises were often worked out between drivers and community members.[17]

The cluster of interlocking relationships and roles constituting the slave community enabled many to survive the hardships of slavery. Some people were connected by blood, but most were joined by a shared condition and a common place in the power structure. Though all did not agree on the best ways of coping with their situation, the slave community provided important support, helping sustain them in the face of continual assaults on their dignity and humanity. The institution of slavery was predicated on the assumptions that the enslaved were subhuman and powerless, valuable only for the work they produced.

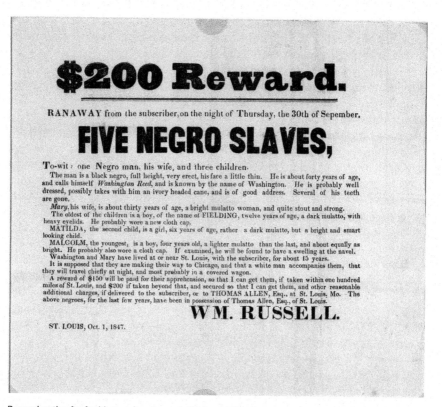

Reward notice for fugitive enslaved people, St. Louis, October 1, 1847.

Though, like any human group, the slave community had conflicts, tensions, betrayals, and animosities, it was in the slave quarters that African Americans were likely to find recognition for their accomplishments, respect for their strength of character and virtue, compassion for their suffering, and love. The community was important because it contradicted slavery's message and provided a partial shield from the institution's most devastating effects.

The family was central to the formation of the community, and its maintenance became far more possible as more Black women were added to the African American population by the late eighteenth and early nineteenth centuries. The historian Ann Malone found that in Louisiana, two-thirds of the enslaved in the 1830s and nearly three-quarters in the 1840s lived in what she called simple family households. Such households were composed of a couple with or without children or a single parent, usually a mother, with children. Family and household composition were greatly influenced by the actions of the slaveholders, who responded to economic difficulties and opportunities by buying or selling people. Therefore, household composition statistics are an incomplete indication of the history of family formation and dissolution. Still, enslaved people's difficulties and adaptations to adversity are reflected in Malone's finding that fewer than one in five lived alone and fewer than one in ten lived in households of more than two generations. This household data gives little information about the family relationships that may have linked separate households and different plantations, but it confirms earlier studies which found that the nuclear family structure of parents and children was the most common family form among enslaved people throughout the South before the Civil War.[18]

Slave marriages had no legal standing, and all such unions took place at the pleasure of slaveowners. Planters often encouraged marriages between enslaved people on their own plantations, since those who married off the plantation would inevitably want the privilege of visiting spouses elsewhere, removing them from the owner's direct control. Some owners acquiesced to the enslaved people's choices of partners from other plantations and attempted to arrange a hire or purchase to unite the couples. When a Colonel Barsdale of Virginia, for example, received a letter asking that he consider hiring or selling an enslaved woman, the request came from a planter whose enslaved blacksmith Israel seemed "much attached to her." Large plantations offered the greatest opportunities for enslaved people to find partners in their local community, but even there, many sought partners elsewhere. The selection of a partner living off one's plantation limited the time a couple could spend together and increased the likelihood of permanent family separation. Since any offspring became the property of the mother's owner, it also made the father less able to influence his children's upbringing. Yet, many enslaved people chose marriage partners from other plantations, thereby exercising some control over their lives, and many marriages of enslaved people were carried on at a distance.[19]

Family life for enslaved people was always problematic, since they had no legal rights to protect a family or keep it intact. In marriages between free people, husbands controlled their wives' property and were assumed to protect their rights, standing as the legal representatives of the family. Marriages of enslaved people put husbands and wives on an equal footing, neither had any property rights or legal standing. Slaveowners had absolute authority to separate the family and discipline or reward any family member, theoretically making parental authority and marriage rights tenuous and easily abrogated. Many families were devastated by the internal slave trade that transported enslaved people from the eastern Upper South to the plantations of the western Lower South. Even under these circumstances many families managed to maintain contact for decades, many had the emotional support of family members, and some maintained extended kinship networks.[20]

When forced sales made separations unavoidable, some people maintained symbolic contact with lost family members through the names they chose for their children. Many followed African traditions, naming children for their grandparents or other relatives. Although many sons were named after their fathers, enslaved women whose children were fathered by white men were likely to name sons after male relatives. Elizabeth Keckley was separated from her mother at age fourteen and taken from Virginia to North Carolina, where she eventually had a son by a white man to whom she was hired out. The child was named George, not for his white father, but for his Black grandfather, whom Elizabeth had barely known.[21]

The gender assumptions of the white society combined with the laws regulating the slave system and the conditions of servitude to diminish enslaved men's roles as husbands and fathers. Enslaved women, on the other hand, were often allowed time during the workday to care for their children. Sometimes children were brought to the fields with their mothers, who nursed them and tended to their needs during work breaks. On a few of the larger plantations, enslaved women ran nurseries for the estate's children, often including the white children. On most of the smaller farms, mothers provided care for their own children and were sometimes given time off from work to do so. Often husbands worked longer hours to make up for the time allowed their wives for child care.

Although enslaved parents could frequently make arrangements for caring for their children, when the demands of work were especially great or when an owner insisted on

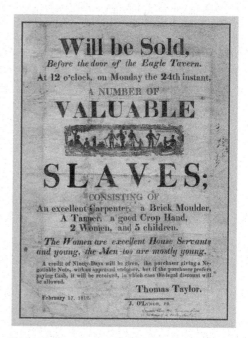

Enslaved persons sale notice, Richmond, February 17, 1812.

maintaining a steady work pace, the children were often left on their own for much of the day. Frederick Douglass characterized the early years of an enslaved child's life as relatively carefree, spent in play and generally in close association with the white children of the plantation. Before age eight or nine, enslaved children were not generally expected to do demanding work, and Douglass described his childhood as a happy time. Others remembered their early years in slavery differently, recalling that the work of the plantation was so demanding that parents had little time for child care until evening or Sunday, the traditional rest day. As J.W.C. Pennington recalled, his childhood was marked by a "want of parental care" as his parents "were not able to give any attention to their children during the day." By necessity, parenting was a community responsibility, with other adults filling in for parents where possible and taking complete responsibility for children separated from their parents. Among enslaved people, the process of informal adoption helped to provide for children whose parents were absent or incapacitated.[22]

Women in Slavery

Slavery was harsh for all enslaved people, but not all experienced the hardships in the same way. "Slavery is terrible for men," explained formerly enslaved **Harriet Jacobs**, "but it is far more terrible for women." Her belief was based on the fact that enslaved women were often forced to endure all the hardships and indignities imposed on men but were also regularly subject to sexual exploitation. The history of slavery is filled with the stories of owners sexually abusing enslaved women, and plantations were populated with the offspring of such relationships. From trading block to whipping post, enslaved women's modesty was not respected; they were stripped and exposed to public view. Sexual relationships with enslaved women marked young white boys' passage into puberty and satisfied the owners' lust. Occasionally women could exercise some control over these exploitations. Harriet Jacobs made a conscious decision to take a white lover to shield her from other white men and to give some protection to her child. The vast majority had no choice but to submit to the sexual demands of white men.[23]

Enslaved women were also vulnerable to the anger of white women who could not punish their husbands, the slaveowners, but could and did punish the enslaved for these relationships. As a child, Patsey told Solomon Northup, she had been a great favorite around the Epps household in Louisiana. She was proud of the fact that her father was an African, carried, she said, to slavery in Cuba before being sold to South Carolina. She was a skilled teamster and rail-splitter, a speedy runner, an accomplished horsewoman, and the fastest cotton picker on the plantation. She was also the unwilling sexual favorite of frequently drunken Edwin Epps and paid dearly for this in severe whippings at the behest of Epps's extremely jealous wife. Many white people believed that Black women were highly sexual and promiscuous, and white men used these stereotypes to absolve themselves of responsibility in these sexual associations. Thus, enslaved women were vulnerable to abuse by planters and punishment by planters' wives and suffered from the stereotypes that protected white men from guilt.[24]

Both women and men did heavy labor in the fields with little accommodation to gender differences. The specific nature of the work depended on the crop being grown and the time of year, but generally both males and females spent long days in strenuous work. Indeed Solomon Northup reported that some cotton and sugar plantations were worked entirely with female labor. When extra hands were needed at Ford's lumber operation, four Black women—Charlotte, Fanny, Cresia, and Nelly—were sent to help the men. They were "excellent choppers," according to Northup, "equal to any man" at piling logs. On the largest plantations enslaved people's lives were likely more regimented than on small farms or in urban areas. Northup recalled that each workday on the large cotton plantations in Louisiana began with the blowing of a horn about an hour before dawn. After a hurried breakfast (typically warm cornmeal cake) the enslaved laborers filled gourds with water, packed lunches of cornmeal cake and, occasionally, cold bacon, and went off to the fields to work.[25]

During March and April the ground was prepared for planting. Where Northup labored, a mule pulling a large plow made a straight furrow; a young woman followed sowing cotton seeds from a huge sack hung around her neck. Then came another mule pulling a harrow, which covered the seed. In one pass two mules, two mule drivers—most often men but sometimes women—and one planting woman could plant a row of cotton several hundred yards long. This was the beginning of the process which by fall produced the tens of thousands of pounds of cotton that were the foundation of the South's economy. After planting came the hoeing season, which lasted from April until July, during which time enslaved people worked their way down each row, cultivating and keeping weeds from choking the growing cotton plants. In August enslaved men and women began picking the cotton, the hardest part of the process, as each picker worked with a huge sack on a strap slung around the neck and shoulders. An experienced hand was expected to pick about two hundred pounds of cotton each day.[26]

Landscape architect, abolitionist, and sometime journalist Frederick Law Olmsted reported seeing plantations on which thirty plows and thirty to forty people with hoes, mostly women, moved together across the wide fields of Mississippi well into the night. Often he saw a Black slave driver walking along,

Enslaved women and men alike were forced to labor on plantations.

Harriet Jacobs

Harriet Jacobs, in a photograph from 1894.

Harriet Jacobs was born into slavery in Edenton, North Carolina, around 1813. At age 14 she became the property of the young child of a Dr. Norcom, whom in her autobiography she called Dr. Flint. She first escaped to her grandmother's house nearby and spent seven years hiding in the attic crawlspace, from where she could observe her two children at play. Still pursued by Norcom, she eventually escaped to Boston, where she was reunited with her children, with the aid of their father, a white man of higher status than Norcom. She wrote her autobiography, Incidents in the Life of a Slave Girl, *under the pseudonym of Linda Brent, and it was published in 1861. In the following excerpt she describes the particular dangers enslaved female domestic servants faced.*

I now entered on my fifteenth year—a sad epoch in the life of a slave girl. My master began to whisper foul words in my ear. Young as I was, I could not remain ignorant of their import. I tried to treat them with indifference or contempt. The master's age, my extreme youth, and the fear that his conduct would be reported to my

brandishing a whip and cracking it over the heads of the workers. After their work in the fields, the enslaved laborers had additional tasks, such as gathering wood for supper fires, feeding the animals, and carrying heavy sacks of cotton to be stored or ginned. Workers had little time to do things for themselves or their families, for at least some planters insisted that the pickers be in bed by ten in the evening and forced them to the fields before daylight. One planter told Olmsted, grandmother, made him bear this treatment for many months. He was a crafty man, and resorted to many means to accomplish his purposes. Sometimes he had stormy, terrific ways, that made his victims tremble; sometimes he assumed a gentleness that he thought must surely subdue. Of the two, I preferred his stormy moods, although they left me trembling. He tried his utmost to corrupt the pure principles my grandmother had instilled. He peopled my young mind with unclean images, such as only a vile monster could think of. I turned from him with disgust and hatred. But he was my master. I was compelled to live under the same roof with him—where I saw a man forty years my senior daily violating the most sacred commandments of nature. He told me I was his property; that I must be subject to his will in all things. My soul revolted against the mean tyranny. But where could I turn for protection? No matter whether the slave girl be as black as ebony or as fair as her mistress. In either case, there is no shadow of law to protect her from insult, from violence, or even from death; all these are inflicted by fiends who bear the shape of men. The mistress, who ought to protect the helpless victim, has no other feelings towards her but those of jealousy and rage. . . . Even the little child, who is accustomed to wait on her mistress and her children, will learn, before she is twelve years old, why it is that her mistress hates such and such a one among the slaves. Perhaps the child's own mother is among those hated ones. She listens to violent outbreaks of jealous passion, and cannot help understanding what is the cause. She will become prematurely knowing in evil things. Soon she will learn to tremble when she hears her master's footfall. She will be compelled to realize that she is no longer a child. If God has bestowed beauty upon her, it will prove her greatest curse. . . . My master met me at every turn, reminding me that I belonged to him, and swearing by heaven and earth that he would compel me to submit to him. If I went out for a breath of fresh air, after a day of unwearied toil, his footsteps dogged me. If I knelt by my mother's grave, his dark shadow fell on me even there. The light heart which nature had given me became heavy with sad forebodings.

Source: Harriet A. Jacobs, *Incidents in the Life of a Slave Girl,* edited by Lydia Maria Frances Child (Boston, 1861), 44–46.

"Well, I don't never start my niggers 'fore daylight except 'tis in pickin' time, then maybe I got 'em out a quarter of an hour before," in this way, confirming his self-image as a kind slaveowner. Other owners sent their enslaved laborers to the fields as early as necessary to get the day's work done. No matter what time enslaved people began their day, the work was constant. "I keep 'em right smart to work through the day," Olmsted's informant declared.[27]

Brutal Labor and Resistance

Solomon Northup described the same brutal conditions in Louisiana that historian Edward Baptist found in Alabama and Mississippi. Owners and overseers set quotas for the amount of work to be done, generally taking into account the experience, skill, and strength of the individual, and workers who did not make their quotas were generally whipped. According to Solomon Northup, the most accomplished laborers picked cotton with extraordinary quickness. Patsey, for example, used both hands and could easily pick five hundred pounds of cotton in a single day. When darkness forced pickers from the fields, the day's production was weighed, a process which provoked extreme anxiety for the workers. Those who had not picked their quota were whipped, and those who had picked substantially more than expected had their quotas raised. Often workers cooperated and reduced their pace to protect weaker or slower pickers. The fastest and cleverest could always be expected to make their quotas, but others were never able to pick the standard poundage and after repeated beatings were finally removed from the fields, sold, or given other jobs to do. Enslaved workers on cotton plantations generally worked in large gangs, moving through the fields from morning to night, under the threat of the overseer's whip.[28]

In the rice fields of South Carolina and the Low country of Georgia, enslaved people often worked under a task labor system, focused less on the amount of time they labored than on the tasks they completed. Ben Horry, enslaved on the Brookgreen plantation in South Carolina, explained that as soon as the fall rice harvest was completed, workers started readying the fields for the next season. Using mules and oxen, they plowed under the remains of the harvested rice plants before winter arrived. They plowed the fields again in the spring, cut deep trenches into the soil, planted the new rice, and flooded the fields. Then, as the fields were alternately drained and flooded, enslaved people worked in water or thick mud for the rest of the season, finding respite during the summer only when they moved to higher ground to plant and tend the crops that supplied food for the plantation. In midsummer, when the fields were drained, the workers toiled long days in intense heat, with thick mud making their every movement an effort. During the harvest season they gathered the grain with rice hooks and threshed the rice by hand, pounding and fanning it in baskets designed like those used in African rice culture to make it ready for market.[29]

The flies and mosquitoes, the disease and fungal infections, and the general discomfort of working long hours in wet soil in heat and humidity combined to make rice cultivation onerous work. John Brown, an enslaved man who worked in the rice fields of Georgia, thought that rice cultivation was the most unhealthful of all slave agricultural work. He contended that working knee-deep in the foul-smelling water that reflected the heat brought on fevers and contributed to sunstroke. With the constant dampness causing cracks in their skin that allowed insects to lodge just under the flesh, enslaved workers suffered infection, rheumatism, asthma, consumption, and other painful and chronic maladies. Brown also recalled the danger from the water moccasins, which were always plentiful in Low-country rice fields. Generally, he said, rice work was "very much more trying than either cotton or tobacco cultivation." Yet the task system employed on most rice plantations provided enslaved people with some degree of autonomy. A skilled rice worker might complete the assigned work some hours before sundown and then have time to perform personal tasks, to grow, gather, or hunt food for his or her own family, to develop a skill that might provide some personal or family advantage, to handle other family matters, or to rest. Completing one's task early could be a backbreaking proposition, but enslaved people generally preferred the task system of rice over the gang labor of cotton.[30]

Enslaved workers employed in cotton production, although forced to labor in gangs, also found ways to exercise some control over the nature and pace of their work. Many sang their way through the ordeal of gang labor. White observers agreed that enslaved laborers seemed to sing all the time they worked. Although a few of the enslaved reported, "Dey didn't allow us to sing on our plantation, cause if we did we just sing ourselves happy and get to shouting and dat would settle de work," slave songs were never successfully banned. These songs ranged from field hollers like "The Carolina Yell," described as "a loud musical shout, rising and falling, and breaking into falsetto," to more structured combinations of words and complex rhythms. Songs

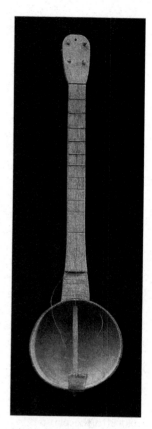

A banjo, from the late 1850s, constructed from the head of a gourd. When in use it would have had a piece of skin stretched across its opening and four strings running from the tuning pegs to the metal tailpiece at its base. Banjos derive from West African musical instruments.

sung during work helped encourage a sense of community among those sharing the hardship of agonizing labor. They helped pass the time during boring work and distracted attention from painful work, but they had an even greater practical value. Working to music set the rhythm for that work. Since on cotton plantations fast workers often amplified an owner's frustration with slower workers and increased the likelihood of their punishment, it was useful for all workers to maintain a moderate but steady pace. Work songs helped to coordinate a common pace, allowing the slowest workers to keep up without alerting the owner or overseer. This singing also often convinced white owners that their enslaved laborers were contented and relieved some of their anxieties about the possibility of slave rebellions.[31]

Enslaved people could also exercise control over their work by running away for a few days. There were many reasons why enslaved workers left their plantations without permission, including visiting friends and family, courting potential partners, or being angry at owners, but they also ran away to the woods or swamps to rest from their labor when they were exhausted or ill. When Patsey was sick and could not keep up her usual fast pace picking cotton, Northup reported, she ran away. Facing whippings for picking too slowly or too little, Patsey stayed away nearly all summer to recover from her illness, living in the woods a short distance from the plantation and depending on the other workers to share what little food they had. Her respite was bought at the price of a severe beating, five hundred lashes being the standard punishment at that time in Louisiana for running away. Across the South whipping was universally employed as the punishment for an infraction of the rules, the severity determined by the type of infraction and the mood and temperament of the owner or overseer. Northup reported that fifty lashes might be administered for a minor annoyance such as a leaf found in the cotton bag, and one hundred lashes for the offense of "standing idle in the field." Other punishments ranged from longer work hours or loss of the privilege of visiting one's family to more horrifying measures like the amputation of limbs or gruesome, terrifying mutilations that resulted in death. The last was meant to serve as a lesson to other enslaved people. For controlling workers, each plantation functioned as an independent fiefdom.[32]

Most enslaved people who ran away did so for a short periods and remained close to the plantation, but some runaways intended to stay away and established wilderness settlements called maroon communities. Often located in mountains or swamps, there were early **maroon** settlements in all colonies with slavery. Africans were most likely to run away, especially the newly arrived—some almost as soon as they landed—and they typically left in groups. Historian Sylviane A. Diouf identified two types of autonomous settlements: borderland maroons on the wild fringes of plantations and hinterland maroons in secluded, hard-to-reach wilderness areas. Borderland communities generally obtained some of their sustenance by stealing from nearby plantations; others were self-sustaining. The largest of these settlements, in the **Great Dismal Swamp** along the border of Virginia and North Carolina covering two thousand square miles, existed from the early 1700s until after the Civil War, sheltered generations of runaways and their descendants, and had an estimated number of residents ranging from hundreds to more than two thousand.[33]

Another way for enslaved people to exert a measure of control over their situations was by gathering information. Henry Clay Bruce, recalling his experience, explained that every plantation had its own spy network. People who worked in the main house were particularly well situated to acquire valuable information about the owner, his family, his political concerns, and his financial matters. On their breaks from duties in the owner's house, enslaved domestic

After the Sale, Slaves Going South from Richmond (1853) by British painter Eyre Crowe. Richmond was the largest slave-trading center in the Upper South.

workers often brought news of local, regional, and national events to the slave quarters. News that someone was to be to be sold or punished, or information about friends or relatives on neighboring plantations, might provide the fore-warning that allowed a timely escape or the formulation of a plan of action.[34]

Years later, Booker T. Washington reported that what he called the "grape-vine telegraph" was a regular and reliable conveyer of information for both enslaved and free Black men and women. Networks of informants included people newly purchased or hired out from other areas, artisans and domestic workers who came into regular contact with white people, and any African Americans who traveled to nearby areas or to towns and cities. Slave drivers or personal servants often accompanied planters on business trips or vacations, sometimes even to the free states. Body servants attended the southern planters who regularly visited northern border cities like Cincinnati, and often visited local Black Americans while their owners did business. The Dumas Hotel in Cincinnati was a favorite gathering place where southern enslaved people and Ohio free Black people mingled, despite the attempts of many slaveholders to discourage such associations. The enslaved people returning from such trips faced lengthy interrogation by their fellows, seeking word of family members who had gone north, or simply wanting news from the outside world. Informa-tion helped break the isolation of the plantation, gave enslaved people a broader sense of the world, and equipped them with important strategic knowledge. If a cotton broker was about to make an appearance to bid on the plantation's produce, enslaved workers knew that the owner might be under special pressure to get the crop baled and shipped to market. As the contract date approached, a planter's dependence on the laborers' efficiency increased, and though his anxiety might lead to additional whippings, it also provided an opportunity they could sometimes exploit to their advantage. At such critical times a work slowdown could be especially effective.[35]

The internal slave trade threatened the stability of enslaved families, but it also provided a valuable source of information on distant family members. New workers brought into an area often carried news of loved ones left behind. Although many plantation laborers lived in relatively isolated areas of the country, the business and social life of the plantation provided many opportunities for the exchange of information. The plantation business brought in new supplies of workers and necessitated contacts with buyers and shippers for agricultural products, and the plantation's social life often brought the personal servants of slaveowners together. Typically, enslaved people from neighboring plantations might gather for holidays like Christmas and, ironically, Independence Day. Through informal networks of information, many people managed to maintain family ties. Willie Lee Mathis of Cincinnati, for example, kept in touch with her mother, enslaved in Virginia, for thirty years. Others smuggled letters to children, parents, and other relatives in bondage in many areas of the South. Contacts between enslaved people and free Black people, North and South, provided information that enabled some people to escape from slavery. These links created the hazardous informal route to freedom that became known as the Underground Railroad. Contacts with the world beyond the plantation, as well as cultural memories, family, and other forms of resistance, sustained the hope of freedom for African Americans through desperate times.[36]

Who, What, Where

Creole languages p.119

Great Dismal Swamp p. 138

Harriet Jacobs p. 132

Maroon p. 138

Solomon Northup p.125

Ring shout p. 127

Nat Turner p. 122

Denmark Vesey p. 122

REVIEW QUESTIONS

5.1 What were the consequences of violent resistance by enslaved Black persons against slavery and slaveholders?

5.2 How did the community that revolved around the slaveholder contrast with the one that existed among the enslaved people?

5.3 How did African Americans adapt Christian beliefs to their circumstances?

5.4 How did community relationships aid the survival of enslaved people?

5.5 How was slavery different for Black women?

5.6 How did the brutality of plantation life fuel resistance?

For additional digital learning resources please go to **https://www.oup.com/he/horton1e**

Free People of Color and the Fight against Slavery

Three Sisters of the Copeland Family, an 1854 painting by William Matthew Prior shows Eliza, Nellie, and Margaret Copeland, the fashionably dressed daughters of Samuel Copeland, a secondhand-clothing dealer and real estate investor from Chelsea, Massachusetts.

6

CHAPTER OUTLINE

David Walker, William Lloyd Garrison, and the *Liberator*

6.1 Contrast David Walker and William Lloyd Garrison's approaches to abolitionism.

Integrated Abolitionism

6.2 Explain the goals and methods of antislavery organizations.

Black National Conventions

6.3 Summarize the impact of the Black national conventions.

Building an Antislavery Movement

6.4 Appraise the development of the antislavery movement.

The Underground Railroad

6.5 Analyze the ways that the Underground Railroad fit in with existing networks of enslaved and free people.

Militant Abolitionism and Political Power

6.6 Understand the controversy over nonviolence and political participation among abolitionists.

FREEDOM FOR AFRICAN AMERICANS during the era of slavery was an ambiguous status between slavery and full citizenship. It was also precarious, especially in the South, where it generally depended on the sufferance of white authority. There, in reaction to slave revolts and other perceived threats, advocating freedom for African Americans and organizing against slavery became progressively more difficult, even dangerous, during the nineteenth century. In the North, where Black freedom was more secure, Black communities established organizations that created the foundation for political action designed to broaden their own freedom and to secure the liberty of those enslaved in the South. Protest organizing in northern Black communities was aided by African Americans' increasing independence from white control and oversight. More than 70 percent of Black people in Philadelphia and more than 80 percent in Boston lived in independent households by 1820. New York City had a smaller percentage that year, about 60 percent, due to New York State's gradual emancipation provision. The state finally ended slavery completely on July 4, 1827. African Americans celebrated with parades and festivals, and as the last enslaved people began to move out of the homes of former white owners, the number of independent Black households grew. Many Black families that had been torn apart by bondage were reunited, although poverty and the demand for live-in servants still meant that some Black Americans lived in white households. Yet, in New York as elsewhere, the early decades of the nineteenth century brought increasing numbers of independent Black households and a growing Black community committed not only to mutual support but also to the struggle for civil rights and Black freedom.[1]

David Walker, William Lloyd Garrison, and the *Liberator*

In Boston in 1826 African Americans joined to form the **Massachusetts General Colored Association**, one of the first specifically antislavery Black organizations. One of the group's founding members was **David Walker**, a free Black man who came to Boston from North Carolina in the mid-1820s. Walker had never been enslaved, but his life and travels in the South had made him intimately familiar with slavery's inhumanity. He described a slaveowner forcing a son to whip his own mother to death and another forcing a husband to beat his pregnant wife until she aborted their child. In Boston, Walker became a community activist, working for abolition and racial justice. In 1827 Samuel Cornish and John Russworm of New York gave Black Americans a public voice when they founded

Timeline

Chapter 6

1822
Denmark Vesey's slave revolt thwarted; South Carolina passes Negro Seaman Acts.

1823
Alexander Lucius Twilight graduates from Middlebury College, the first Black

college graduate in the United States.

1827
John Russwurm and Samuel Cornish begin publishing *Freedom's Journal*, the first Black-owned newspaper.

1829
David Walker publishes his *Walker's Appeal to the Colored Citizens of the*

World, urging enslaved people to overthrow slavery. Slavery abolished in Mexico.

1830
First national convention of African Americans held in Philadelphia.

1831
Nat Turner leads slave revolt in Virginia.

Freedom's Journal, the nation's first African American newspaper, and Walker became its Boston agent.[2]

The next year, in a militant speech before the Massachusetts General Colored Association, Walker called for the formation of Black organizations to "protect, aid and assist each other to the utmost of our power," and advocated the use of "every scheme we think will have a tendency to facilitate our salvation." In 1829 Walker expanded this message with his publication of *David Walker's Appeal to the Coloured Citizens of the World*, even sending it into the slave South. He condemned the hypocrisy of all those, especially Christians, who professed to love liberty yet supported slavery. He challenged the Jeffersonian thinking that called for freedom while profiting from human bondage and arguing that Black people were intellectually inferior, and he contended that enslaved people, inflamed by the same thirst for liberty that had moved American Revolutionary patriots, would be justified in revolting against their owners. He saw education as a force for racial defense and uplift, believing it would produce revolutionaries. Southern slaveholders had vivid memories of earlier rebellions and Walker's *Appeal* exacerbated their fear.[3]

A few years later, in 1831, another strong antislavery voice came from Boston when **William Lloyd Garrison** began to publish his newspaper, the *Liberator*. Garrison, a white man, had good antislavery credentials. He had edited a political reform newspaper in Vermont, worked with Quaker activist Benjamin Lundy in Baltimore editing the *Genius of Universal Emancipation*, and been jailed on a conviction of libel for accusing a New England shipowner of engaging in the illegal slave trade. Garrison spoke so passionately against slavery that many who had not met him assumed him to be Black. Garrison counted more Black Americans among his friends than did most white reformers of his day. He valued the opinions of his Black associates and regularly sought their advice. When he was working out his positions on immediate

William Lloyd Garrison begins publishing the *Liberator*.

1833
British Emancipation Act abolishes slavery in the British Empire, including Canada.
American Anti-Slavery Society established.

1838
Frederick Douglass escapes from slavery in Maryland.

1839
Slave rebellion aboard the ship *Amistad*. Supreme Court decision in 1841 frees the survivors.
Liberty Party formed in New York State.

1845
Frederick Douglass publishes *Narrative of the Life of Frederick Douglass*.
United States annexes Texas.

1846–1848
Mexican–American War

1849
Harriet Tubman escapes from slavery in Maryland.

1853
First issue of the *Provincial Freeman* appears, first newspaper in North America edited by a Black woman.

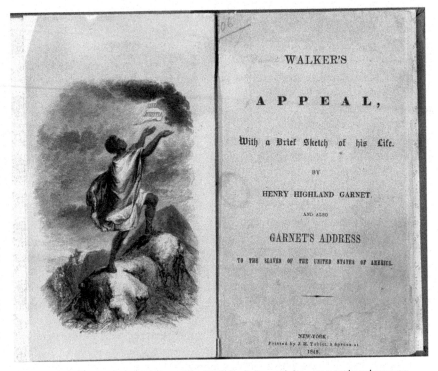

The frontispiece of this 1848 edition of David Walker's *Appeal* shows an enslaved man on top of a mountain, with his hands raised in appeal for *"libertas justitia"* (liberty and justice). The title page indicates that the volume also includes writings of the noted Black abolitionist Henry Highland Garnet.

emancipation and African colonization, he often did so with African American friends who criticized and helped him shape his ideas. James Forten and other Black friends from Philadelphia provided a sounding board for some of Garrison's early fiery speeches. Speaking before Black audiences in New York, New Haven, and Hartford helped him perfect his delivery, which a newspaper in 1830 had described as a bit stiff but admirable in "literary composition and 'philanthropic' concern." His speechmaking improved, and later that year one enthusiastic observer said that when he spoke, people felt as though they had "heard the groans and viewed the lacerated bodies of the poor sufferers." With the power of an evangelical preacher, Garrison repeatedly announced, "I will not equivocate. . . . I will not retreat a single inch—And I WILL BE HEARD." In his newspaper Garrison demanded both the abolition of slavery and the "improvement of the condition of the free people of color." It is no wonder that African Americans came to think of this most unusual white man as a "dearest friend."[4]

Garrison was so influential that those who subscribed to his ideas about immediate emancipation, anti-colonization, and not participating in traditional political organizations came to be known as Garrisonians. Since he was a pacifist, Garrison had misgivings about the prospect of African American violence in opposition to slavery. Walker's call for a slave revolt put Garrison in a difficult position, but after some hesitation, he published portions of the *Appeal* in his newspaper. Rumor had it that Walker's southern agents had distributed his pamphlet in the South. In December 1829 Walker sent thirty copies to Richmond, where they were sold for twelve cents or given away to those who could not afford the price. Many believed that Black sailors carried copies south, sewn into the linings of the clothing Walker sold in his secondhand clothing store. The *Appeal*'s publication in the *Liberator* gave it a wider circulation and a much higher visibility. In 1831 Nat Turner's deadly slave revolt in Virginia confirmed planters' fears that antislavery propaganda from the North was creating dangerous unrest among enslaved people. State laws requiring the confinement of free Black sailors when their ships were in port continued to be enforced in the South, despite the fact that a federal court had declared South Carolina's **Negro Seaman's Acts** unconstitutional in 1823. In a further effort to protect their ownership of human property, southern authorities placed a price on Walker's head and offered substantial rewards for Garrison, his publisher, or any of the *Liberator*'s agents. The mayor of Savannah, Georgia, wrote to the mayor of Boston asking that Walker be arrested and that his writing be suppressed, but Walker's pamphlet had caused less controversy in the North than in the South, and Boston's mayor, unfamiliar with Walker and his writing, denied the request.[5]

The strength of southern animosity toward David Walker led many in the Black community to suspect foul play when, later in 1831, he was found dead near the doorway of his clothing shop on Boston's Beacon Hill. In 1835 William Lloyd Garrison felt proslavery's wrath when he was attacked by anti-abolitionist forces, seized, and dragged through Boston's streets at the end of a rope. Local Black Americans saved him in a daring wagon rescue, and city authorities placed him in protective custody.[6]

Integrated Abolitionism

The violent opposition of southern slaveholders and their sympathizers did not deter the abolitionists, however. In 1832 William Lloyd Garrison and other abolitionists organized a meeting at the African Meeting House that established the **New England Anti-Slavery Society**. Several Black Boston residents were among those signing the society's organizing documents. The Massachusetts General Colored Association became an auxiliary to this new society, and prominent Black Bostonians John T. Hilton, Samuel Snowden, and Charles Lenox Remond assumed leadership positions. When, at Garrison's instigation, a national antislavery organization was formed in Philadelphia in 1833, seven Black men were among the sixty delegates at the founding convention. During the 1830s and 1840s abolitionists created a vast network of antislavery organizations that linked cities and towns in the

North and Midwest, joined Black communities in coordinated efforts, and tied Black organizations to integrated groups. Their grassroots efforts were so successful that by the early 1840s, these radical abolitionists claimed one thousand organizations with five hundred thousand members. Integrated organization was facilitated by the relatively high and rising Black literacy that made pamphlets, newspapers, and handbills effective conduits of information in urban Black communities. In 1850 the U.S. Census reported that nearly half of free Black adults could read and write; by 1860 the majority counted were literate. Effective propaganda gained international support for the antislavery cause. Successful organizations also helped enslaved southern Black Americans escape to freedom.[7]

In 1839 this network of antislavery organizations joined together to work for the freedom of fugitives from slavery in a celebrated international case. Fifty-three people had been captured in Africa and shipped to Cuba aboard a Spanish ship called the *Amistad*, despite the fact that in 1817 Spain had signed a treaty with England outlawing the Atlantic slave trade. Off Cuba the Africans killed the captain and some members of the crew, took over the ship, and attempted to return home. Eventually they were tricked by the crew into sailing into U.S. waters. They were captured, arrested, charged with murder, and imprisoned in Connecticut. The abolitionists went into action with a flurry of activity and publicity. They printed regular accounts in antislavery newspapers; visited the captives; and raised money for their defense, collecting donations at meetings, staging a play in New York, and commissioning and copying a portrait of the group's charismatic leader, **Joseph Cinque**. After sustained effort their case made its way to the U.S. Supreme Court, where former president John Quincy Adams and several prominent abolitionists defended the Africans. The court declared that the defendants had been kidnapped and set them free. In November 1841, finally, the thirty-five people who had survived this ordeal returned to Africa.[8]

Although antislavery societies brought Black and white activists together, African Americans did not abandon all-Black organizations. In 1829 an increase in Cincinnati's African American population had triggered white fears,

Enslaved Africans, led by Joseph Cinque, kill Captain Ramon Ferrer during an insurrection on-board the Spanish slave ship *Amistad*, off the coast of Cuba in July 1839.

resulting in a deadly assault on the city's Black community. Despite a successful defense, many Black Americans were driven from the city, some to Canada. Cincinnati officials, bowing to local racist pressure, promised stricter enforcement of Ohio's exclusionary racial laws. Ohio had passed these laws earlier in the century in an attempt to limit Black migration to the state. They required Black migrants to register with the county, certifying that they were free, and to post a five-hundred-dollar bond to ensure that they would not become dependent on local charity. Anyone who knowingly hired or harbored fugitives from slavery could be fined. Other western states also had restrictive laws: Illinois threatened bondage for any Black migrant attempting to settle permanently in the state. Black migrants were barred from settling in Michigan, Indiana, Wisconsin, and Iowa. Oregon also prohibited Black people from owning land, and banned further Black immigration when the territory became a state in 1859. In western states generally, Black Americans were prohibited from voting, serving on juries, giving testimony in court cases involving white people, or attending public schools. Though these laws were irregularly enforced, they made African American freedom especially precarious in those states.[9]

Black National Conventions

In response to the Cincinnati riots and attacks on Black civil rights throughout the North, African American delegates from nine states, including New York, Pennsylvania, Maryland, Delaware, and Virginia, met in Philadelphia in 1830 in their first national convention. The delegates meeting at the Mother Bethel Church chose the Philadelphian Reverend Richard Allen, then seventy years old, to preside over the convention. The main topic on the agenda of this first meeting was the establishment of a Canadian settlement for refugees from American slavery, hostility, and discrimination. Delegates constituted themselves as **The American Society of Free Persons of Colour**, met annually for six years, then revived their national meetings again in the 1840s. Delegates came from local auxiliary societies organized to combat slavery and its ancillary effects on free Black people.[10]

The conventions provided a national forum for African Americans and helped coordinate the actions of the local, state, and regional conventions and organizations of which they were an outgrowth. They also provided opportunities for Black leaders to discuss and pass public resolutions on issues concerning their communities and to devise strategies for addressing them. The major concerns of these groups were opposition to slavery, the achievement and protection of civil rights, and the advancement of the race, especially through education and moral reform. The national conventions continued the determined opposition of most Black organizations to the African settlement program of the American Colonization Society. Yet their support for Canadian settlements remained strong, especially after **Canada** abolished slavery in 1833 and refused to return fugitives from slavery to the United States.[11]

Some African Americans also considered Haiti an appropriate place for possible settlement. Enslaved people had forged Haiti into the first independent Black nation in the Western Hemisphere through their successful violent revolt against French colonial forces, making it a symbol of black freedom and power. In the early 1820s Haitian president Jean-Pierre Boyer invited Black Americans to settle in his country, offering free land, four months' provisions, and financial assistance. Haiti needed skilled farmers, and Boyer hoped that Black Americans could form a stable rural population. Interest in Boyer's proposal was strong in Black communities in the United States. Prince Saunders, a former teacher in Boston's Black school, became a strong advocate of the project and worked with Haitian official Jonathan Granville to recruit African Americans for an American-Haitian settlement. Granville toured New York, Philadelphia, Boston, and Baltimore, speaking to large and enthusiastic Black audiences. With Saunders, Granville established the Haitian Emigration Society at a mass meeting in Philadelphia in 1824, and within a few weeks, 60 African Americans set sail from Philadelphia, 120 from New York, and 21 from Baltimore. During the next two years, six thousand Black Americans made the voyage to Haiti, and by the end of the decade, Black communities in the United States had sent between eight and thirteen thousand emigrants.[12]

The venture was not entirely successful, however, and many African Americans returned within a few years. The Haitian government complained that these settlers were not willing to work the land but preferred to rent or sell their holdings and move into the cities. There the language and cultural differences between Catholic French-speaking Haitians and Protestant English-speaking African Americans created an uncomfortable urban coexistence. The most successful and longest-lasting settlement was located in an isolated section of the present-day Dominican Republic. There Black Americans created an English-speaking enclave that retained its American identity well into the twentieth century. The reaction of the thousands of migrants who returned to the United States, however, for whom the French culture seemed too foreign, suggests the degree to which these Black people were American in their identity and cultural expectations. By this time, almost all Black Americans had been born in the United States, and most were several generations away from an African or Caribbean regional or cultural identification. This experience further strengthened the resolve of most Black Americans to remain in the United States.

The plan of the American Colonization Society to settle Black Americans in Liberia was especially unpopular because most of the society's members were prominent slaveholders who, it was believed, simply wanted to remove free Black people from the country. Delegates who met in the national Black conventions during the 1830s were particularly opposed to African colonization. In their broad program, they presented a united front—opposing colonization and slavery and supporting moral reform and racial uplift. Yet the records of these conventions make it clear that free Black Americans had diverse opinions. All agreed on general aims but not always on the strategies for their accomplishment. Some favored separate all-Black organizations and institutions as the major vehicles—advocating establishing all-Black schools and encouraging Black people to patronize Black businesses—believing that only Black-controlled groups could properly speak for and serve the African American community. Others believed true equality could only come through integrated facilities, organizations, and institutions. Some were committed to bringing about changes through the nonpolitical action of "moral suasion," holding fast to the Garrisonian approach of nonviolence and not participating in inevitably corrupt partisan politics. Others, especially by the 1840s, believed that African Americans would only gain their rights as Americans and have the power to force the society to abolish slavery through participating in politics and forging political alliances.

From the beginning, convention delegates were concerned with establishing the means for independent Black achievement in order to escape the restrictions of racial discrimination. Austin Steward, formerly enslaved delegate from New York State, believed that farming could provide the independence that African Americans needed. To this end he supported the establishment of rural communities in Canada and moved his family to the Wilberforce Colony in Upper Canada for a time, to aid this enterprise. By the end of the 1840s there were such Black settlements in Hamilton, Toronto, Chatham, Montreal, and other areas of eastern Canada, and a growing Black community on Canada's West Coast. African Americans who found security in their new Canadian homes urged others to follow; some prospered in these new settlements. **Mary Ann Shadd**, daughter of a prominent Philadelphia Black abolitionist family, opened a school for Black students in Windsor, just across the border from Detroit, in 1851. During the next decade she edited a newspaper, the *Provincial Freeman*, becoming the first Black female newspaper editor in North America. She also published a guide to Canada for fugitives who had escaped from slavery in the United States, and became one of Canada's most effective and prominent abolitionist speakers. In 1856 she married Thomas J. Cary, a Black businessman from Toronto. She was determined to remain in Canada herself and passionately urged others to emigrate. "Your national ship is rotten and sinking," she told Black Americans. "Why not leave it?"[13]

Canada did seem a haven to many fugitives whose freedom was insecure in the United States. This was true for Henry Bibb, another influential advocate of Canadian emigration. Bibb, born in slavery in Kentucky in 1815, attempted many escapes, but he was recaptured as he attempted to rescue his family. He was finally sold south to New Orleans and then into Texas and what was known as Indian Territory, where he became enslaved by a Native American owner. In 1841, he escaped again, this time to Detroit, but by then he had given up any hope of rescuing his wife. She had been resold, and her new owner had made her his concubine. In 1848 Bibb married Black abolitionist Mary Miles, and the couple was forced to flee to Canada when a new federal Fugitive Slave Law was passed in 1850. The Bibbs settled in Sandwich, Canada West (present-day Ontario), where she opened a school and he edited the *Voice of the*

Reward posters for fugitive enslaved people often contained detailed descriptions of runaways.

Fugitive, an antislavery weekly newspaper that advocated the emigration of Black Americans to Canada. Through the efforts of the Bibbs, Mary Ann Shadd Cary, Austin Steward, and other Black Americans who had come to see Canada as a land of freedom and opportunity, many Canadian Black settlements were established in the three decades before the American Civil War ended slavery in the United States.[14]

Although many African Americans came to believe that emigration was their only route to security and independence, most were determined to achieve full freedom in the United States. Richard Allen, for example, argued that independence might also be achieved through practical training in the mechanical trades. When a group of white abolitionists, including William Lloyd Garrison, Benjamin Lundy, and New York businessman Arthur Tappan, attended the second national convention to propose the establishment of a manual labor school, delegates received them enthusiastically. These schools, where students supported their education by learning and practicing trades, were popular institutions with reformers at the time. In fact the emphasis on the importance of Black education for racial uplift was part of a general moral reform movement that linked Black and white reformers in a commitment to antislavery, temperance, and other moral causes.

The convention endorsed the proposal for a racially integrated college and appointed editor Samuel Cornish to head fundraising for the project. Integrationists also prevailed on decisions about the administration of the college, though it was agreed that African Americans should be in the majority on the board of trustees. When the residents of New Haven, Connecticut, the home of Yale University, learned that the new college was to be located in their city, they quickly organized in opposition. After a town meeting denounced the idea as promoting abolitionism and disorder, white mobs attacked Black Americans in New Haven and vandalized wealthy white abolitionist Arthur Tappan's home. This hostile reaction discouraged the initiative for a college in New Haven, but Black leaders remained interested in promoting education generally and in manual labor schools in particular. Especially as African Americans faced increased competition for low-level jobs from Irish immigrants in the 1840s and 1850s, there was heightened support for the establishment of educational institutions providing a combination of traditional and practical education.[15]

Although a Black-controlled school of higher education was not established during this period, the cooperation between white and Black abolitionists did lead to the integration of a few institutions established and controlled by antislavery reformers. In 1823, Alexander Lucius Twilight graduated from Middlebury College, becoming the first Black college graduate in the United States. After 1830 integrated schools such as Oneida Institute and New York Central College in New York State and Oberlin Collegiate Institute in Ohio educated a small but growing number of African American students. Oneida Institute, for example, with a student body of just over one hundred, under the presidency of white abolitionist Beriah Green and supported by the largess of Arthur Tappan and his brother Lewis, educated fourteen Black students between 1832 and 1844. Oberlin had educated one hundred African American students by the 1860s.[16]

Building an Antislavery Movement

Abolitionists' commitment to Black education brought many people into the antislavery movement at a young age. In Cincinnati white abolitionist students from Lane Seminary taught Black students, mixing lessons in reading and writing with moral and antislavery messages. In Boston Black choirs and youth groups, such as the Juvenile Garrison Independent Society, participated in abolitionist programs and conventions. It was common for whole families to be involved in the public programs held by Black communities to protest slavery and racial discrimination. Walker Lewis of Boston was a founding member of the Massachusetts General Colored Association and a close associate of David Walker. Lewis's father, Thomas Lewis, had helped found Boston's African Society, an organization that in the early nineteenth century provided aid to African Americans in need and protested against slavery. Thomas Lewis also helped establish the African Masonic Lodge in Boston, where David Walker was a member during the 1820s. By the 1840s, when Simpson H. Lewis joined the Boston Committee of Vigilance to protect fugitives from slavery, three generations of the Lewis family had been active in antislavery and civil rights efforts. The Black Snowden family, both men and women, was also active in antislavery work. Samuel Snowden was elected as a counselor to the New England Anti-Slavery Society in 1833, his two sons were part of a group that armed itself against slave catchers, and his daughters were members of the Boston Vigilance Committee. Women were critical to the antislavery movement in many ways. They held the bazaars and fairs that raised money, providing a major source of financial contributions. Women organized many auxiliaries to male groups, but they also participated in the meetings of the major integrated antislavery associations and were especially active in the moral reform movement. The Female Moral Reform Society, an interracial organization formed in New York in 1834, had sixty-one chapters in New England alone by 1841, and its bimonthly magazine was supported by three thousand subscribers.[17]

The campaign against slavery in America created organizations and networks that connected cities and regions, transcended generational divides, crossed racial divisions, and brought men and women together in coordinated and shared efforts. The crossing of so many boundaries often resulted in strong differences of opinion regarding strategy, and it was on the issue of all-Black organizations that the Black national convention movement foundered in 1835. A strong Philadelphia faction, led by William Whipper, believed that separate organizations undermined arguments for racial integration in American society. Other delegates, especially those from New York, argued that exclusively Black groups, in addition to integrated groups, were necessary to fully represent the interests and views of African Americans. The 1835 convention, dominated by the Philadelphia delegation, formed the American Moral Reform Society, and subsequent meetings became embroiled in debates over this issue. The most extreme position was taken by Whipper, Robert Purvis, and other Garrisonians from Philadelphia who objected to any reference to race and opposed the designation of "free people of color" as unwarranted exclusivity. After years of contention the American Moral Reform Society discontinued its meetings in 1841. Although many Black activists may have understood the philosophical principle of the moral reformers, most believed their position to be unrealistic and impractical. Samuel Cornish excoriated them for engaging in trivial debates that distracted them

The large woodcut image of a supplicant enslaved man in chains appears in a 1837 publication of the American Anti-Slavery Society, along with John Greenleaf Whittier's antislavery poem, "Our Countrymen in Chains." The design was originally adopted in the 1780s as the seal of the Society for the Abolition of Slavery in England.

from more important endeavors. "They are quarreling about trifles," he said, "while their enemies are robbing them of diamonds and of gold." Although willing to work with white reformers, most African Americans believed it was important to maintain Black organizations in order to be free from the constraints of integrated groups and the subtle prejudice and discrimination they suffered in them. Integrated organizations were more likely to accept gradualist positions and counsel patience, and, given the strength of northern prejudice toward interracial association, there was a greater danger of mob attacks on integrated meetings and economic reprisals on participants.[18]

There were also benefits to working in the integrated antislavery movement, however. Through these groups African Americans asserted their right to equal participation in the society in a concrete way. They also gave Black activists access to far greater financial resources and a much wider audience, and white reformers were educated by their contact with Black Americans. Within the first year of organizing, the integrated **American Anti-Slavery Society** had forty-seven local societies in ten northern and western states. Although Garrison himself came from a modest background, some prominent white abolitionists—Gerrit Smith and Arthur and Lewis Tappan of New York, and Wendell Phillips of Massachusetts, for example—were wealthy men who could lend their names, political connections, social networks, and economic resources to the cause. The Tappans underwrote the educational efforts at Oneida Institute, and Smith was the primary supporter of New York Central College. With the assistance of Black abolitionists James McCune Smith and Charles B. Ray, Gerrit Smith purchased and distributed more than three thousand land titles for farms in upstate New York near Lake Placid to African Americans from eastern cities. This created thousands of qualified Black voters able to meet New York State's property requirement. These were urban workers, cooks, waiters, coachmen, and barbers, ill-prepared for farming. The land was poor, either low and swampy or rocky mountain slopes, and the winters were harsh, but the settlers established farms, raised sheep, and initiated a wool trade with Canadian towns. Many of them voted in state and national elections.[19]

Perhaps the greatest contribution of integrated abolition was that it enabled African Americans to speak to sympathetic white audiences. The American Anti-Slavery Society and its supporters published flurries of pamphlets, sermons, and newspapers, but their most effective agents were antislavery speakers. They crisscrossed the North, made forays into the West, and spoke to large gatherings in major cities and more intimate meetings in small villages. Both Black and white Americans, men and women, became antislavery speakers, enduring the hardships of long periods away from home. They lived on subsistence wages and the kindness of supporters, collected money for the cause, encouraged local chapters, and often suffered vilification from hecklers and attacks and objects thrown by hostile mobs. The most popular speakers by the early 1840s were African Americans who had been enslaved, many of whom were still fugitives. For many white people attending these lectures, it was the first time they had heard a Black speaker.

The first full-time paid Black traveling abolitionist speaker was free-born Charles Lenox Remond, employed by the Massachusetts antislavery society in 1838. Yet the best-known Black American abolitionist was a man who escaped from slavery and was hired by the American Anti-Slavery Society in 1841. Born Frederick Bailey on Maryland's eastern shore in 1818, **Frederick Douglass** grew up on the plantation of Edward Lloyd, former governor of Maryland and U.S. senator. With a hunger for knowledge encouraged by his grandmother, Douglass seized every opportunity to learn to read and write. From his young white playmates being tutored by a teacher from New England, from his owner's sister-in-law who tutored him directly, and through his own efforts, Douglass acquired the beginnings of the education that he continued to expand throughout his life. When, as a young man, he was hired out in Baltimore, his curiosity about the world turned to a determination to secure his own freedom. At twenty, in the late summer of 1838, with the help of a free Black woman named Anna and carrying identification papers borrowed from a Black sailor, Douglass escaped.[20]

Traveling through Philadelphia and continuing northward, Douglass made his way to the New York home of Underground Railroad activist David Ruggles, where Anna later joined him and they were married. The couple moved farther north, settling in New Bedford, Massachusetts, where Douglass worked as a dock laborer. He became a lay preacher in the African Methodist Episcopal Zion church and attended local antislavery meetings, where he occasionally told the story of his own bondage. In August 1841 he attended an antislavery convention on Nantucket Island. White abolitionist William C. Coffin had heard him speak to a small gathering in New Bedford and asked him to give his personal testimony to the Nantucket meeting. Douglass was nervous standing before the crowd, but soon his powerful story captured and greatly moved the audience. William Lloyd Garrison and the other prominent abolitionists were so impressed that they offered him a position as an antislavery agent for the Massachusetts Anti-Slavery Society. Late that fall Douglass, Anna, and their two children moved to Lynn, Massachusetts, a Quaker community near Boston that was believed to be safe for fugitives. Over the next two years Douglass gave antislavery speeches in more than sixty towns in

This 1848 daguerreotype is a rare image of Frederick Douglass as a young man.

New England and became an accomplished speaker whose power to affect and inspire his audience had few equals.[21] In 1845, Douglass published his *Narrative of the Life of Frederick Douglass*, which introduced readers firsthand to the horrors of slavery. It sold tens of thousands of copies at home and abroad.

The Underground Railroad

As abolitionists continued formal organizing, less structured, more spontaneous activity, carried on in secret, liberated thousands of people from bondage. The modern technology of the steam locomotive provided the terminology for this **Underground Railroad**. Its safe houses were called stations, its operators were called conductors, and the fugitives were called passengers. Its function became legendary, and white as well as Black Americans participated. Although some of its work was directed and financed by formally organized abolitionist societies, Underground Railroad activity extended far beyond the formal organizations. Its varied action included everything from raids on southern plantations, to desperate bids for freedom by individuals. Fugitives in maroon communities and Black Americans allied with the Seminole Indians of Florida struck from the cover of swamps and protective wilderness at the plantations of Georgia and South Carolina. Fugitives moved south as well as north. From the regions of the Deep South or the Southwest, many fugitives fled toward Mexico, which had abolished slavery in 1829, or westward into the frontier territories.

In the southern interior, fugitives might seek temporary safety in deep woods, swamps, or mountains. In the Upper South, the North was the logical favored destination. The mythology of the Underground Railroad has emphasized the efforts of northern white abolitionists, mainly Quakers. While their support was important, the Underground Railroad radiated out from the South in all directions, and escape was generally initiated by the enslaved people. The first hours and the first few miles, before a runaway reached the relative safety of free territory or a protective community, were most critical. Generally unfamiliar with areas outside the immediate proximity of the plantation, fugitives were at a great disadvantage, easy prey for pursuers with tracking dogs or local patrols that routinely stopped Black people unescorted by white owners. In this early phase fugitives depended on other enslaved people, friends, and family to shelter, feed, and guide them on their way. Later, in southern towns or in the North, contact with the free Black community became increasingly significant, and along with it an increased possibility for contact with organized Underground Railroad activity.

James Williams escaped slavery in Virginia, headed north, and finally reached Carlisle, Pennsylvania, where he found a number of free Black Americans. When he inquired about employment, they surmised that he was a runaway from the South. "They knew that I was from Virginia, by my pronunciation of certain words [and] that I was probably a runaway slave," he recounted.

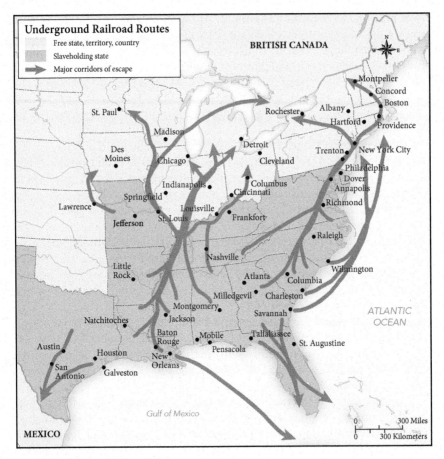

Map 6.1 Underground Railroad Routes

He confided in these people, placing his fate in their hands in part because they were Black. Later Williams explained that he was informed "that I need not be alarmed as they were friends, and would do all in their power to protect me." They sheltered him and "treated [him] with the utmost kindness." He was taken by wagon to Harrisburg to meet others, and from there he was taken to Philadelphia. To this point Williams had been cared for by strangers concerned for his safety. Only in Philadelphia did he contact the formally organized Underground Railroad.[22]

The Philadelphia Vigilant Association, formed in 1837, specialized in assisting fugitives and maintained contacts throughout the North. Through its resources Williams traveled to New York. But apparently Williams's owner was so determined that he be recaptured that he had employed slave catchers who searched for the fugitive as far north as Boston. When they were seen in

New York, the New York Committee of Vigilance arranged for Williams to be sent to England. By this time, Williams was under the protection of the formal underground, with international connections.[23]

Such Black abolitionists as Jacob C. White and William Still in Philadelphia, David Ruggles in New York, and Leonard Grimes and Lewis Hayden in Boston, major figures in underground activities, represent the range of personal experiences that people brought to this dangerous and demanding work. The White family was important to much of Philadelphia's Black abolitionist action. Jacob was a wealthy businessman and longtime activist, and his wife, Elizabeth, was a member of the Female Vigilance Committee. Jacob operated a free-produce store and led a boycott of cotton, sugar, rice, tobacco, and other products grown with enslaved labor. Their son, Jacob C. White, Jr., later continued this work. David Ruggles was born free in Connecticut and came to New York City as a teenager. After working in several businesses, he became an agent for the antislavery newspaper, the *Emancipator*, and for the American Anti-Slavery Society. Later he opened a bookstore specializing in antislavery publications. When a proslavery mob burned his store in 1835, Ruggles became an officer in the New York Committee of Vigilance, the chief arm of the city's antislavery underground. Over the next five years he and his associates facilitated the escape of more than six hundred fugitives, before poor health finally forced him to limit his underground work.[24]

Leonard Andrew Grimes was born in northern Virginia in the small town of Leesburg in the early winter of 1815. He was free, and although his racially mixed heritage was readily apparent to many, he was light enough sometimes to be mistaken for a white person. As a young boy, he traveled to nearby Washington, D.C., where he worked first at a butcher shop and then for a druggist, before a slaveholder hired him to be a hack driver. In this employ, Grimes traveled through the South, where his observations led him to hate slavery and encouraged him to become active in the Underground Railroad. He saved his money and prospered in his business while using his wits, his funds, and his horse-drawn hacks to assist fugitives to escape from bondage. After aiding one family that escaped to Canada from Virginia, Grimes was arrested in Richmond, found guilty of "stealing slaves," and sentenced to two years in prison. His prison term was hard on him both physically and emotionally, but after serving his time, he emerged with his spirit intact and a powerful devotion to religion. He became a preacher and traveled north, settling first in New Bedford, where he ministered to a small congregation for two years. Then, in 1846, the Twelfth Baptist Church in Boston called Grimes to be its minister. From this pulpit he continued his abolitionist work, becoming a major leader of underground activity in the city. His church attracted so many runaways that it become known as the fugitive slave church.[25]

For most free Black men and women involvement in the Underground Railroad was a natural outcome of their personal relationships. Since nine of every ten African Americans were enslaved, almost every free Black person

PROFILE

William Still

William Still, abolitionist and leader of the Underground Railroad in Philadelphia.

WILLIAM STILL'S PARENTS HAD lived in slavery. His father freed himself by self-purchase, but his mother, who escaped in 1807, was forced to leave her two sons behind. Fourteen years later, William was born in New Jersey. As an adult, Still became one of the nation's most important abolitionists. In Philadelphia he operated an elaborate network of safe houses and conductors, part of the country's most extensive Underground Railroad system.

In a letter written on August 8, 1850, William Still described an astounding encounter in his Philadelphia office with a man from Alabama who called himself Peter Freedman. As Freedman's story about his family, who had come north some years before, progressed, Still recognized much of the detail. "My feelings were unutterable," he explained. "I could see in the face of my newfound brother, the likeness of my mother" Peter had been left in slavery when his mother escaped, and the brothers had never met. "I told him I could tell him all about his kinfolk," William recalled, and the next day Peter was reunited with the family. Their father was dead by this time, but Peter met five brothers and three sisters that he had never known.

Slavery, central to southern social and economic life and a legal and political fact of American life, regularly created hardships for families. This family's struggle was not over, however. Peter had left a wife and children in Alabama and was determined they be free. They escaped to Indiana on the Underground Railroad but were recaptured and returned to slavery. When Peter attempted to purchase their freedom, their owner demanded the almost impossible sum of five thousand dollars. Peter began a lecture tour, telling his story to abolitionist gatherings and raising money for their freedom. Four years later, in October 1854, he accomplished his goal and settled his family on a ten-acre farm in Burlington, New Jersey. Peter died in 1868, but William Still continued his Underground Railroad and civil rights work in Philadelphia throughout the Civil War. During and after the war, he raised funds for freed people in the South. He lived into the twentieth century, dying in 1901.

_____

Source: "William Still to James Miller McKim," Philadelphia, August 8, 1850," in *The Black Abolitionist Papers*, ed. Peter C. Ripley, Roy E. Finkenbine, Michael F. Hembree, and Donald Yacovone, vol. 4 (Chapel Hill, NC: University of North Carolina Press, 1991), 53–58.

either had been enslaved or had family members or friends in slavery. As one historian explained, "Practically every clump of Negro settlers in the free states was an underground depot by definition." Fugitives were some of those most directly involved in Underground Railroad activities, thereby risking their own recapture. Lewis Hayden was a fugitive from Kentucky who settled in Boston, opened a small clothing shop, and became active in antislavery and the underground. He often sheltered fugitives in his home and confronted slave catchers who attempted to capture people under his protection. The story of **Harriet Tubman**, Underground Railroad conductor, is legendary. Born in slavery in 1822 on Maryland's Eastern Shore, Tubman was the property of one of the area's largest plantation owners. At six years of age, she was doing domestic work, and by her teens, she worked full-time in the fields doing heavy labor. An overseer struck Tubman in the head while she was attempting to protect another enslaved person from punishment. Her injury from the blow was life-threatening, and, thereafter, she suffered short episodes of unconsciousness.[26]

When her owner died and it became clear that his enslaved property would be sold away from the area and possibly into the Deep South, she determined to escape. In 1849, after one abortive attempt with her brothers and a failure to convince her free Black husband to follow her, she set out alone and reached Philadelphia. There she found domestic work and soon decided to devote her life and the little money she was able to accumulate to freeing her family and others from slavery. She was aided in this project by a network of antislavery activists including William Still, the leader of the Underground Railroad in Philadelphia. In late 1850 Tubman traveled to Baltimore on the first of many clandestine ventures into the South. This first trip was occasioned by word that her sister and her sister's two children were about to be sold at auction and separated from their husband and father, a free Black man on Maryland's Eastern Shore. The husband successfully bid on his family, and before payment was due, he spirited them away while the auctioneer was at dinner. He then brought them to Baltimore, where Tubman waited to escort them to freedom.

With elaborate plans that included rescues on Saturday evenings so as to delay the publication of advertisements for fugitives until Monday morning newspapers, or during Christmas work breaks to postpone detection of their absence, Tubman faced the dangers, including potentially her own recapture, with bravery, cunning, and faith in God's protection. During the 1850s, Tubman made at least twelve trips into slave territory, rescuing members of her family and others, personally conducting to freedom as many as sixty to eighty people and aiding many others. Although white abolitionists contributed much to the movement, as white activist James G. Birney observed, "such matters [as the direct contact with and assistance of fugitives] are almost uniformly managed by the colored people, I know nothing of them generally till they are past." Birney understated the role of white reformers, but it was true, nevertheless, as Cincinnati Quaker Levi Coffin remembered, "fugitives often passed through [town] generally stopping among the colored people."[27]

Even so, at its most organized levels the Underground Railroad was very much an interracial enterprise. It was most formally organized and most interracial in the North, where the law and local sentiment were less hostile toward antislavery activity, but some white antislavery activists were willing to go South, risking their freedom, even their lives, to assist fugitives. Calvin Fairbank and Delia Webster, white students at Oberlin College, were arrested and jailed for aiding escaping fugitives from Kentucky (one of whom was Lewis Hayden). Many of these fugitives worked to win their release, but Fairbank became so notorious for his actions that Kentucky finally sentenced him to fifteen years in prison, where he was tortured mercilessly.[28]

Left to right: Harriet Tubman; Gertie Davis (Tubman's adopted daughter); Nelson Davis (Tubman's second husband); Lee Cheney; "Pop" Alexander; Walter Green; Sarah Parker ("Blind Auntie" Parker); and Dora Stewart (granddaughter of Tubman's brother, John Stewart).

Jonathan Walker, a white New England sea captain, was apprehended off the Florida coast in the summer of 1844 with fugitives whom he was attempting to transport to freedom in the Bahamas. His ship was captured, and he was arrested and taken to Pensacola. He was jailed, fined, whipped, and branded with a double S for "slave stealer." After seven months several of his friends, including a number of free Black Americans, secured his release from prison. Frederick Douglass praised Walker's actions, saying that abolitionists would make the double S a symbol for "slave-savior."[29]

Fugitives often sought the assistance of seamen whom they thought to be particularly willing to provide aid. With cosmopolitan knowledge and access to the means of long-distance travel, sailors could provide a fugitive with valuable services. After Frederick Douglass escaped slavery in Baltimore with false seaman's papers, another sailor in New York City facilitated his contact with the vigilance committee. The culture of seagoing men often encouraged defiance of shoreside social, legal, and even racial conventions. Perhaps it is too much to say that "there seemed to have been an entire absence of prejudice against the blacks as shipmates among the crew," as one nineteenth century observer claimed, but historian William Jeffrey Bolster has documented the interracial comradeship on shipboard and the willingness of sailors, Black and white, to assist fugitives. White southerners always regarded sailors with suspicion. One southern newspaper asserted that sailors actually kidnapped enslaved people who might otherwise be unwilling to leave the South.[30]

Seamen and river boatmen were also crucial to the underground communication network that kept free Black Americans in the North in touch with friends and relatives in southern slavery. In their regular trips up and down the Mississippi River or the Atlantic coast, these men often carried personal messages and antislavery literature and provided information to southern free and enslaved Black people, breaking the isolation of southern society. Information about routes of travel, underground contacts in northern communities, and antislavery activities buoyed those held in bondage and helped to make escape a more realistic aim.[31]

This communication network facilitated personal interaction across the line of the cotton curtain. When Henry Williams escaped from slavery in Louisiana during the 1830s, he left his wife behind. He settled in Cincinnati, where he was able to secure work and establish a new life in freedom. After several years Henry met and married a woman from a neighboring town. Members of his church who considered him already married were outraged. The congregation charged Henry with bigamy, and he was accused of having deserted his wife in slavery. The church demanded a signed release from her before it would sanction the new marriage. This posed a difficult and dangerous situation for a fugitive from slavery, who might face re-enslavement if he returned to the South. The underground communication network provided the answer to Williams's dilemma. He sent a message to his first wife by way of a boatman who regularly traveled to southern port cities on the Mississippi River. The boatman obtained her X and her enthusiastic expression of support for dissolving the marriage. The church was satisfied and recognized Williams's new marriage.[32]

The Underground Railroad was organized groups and extensive communication networks, but it could also be specific, sometimes isolated, acts of conscience that transcended political philosophy. The Chief Justice of the Ohio Supreme Court, Joseph R. Swan, in his legal opinion supporting the constitutionality of the 1850 Fugitive Slave Law, explained, "As a citizen I would not deliberately violate the Constitution or the law." Yet, if confronted by a fugitive from slavery pleading for protection, the chief justice admitted, "I might momentarily forget my allegiance to the law and the Constitution and give him covert [sic] from those who were on his track."[33]

For African Americans the fight against slavery was both personal and philosophical. It was about the liberty promised by the Revolution and the Declaration of Independence, and the freedom denied to family and friends bound in slavery. It was also about defending Black people from an institution that by its very existence threatened the human rights of all African Americans. Resistance to slavery not only included overt physical confrontation with owners and overseers but also meant defeating slavery's attempts to control its victims and to hold them in debilitating isolation. The underground communication network was as much a part of antislavery activity as the Underground Railroad or formal abolitionist protest. In both formal and informal ways, Black Americans, often joined by progressive white supporters, engaged in a long-term agitation against slavery.

Militant Abolitionism and Political Power

A call for a meeting in Buffalo, New York, in 1843 to reconvene the Black national convention sparked a great deal of debate among Black leaders. Their philosophical differences had become more public, their disagreements over strategy more strident, and meeting in New York State signaled a change that was partly generational, partly a reflection of changing political and social circumstances. All but one of the previous meetings had been held in Philadelphia, which, like Boston, was a stronghold of Garrisonian opinion. Many Black people had grown impatient with the tools of moral suasion, nonparticipation in politics, and nonviolence that had been so influential in the previous decade. **Pacifism** had always been a controversial philosophy among Black Americans. Many of their most loyal allies, including Quakers and William Lloyd Garrison, were pacifists, but few African Americans were committed to this belief. In 1837 a meeting of Black New York residents had challenged the theory of nonviolence as impractical for "persons who are denied the protection of equitable law, and when their liberty is invaded and their lives endangered by avaricious kidnappers." Samuel Cornish, editor of New York's *Colored American*, confessed that when faced with kidnappers or "a midnight incendiary with a lighted torch in his hand" he had trouble believing in the virtue of "using moral weapons."[34]

From the start it was clear that nonviolence would be a major point of contention at the 1843 meeting. Fearing acrimonious debate and conclusions they could not support, the Philadelphians opted not to attend. Samuel Davis of Buffalo, chair of the convention, opened the meeting by urging Black Americans not to wait for others to act on their behalf. Citing uprisings in Greece and Poland as illustrations of the need to strike for liberty, he asserted that "if we are not willing to rise up and assert our rightful claims, and plead our own cause, we have no reason to look for success." On the second day, **Henry Highland Garnet** took the podium and delivered a rousing speech, one of the most militant calls for slave uprisings since David Walker's *Appeal*. He argued that patience should be no virtue for Black people and proposed a resolution urging African Americans to wait no longer for freedom and justice. The time for action had come, he declared, and for free Black Americans this meant the use of violence if necessary to defend their rights, their families, and the freedom of those who had been held in bondage. For people in slavery this might mean open rebellion to secure freedom. "You cannot suffer greater cruelties than you have already. Rather die freemen," he urged, "than live to be slaves."[35]

Other New Yorkers echoed Garnet's sentiments and supported his call to action, but the Boston delegates and other Garrisonians dissented. Frederick Douglass and Charles Lenox Remond pointed out that openly encouraging slave rebellions simply provided an excuse for proslavery retaliation against both enslaved and free Black Americans. They argued that it was reckless to jeopardize the entire abolitionist movement with such calls. Other delegates made counterarguments, sentiment was closely divided, and the resolution failed by just one vote.[36]

A second issue—the wisdom of Black involvement in partisan politics— also sharply divided Black opinion. Garrison urged abolitionists not to participate in politics, arguing that party politics required compromises that would dilute antislavery principles and voting expressed tacit approval for the constitutional system that sanctioned slavery. Nevertheless many Black abolitionists voted, and African Americans were powerful advocates for political reform even in states that prohibited Black voting. In New York State the fact that there were property requirements for Black voters but not for white voters made some African Americans more determined to participate in politics, if only to challenge this law.

In 1839 abolitionists from western New York had organized the **Liberty Party**, and antislavery hopes for political power were raised when the new party ran antislavery men for state and national offices. The Liberty Party nominated a former Kentucky slaveholder turned Ohio abolitionist, James G. Birney, for the presidency and attracted considerable Black support. The *Colored American* endorsed the party's national slate, calling Birney "a better man in every possible respect to be President of the United States" than current Democratic President Martin Van Buren or Whig candidate William Henry Harrison. Black delegates attended the party's convention in 1840, but Black support was equivocal. At the 1840 New York State convention of African Americans, a resolution endorsing the party was hotly debated before it was

DOCUMENTING BLACK AMERICA

Henry Highland Garnet

Henry Highland Garnet, a formerly enslaved antislavery activist.

Henry Highland Garnet's "Address to the Slaves" delivered in Buffalo, New York in 1843.

. . . SLAVERY! How much misery is comprehended in that sinful word. What mind is there that does not shrink from its direful effects? Unless the image of God is obliterated from the soul, all men cherish the love of Liberty. . . .

Brethren, it is as wrong for your lordly oppressors to keep you in slavery, as it was for the man thief to steal our ancestors from the coast of Africa. You should therefore now use the same manner of resistance, as would have been just in our ancestors, when the bloody foot print of the first remorseless soul thief was placed upon the shores of our fatherland. . . . Brethren, the time has come when you must act for yourselves. It is an old and true saying, that "if hereditary bondmen would be free, they must themselves strike the blow," You can plead your own cause, and do the work of emancipation better than any others. . . .

finally withdrawn. Though strongly opposed to slavery, the Liberty Party attempted to broaden its appeal beyond antislavery circles by linking the evil of slavery with the injustice of poverty. "Pity not only the enslaved poor and the colored poor, but all poor," urged a broadside advertising its meeting in Peterboro, New York, in 1846. Though some remained wary of any political party's ability to remain ardently antislavery, Black support for the Liberty Party was substantial throughout the 1840s. Several Black Americans traveled the campaign circuit, combining stories of their experience in slavery with a partisan political message. In 1844 the minister and formerly enslaved Jermain Wesley Loguen agreed to merge fund-raising efforts for his church in Bath, New York,

Look around you, and behold the bosoms of your loving wives, heaving with untold agonies! Hear the cries of your poor children!. Remember the stripes your fathers bore. Think of the torture and disgrace of your noble mothers. Think of your wretched sisters, loving virtue and purity, as they are driven into concubinage, and are exposed to the unbridled lusts of incarnate devils. Think of the undying glory that hangs around the ancient name of Africa, and forget not that you are native-born American citizens, and as such, you are justly entitled to all the rights that are granted to the freest. Think how many tears you have poured out upon the soil which you have cultivated with unrequited toil, and enriched with your blood; and then go to your lordly enslavers, and tell them plainly, that YOU ARE DETERMINED TO BE FREE. . . .

We do not advise you to attempt a revolution with the sword, because it would be INEXPEDIENT. Your numbers are too small, and moreover the rising spirit of the age, and the spirit of the gospel, are opposed to war and bloodshed. But from this moment cease to labor for tyrants who will not remunerate you. Let every slave throughout the land do this, and the days of slavery are numbered. You cannot be more oppressed than you have been—you cannot suffer greater cruelties than you have already. RATHER DIE FREEMEN, THAN LIVE TO BE SLAVES. Remember that you are THREE MILLIONS. . . .

Let your motto be RESISTANCE! RESISTANCE! RESISTANCE!—No oppressed people have ever secured their liberty without resistance. What kind of resistance you had better make, you must decide by the circumstances that surround you, and according to the suggestion of expediency. Brethren, adieu. Trust in the living God. Labor for the peace of the human race, and remember that you are three millions.

Source: Henry Highland Garnet, "An Address to the Slaves of the United States of America, delivered at the National Convention of Colored Citizens, Buffalo, New York, August 16, 1843," in Henry Highland Garnet, *Walker's Appeal, with a Brief Sketch of His Life* (New York: J.H. Tobitt, 1848), 90–96.

with tours on behalf of the Liberty Party. One contemporary recalled the effectiveness of Loguen's presentation in the small town of Courtland, maintaining that "no prayer ever made . . . melted the people like that." Liberty Party officials did remain committed to broadening the Black franchise, not incidentally, increasing the number of their potential supporters. After his unsuccessful 1840 presidential candidacy, Birney wrote to Lewis Tappan suggesting a petition campaign to secure equal suffrage for Black people in New York State. This was the context for abolitionist Gerrit Smith's distribution of farmland in upstate New York to Black families, allowing more Black people to meet the property requirement for voting.[37]

The establishment of the Liberty Party seemed to many to indicate the growing power of the antislavery movement, but there were also ominous indications that slavery was expanding its territory and its power. In 1836 prominent slaveholders in northern Mexico rebelled against their government's restrictions on slavery and established the independent republic of Texas. In 1845 the United States annexed Texas as a slaveholding territory with the prospect of statehood. In his address to the Buffalo convention in 1843, Henry Highland Garnet had anticipated just such an expansion of slaveholder influence, warning of the "propagators of American slavery spending their blood and treasure, that they may plant the Black flag in the heart of Mexico and riot in the halls of Montezuma." When President James K. Polk asked Congress to declare war against Mexico in 1846, Black Bostonians denounced "any war which may be occasioned by the annexation of Texas, or . . . any other war . . . designed to strengthen or perpetuate slavery." Douglass scolded Massachusetts, "the brightest of every other state," for becoming "the tool of Texas" when it offered men to fight and die in the unjust war, a war he saw as a hypocritical ruse to rob Mexico. African Americans were alarmed that the slave power seemed strong enough to push the federal government into a proslavery war.[38]

Meanwhile Black Americans in the late 1840s in northern cities worried about the wave of immigration that increased job competition among those at the bottom of the economic ladder. Economic competition threatened to create racial violence and provided potential converts for the anti-abolitionist Democratic Party. As national political parties took up contentious issues directly related to the antislavery cause, and members of Black communities felt under increasing political and economic attack, Black abolitionists debated the most expeditious course of action. There were many disagreements over specific strategies, but all agreed that their responsibility to those still suffering under slavery and to those growing up in the limited northern freedom demanded their steadfast commitment to racial justice.

Who, What, Where

REVIEW QUESTIONS

6.1 How did David Walker's and William Lloyd Garrison's approaches to abolitionism differ?

6.2 What were the goals and methods of antislavery organizations?

6.3 What impact did the Black national conventions have on the fight against slavery?

6.4 How did the fight against slavery develop into an integrated abolitionist movement?

6.5 How did the Underground Railroad fit in with existing networks of enslaved and free people?

6.6 Why was there a debate over nonviolence and political participation among abolitionists?

For additional digital learning resources please
go to **https://www.oup.com/he/horton1e**

From Militancy to Civil War

Ent'd according to Act of Congress. A. D. 1863, by W. T. Carlton, in the Clerk's Office of the District Court of the District of Mass.

On December 31, 1862, African Americans, both free and enslaved, held watch meetings for the Emancipation Proclamation that symbolically abolished slavery in Confederate-held areas on the new year.

7

CHAPTER OUTLINE

BY THE 1847 national Black convention, debates were more pessimistic, more militant, and even more bellicose. Educate your sons in the "art of war," urged one resolution. Calls for patience and faith in rational debate were replaced by arguments favoring the use of violence to discourage slaveholding and the kidnapping of free Black Americans. The next year in Cleveland, the convention passed resolutions advocating women's rights and the right of violent self-defense. The delegates supported speakers who urged that additional committees of vigilance be formed "to measure arms with assailants without and invaders within." Black activists in Ohio reinforced that message in 1849 when their meeting urged "the slave [to] leave [the plantation] immediately with his hoe on his shoulder" and made plans to publish five hundred copies of a volume pairing Walker's *Appeal* with Garnet's 1843 address. Even Frederick Douglass, previously opposed to violence in the antislavery cause, could see justice in enslaved people's killing slaveholders. In the winter of 1849 Douglass asked, "Who dare say that the criminals deserve less than death at the hands of their long-abused chattels?"[1]

Events during the 1850s confirmed Black Americans' growing conviction that the federal government was unlikely to support the cause of freedom. The U.S. victory over Mexico brought large tracts of land under federal authority, again raising the inflammatory question of whether the new lands would be open to slavery. This issue had broad political consequences, since the common wisdom among northern white working men was that their labor was cheapened and their opportunities severely limited in regions that tolerated slavery. Although most white workers would not disturb slavery in the South, they were strongly opposed to allowing slavery in the western territories, fearing it would deprive white working people of access to the new lands that were the core of the American future. White southerners agreed that the nation's future lay in the western territories but asserted their right to bring slavery, an institution basic to their way of life, into that future. To forestall a clash between regions, Kentucky representative Henry Clay engineered a political compromise in Congress. California would be admitted as a free state, but the other southwestern territories taken from Mexico would be organized without a decision on slavery. For the antislavery forces, the compromise promised the abolition of the slave trade in the nation's capital. For proslavery interests, the compromise offered the strictest Fugitive Slave Act ever enacted, far stronger than the 1793 provision. This measure was so harsh that even President Millard Fillmore, who signed it into law in the fall of 1850, questioned its constitutionality.[2]

The Fugitive Slave Law of 1850

The Fugitive Slave Law of 1850 infuriated African Americans, who considered it definitive evidence that proslavery forces had taken over the federal government. This new law made it easier for slaveholders to retrieve runaways who

Timeline

Chapter 7

1848
William and Ellen Craft escape from slavery in Georgia.

1850
Fugitive Slave Law passed.

1852
Harriet Beecher Stowe publishes *Uncle Tom's Cabin*.

1854
Congress passes the Kansas-Nebraska Act; fugitive Anthony Burns returned to slavery from Boston; Republican Party formed.

1856
Margaret Garner and other fugitives from Kentucky find sanctuary in Ohio.

1857
Dred Scott v. Sanford

1858
Senatorial election debates between Abraham Lincoln and Stephen A. Douglas

sought asylum in the North. They were not required even to bring an accused fugitive before a court but could take possession of their human property simply by presenting an affidavit drawn up by a southern court, with a physical description of the runaway, to any federal commissioner. Further, any bystander who refused to help recover a fugitive could be fined one thousand dollars and sentenced up to six months in jail. This law not only struck down northern states' personal liberty laws, which prohibited the use of local and state officials or facilities in the capture of fugitives, but it even threatened the freedom of Black Americans who were legally free. Since alleged fugitives could not speak in their own defense, free Black men and women could more easily be kidnapped into slavery. Thus, even where abolitionists were strongest, no African American was beyond the reach of the slave power.[3]

Free Black groups immediately swore to defy the new federal law. Meeting in Chicago only a few days after its passage, African Americans strongly denounced it. The city council in Chicago called it unconstitutional, deemed its supporters traitors, and refused to order city police to enforce it. At Boston's Faneuil Hall, abolitionists vowed that no fugitive would be taken from that city, and Frederick Douglass asserted that the streets "would be running red with blood" before the law could be enforced in Boston. Black Americans in Pittsburgh, stating their intention to make the recovery of fugitives in that city a costly proposition, bought one store's entire inventory of handguns and knives. In Cazenovia, a town in the middle of New York State, abolitionists and fugitives met defiantly in a "Fugitive Slave Convention" and called for slave rebellion. Anticipating a confrontation, leaders in Ohio and Massachusetts called for the formation of Black military companies to be ready to take up arms against slavery.[4]

Despite such strong reactions, the federal government, prodded by southern political pressure, was determined to enforce the law. James Hamlet, who was arrested in New York City and taken to Baltimore, had the dubious distinction of being the first person to be returned to slavery under its provisions. Hamlet, the son of a free mother, asserted that his enslavement had been illegal. He had lived in New York for three years with his wife and two children, but, under the

in Illinois. Douglas wins election.

1859
John Brown leads twelve white and five Black resistance fighters in an abortive raid at Harpers Ferry, Virginia.

1860
Abraham Lincoln elected president; South Carolina becomes first southern state to secede from the Union.

1861–65
Civil War. Over 180,000 African Americans serve in combat roles and 200,000 as support troops.

1863
Abraham Lincoln issues the Emancipation Proclamation; Black Union soldiers fight their first major Civil War battle at Port Hudson, Louisiana.

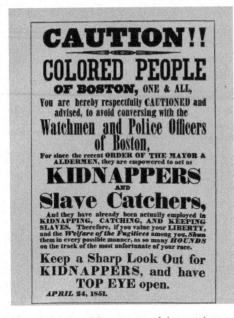

A poster warning of the presence of slave catchers in Boston.

new law, he was prohibited from testifying in his own defense, and the New York abolitionists had been unable to prevent his capture and return. Instead they collected the eight hundred dollars demanded by Hamlet's owner, bought his freedom, and returned him to the city. Others were not so fortunate and were returned to slavery from northern cities during the early 1850s. Many, even those who had lived in the North for several years, fled to Canada. Communities closest to the South felt this emigration most acutely. According to contemporary accounts, small towns in southern Pennsylvania were "almost deserted of black fellows, since they have heard of the new law. It is supposed that more than a hundred have left for Canada and other parts." The Black population of Columbia, Pennsylvania, decreased by more than half in a matter of months. One observer in Pittsburgh reported that "nearly all the waiters in the hotels have fled to Canada." According to his tally, "Sunday 30 fled; on Monday 40; on Tuesday 50; on Wednesday 30 and up to this time the number that has left will not fall short of 300." Fugitive or free, Black individuals not well known in their local communities were especially vulnerable to capture or kidnapping. Things were not much better farther north—in Buffalo one Black church lost 130 members of its congregation, Rochester's Black Baptist church lost 114 members, and Boston's Twelfth Baptist Church and Hamilton Street Church in Albany, New York, each lost one-third of their members to Canadian migration. Shortly after the fugitive slave provision was signed into law, the Anti-Slavery Society of Canada estimated that between four and five thousand African Americans had crossed the Canadian border, and many of these were free Black men and women.[5]

Most Black Americans, however, did not go to Canada. African Americans were critical in the fight against the Fugitive Slave Law and the historical record is filled with their defiance of authority, as they endangered themselves and their property in attempts to prevent the recapture of fugitives. Before the passage of the new law, William Craft and his wife, Ellen, had escaped slavery in Georgia. They had made their way to Philadelphia and then to Boston, using an ingenious disguise, with the light-complexioned Ellen posing as an ill young white man and the darker William as her enslaved attendant. After their escape, they traveled widely as antislavery speakers, mesmerizing audiences with their story. While in Boston, the couple stayed with Lewis Hayden, an active abolitionist who had also escaped from slavery. Though one of the best-known centers of antislavery activity in the country, Boston was not beyond slavery's reach. In early November 1850 the *Liberator* warned of "the appearance of two prowling villains . . . from Macon, Georgia, for the purpose of seizing William and Ellen Craft, under the infernal Fugitive Slave Bill, and carrying them back to the hell of Slavery."[6]

Abolitionist pressure led to the temporary arrest of the slave hunters, but eventually they descended on Hayden's home intending to recover the fugitives. Hayden confronted the slave hunters on the front porch of his house, where he had placed barrels of explosives. He made clear his intention to blow up the house and anyone who might enter rather than allow the fugitives to be taken back to slavery. Meanwhile a number of Boston's Black activists met to consider their course of action, and it was the overwhelming sense of the meeting that the fugitives would not be taken without a fight. Yet, realizing it was only a matter of time before the federal government would prevail even in Boston, abolitionists raised funds to send the Crafts to England, where they were taken in by British abolitionists and remained safe from capture.[7]

In Springfield, Massachusetts, John Brown, a deeply religious—some said fanatical—white activist, organized the **League of Gileadites**. This group of Black men and women armed themselves and intended to act as a guerrilla force to defend fugitives and attack slavery. Defiant abolitionist action spread across the North, but federal officials grew more determined as resistance increased. When an integrated group of abolitionists led by Lewis Hayden successfully rescued a fugitive named Shadrach Minkins from his confinement in a Boston courtroom, President Fillmore ordered the prosecution of the rescuers. Eight Bostonians, four Black and four white, were arrested, but none was convicted. In Syracuse, New York, in a case that became known as the Jerry Rescue, William ("Jerry") Henry, a fugitive from Missouri, was arrested, but abolitionists rescued him from authorities and delivered him to Canada.[8]

Resistance in many northern cities made enforcing the Fugitive Slave Law costly. In New York City two hundred policemen were required to guard a single chained fugitive and return him to slavery. An attempt to recapture a fugitive in Christiana, Pennsylvania, resulted in the "Battle of Christiana," which left one slaveholder dead and another injured. The failed rescue of **Anthony Burns**, a fugitive from Georgia, in Boston in 1854 was one of the most dramatic and costly actions. Several hundred abolitionists armed with stones, ax handles, guns, and knives attacked a federal courthouse and murdered a U.S. deputy marshal. It took two military companies to quell the violence. Thousands of antislavery supporters came from the surrounding area to witness Burns's trial and return to slavery, proceedings that required more than two thousand police and military troops and cost the federal government one hundred thousand dollars.[9]

The legal arguments of abolitionists, including Ohio governor Salmon P. Chase, supporting **Margaret Garner** in her tragic case did not prevent her return to slavery. Although state authorities indicted Garner for murder, federal law and the slaveholder's perspective prevailed. The court upheld the owner's right to his human property, implicitly redefining the child's murder as property theft.

Margaret Garner

THE MODERN MEDEA—THE STORY OF MARGARET GARNER.—Photographed by Brady, from a Painting by Thomas Noble.—[See Page 318.]

Margaret Garner, fugitive from slavery, tried to kill her children rather than submit them to re-enslavement.

IN 1987 BLACK writer Toni Morrison took the literary world by storm with a wrenching and haunting novel. *Beloved* was the story of Sethe, a fugitive from slavery who killed her baby rather than allow the child to grow up under slavery. The novel and the movie made from it were loosely based on an actual incident in 1856. Margaret Garner, her husband, their four children, and her in-laws escaped from slavery in Kentucky. It was winter, and they walked across the frozen Ohio River to the free state of Ohio. There, they joined nine other fugitives from Kentucky and made their way to Cincinnati. Within sight of slave laborers across the river, Cincinnati was a virtual magnet for runaways. They were drawn there and to other towns on the north side of the river by the hope of safety within a free Black community and aid from abolitionists. Nevertheless, slave catchers trapped Margaret and her children, but before they could seize her, she cut her baby girl's throat and severely injured two of her other children. "If they had given me time," Margaret later said, "I would have killed them all." The prospective return of her children to slavery was too much for her to bear. The best efforts of Cincinnati abolitionists could not prevent her being returned to the South. Still, Margaret was determined that she and her children not be re-enslaved. On a ship bound for their sale in the deep South, she threw one child overboard and leaped in herself. Sailors pulled Margaret from the water still alive, but the child drowned.

One can hardly imagine a slavery so horrible that a mother would kill her children to save them from it. Defenders of slavery often claimed that the enslaved were contented. They contended that owners were benevolent, and they romanticized the owner–slave relationship. The power of Margaret Garner's tragic story was not lost on the abolitionists. They told it again and again as heartbreaking proof of the inhumanity of slavery and the incredible lengths to which some would go to free themselves and those they loved from its grip.

This case further inflamed northern opinion against the Fugitive Slave Law. The Ohio legislature, calling the law unconstitutional, ordered state officials to remove fugitives from the custody of federal authorities upon the state's issuance of a writ of habeas corpus.[10]

Growing Opposition

Attempts to enforce the Fugitive Slave Law heightened African American resistance, strengthened abolitionist resolve, and seemed to increase northern opposition to the inhumanity of keeping human beings in bondage. Highly publicized cases of fugitives from slavery gave human form to what previously had been abstractions in the minds of many white northerners. Seeing some of these people returned to slavery evoked the sympathy of many formerly apathetic people, and the tragedies attending the enforcement of federal law galvanized the abolition movement. **Harriet Beecher Stowe** was a writer from a northern white abolitionist family whose sister urged her to use her literary talent to combat the Fugitive Slave Law. Stowe's 1852 novel *Uncle Tom's Cabin* caught the imagination and stirred the emotions of northern readers. Her melodramatic depiction of the plight of the fugitive and the horrors of slavery became the single most influential piece of antislavery literature in the century. Its authenticity was bolstered by consultation with people who had actually experienced slavery. Prominent among them was Frederick Douglass, whom Stowe admired and with whom she developed a close friendship. Douglass was effusive in his praise of Stowe's intelligence, philosophy, and character, and he called her novel "*the master book of the nineteenth century.*"[11]

The moral discomfort this book caused in the North was not strong enough to unite northern white Americans in the antislavery cause. It and the Fugitive Slave Law did, however, convince many northerners that the expansion of slave power posed a threat to the civil rights of *all* Americans. *Uncle Tom's Cabin* sold out its first printing of five thousand copies in the first two days and sold three hundred thousand copies in the United States and two hundred thousand copies in England during the first year. *The Times* of London reported on its wild popularity among the British. Lord Palmerston, who became British prime minister during the 1860s, claimed to have read the entire book three times, the only

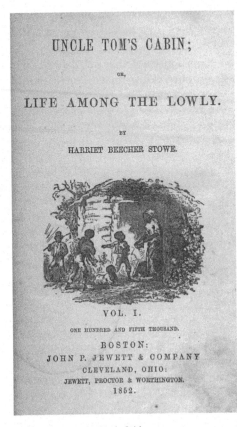

UNCLE TOM'S CABIN;

OR,

LIFE AMONG THE LOWLY.

BY

HARRIET BEECHER STOWE.

VOL. I.

ONE HUNDRED AND FIFTH THOUSAND.

BOSTON:
JOHN P. JEWETT & COMPANY
CLEVELAND, OHIO:
JEWETT, PROCTOR & WORTHINGTON.
1852.

Title page of *Uncle Tom's Cabin.*

novel he had read in thirty years. This book's impact was so powerful that it influenced British authorities to keep the Canadian border open to people fleeing from slavery. Partly because of Stowe's novel and partly in response to the fugitive slave cases, many northerners who had supported slaveholders' property rights were forced to confront the morality of their position.[12]

The novel was widely read even in the South. In the stores in Charleston, South Carolina, it sold out quickly, though reaction was decidedly negative. "I would have the review as hot as hellfire, blasting and searing the reputation of the vile wretch in petticoats who could write such a volume," the editor of the *Southern Literary Messenger* wrote to instruct his book reviewer. In the two years after the publication of *Uncle Tom's Cabin*, southern authors wrote at least fifteen novels whose premise was that slavery was more benevolent than Stowe's depiction. Many argued that slavery compared favorably to the conditions of free labor in the North. Clearly, Stowe's novel accentuated the growing rift between North and South, and it led President Lincoln a decade later to address Stowe as, "the little lady who wrote the book that made this great war."[13]

By the 1850s most of the South had become virtually a police state that barred dissent, requiring concurrence with slavery as the price of social acceptance and individual safety. Slavery was claimed to be a superior, more progressive, more humane system than free labor. The abolitionist arguments that the South was controlled by proslavery forces bent on shaping national policies to their needs was made more credible by southern reactions to the rise of antislavery in the North. White northern anxiety strengthened with each southern attempt to block the delivery of the U.S. mail for fear that it carried antislavery literature. Each act of violence meant to prohibit the public expression of antislavery ideas, and each reward for killing antislavery leaders offered or sanctioned by southern legislators, heightened northerners' concerns about their own rights. By the middle of the nineteenth century, northern support for the antislavery cause had broadened to include those "likely to be more concerned for the welfare of white men than they were for the rights of free black men and slaves."[14]

Sectional disputes erupted in violence as Congress began to organize the Kansas and Nebraska territories. Although the Missouri Compromise of 1820 had prohibited slavery in the territories held by the federal government north of the southern border of the slave state of Missouri, the question was opened again in the 1850s. The gold discovered in California in 1848 had spurred the desire for constructing a transcontinental railroad to the West Coast. When the U.S. Senate began to organize the territories in preparation for this construction, an agreement was struck between southern Democrats and the chair of the Committee on Territories, Illinois Senator Stephen A. Douglas. In return for the southerners' support for a railroad route through Chicago in his home state, Douglas's bill left the issue of slavery's existence in the territories to the settlers, effectively rescinding the Missouri Compromise. The bill outraged African Americans. Many gathered in Philadelphia to denounce it, and all over the North abolitionists condemned Senator Douglas as a "sectional traitor." Angry antislavery supporters burned Douglas in effigy, and when he tried to explain the bill to a Chicago audience, he was hooted down. **The Kansas-Nebraska Act** was signed into law in the spring of 1854, and *Frederick Douglass' Paper* lamented the triumph of "the audacious villainy of the slave power" over "the most explicit and public pledges of both the great parties."[15]

The **popular sovereignty** provision of the Kansas-Nebraska Act set the stage for a confrontation between antislavery and proslavery forces who rushed

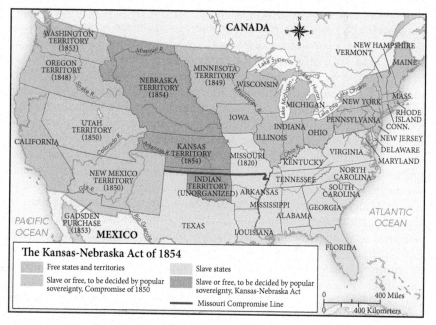

Map 7.1 The Kansas-Nebraska Act of 1854

to settle Kansas. Planters sponsored proslavery emigrants from Missouri, who flooded into Kansas and were confronted by **Free-Soilers** from New England and New York. Frederick Douglass proposed raising funds to encourage Black emigration to Kansas, but scarcity of resources discouraged such efforts. A large Black migration would have been an especially risky project, since Black settlers in the territory were often in mortal danger from proslavery forces. White Free-Soilers who took up residence in Kansas ultimately did battle with "border ruffians" from Missouri in bitter unrestrained conflicts that earned the territory the name **Bleeding Kansas**. In 1856 warring forces killed some two hundred people. Despite his shocking execution of five men at Pottawatomie Creek, white abolitionist *John Brown* became a heroic figure in some antislavery circles for his battles in Kansas against supporters of slavery.[16]

At the same time, in February 1854, a diverse group of abolitionists, Liberty Party people, Free-Soilers, and disaffected Whigs formed a new political party. They were joined by some northern Democrats appalled at the growing influence of southern planters within the Democratic Party. Within two years, this new **Republican Party** ran John C. Frémont as its first presidential candidate. Mainstream Republicans sought to keep the western territories free from slavery, and the party's slogan, " Free Labor, Free Soil, Free Men," was attractive to both African Americans and to land-hungry white workers. Yet the Republican plan was for slavery's containment within the borders of the South, not for its abolition. Especially troubling was the link between this Free-Soil stand and the philosophy of white supremacy, as Frederick Douglass noted in his 1856 essay, "The Unholy Alliance of Negro Hate and Anti-slavery."[17]

The pervasiveness of racism encouraged Republicans to filter their message through appeals to white racial chauvinism. Many of those attracted to the new party were also those who packed audiences in **blackface minstrel shows**. In these immensely popular performances by white men such as T.D. Rice, Dan Emmett, and Dan Bryant, working-class northern white men could measure their self-worth against caricatured degraded images of Black people. Before the Civil War these performances by white actors who darkened their faces to assume stereotypical Black styles became the embodiment of white ambivalence toward the interracial American culture. Many white people were attracted to Black music, dance, and humor but feared and disdained Black people. Appealing to this constituency while maintaining an antislavery stance was no simple proposition. Thus the platform of the Republican convention in 1856 committed the party to freedom in Kansas but was silent on other issues of interest to African Americans, such as the Fugitive Slave Law, slavery in the District of Columbia, the interstate slave trade, and the abolition of slavery.[18]

Most African Americans were more inclined to support the Liberty Party. It stood for abolition and civil rights for Black people, included several prominent African Americans in its leadership, and by 1855 was considering changing its name to the Radical Abolition Party. But the Liberty Party had no chance of electing candidates to office. The Republican Party was not an antislavery party, but it might at least be successful in limiting slavery's spread and curbing its power. Given the practical political choice between Republicans and

Democrats, the "avowed supporters of the enslavement of [the] race," there really was no choice. In Boston, African Americans, including Garrisonians, resolved to give Frémont their qualified support. As one speaker made clear, "We do not pledge ourselves to go further with the Republicans, than the Republicans will go with us." Before the November elections Black meetings in Brooklyn, New York; throughout New York State; and in Ohio and Pennsylvania endorsed the Republican Party and its candidate, but their ambivalence was apparent. As one delegate from New York put it, "[W]e do not for a single moment endorse all the political tenets of that party."[19]

Even qualified political support from African Americans was a mixed blessing for the Republicans, and they came under harsh criticism from their opponents. Black activists, on the other hand, were encouraged when the Democrats attacked the party as "Black Republicans" and accused it of favoring radical abolitionists and race-mixing. Republican candidates made a respectable showing in the election of 1856. Frémont lost to the Democratic presidential candidate, James Buchanan, by fewer than half a million votes out of a total of four million cast. Frederick Douglass took hope from these results. "We have turned Whigs and Democrats into Republicans," he wrote to New York abolitionist Gerrit Smith; "we can turn Republicans into Abolitionists." Others, less optimistic about political change, concluded that "the peaceful annihilation of slavery [was] hopeless" and that the slaveholder's "execution only waits the finish of the training of his executioners."[20]

Dred Scott v. Sanford

A Supreme Court case in the fall of 1857 made it even more difficult for African Americans to be optimistic about ending slavery and about their future. After a series of decisions and reversals in lower courts, a case involving a Virginia-born enslaved man named **Dred Scott** reached the high court. Scott brought suit against his owner, demanding freedom on the basis of their having lived in the free territories of Wisconsin and Illinois for a number of years. Scott had originally brought his case in Missouri, where others had been successful in similar actions, but, after winning his case initially, he lost on appeal, and the case moved to the Supreme Court. In his opinion in this case, southern-born Chief Justice Roger B. Taney went far beyond the simple decision. Taney declared that Congress had no authority to exclude slavery from the territories, essentially striking down the central plank in the Republican platform and finishing off the Missouri Compromise. Further, he stunned African Americans by attacking them directly, declaring that they were not and could not be American citizens and thus had no rights guaranteed under the U.S. Constitution—or, as Taney put it, they "had no rights which the white man was bound to respect."[21]

The Department of State, under Secretary Lewis Cass of Michigan, responded quickly and denied passports to Black Americans, a change in policy despite the department's insistence to the contrary. Defiantly the *Boston Daily Bee* pointed to several instances in which Black people previously had received passports. Protesting the Supreme Court's decision, the Massachusetts legislature

Dred Scott, Harriet Scott, and their daughters Eliza and Lizzie, newspaper article on the family, 1857.

instructed its secretary of state to issue passports to Black citizens of the state. African Americans continued to exercise a right of citizenship by voting in five New England states and in New York (with property requirement restrictions). Many white citizens also denounced the court decision, and many state and federal officials expressed outrage at the obvious inequity.[22]

This federal assault on their rights led some Black Americans to reconsider emigration. In the summer of 1858 a group of Black people, led by militant abolitionist Henry Highland Garnet, established the African Civilization Society to encourage settlement of Black Americans in Liberia, which had become an independent West African nation in 1847. The society was not racially restricted and counted several white reformers as part of its membership, but unlike the earlier American Colonization Society, this was largely a Black-controlled venture that condemned slavery and American hypocrisy and focused on expanding opportunities for Black freedom and independence. It also reflected the desire of society members, many of whom were Black ministers, to spread the faith among West Africans. But African colonization was not popular with many African Americans, some of whom reasoned that emigration to Canada or the West Indies was more practical for continuing the fight against slavery. James T. Holly, born free in Washington, D.C., returned from a visit to Haiti in the mid-1850s with glowing reports of the opportunities there for African Americans willing to take up residence. Perhaps aware of the earlier attempt at Haitian settlement, few Black Americans agreed to emigrate there, but Canadian emigration continued.[23]

As the decade progressed, emigration seemed less likely and the sequence of events encouraged African Americans to prepare themselves for military action. Black activists in Boston had petitioned the Massachusetts legislature in 1855 to charter a Black military company, and when their request was denied, they had formed the Massasoit Guard without state sanction. In November 1857, after the Dred Scott decision was announced, the guard, armed and in full uniform, paraded through the streets of Boston. At a meeting of Massachusetts African Americans in 1858, Black lawyer Robert Morris called on his fellows to stand together against the federal attack: "If any man comes here to New Bedford and they try to take [any fugitive] away, you telegraph us in Boston, and we'll come down 300 strong, and stay with you; and we won't go until he's safe." Cincinnati African

Americans formed the Attucks Guards, named for Crispus Attucks, the Black sailor who was the first to die in the American Revolution. African Americans in New York also called one of their units the Attucks Guards. Black activists in Ohio demanded that racial restrictions be removed from the state militia, and the Ohio convention of 1857 resolved that independent military companies should be established wherever Black men were denied places in the state militia. In cities and towns in the North, African Americans anticipated war and readied themselves. "Captain" J.J. Simmons of the New York City unit prophesied that soon northern Black military units would be called to march through the South with "a bible in one hand and a gun in the other."[24]

John Brown's Raid at Harpers Ferry

Through the spring and summer of 1858, a group of Black and white abolitionists met in the United States and Canada to discuss the feasibility of attacking slavery directly. John Brown, the leader of Kansas abolitionist guerrilla forces, devised a daring plan to strike against slavery in Virginia. With the financial backing of wealthy abolitionists from New England and New York, Brown gathered a band of eighteen men—thirteen white and five Black. As what began as plans for a small guerrilla action grew to plans for a full scale assault, African Americans' doubts about the wisdom of the scheme also grew. Although Frederick Douglass had taken part in the early discussions, by the time of the raid he was convinced it was a noble folly. Later, Douglass wrote that although he had prior knowledge of the raid, he had never intended to join it. "Let every man work for the abolition of slavery in his own way," he declared. "I would help all and hinder none."[25]

On October 16, 1859, Brown and his men raided the federal arsenal at **Harpers Ferry**, Virginia, in an effort to obtain weapons and ammunition to arm the people enslaved on nearby plantations. With this expanded force, Brown intended to move against the slaveholders, freeing their enslaved laborers and enlisting some in a vast abolitionist army. Despite their doubts many Black men and women encouraged the mission and supported it—including Harriet Tubman, who, though not fulfilling Brown's desire for her to take part in the raid, did help recruit participants. The five African Americans among Brown's twenty-one men at Harpers Ferry were: Shields Green, a fugitive from South Carolina; Osborne Anderson, a printer from Chatham, Canada; Lewis Sheridan Leary, from Oberlin, Ohio; Leary's nephew, John Copeland, a student at Oberlin College; and Dangerfield Newby, a freedman from Virginia. Forty-four-year-old Newby, the oldest of the five, had personal reasons for participating in the raid. Newby hoped to free his wife, Harriet, and their six children, who were enslaved in Virginia near Harpers Ferry. In April Harriet had written to him begging that he come for them:

> It is said Master is in want of money. If so, I know not what time he may sell me, and then all my bright hopes of the future are blasted, for there has been one bright hope to cheer me in all my troubles, that is to be with you. If I thought I should never see you this earth would have no charms for me. Come this fall without fail money or no money. Do all you can for me, which I have no doubt you will. The children are all well. The baby cannot walk yet. You must write soon and say when you think you can come.[26]

John Brown stops to kiss a Black child on his way to his execution in this romanticized depiction from 1884.

Newby never reached his family. John Brown and his raiders were trapped by federal troops under the command of U.S. Colonel Robert E. Lee, and most of Brown's men, including Newby, were killed. Brown and four others, Copeland and Green among them, were captured, tried, convicted of treason, and sentenced to be hanged. Anderson escaped, while authorities sought other conspirators. A telegraph operator in Philadelphia warned Frederick Douglass three hours before delivering to the sheriff an order for Douglass's arrest. Douglass escaped to Canada and, near the end of November, sailed for England, where he would remain for six months. Several of Brown's financial backers also fled to Canada.[27]

The raid on Harpers Ferry shocked the South and confirmed southern beliefs that only a strong proslavery federal government could protect slavery from abolitionist aggression. Among African Americans, John Brown was a hero. In a letter to his wife, Mary, a group of Black women from New York called him "our honored and dearly-loved brother." On the day of Brown's execution, Black Americans in Cincinnati, Pittsburgh, Philadelphia, and New York mourned his death. Three thousand gathered in Boston's Joy Street Church to hear the formerly enslaved Reverend John Sella Martin condemn slavery and praise noble efforts to end that evil institution. A solemn crowd in Detroit listened to a message on "Brown's Christian Fortitude" and his devotion to antislavery and heard the Brown Liberty Singers offer a musical selection entitled "Ode to Old Capt. John Brown."[28]

Reaction to John Brown's raid and his martyrdom reflected the growing conviction among abolitionists that only violence would bring an end to slavery. One Black abolitionist from Boston, John Rock, expressed his certainty that "sooner or later, the clashing of arms will be heard in this country" and contended that "the black man's service will be needed . . . to strike a genuine blow for freedom [with a] power which white men 'will be bound to respect.'" In early December 1859 broadsides called Black Canadians to local meetings to consider ways to honor "Brown and his confederates . . . martyrs to the cause of Liberty," and Thomas Hamilton, editor of the *Weekly Anglo-African*, compared Brown's raid with Nat Turner's slave rebellion, the deadliest of nineteenth-century North America.[29]

Abraham Lincoln's Election and the War

By the end of the 1850s sectional considerations pervaded virtually every political decision in America, and all sectional considerations involved slavery either directly or indirectly. Confrontations grew more antagonistic, and violence reached even into the halls of Congress when a supporter of slavery attacked and beat Massachusetts senator Charles Sumner on the floor of the Senate chamber. Gun and knife fights broke out in the House of Representatives, and one congressman was killed by political rivals. In the presidential election year of 1860, sectional animosities split the Democratic Party between proslavery southerners who selected James G. Breckenridge of Kentucky as their standard bearer and northern Democrats who remained loyal to Stephen A. Douglas. Other southerners who refused to accept Breckenridge formed the Constitutional Union Party under the leadership of John Bell of Tennessee. Republicans nominated the politically moderate Abraham Lincoln as their presidential candidate.

African Americans continued to view Republicans as essentially the lesser of potential political evils. They found the Democratic proslavery position completely unacceptable, but they were also realistic about the shortcomings of the Republican Party. Black abolitionists had observed the Republican rush to denounce John Brown and disassociate themselves from his raid. They had angrily noted Massachusetts Republican Governor Nathaniel P. Banks's veto of legislation allowing Black Americans to enlist in the state militia. They knew that despite the Black support that had helped elect Republican Governor Edwin D. Morgan in New York, he had failed "to utter an antislavery sentence" during his annual message. Republicans had introduced a bill to repeal the Fugitive Slave Act, but it had failed when twelve Republicans voted against it and forty-three abstained. Further, in an effort to combat the "black Republican" label, some Republicans had declared themselves "a white man's party."[30]

Some Black leaders argued that the Republicans' pretense of friendship was more dangerous to African American rights than the Democrats' animosity. John Rock asserted that Republicans "[aimed] to place white men and white labor against black men and black labor" and thus were "no better than" the Democrats. Others considered Abraham Lincoln and his moderate wing of the Republican Party to be only Free-Soilers, not genuinely antislavery. Although Douglass and other Black leaders expressed their misgivings, African Americans in New York, Brooklyn, Boston, and several other northern cities formed Republican clubs, and the vast majority of Black voters cast their ballots for the victorious Lincoln.[31]

Lincoln's election precipitated a crisis. Before he could take office, South Carolina demanded that President Buchanan remove federal troops from the forts in Charleston Harbor and led the seven states of the lower South (South Carolina, Mississippi, Florida, Alabama, Georgia, Louisiana, and Texas) in declaring their withdrawal from the United States. On February 4, 1861, representatives from all the seceding states—except Texas, whose delegates arrived later—met at a constitutional convention in Montgomery, Alabama, to define the political structure of the **Confederate States of America**. Lincoln reacted cautiously during his first days in office, trying to hold on to the slave states of the Upper South. In his inaugural address he firmly opposed the right of states to withdraw from the federal union but pledged that he would not interfere with slavery, the institution that was the foundation of southern economic and social life. Attempted conciliation did not dissuade the states of the Confederacy, and war came on April 12, 1861, when Confederate batteries in Charleston Harbor opened fire on the federal Fort Sumter. Within days Lincoln issued a call for seventy-five thousand volunteers to put down the rebellion in South Carolina. Fearing a federal invasion that would threaten slavery, four states of the Upper South (Virginia, Arkansas, Tennessee, and North Carolina) withdrew from the United States, leaving Maryland, Delaware, Kentucky, and Missouri as the only slave states loyal to the U.S. government. Lincoln's increased need for federal troops was exacerbated by the fact that almost one-third of the nation's army officer corps, including important West Point–trained men, left to fight with the rebellion against the United States. During the first year of the war the U.S. Army expanded from just over sixteen thousand men to more than seven hundred thousand. Black

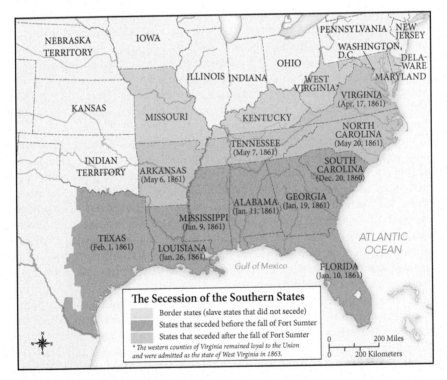

Map 7.2 The Secession of the Southern States

men volunteered immediately, but the federal government refused them, and not one of the new recruits were African American.[32]

African Americans in Washington, D.C., Pittsburgh, Boston, New York, and elsewhere, answered Lincoln's call. Through their military units and as individuals, they sent letters and petitions to the War Department expressing their eagerness to serve, but all their offers were rejected. Most white Americans and government officials, including Lincoln, questioned Black Americans' bravery. Many believed that formerly enslaved people in particular would be too submissive and cowardly to be good soldiers. One white corporal from a New York regiment bluntly summed up the general feeling among white recruits: "We don't want to fight side and side with the nigger. We think that we are a too superior race for that." Outraged Black leaders pointed to the fact that Black troops had served with distinction in the American Revolution and in the War of 1812. "Colored men were good enough . . . to help win American independence," Douglass noted angrily, "but they are not good enough to help preserve that independence against treason and rebellion." Why would the American government attempt to fight "rebels with only one hand?"[33]

Before the war many radical abolitionists had supported the idea of disunion—that is, withdrawing the free states from their union with slaveholders. Frederick Douglass had begun to reconsider when Lincoln's election had brought, as Douglass wrote, "at least an antislavery reputation to the Presidency." He was less hopeful, though, when Lincoln attempted to compromise with the South by proposing constitutional protections for slavery. "If the Union can only be maintained by new concessions to the slaveholders," Douglass had declared, "let the Union perish." Southern secession, however, changed abolition's prospects—southern slavery was no longer protected by the military might of the United States. Slave rebellion had a much better chance of success, and runaways might be safe in free states. Despite Abraham Lincoln's equivocation, African Americans agreed that the war ignited by the firing on Fort Sumter was "a war for and against slavery," and the United States could not win it without destroying slavery. Yet federal military commanders continued for two years to refuse the thousands of Black men who volunteered to be soldiers.[34]

The South recognized the value of Black participation in the Confederate war effort. Slave labor produced most of the food for the troops, and the Confederacy impressed free and enslaved Black men into service as laborers, teamsters, cooks, and servants to support southern troops. Despite their value to the southern war effort, however, U.S. commanders continued to return runaways to their southern owners. Recognizing the value of enslaved people to the Confederate war effort, early in the war General Benjamin Butler extended the definition of contraband of war—military goods shipped to a participant and liable to seizure by the other side. Since the South considered them property, he labeled three people who had escaped from Virginia to federal lines in Maryland as **contraband** that did not have to be returned to their owners. Within three months approximately nine hundred contrabands lived and worked with Butler's Massachusetts troops. The policy disputes this occasioned were finally resolved when Congress passed the Confiscation Act in August 1861. This act set people enslaved by Confederates free once they came under the control of federal forces, but it did not free those who might escape from slaveholders in states such as Delaware and Maryland, which had remained loyal to the United States. African Americans were insulted by the government's refusing their service, and many, like Henry Cropper of the Philadelphia Black military company, urged African Americans to maintain their dignity and self-respect by withdrawing their offer.[35]

Meanwhile the early years of the war brought enormous losses to the United States. At Shiloh, Tennessee, in April 1862, sixty-three thousand United States troops fought the largest battle in American history and suffered more than thirteen thousand casualties. The United States lost sixteen thousand dead, wounded, or missing two months later, during the Seven Days Battle in Virginia, and more than fourteen thousand at the Second Battle of Manassas. By early summer 1862 it was clear that this would not be a short and relatively painless war. In the face of such losses, and with support for the Confederacy said to be building in Britain and western Europe, Congress and the president decided to take desperate measures. In July Congress passed legislation allowing the president to enlist Black troops should he deem it "necessary and proper for the suppression of this rebellion." By November the first Black regiment had been raised, composed of men formerly enslaved in South Carolina who had been recruited after escaping to freedom within U.S. lines. Thomas Wentworth Higginson, a white abolitionist who had participated in a daring attempt by Black abolitionists to rescue a fugitive in Boston before the war, was appointed to command these troops. By year's end the First South Carolina was engaged in combat along the Georgia–Florida border. Witnessing their courage and ability, Higginson wrote, "Nobody knows anything about these men who has not seen them in battle. . . . No officer in this regiment now doubts that the key to the successful prosecution of this war lies in the unlimited employment of black troops."[36]

The Emancipation Proclamation and Black Soldiers

In the summer of 1862, Lincoln had announced his intention to strike directly at slavery in the South, to redirect and rejuvenate the war effort, to enlist northern antislavery sentiment, and to make it more difficult for the British and Europeans to support the Confederacy. The president was true to form; Lincoln's timing and words were cautious: a U.S. victory would precede the public announcement, and he would pursue his political and military purpose with the least disruption for slaveholders in loyal states. In September, General George McClellan, commander of the U.S. Army of the Potomac, defeated Confederate forces under Robert E. Lee at Antietam Creek in Sharpsburg, Maryland. Lincoln moved swiftly, and five days after the victory, on September 22, he made the preliminary announcement of his Emancipation Proclamation. As of January 1, 1863, all enslaved people in areas controlled by people in rebellion against the United States would be declared "forever free." The declaration of freedom did not apply to those held by people loyal to the United States or to those held by rebels who had been subdued before January 1, 1863. Though certainly a limited emancipation, it reinforced Congress's abolition of slavery in the District of Columbia the previous April and seemed to be part of an abolitionist trend.

African Americans had waited anxiously for the promised New Year's proclamation. They were not confident of Lincoln's commitment. He had denounced slavery but had protected it to secure southern loyalty to the United States before the war. He had finally enlisted Black men into the military but had promised emancipation only to those held by Confederates. In August 1862 he had been the first American president to invite a delegation of African Americans to meet with him at the White House, but he had told them that Black people were a burden on the nation and it would be better if they left the country and settled in Africa or the West Indies. Across the North, African Americans in small towns and large cities held mass meetings to await the proclamation. When it came, they broke into wild celebration, greeting it with singing, dancing, prayers, lofty rhetoric, and plain speaking about family and friends still in slavery. News of the proclamation came quickly to enslaved people in the East, but it took much longer to reach the West. When the U.S. Army finally informed people in Texas on June 19, 1865, after the war had ended, enslaved people seized their freedom and soon added June 19, called **Juneteenth**, to other African American freedom celebrations. Eventually, Juneteenth became the best-known freedom commemoration, celebrated well into the twenty-first century.[37]

Although it was a half-way measure, the Emancipation Proclamation transformed the war's purpose and made Lincoln the "Great Emancipator." The war's new moral objective and the dedication and success of Black soldiers influenced racial sentiment in the North. By late winter 1863, a second Black unit from South Carolina commanded by Colonel James Montgomery, had been formed, and in March some of Montgomery's and Higginson's African American troops captured and occupied the Confederate stronghold of Jacksonville, Florida. General David Hunter informed his superiors that his Black troops were "hardy, generous, temperate, strictly obedient, possessing remarkable aptitude for military training, and deeply imbued with that religious sentiment which made the soldiers of Oliver Cromwell invincible." He also wrote that he had detected the racist attitudes of many of the white soldiers who had come into contact with Black troops, "rapidly softening or fading out." Newspapers challenged racial bigots with the "facts" of "good conduct and gallant deeds of the men they persecute and slander." One white Illinois soldier who had voted Democratic before the war wrote to his wife, "So long as [my] flag is confronted by the hostile guns of slavery. . . I am as confirmed an abolitionist as ever was pelted with stale eggs." In the Eighty-sixth Indiana Regiment one officer reported that although many of his men had denounced what they called an "abolition war," by March 1863 they were expressing support for emancipation and for Black combat troops. An Indiana sergeant who admitted that he did not like free Black men declared himself in favor of the Emancipation Proclamation if it would end the war. A poll of one Iowa regiment showed that only one-quarter of the white soldiers opposed the proclamation, while half favored it, and the rest registered no opinion.[38]

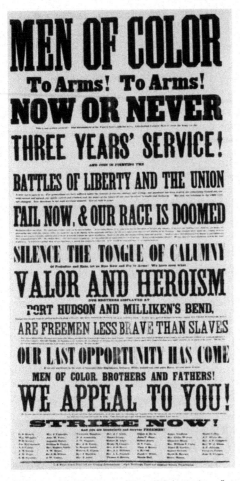

A recruitment poster urges "Men of Color to Arms."

There was still resistance to Black men's participation in the war, however. In Pennsylvania the governor refused to recruit them, and John Mercer Langston's offer to raise Black troops in Ohio met an icy response from Governor David Tod. "Do you know Mr. Langston," Tod asked, "that this is a white man's government; that white men are able to defend and protect it?" He continued, "When we want you colored men we will notify you." Yet, now that Lincoln had committed the nation to the cause of freedom and Congress had authorized raising Black troops, there seemed reason for optimism. In January 1863 Governor John A. Andrew of Massachusetts was authorized to form the Fifty-fourth Massachusetts Volunteers, the first Black military regiment recruited from the North. Governor Andrew, an abolitionist, placed Colonel Robert Gould Shaw, a young man from a prominent white abolitionist family, at its head. He also appointed several Black leaders, including Frederick Douglass, Charles Lenox Remond, Thomas Morris Chester, and Martin Delany, as recruiting agents, but the effort was slow at first. Many Black men were reluctant to join a force that had recently rejected their offers to serve. Chester presided over a meeting in Harrisburg, Pennsylvania, where Black men demanded a guarantee of fair treatment. If they were to serve, it must be with dignity and equality. Although most state and local officials accepted Black military assistance only under the most dire circumstances, by April, thirty or forty men a day were enlisting in the Massachusetts Fifty-fourth.[39]

African Americans who enlisted were refused positions as officers, and Black men in uniform risked being attacked and harassed by northern white people. A white gang and policemen attacked Corporal John Ross in the streets of Washington, D.C., in the summer of 1863, and one police officer explained that he would shoot a "nigger recruit" as easily as he would a mad dog. The greatest insult Black soldiers faced, however, came from the Confederacy.

In May, the Confederate congress resolved that any Black U.S. troops captured would be killed or enslaved, not treated as prisoners of war. White officers leading Black troops were to be treated as criminals and might be executed. Chester gave up his recruiting efforts in disgust and left the United States for Britain in the fall of 1863, but African Americans continued to enlist despite the injustices they faced.[40]

As an added insult, Black troops were expected to serve for inferior pay. Initially, the War Department pledged equal pay, and the first recruits enlisted with that understanding. But until 1864, when Congress actually authorized equal pay, Black troops were paid at a rate less than half that paid to white soldiers. A white private was paid thirteen dollars per month plus a uniform allowance, and a regimental sergeant received twenty-one dollars per month plus allowances, while Black men at all non-commissioned ranks earned only ten dollars per month, from which three dollars were subtracted for uniforms. Black soldiers, their families, and many of their white officers complained bitterly, pointing out that soldiers could not provide for their families on this substandard pay. Black civilians employed by the military could earn as much as twenty-five dollars per month. Some Black soldiers' wives and children were forced into poorhouses while their men were defending the country. Some Black men refused to serve without full pay, some requested discharges so they could support their families, and others served without pay rather than accept inferior pay. For more than a year almost all of the Fifty-fourth Massachusetts refused to accept unequal pay. Protest was widespread, with Black regiments from Michigan, Kansas, Rhode Island, and South Carolina joining in. The Black women of Boston held fairs to raise money and gather supplies for soldiers' families. Black soldiers resented both the pay differential and the symbolic refusal to recognize their role as soldiers that it represented: it was about more than money. "To say we are not soldiers [even if they paid] us $20 would be injustice," wrote one Black corporal from the Fifty-fourth Massachusetts, "for it would rob a whole race of their title to a manhood." Pay inequities rooted in practicality and prejudice were not easy to change. One white New Yorker expressed the prevailing sentiment: "[I]t is unjust in every way to the white soldier to put him on a level with the Black." Black protest met a swift military response. In the fall of 1863, when one company of the Third South Carolina Volunteers, led by Sergeant William Walker, refused to perform their duties until they were properly paid, the army charged the entire company with mutiny and executed Sergeant Walker.[41]

Although not admitted as soldiers, Black women also served the war effort. *Provincial Freeman* editor Mary Ann Shadd Cary moved from Canada to Indiana during the war to help in Black recruitment. Harriet Tubman, the famous Underground Railroad conductor, expanded her activities to include recruiting, cooking, nursing, spying for the government, and leading a band of scouts, often behind enemy lines. In March 1863 she helped plan and lead an expedition that brought from seven hundred to eight hundred people out of slavery. Thousands of other Black women did everything from camp chores to taking up arms when circumstances warranted. **Susie King Taylor**, born into slavery in Georgia, worked as a teacher of freed people and as a nurse during the war. She spent part

Susie King Taylor (1848–1912)

Susie King Taylor, Civil War nurse.

Susie King was born in slavery on an island off the coast of Georgia and from age seven lived with her grandmother in Savannah. She learned to read and write at a school secretly taught by free Black women. She was fourteen years old at the beginning of the Civil War, when enslaved people in her area came under the protection of federal troops. She later married the formerly enslaved Edward King, a sergeant in the U.S. First South Carolina Volunteers, and worked for the regiment as a volunteer laundress, nurse, and teacher. She eventually settled in Boston, did veterans' relief work, and published her memoir.

My great-great-grandmother was 120 years old when she died. She had seven children, and five of her boys were in the Revolutionary War. She was from Virginia, and was half Indian. . . . My great-grandmother . . . was one hundred years old when she died. . . . She was the mother of twenty-four children, twenty-three being girls. She was one of the noted midwives of her day. . . .

After I had been on St. Simon's [Island] about three days . . . Commodore Goldsborough . . . wished me to take charge of a school for the children on the island. I told him I would gladly do so, if I could have some books. . . . and in a week or two I received two large boxes of books and testaments from the North. I had about forty children to teach, beside a number of adults who came to me nights, all of them so eager to learn to read, to read above anything else. Chaplain French, of Boston, would come to the school, sometimes, and lecture to the pupils on Boston and the North. . . .

[Beaufort, S.C.] On the first of January, 1863, we held services for the purpose of listening to the reading of President Lincoln's proclamation by Dr. W. H. Brisbane, and the presentation of two beautiful stands of colors, one from a lady in Connecticut. . . . It was a glorious day for us all, and we enjoyed every minute of it, and as a fitting close and the crowning event of this occasion we had a grand barbecue. . . . The soldiers had a good time. They sang or shouted "Hurrah!" all through the camp, and seemed overflowing with fun and frolic until taps were sounded, when many, no doubt, dreamt of this memorable day. . . .

I learned to handle a musket very well while in the regiment, and could shoot straight and often hit the target. I assisted in cleaning the guns and used to fire them off, to see if the cartridges were dry, before cleaning and reloading, each day. I thought this great fun. I was also able to take a gun all apart, and put it together again. . . . I taught a great many of the comrades in Company E to read and write, when they were off duty. Nearly all were anxious to learn. My husband taught some also when it was convenient for him. . . . I gave my services willingly for four years and three months without receiving a dollar. I was glad, however, to be allowed to go with the regiment, to care for the sick and afflicted comrades. . . .

On February 28, 1865, the remainder of the regiment were ordered to Charleston, as there were signs of the rebels evacuating that city. Leaving Cole Island, we arrived in Charleston between nine and ten o'clock in the morning, and found the "rebs" had set fire to the city and fled, leaving women and children behind to suffer and perish in the flames. The fire had been burning fiercely for a day and night. When we landed, under a flag of truce, our regiment went to work assisting the citizens in subduing the flames. It was a terrible scene. For three or four days the men fought the fire, saving the property and effects of the people, yet these white men and women could not tolerate our black Union soldiers, for many of them had formerly been their slaves; and although these brave men risked life and limb to assist them in their distress, men and even women would sneer and molest them whenever they met them. . . .

At the close of the war, my husband and I returned to Savannah. . . . A new life was before us now, all the old life left behind. After getting settled, I opened a school at my home . . . as there was not any public school for negro children. I had twenty children at my school, and received one dollar a month for each pupil, I also had a few older ones who came at night. . . . On September 16, 1866, my husband, Sergeant King, died, leaving me soon to welcome a little stranger alone. He was a boss carpenter, but being just mustered out of the army, and the prejudice against his race being still too strong to insure him much work at his trade, he took contracts for unloading vessels, and hired a number of men to assist him. He was much respected by the citizens, and was a general favorite with his associates.

Source: Susie King Taylor, *Reminiscences of My Life in Camp With the 33d United States Colored Troops, Late 1st S.C. Volunteers* (Boston, 1902), 1, 21, 26, 42, 54.

of her time with her husband's unit, the First South Carolina Volunteers, doing the laundry and learning to handle a gun.[42]

Men, women, and children flocked to the Union lines to escape slavery as the U.S. Army moved through the South. Commanders quickly learned that Black enlistees were far more willing to serve if the army guaranteed the protection of their families, and small shanty settlements of civilians sprang up on the fringes of military camps. The wives of Black soldiers often did cooking and laundry for the officers, and although this allowed Black women to be close to their husbands, it posed problems as well. White men in authority generally regarded Black women as inferior and fair game for sexual exploitation. At one camp the harassment was so bad that a Black soldier complained, "We have a set of officers here who apparently think that their commissions are license to debauch and mingle with deluded freedwomen, under cover of darkness."[43]

About 29,000 Black sailors (about one-quarter of the navy) and more than 186,000 African American soldiers, in 166 Black regiments, fought for the United States during the Civil War. One in every five Black adult males in the entire country served in the U.S. forces, constituting one-tenth of the nation's military force. About half those who served were formerly enslaved. In battle Black troops were often given the most dangerous jobs. Coupled with the Confederate treatment of captives, this resulted in a casualty rate for African American soldiers that was roughly twice that of white troops. Despite their sacrifices and their service in previous wars, Black troops were continually challenged to prove

Charge of the Fifty-fourth Massachusetts Colored Regiment on Fort Wagner, South Carolina, July 1863.

their courage and capability in battle. African Americans fought their first major Civil War battle at Port Hudson, Louisiana, in May 1863. The First and Third Louisiana regiments, a Native Guard composed of free, educated, affluent Black men from New Orleans, advanced under the command of Black officers who gave orders in both English and French. Seven successive charges on Confederate fortifications left one of every five Black soldiers dead or wounded. The siege by white and Black regiments lasted for forty-eight days, and the United States lost nearly ten thousand men. Witnesses were effusive in their praise of the Black troops. "No regiment behaved better than they did," reported one white officer. "Nobly indeed, they have acquitted themselves," read the *New York Times*, and poet George H. Boker commemorated their heroism with a verse distributed in English and German.[44]

About the same time, two regiments of African Americans beat back a Confederate attack at Milliken's Bend on the Mississippi River near Vicksburg. At one point, 840 Black soldiers and 160 white soldiers defended the U.S. position against almost two thousand Confederates. The Confederate advance pushed U.S. forces to the edge of the river, and Confederates summarily executed captured Black troops. Finally, with the arrival of a gunboat, the U.S. forces made a desperate stand, with soldiers using their rifles as clubs in hand-to-hand combat. Even the defeated Confederates praised this predominately Black force, and one U.S. officer declared that "[b]y their coolness and determination in battle," Black men had moved themselves into "high standing as soldiers." Finally that summer, the famous assault by the Fifty-fourth Massachusetts at Fort Wagner in Charleston Harbor brought further proof of Black valor. They suffered enormous losses in this futile attack on the Confederate stronghold, but they fought with courage and skill. Leading the charge, Colonel Shaw fell on the ramparts and was killed. For his part in the attack, Sergeant William H. Carney received the Congressional Medal of Honor, and the *New York Tribune* praised the Fifty-fourth's performance in this "test of black troops." The *Tribune*—apparently ignorant of the Black soldiers who had fought in that famous Revolutionary War

Sergeant W.H. Carney, Company C, Fifty-fourth Massachusetts Colored Regiment, awarded the Congressional Medal of Honor.

battle—compared the bravery of the Fifty-fourth at Fort Wagner to the courage of white troops at the battle of Bunker Hill. Harriet Tubman poignantly described the battle from her vantage point at a camp about a mile away:

> And then we saw the lightning,
> and that was the guns;
> and then we heard the thunder,
> and that was the big guns;
> and then we heard the rain falling,
> and that was the drops of blood falling;
> and when we came to get in the crops,
> it was the dead that we reaped.[45]

By the end of the summer of 1863, Abraham Lincoln was convinced of the value of enlisting Black troops and urged General Ulysses S. Grant to increase enlistments, saying, "I believe [they are] a resource which, if vigorously applied now, will soon close the contest." Finally, the federal government had acceded to Black demands that African Americans be relied on to strike a blow for freedom.[46]

Who, What, Where

Blackface minstrel shows p. 180	Harpers Ferry p. 183
Bleeding Kansas p. 180	Juneteenth p. 189
John Brown p. 180	Kansas-Nebraska Act p. 179
Anthony Burns p. 175	League of Gileadites p. 175
Confederate States of America p. 186	popular sovereignty p. 179
contraband p. 187	Republican Party p.180
Free-Soilers p. 180	Dred Scott p. 181
Fugitive Slave Law of 1850 p. 172	Harriet Beecher Stowe p. 177
Margaret Garner p. 175	Susie King Taylor p. 191

REVIEW QUESTIONS

7.1 How did African Americans react to the Fugitive Slave Law?

7.2 In what ways did African American resistance to slavery evolve during the 1850s?

7.3 How did the Dred Scott decision affect opponents of slavery?

7.4 What were the motives for African Americans to join John Brown and to support militant abolitionism?

7.5 Why did African Americans have a complex relationship with the Republican Party? Why did Lincoln issue the Emancipation Proclamation, and how did this change the nature of the war?

7.6 How were Black Union soldiers treated differently than white Union soldiers?

For additional digital learning resources please go to **https://www.oup.com/he/horton1e**

From Reconstruction to Jim Crow

A print celebrating the ratification of the Fifteenth Amendment in February 1870.

CHAPTER OUTLINE

The War's End and Lincoln's Assassination

8.1 Understand the impact of Lincoln's changing views on race and equality on Black Americans.

Aid for Freed People

8.2 Summarize the various types of aid that freed people received after the war and analyze their effectiveness.

Black Politics and Black Politicians

8.3 Appraise the impact Black voters had on the South during Radical Reconstruction.

Progress and White Terrorist Backlash

8.4 Describe the methods and intentions of various white terrorist organizations that arose during Reconstruction.

Emigration from the South

8.5 Understand the reasons that many newly freed people chose to emigrate from the South.

Legalized Racial Control

8.6 Appraise how the resurgence of Democratic control in the South led to racial discrimination and segregation. Understand the consequences of *Plessy v. Ferguson* for Black Americans.

THOMAS MORRIS CHESTER was born in 1834 in Harrisburg, Pennsylvania, to a mother who had escaped slavery in Baltimore, Maryland, and a father, a restaurateur, who was the local agent for the *Liberator*. As a young man Chester became discouraged about the prospects for Black citizenship and joined the **African Colonization Society**, condemned by many African Americans as a "vicious" and "nefarious" plot to "drain the country of the most enlightened part of our colored brethren." He argued that emigration to Africa was a practical alternative to racial injustice in America and emigrated to Liberia, where he worked as a teacher and a newspaper editor for ten years.[1]

The promise of Black military involvement in the war, however, convinced Chester to return to live in the United States. He led African Americans in Harrisburg in demanding full citizenship rights in return for service, was a recruiter for the Fifty-fifth Massachusetts Regiment in the spring of 1863, and became the captain of a state militia company formed to defend the city from possible Confederate attack. Disturbed by the limits the government placed on African Americans' participation in the war and by their unequal pay, Chester set off for Britain late that year in the vain hope of finding a way to finance training in law, working as an antislavery speaker and advocate for the U.S. cause. Upon his return to the United States in 1864, he took the influential and dangerous position as war correspondent for the *Philadelphia Press*. From Virginia and North Carolina, he wrote candid and dramatic accounts of the Black troops, providing abundant evidence of their courage and honor in battle and reminding his readers that Black fighting men suffered special hardships. Except in a few special cases in which Black doctors and ministers became officers late in the war, African Americans remained restricted to the enlisted ranks. They endured racial injustice, even from some of their own white officers. Chester's reports condemned those "wrongs which . . . exhibit a disgraceful depth of depravity, practiced by dishonest men, in the name of the Government."[2]

Perhaps Chester's news stories contributed to a change in public sentiment and influenced federal legislators: in June 1864, Congress passed a law equalizing pay, arms, equipment, and medical services for Black troops, though the new pay rate was made retroactive only to January 1, 1864. However, Black troops still faced special hazards. Southern commanders took few Black prisoners and executed many of those they did take. At **Fort Pillow**, Tennessee, in the spring of 1864, Confederate forces commanded by General Nathan Bedford Forrest murdered hundreds of captured U.S. troops, about half of whom were African Americans. Reportedly Forrest, whose short

Timeline

Chapter 8

1861
Port Royal Experiment begins on coastal island in South Carolina occupied by U.S. troops.

1864
Fort Pillow Massacre

1865
President Abraham Lincoln assassinated; Vice President Andrew Johnson, a Democrat, succeeds him; Confederate forces surrender; slavery is abolished by the Thirteenth Amendment. Congress establishes the Freedmen's Bureau.

1866
Congress passes Civil Rights Bill; Congress passes the Fourteenth Amendment, removing racial restrictions on U.S. citizenship; Ku Klux Klan formed in Pulaski, Tennessee; Fisk University founded.

1867
Howard University, Morehouse College, and Morgan State University founded.

1868
President Johnson is impeached by U.S. House of Representatives, but Senate fails to muster votes needed to remove him.

1868
Fourteenth Amendment is ratified, promising citizenship to all people born or naturalized in the U.S. and equal protection of the laws to everyone in the nation;

temper was well known to his men, had been angered by the fort's refusal to surrender and was further incensed by the taunts of Black soldiers. The Confederates, with more than twice as many men, overran the garrison and then conducted a bloody massacre. Although some Confederate soldiers were reluctant to indulge in the carnage, Forrest "ordered [the captured U.S. troops] shot down like dogs." "Kill the last damned one of them," Forrest reportedly demanded, and his men complied,

Confederate soldiers slaughtering African American Union soldiers at Fort Pillow, Tennessee, in April 1864.

clubbing the wounded to death, burning some alive, and nailing others to walls. Many of the victims ran into the river but were shot before they could escape, "their heads presenting 'beautiful' targets." At one point the killing was so furious that even Forrest seemed to have had second thoughts, as one of his men wrote that "if General Forrest had not run between our men and the Yanks with his pistol and sabre drawn not a man would have been spared." Later Forrest observed that "the river was dyed with the blood of the slaughtered for 200 yards." Chester called the Confederate atrocities at Fort Pillow "evidence of Southern barbarism and inhumanity," and northern newspapers carried outraged headlines of the "Fort Pillow Massacre." *The New York Tribune* referred to Forrest, who had been a slave trader before the war and would be one of the organizers of the Ku Klux Klan after it, as "BUTCHER FORREST." Less

John W. Menard of Louisiana becomes first African American elected to Congress.

1870

Hiram Rhodes Revels becomes the first African American U.S. senator; Fifteenth Amendment to the Constitution is ratified, removing racial restrictions on voting.

1872

Most ex-Confederates pardoned by U.S. General Amnesty Act.

1875

Congress passes Civil Rights Bill, pledging equal access to public accommodations regardless of race.

1877

Last occupying federal troops withdrawn from the South.

1880

Thousands of Black "exodusters" migrate from the South to Kansas.

1883

U.S. Supreme Court declares Civil Rights Law of 1875 unconstitutional.

1896

In *Plessy v. Ferguson*, U.S. Supreme Court declares "separate but equal" public facilities to be constitutional.

than a week after the massacre, twelve hundred Black troops in Memphis fell on their knees to take a solemn oath of revenge. "Remember Fort Pillow" became their rallying cry.[3]

The War's End and Lincoln's Assassination

By the summer of 1864 the tide of the war had turned. U.S. military victories in Atlanta and in Virginia's Shenandoah Valley made the Democrats' contention that the war should be abandoned less convincing, and northern acceptance of the Emancipation Proclamation and federal recruitment policies contributed to Lincoln's re-election that fall. Eighty percent of the federal army voted for him, and those African Americans who could vote gave him their overwhelming support. By the time Abraham Lincoln delivered his second inaugural address in January, the conflict was almost over. Confederate desertions were high and increasing; southern soldiers were low on ammunition, food, shoes, and other vital supplies. They were losing the hope of victory, and some wives and other family members suffering hardships at home encouraged their men to desert. Many poor white southerners questioned the disproportionate sacrifices they were making in what they began to consider a rich man's struggle to maintain a rich man's privilege.[4]

A desperate situation called for desperate measures, and Confederate army officers with the support of their commander, Robert E. Lee, proposed the recruitment of enslaved men into the southern military. As Richmond was increasingly threatened by U.S. troops, Virginia's governor lobbied for the conscription of Black soldiers. One staunch slavery supporter contended that all the slaveholders he knew would support giving freedom to enslaved men who would fight in the military. A bill to that effect was hotly debated in the Confederate Congress, and reaction was intense. Although enlisted men generally supported the measure, one southern soldier spoke for many. He wrote to his mother saying that he was considering deserting the Confederate army because "I did not volunteer my services to fight for a free Negroes country but to fight for a free white mans country & I do not think I love my country well enough to fight with black soldiers." Nevertheless, the bill authorizing the recruitment of three hundred thousand enslaved men to serve the South narrowly passed and became law in the Confederacy on March 13, 1865, three weeks before the war's end. Ironically, the slaveholders who had claimed that the enslaved did not desire freedom offered them freedom in return for their fighting in the war to maintain slavery. In the end, the Confederate recruitment of Black men was a failure. Enslaved men constituted two small companies of hospital workers and forty to sixty trainees, none of whom saw combat. Even had these enslaved men fought, they would have been a tiny token force among about one million total Confederate soldiers, but the war was over before they were sent into combat.[5]

The Confederate capital at Richmond fell in early April 1865 to a U.S. force including five thousand Black infantry and eighteen hundred Black cavalrymen. In Boston, Frederick Douglass told an audience gathered at Faneuil Hall that the occupation of Richmond meant "the fall of the rebellion" and the start of "the upbuilding of liberty through the Southern States." Most African Americans agreed, especially those in the South, roughly 40 percent of the region's population. As Jefferson Davis and his political entourage withdrew, white southerners in Richmond were near panic. One Richmonder captured their mood on the night of the evacuation: "We walked the streets like lost spirits 'til nearly daybreak." Robert Lumpkin, a well-known local slave dealer, tried to remove his human property before the U.S. troops arrived. Unsuccessful, he returned them to the holding pens known locally as Lumpkin's jail. There he spent the night with a Black woman who was his property, the mother of his two children, and soon to be his wife.[6]

Although conditions were changing rapidly and African American hopes were high, indignities remained. Black troops had led the advance on Richmond, but their white commanders ordered them halted to allow white troops to overtake them and enter the city first. "History will show," wrote the editor of Philadelphia's *Christian Recorder*, "that [the Black troops] were in the suburbs of Richmond long before the white soldiers, and but for the untimely and unfair order to halt, would have triumphantly planted their banner first upon the battlements of the capital of 'ye greate confederacie.'" Black soldiers deeply resented being denied the opportunity to lead the conquering forces into the Confederate capital. They understood the symbolism of being first to "tear down Jeff. Davis' nest." Nonetheless Black soldiers, some of whom had been enslaved in Virginia and were coming home to liberate their people, took great pride in being part of the occupying force. Garland White had escaped from slavery in Virginia and settled in Ohio before the war. Upon his return as chaplain with the Twenty-eighth U.S. Colored Troops, he addressed the large crowd, "one huge sea [of] black faces" filling the street. Thomas Morris Chester noted the enthusiasm and pride of the city's Black population as they watched African American soldiers march through the streets of Richmond. Amid much congratulatory handshaking and backslapping, they sang out boldly, "Richmond town is burning down, High diddle diddle inctum inctum ah." Black women, and some white women too, raided Confederate food supplies, seizing flour, coffee, sugar, and whatever they could find. President Lincoln, a master of symbolic expression, walked the streets of Richmond a few days later. After greeting Black soldiers and civilians, he entered the Confederate White House and sat in Jefferson Davis's chair.[7]

Lincoln returned to Washington on April 9, and on that same day, the southern forces under Robert E. Lee surrendered to General U.S. Grant at Appomattox Court House. By the time of their surrender, the Confederate forces had lost more than a quarter of a million men to death from combat, accident, or disease. The southern economy was devastated, its money was worthless, and it had lost much of its slave property. The federal forces lost more than three hundred seventy thousand of their total force of about two million. Of those who died, thirty-seven thousand were Black men, of a total of approximately one hundred ninety thousand who served. Two days after Lee's surrender, Lincoln made a public speech outlining the pressing postwar and post-emancipation problems that faced the United States government and the American people. He spoke of molding a new government in the South from the "disorganized and discordant elements" of "Jefferson Davis's fugitive government," and of providing the vote to literate Black men and Black veterans. Among those listening to Lincoln's speech was John Wilkes Booth, an actor, a southerner, and a believer in the Confederate cause. Booth was furious at the Confederacy's defeat, and doubly furious that Lincoln now seemed to embrace the Radical Republican stand on race. "That means nigger citizenship," Booth believed, and he told a friend, "That is the last speech [Lincoln] will ever make."[8]

That was no idle threat. On the evening of April 14, the Lincolns were watching a play at Ford's Theater in Washington when Booth suddenly appeared at the rear of the presidential box, aimed, and shot the president. Abraham Lincoln died at 7:22 the next morning, the first president in American history to be assassinated. Most African Americans felt Lincoln's death as a personal loss. Even though the *Emancipation Proclamation* had been more a military and political document than a humanitarian act, it had great symbolic significance, and formerly enslaved people had come to see Lincoln as their friend and ally. The Twenty-second Regiment of African American troops took their stations along Pennsylvania Avenue as the president's funeral precession moved from the White House to the Capitol. Thousands of Black people lined the railroad tracks as the funeral train returned Lincoln's body to his hometown of Springfield, Illinois. Soon after the funeral, the Twenty-second Regiment joined the search for Booth. Frederick Douglass recalled the tragedy "as a personal as well as a national calamity; on account of the race to which I belong and the deep interest which that good man ever took in its elevation."[9]

Lincoln had led the nation through its greatest crisis. He had come to appreciate the value of Black men's service during the war, had publicly acknowledged their role in winning the war, and had even cautiously suggested in private to the governor of Louisiana that in some of the states "the very intelligent [newly freed Black men] and especially those who fought gallantly in our ranks" might be enfranchised. Lincoln was certainly not an unequivocal supporter of African American civil rights, but this did represent a change from his stand in the 1850s, when he had questioned the federal government's power to secure emancipation, and from his willingness in 1860 to support the constitutional protection of southern slavery. It is impossible to know what Lincoln's postwar policies might have been. He had not

Champions of Liberty (1865) print produced following Lincoln's assassination, depicting his elevation in status to match that of the nation's revered first president.

totally abandoned the possibility of colonization in Africa or the West Indies, but he had proved himself able to learn from experience and to take advantage of changing conditions. Furthermore, he seemed open to arguments for racial justice, something that could not be said of his successor, Vice President Andrew Johnson, a former Democrat from Tennessee. Johnson's presidency was short-lived and highly contentious, coming as it did at this critical moment for African Americans and the nation.[10]

Aid for Freed People

The most immediate problems facing the nation were food and labor shortages in the South. Mounting numbers of freed people were walking off plantations with little more than what they wore or could carry. Many white southern workers and small farmers had been ruined by the war; their jobs were gone and their farms were destroyed. The sheer magnitude of human need threatened to overwhelm the resources of the U.S. Army and the federal government. Initially during the war, private groups had taken on much of the relief work, feeding, clothing, counseling, and providing education to freed Black and poor white people. Many Black soldiers, too, learned to read and write in schools established by these private charities in the occupied South. One of the most successful social welfare projects, the **Port Royal Experiment**, was begun early in the war on an island off the coast of South Carolina. In November 1861, planters fled, U.S. troops occupied the coastal islands, and ten thousand enslaved laborers on 195 plantations were suddenly free. Beginning the following spring, thousands of abolitionist teachers, missionaries, medical professionals, and legal advisors, both Black and white, came from New England, New York, and Pennsylvania to aid the freed people.[11]

Many freed people enthusiastically welcomed those who traveled south to assist their transition from slavery to freedom. Medical needs and a thirst for education brought freedmen of all ages flocking to the northern reformers, who established hospitals, welfare centers, and schools. Enslaved people had been denied access to learning, and in most places in the South it had been illegal for them to acquire even a rudimentary education. Now that slavery was over, many Black people were determined to get an education, viewing learning as a symbol of freedom. Parents wanted to learn to read and write, and they sought more extensive instruction for their children. The large numbers of enthusiastic students gratified and overwhelmed the teachers. Many conservative white southerners found the prospect of education for formerly enslaved people both ridiculous and disturbing. As throngs of African Americans of all ages flocked to the schoolhouse, one white man in Louisiana remarked, "I have seen many an absurdity in my lifetime, but this is the climax of absurdities." Others feared that educated Black Americans might challenge the traditional system of white supremacy. They were right to be concerned, for African Americans generally saw acquiring an education as both a racial responsibility and a means to racial equality. "I'm going to school now to try to learn something which I hope will enable me to be of some use to my race," explained one young Black man in

Augusta, Georgia. "The Lord has sent us books and teachers," he continued, "we must not hesitate a moment, but go on and learn all we can."[12]

Freed people found Black teachers especially inspiring. Charlotte Forten, the twenty-five-year-old granddaughter of James Forten, Black abolitionist and wealthy Philadelphia sailmaker, was among the zealous reformers who took the first tentative steps toward postwar Reconstruction at Port Royal. Forten taught school, nursed wounded soldiers, counseled freed people on legal and political matters, and played the piano for their entertainment. Some abolitionists, such as Laura Towne, fervent white Garrisonian from Philadelphia, became part of the community. Reformers continued to serve the Black population of the sea islands for almost forty years. Their devotion saved lives and educated thousands, and their letters to northern friends and colleagues gained enthusiastic support and assistance for their work. Their efforts also encouraged public backing, which came in March 1865 when the Congress established the Bureau of Refugees, Freedmen, and Abandoned Lands, known simply as the Freedmen's Bureau, in the War Department.

The **Freedmen's Bureau** expanded the work of private charities both programmatically and geographically, opening local offices to extend aid to freed Black and poor white people throughout the South. The Freedmen's Bureau issued thirteen million food rations of corn meal, flour, and sugar during its first fifteen months. It oversaw thousands of schools and helped formerly enslaved workers negotiate labor contracts, legalize marriages, and become taxpayers, voters, business operators, and landowners. Freedmen's Bureau officials took complaints from freed people who were victimized by former slaveholders, negotiated with white people, and tried to resolve community and family conflicts among Black people.[13]

With limited resources and unreliable political support, the Freedman's Bureau attempted to reconstruct the social system as well as the southern economic and political system. This involved many difficulties and uncertainties. Most Black people had definite ideas about the meaning of freedom, and at least in the short run, it meant being freed from the place they had been bound to by slavery. For many the first priority was reuniting with family members from whom they had been separated or trying to find family members who had

The Freedmen's Bureau by A.R. Waud (1868) A Freedman's Bureau agent, wreathed in the American flag, stands between an angry mob of white men and armed black freedmen.

been sold away during slavery. People walked hundreds of miles, questioned people from the areas where their relatives were last known to reside, and followed rumors of loved ones to distant places, hoping to reunite their families. Black newspapers for at least the next forty years carried pleas for information about lost family members. Such ads appeared in the *Colored Tennesseean* on August 12, 1865, and in the *Anglo-African* on August 19, 1865:

> Information Wanted, of Caroline Dodson, who was sold from Nashville, Nov. 1st, 1862, by James Lumsden to Warwick, (a trader then in human beings), who carried her to Atlanta, Georgia, and she was last heard of in the slave pen of Robert Clarke, (human trader in that place), from which she was sold. Any information of her whereabouts will be thankfully received and rewarded by her mother. Lucinda Lowery, Nashville.[14]

> Andrew Dennis and Richard Dennis, generally called Dick. When last heard from some six years ago they resided in Georgia. It is supposed they joined the Union Army. Their mother, brother George and sister Cecelia are residing in San Francisco and wish information respecting them.

> Mrs. Thos. L. Johnson who was sold away from Georgetown, D.C., when quite a child and who, at the breaking out of the war, was taken to Richmond, is very desirous of finding her father, Joseph Thompson, who for many years was a gardener in and around Washington.[15]

Some planters lamented the "disloyalty" of people they had formerly enslaved, whom they saw as "deserting" the plantation when their labor was desperately needed. Some U.S. Army officers observed that multitudes of Black people were wandering the roads as "vagabonds," confirming white fears that freed people would become an idle, vagrant people who would only work if compelled. Under these circumstances the Freedman's Bureau was under great pressure from southern planters and northern textile manufacturers to stabilize the southern work force, reverse the flow of former laborers from plantations to southern cities, and rebuild the agricultural system. Thus, bureau officials expended a great deal of effort persuading freed people to sign labor contracts with planters, often their former owners.

Many freed people asserted that generations of forced unpaid labor had earned them the right to possess the land they had worked. At war's end there were a few politicians and military men, such as General Rufus Saxton, head of the Freedmen's Bureau in South Carolina, Georgia, and Florida, who urged that freed people be provided with small farms carved from the tens of thousands of acres Confederate planters had abandoned. This would have established an independent class of African Americans and the foundation for a Black southern economy less dependent on the largess of the federal government or the southern white patronage. Black Americans understood how important land ownership was—for them, as for most Americans, it represented stability, independence, and opportunities for the future. As one freedman from Mississippi confided, "all I wants is to git to own fo' or five acres [of] land [that] I can build me a little house on and call my home." "Gib us our own land and we take care ourselves," one freedman explained, "but without land, de ole massas can hire us or starve us, as dey please." A song, sung to fugitives by Harriet Tubman during the Civil War, expressed the expectations of the formerly enslaved. "Come along! Come along! don't be alarmed, Uncle Sam is rich enough to give you all a farm." National wealth notwithstanding, none but the most radical Republicans considered permanently redistributing confiscated Confederate land to freedmen. Senator Charles Sumner from Massachusetts proposed legislation to provide homesteads to freed people, but even his colleague from the same state, fellow radical Henry Wilson, would not support it. Wilson argued that passing the measure would show special favor to Black people, to which Sumner replied that slavery had already placed Black Americans in a uniquely unfavorable position. In the House of Representatives, Pennsylvania's Thaddeus Stevens introduced a bill calling for the distribution of forty acres of confiscated land to freed people, but there too most members opposed it. The strength of southern opposition to which Congress acquiesced extended even to selling land to African Americans, as was reported by Whitelaw Reid shortly after the war:

> The feeling against any ownership of the soil by Negroes is so strong [among white people] that the man who should sell small tracts to them would be in actual personal danger. Every effort will be made to prevent Negroes from acquiring land; even the renting of small tracts to them is held to be unpatriotic and unworthy of a good citizen.[16]

Andrew Johnson, the new president, was even more resistant than Congress to the idea of redistributing land to Black Americans. Johnson had controlled the process of reconstruction in the months immediately after Lincoln's assassination and had proven himself willing to concede power to the defeated Confederates. Former slaveholders asserted their authority over the formerly enslaved with special state laws called "black codes," based on the old slave codes and vagrancy laws. Although these laws recognized Black Americans' rights to legally marry, use the courts, and own property, they also limited their economic and political opportunities and civil rights. Racially discriminatory vagrancy laws restricted Black people's movements and reduced Black workers to near-slavery conditions. Under Mississippi's harsh black codes, for example, unemployed Black people and those unlawfully assembled, or white individuals associating with them, were subject to fines and imprisonment. If Black people could not pay the fine, they would be hired out to someone who could pay. Leaving before the fulfillment of a labor contract without good cause carried forfeiture of the year's wages and return to the employer. Additionally, interracial marriage was penalized by life in prison. Congress was so outraged by this apparent attempt by former slave owners to continue slavery under the name of freedom that moderate Republicans united with radicals to wrest control from the president and institute a more liberal congressional reconstruction, sometimes called

Radical Reconstruction. Before the war, education for enslaved people had been illegal, and even free Black people had played almost no role in southern politics. Now Radical Reconstruction extended education for African Americans, protected Black voting rights, and encouraged Black Americans to hold political office. Yet, most African Americans remained landless, and the few Black people who had been settled on confiscated land soon found themselves dispossessed. Hopes that the government would deliver forty acres and a mule were dashed on hard political reality. Congress voted to return almost all Confederate land to prewar owners, leaving the economic power structure of the South largely intact. Without the provision of land to freed people, emancipation was unlikely to bring fundamental or lasting economic change.[17]

One of the most significant and longest lasting efforts during these years was the establishment of a number of Black colleges in the South. Some schools, notably Howard University in Washington, D.C., begun in 1867, were founded with the aid of the federal government and received some public support, but the vast majority were formed by northern missionary groups. Starting with **Fisk University** in Nashville in 1866, and Morgan College in Baltimore and Morehouse College in Atlanta the following year, Black higher education was off to an impressive start. By 1895, there were forty colleges educating a predominantly Black student body. These colleges were the intellectual centers of southern Black life, and their graduates became the teachers of generations of African American leaders.[18]

Black Politics and Black Politicians

Once in control, in 1867, the Republican Congress divided the former Confederacy into five military districts and declared Black suffrage to be one important precondition for reinstating the rights of southern states in the federal union. Initially the southern state governments under Reconstruction were dominated by an alliance of northern migrants and southern loyalists. Most white southerners disdainfully called these northerners carpetbaggers and derided the loyalists by calling them scalawags. With Black voters providing a solid base, this Republican alliance controlled southern state governments for nearly a generation. African Americans were generally well represented at the state conventions that drew up new constitutions removing race as an obstacle to voting. They constituted a majority of the eligible voters in South Carolina, Florida, Mississippi, and Louisiana and exercised their greatest political power in these states. In South Carolina, Black people made up more than 60 percent of the delegates to the postwar constitutional convention, including fifty-seven formerly enslaved people. This convention, which also included twenty-seven white southerners, adopted a remarkably progressive constitution in 1868. It abolished racial discrimination in voting, schools, and the militia, and abolished dueling, property requirements for voting or office holding, and imprisonment for debts. This constitution established the state's first free public school system with regular support and reformed the courts by providing for elected rather than appointed

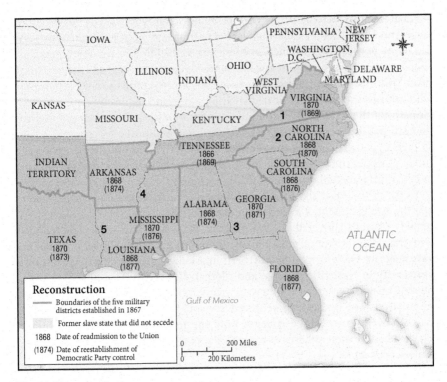

Map 8.1 Reconstruction

judges. Women also gained rights under its provisions, as a married woman's property could no longer be sold to satisfy her husband's debts, and it instituted South Carolina's first divorce law.[19]

There were also important changes at the federal level during Reconstruction, as Congress passed and the states ratified amendments to the nation's Constitution. The **Thirteenth Amendment** (1865) prohibited slavery, the **Fourteenth Amendment** (passed 1866; ratified 1868) nullified the Supreme Court's 1857 Dred Scott decision by banning the use of race as a bar to citizenship, and the **Fifteenth Amendment** (passed 1869; ratified 1870) prohibited the use of race to deny the right to vote. Frederick Douglass celebrated the postwar constitutional changes and expressed great hopes for Black citizenship and the future: "We are a great nation. . . . We are all together now. We are fellow-citizens of a common country. What a country—fortunate in its institutions, in its fifteenth amendment, in its future." The provision of citizenship rights to African Americans was unpopular with President Johnson, with northern Democrats, and particularly with white southerners. These amendments helped Republicans build and sustain their political power in the South. They also escalated the conflict over the control of Reconstruction policy between Congress and Johnson that resulted in the impeachment and near removal of the president in 1868.[20]

Later that year, John W. Menard from Louisiana, where nearly 50 percent of the population was Black, became the first African American elected to the U.S. House of Representatives. However, the House Committee on Elections ruled that, though Menard had been fairly elected, Congress was not yet ready to admit an African American. Menard, whose parents were French Creoles, addressed the House, eloquently defending his right to serve, but the House refused to seat him. In South Carolina, where almost 60 percent of the population was African American, Black people held state and local offices from lieutenant governor, secretary of state, treasurer, and speaker of the house to county sheriff and court clerk. In 1869, the University of South Carolina was opened to all races, and two African Americans were elected to its board of trustees. The next year, the state sent its first African American, Joseph H. Rainey, to the U.S. House of Representatives. Within a year, Rainey was joined by four other Black representatives from Alabama, Florida, and South Carolina. When the South Carolina General Assembly met in the fall of 1872, African Americans took their places as president pro tem of the senate and speaker of the house. Although no state elected a Black governor, Louisiana's lieutenant governor, P.B.S. Pinchback, formerly denied his seat in the U.S. Senate, served as acting governor after the corrupt white governor was removed from office.

Although hundreds of African Americans were elected to state and local offices in the South, they never controlled any state government. Yet the promise held by the dramatic political changes going on in the South drew many African Americans. Some who had moved north before the war returned, and

THE FIRST COLORED SENATOR AND REPRESENTATIVES.
In the 41st and 42nd Congress of the United States.

African Americans in the Forty-First and Forty-Second Congress of the United States, 1872.

The Reconstruction Amendments

These amendments to the U.S. Constitution Article, ratified between 1865 and 1870, provided for the freedom, citizenship, and voting rights of African Americans.

Article XIII

Neither slavery nor involuntary servitude, except as a punishment for crime whereof the party shall have been duly convicted, shall exist within the United States, or any place subject to their jurisdiction.

Congress shall have power to enforce this article by appropriate legislation.

Article XIV

1. All persons born or naturalized in the United States, and subject to the jurisdiction thereof, are citizens of the United States and of the State wherein they reside. No State shall make or enforce any law which shall abridge the privileges or immunities of citizens of the United States; nor shall any State deprive any person of life, liberty, or property, without due process of law; nor deny to any person within its jurisdiction the equal protection of the laws.

2. Representatives shall be apportioned among the several States according to their respective numbers, counting the whole number of persons in each State, excluding Indians not taxed. But when the right to vote at any election for the choice of electors for President and Vice President of the United States, Representatives in Congress, the Executive and Judicial officers of a State, or the members of the Legislature thereof, is denied to any of the male inhabitants of such State, being

many who had been born in the North, went south to work, teach, and share in the new political power. Jonathan J. Wright, for example, had been born in Pennsylvania, studied law, and was the first African American admitted to the bar in that state. The opportunity to work for the Freedmen's Bureau attracted him to South Carolina. There he became a member of the postwar constitutional convention and, a few years later, was elected to the bench of the state supreme court, where he served until 1877. African Americans were powerful in the Republican Party in the South and held high positions in state and regional governments. Voters elected Black men to offices at all levels, from local sheriff to representative in the national Congress, and Black people were in office from the late 1860s throughout the nineteenth century. More than six hundred African Americans served in state legislatures, and by the beginning of the twentieth century, twenty had served in the U.S. House of Representatives and two had served in the U.S. Senate.[21]

twenty-one years of age, and citizens of the United States, or in any way abridged, except for participation in rebellion, or other crime, the basis of representation therein shall be reduced in the proportion which the number of such male citizens shall bear to the whole number of male citizens twenty-one years of age in such State.

3. No person shall be a Senator or Representative in Congress, or elector of President and Vice President, or hold any office, civil or military, under the United States, or under any State, who, having previously taken an oath, as a member of Congress, or as an officer of the United States, or as a member of any State legislature, or as an executive or judicial officer of any State, to support the Constitution of the United States, shall have engaged in insurrection or rebellion against the same, or given aid or comfort to the enemies thereof. But Congress may by a vote of two-thirds of each House, remove such disability.

4. The validity of the public debt of the United States, authorized by law, including debts incurred for payment of pensions and bounties for services in suppressing insurrection or rebellion, shall not be questioned. But neither the United States nor any State shall assume or pay any debt or obligation incurred in aid of insurrection or rebellion against the United States, or any claim for the loss or emancipation of any slave; but all such debts, obligations and claims shall be held illegal and void.

5. The Congress shall have power to enforce, by appropriate legislation, the provisions of this article.

Article XV

The right of citizens of the United States to vote shall not be denied or abridged by the United States or by any State on account of race, color, or previous condition of servitude.

Although most southern Black men and women were illiterate at the end of the war, most Black political leaders were educated. They were former soldiers, abolitionists, businessmen, ministers, lawyers, and teachers. Some were self-taught, like Oscar J. Dunn, who was born in slavery in Louisiana and became lieutenant governor of the state. Others had considerably more formal education, like Francis Louis Cardozo, who was educated in Europe at the University of Glasgow and the London School of Theology. Cardozo returned to his native South Carolina in 1865 to head Avery Institute, the area's largest Black educational institution. He was also a member of the convention that drew up the state's progressive post–Civil War constitution and served as secretary of state from 1868 to 1872 and state treasurer from 1872 to 1877. Jonathan Gibbs, who graduated from Dartmouth College and Princeton Theological Seminary, was the Florida secretary of state from 1868 to 1872 and later served as state

PROFILE

Hiram Rhoades Revels

Hiram Revels, U.S. senator from Mississippi.

BORN FREE IN 1822 IN FAYETTEVILLE, North Carolina, during the height of slavery, Hiram Revels left the South to be educated at a Quaker seminary in Indiana and at Knox College in Illinois. After graduation he became a minister in the African Methodist Episcopal Church, serving congregations in the midwestern and border states. When the Civil War broke out, he helped recruit Black troops for the U.S. Army in Maryland and Missouri. He joined the Republican Party and served on the city council in Natchez and in the Mississippi state senate in the late 1860s. In 1870 Revels was elected to fill the seat recently vacated by former Confederate president Jefferson Davis in the U.S. Senate, becoming the first African American to serve in that body. Mississippi Democrats were furious at the election of a Black man to represent their state, calling him "a thousand dollar darky." Referring to the cost of the war, one northern writer argued that Revels was "a three thousand million Darky," adding, "I hear in his voice the thunders of [Confederate defeats at] Donelson, and Shiloh, and Vicksburg, and Gettysburg and in his footsteps the tread of mightier armies than Napoleon marshalled for the conquest of Europe." Senator Simon Cameron of Pennsylvania recalled ironically that he had once warned Davis that through the justice of God "a Negro some day will come and occupy your seat." The Senate gallery was filled when Senator Revels came forward to take his oath of office. The Philadelphia Press reported, "Never since the birth of the republic has such an audience been assembled under one roof . . . the greatest and the least American citizens."

With Revels formally placed in the Senate, that body set about bringing Mississippi back into the United States as a full partner in the union. After serving in the Senate, Revels returned to Mississippi, at first to minister to an AME church and then to serve as the president of two Black schools, Alcorn Agricultural and Mining College and the newly formed Mississippi State College for Negroes. By the end of his life in 1901, Revels had become conservative, even supporting the Democratic Party and the white supremacist White League. Perhaps the violent end of Reconstruction led him to be afraid for African Americans who continued to resist the inhumane and murderous force of the Ku Klux Klan and other terrorist groups.

Source: Lerone Bennett, Jr., *Black Power U.S.A.: The Human Side of Reconstruction, 1867–1877* (Chicago: Johnson Publishing Company, 1967), 213–14.

superintendent of education. The educational accomplishments of many African American officeholders contradicted the claims of white southerners that illiterate Black people controlled the South. Some African Americans made the point that most of the Black representatives who served at the national level had more formal education than President Andrew Johnson. Working through the Republican Party and political associations such as the Union League, Black leaders and their constituents transformed southern politics, at least for a time.

Although voting was limited to men, Black women were a powerful presence in Reconstruction politics. Before the war, both enslaved and free women had been active participants in Black family, work, and community life. Now that freedom had finally come, they continued to be active. White women sometimes attended political conventions and rallies, sitting quietly at the rear of the room or observing from the gallery, but Black women were known actually to take the floor and participate in the debate. White Republicans in Charleston, South Carolina, became so exasperated that they once asked their Black colleagues to "leave their wives at their firesides." Despite such protests, Black women continued to play important roles in community decision making and participated in every phase of politics but voting. Black Republican organizers traveled the South during the 1860s speaking to Black groups at churches and other community gatherings and urging the men to vote and the women to see that they did. In many places "the voting," as Black people often called it, was a festive occasion, a family day on which women accompanied men to the polling places, where they shared picnic lunches. The female presence was not just symbolic. One observer in South Carolina reported that Black women "appear to have assumed a role more in keeping with their 'place' as they, like the ancient Greek women of Lysistrata, reportedly applied the sanctions of the bedroom to whip male political defectors into conformity with self-interest." In rural Mississippi women threatened similar sanctions. In other places women employed more direct methods of controlling Black male votes. One Black woman in South Carolina attacked her husband with an axe after she learned that he had sold his vote to the Democratic candidate.[22]

African American participation in southern politics was a revolutionary change, but it was only part of the change brought about by emancipation. Deviations from southern traditions governing everyday racial interactions angered and frightened white southerners. Many Black Americans had decided, as one formerly enslaved man in Georgia put it, to take "no more foolishness off white folks," and they were incensed when white people tried to continue the old racial conventions designed to reinforce status distinctions. Addressing a Black man as "boy," a Black woman as "girl," or either as "nigger," was likely to lead to a confrontation. In Helena, Arkansas, when an elderly freedman addressed a white man on the street as "Mr. Powell," Powell followed the prewar convention and replied, "Howdy uncle." The Black man angrily assured him that they were not related and demanded, "Call me Mister."[23]

Progress and White Terrorist Backlash

Black political power in the Reconstruction South could not force changes in land policies needed for long-term economic and social transformation. Most Black southerners were without land, so the best they could manage was to work for white landholders who had little cash but offered shares of the crop in return for their labor. Although **sharecropping** could conceivably have offered an approximation of the family farm, it most often led to debt peonage. White landholders used both legal and illegal means to bind Black sharecroppers to the land through real or contrived indebtedness. Impecunious sharecroppers were forced to rely on credit advanced against the next year's crop to purchase farming supplies. The seed, tools, and teams of mules or horses were purchased on credit, as were the food, clothing, and other necessities that families needed to sustain themselves. The farmers secured credit either at stores the landholder operated on his land or at independent local stores. In either case expenses were generally manipulated to the sharecropper's disadvantage. At the end of the year, when profits were figured and debts were settled, sharecroppers were likely to find themselves in debt. Their debts grew each year, and there was no authority to whom they could appeal. "They said figures didn't lie," reported one Arkansas sharecropper. "You know how that was. You dassent dispute a [white] man's word then." Sharecropping offered some independence compared to the slave gang labor system, but the shift in power was limited. Freed people understood very well that they were farming the white man's land and were forced to play by the white man's rules. Looking back over his life as a sharecropper, eighty-year-old Henry Blacke explained, "no matter how good accounts you kept, you had to go by [the white landowners'] account, and—now brother, I'm telling you the truth about this—it has been that way a long time." Even during the late 1860s and 1870s, when Republicans held

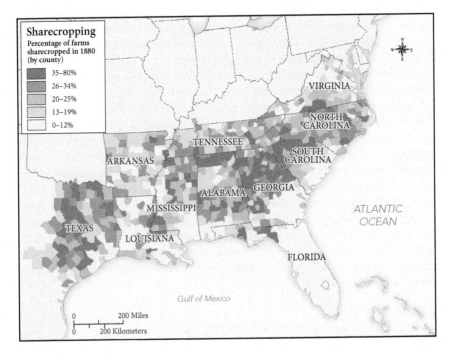

Map 8.2 Sharecropping

political power, southern Democrats often had so much white popular support that the U.S. troops could not protect Black Americans' legal rights.[24]

The organization of political terrorist groups made it extremely difficult to enforce Black civil rights laws. There were many such groups, including the Knights of the White Camellia and the Pale Faces, but the most notorious was the **Ku Klux Klan**, initially formed as a social group in Pulaski, Tennessee, (on Christmas Eve) in 1865. These groups attempted to impose social, economic, and political control on freed people and their allies by intimidating voters and enforcing the southern racial etiquette of white supremacy. They punished Black sharecroppers for questioning white landlords, besieged Black businesses for being too competitive, attacked Black students for displaying too much intelligence, and assaulted white people for encouraging Black aspirations. Few white southerners accepted full emancipation; most refused to acknowledge Black people as citizens and continued to treat them as property, albeit property at large. White "[m]en who are honorable in their dealings with their white neighbors will cheat a Negro without feeling a single twinge of their honor," reported one Freedmen's Bureau official. Such white people believed that their version of southern civilization must be protected by punishing any Black person who showed signs of contesting their control.

Punishment ran the gamut from individual beatings and whippings to massacre. African Americans understood that "to kill a Negro [white southerners] do not deem murder; to debauch a Negro woman they do not think fornication; to take the property away from a Negro they do not consider robbery." As one Black soldier in Mississippi reported to the Freedmen's Bureau, "houses have been tourn down from the heades of women and Children" and none dared complain for fear of their lives. "Report came to [Vicksburg, Mississippi] this morning," he wrote, "that two colored women was found dead side the Jackson road with their throats cut lying side by side." The Klan targeted the churches and their ministers for bolstering Black spirits and the schools and teachers for educating Black children. Before the war white southerners had considered African Americans who could read and write dangerous, and educating them had generally been prohibited. Rates of literacy among southern white people, themselves, were low. Particularly to poor illiterate white people, a Black person with a superior education seemed to be a violation of the natural social order. Education, many argued, would create false pride, raise unrealistic aspirations, and spoil Black people for the work for which they were destined. "The cook, that must read the daily newspaper," one white educator warned, "will spoil your beef and your bread." Underlying these fears was the threat of social equality and the belief that Black men might demand access to white women as the badge of their equality. Southern white women had become the embodiment of southern civilization. The slave system had given white men virtually free access to Black women. In the aftermath of emancipation, southern white men envisioned a post-revolutionary society where Black men asserted the same privileges. This was the nightmare that gave rise to extreme fantasies of racial menace and could bring even law-abiding white people to justify the most grizzly violence.[25]

Between midnight and one o'clock in the morning in May in the early 1870s the Klan descended on the home of Elias Hill, a Black minister severely disabled by rheumatism in both arms and legs. They beat his brother's wife and forced her to show them where Hill was sleeping. They dragged him from his bed, took him to the front yard, and accused him of encouraging "black men to ravish all the white women" in the town. While he protested his innocence, the night riders beat him with their fists and whips, put a gun to his head, and threatened to kill him. After the beating, their real purpose became clear—they demanded that Hill place an ad in the newspaper "to renounce all republicanism and never vote." They threatened to return and kill him if he did not stop preaching republicanism.[26]

Although the Klan drew its foot soldiers from the ranks of poor white southerners, the southern planter aristocracy encouraged, condoned, and sometimes controlled their actions. Democratic leader Wade Hampton of South Carolina explained to his political colleagues that illegal action, even murder, in defense of racial domination was completely acceptable. "Every Democrat must feel honor bound to control the vote of at least one Negro," he argued. Then he elucidated, "Never threaten a man individually. If he deserves to be threatened, the necessities of the times require that he should be killed." This kind of rhetoric encouraged terrorist groups' violent action. In 1876, President Ulysses S. Grant charged that "murders and massacres of innocent men" because of their political opinions had become so frequent as to be familiar. An indeterminate number of Black people in Aiken County, South Carolina, (estimates ranged from 15 to 125) were killed trying to vote, and in Hamburg, South Carolina, white people assaulted Black voters in a "cruel, bloodthirsty, wanton, and unprovoked" attack. The pattern was the same in Louisiana, Mississippi, and everywhere Republicans were strong. In Kentucky alone, more than one hundred Black people were lynched in the first decade after the war.[27]

This Klan violence was not simply randomly directed at African Americans. It was political terrorism designed to restore southern Democratic power. On occasion Klan leaders seemed willing to endorse Black political action if it supported the Democrats. In Memphis the Klan encouraged and agreed to protect sixty-five African

"A COMPANY OF WHITES LAY IN AMBUSH FOR A PARTY OF NEGROES RETURNING FROM CHURCH, KILLED TEN, AND WOUNDED THIRTEEN."

A band of white supremacists fire on a group of Black people returning from church services in Choctaw County, Alabama, August 1, 1874.

Americans who established the Colored Democratic Club in the summer of 1868. Not many Black Americans were willing to support the Democrats, however, and Klan attacks on Republicans, regardless of race, increased so that in 1870 Congress passed the first of a series of Enforcement Acts authorizing the use of federal troops to control Klan violence. In 1871 Congress launched an extensive investigation of the Klan, and in a series of federal trials in Mississippi, South Carolina, and North Carolina, hundreds of white people—some of whom were doctors, lawyers, ministers, college professors, and other professionals—were arrested and indicted. Congress also passed a limited-term law that forced much of the Klan's activity underground, but with the support of the South's most influential citizens, the Klan continued its terrorism throughout the late nineteenth century.[28]

African Americans did not submit meekly to Klan violence. Black judges issued arrest warrants and Black sheriffs jailed white terrorists. Confrontations between Black soldiers or returning veterans and white southerners were common. Black troops arrested the white chief of police in Wilmington, North Carolina, when he refused to surrender his weapon as ordered. Black soldiers in Victoria, Texas, retaliated for the murder of a Black civilian by lynching the white killer, and Black soldiers in South Carolina shot a Confederate veteran who had stabbed a Black sergeant for refusing to leave a railroad car in which white women were seated. Many Black veterans retained their military weapons, and some formed militia units to protect their communities. White southerners made various attempts to disarm the Black community, especially where Black militia units most actively resisted attacks. Often white Republican officials acceded to white petitions to gain the cooperation of prominent local citizens. Disarming these units left Black communities much more vulnerable to terrorist attack.[29]

Though some historians have speculated that Black people were unwilling or unable to defend themselves, there is strong evidence to the contrary. African Americans were most vulnerable and white terrorists were most active in areas of the South where Black Americans were a minority or were just barely a majority of the population. The Klan and other groups were far less active where there were large majority-Black populations. It was clear that white terrorist actions were aimed at the growing Black political power. When white people, including police officers, invaded the Black community in Memphis, Tennessee, in 1866, Black freedmen, many of them veterans, confronted them. In the resulting battle, called a riot by a local newspaper, forty-six Black and two white people died. Also in 1866 a white mob and police attacked hundreds of unarmed Black and white Republicans meeting for a state constitutional convention in New Orleans. After a two-and-a-half-hour confrontation outside the hall, the battle moved inside, where former soldiers led the defense of convention goers, returning the police fire. The massacre of people in the hall and as they escaped from the area left forty-eight Black Americans dead.[30]

Even when they were most vulnerable, African Americans did not submit to intimidation quietly. In 1868, Charles Caldwell, a Black Mississippi politician, who was wounded by a white man, shot and killed his assailant. Such confrontations were common, but Caldwell's acquittal by an all-white jury on the grounds of self-defense was unusual. Those who resisted, however, were likely to pay a heavy price. On Christmas Day almost a decade after his acquittal, Caldwell was shot dead by a white gang. By the mid-1870s terrorist tactics were returning Democrats to power, and there were fewer and fewer protections for southern African Americans. Leaders continued to urge resistance throughout the century. Writing anonymously in an 1885 New York newspaper, one Black Kentuckian counted the number of Black people killed by white attacks. "We cannot stand it any longer," he contended. "We should kill as well as be killed." But African Americans in the South understood the impracticality of armed confrontation with the white people and the dwindling prospects for justice. A political compromise between Republicans and Democrats in the winter of 1877 brought Republican Rutherford B. Hayes into the White House in return for business investment in the South, the withdrawal of the few remaining U.S. occupying troops, and the informal understanding that Black southerners would be left to the mercy of southern Democrats.[31]

By the late 1870s the rapprochement between the political parties, the disarming of the local Black militia, and the reassertion of white control over Black labor had nearly ended Black political influence. Supreme Court decisions in a series of cases from 1873 to 1883 removed federal protection for almost all Black civil rights in the South, leaving terrorists free rein. To make matters worse, in the midst of the national economic depression of 1873, the privately operated Freedmen's Savings Bank failed. The bank had been incorporated by Congress in 1865, to provide financial services and encourage thrift among the freedman, but the speculation of its directors made it one of many institutions to succumb to the economic crisis. It closed its doors in 1874, depriving its depositors—Black individuals, Black churches, and benevolent societies—of most of their hard-earned savings. Bank customers were paid a fraction of their deposits, and these poor people who had trusted their meager accounts to what had seemed to be an institution backed by the federal government lost faith in banks and their government for many generations.[32]

Emigration from the South

In the face of economic hardship, diminishing opportunities, and mounting racial violence, many freed people decided to leave the South. In Louisiana, political activist and former U.S. soldier Henry Adams expressed the feelings of many Black southerners. "This is a horrible part of the country," he lamented. African Americans could not find justice or enjoy the basic rights of citizenship in a society still controlled by white people who had never accepted the demise of slavery. Frustration and pessimism over conditions in the South again led some African Americans to reconsider African emigration. In the spring of 1878, more than two hundred people departed from Charleston, South Carolina, for Africa on the ship *Azor*, chartered by the Black-owned Liberian Exodus Joint Stock Steamship Company. Although their motives are difficult to assess, there were some for whom emigration was a matter of racial pride and nationalism. One such emigrationist was Bishop Henry McNeal Turner, leader of the African Methodist Episcopal Church. He experienced the disappointment and disillusionment of postwar reconstruction in Georgia, became convinced that America offered no future for Black people, and hoped that two or three million

African Americans would establish a humane and just society in the land of their ancestors.[33]

However, though conditions were dismal, most African Americans, like other generations before them, were unable or unwilling to leave the United States. Most remained in the rural South, and those who migrated went to southern cities or to the North. A considerable number dreamed of attaining independence and self-sufficiency by becoming landholders in the West. Some struck out for New Mexico, Arizona, or Colorado. Groups left North Carolina and Mississippi for Nebraska, and a large number moved to Kansas. Henry Adams claimed that ninety-eight thousand Black people had enrolled their names with him to express their intention to migrate to the West. They were called "Exodusters," a name rooted in the biblical Exodus story of the Israelites who escaped from slavery in Egypt that was a foundation of African American Christianity. Led by such men as Adams and the formerly enslaved Benjamin Pap Singleton, they moved their families from the Deep South westward into Kansas in 1879 and 1880. Singleton's real estate company promised affordable land to those who would move west to claim it, enticing several thousand to relocate. Life in Kansas was hard, but many found greater freedom there than they had known in the South. The first group of **Exodusters** arrived in April 1879, traveling up the Missouri River by steamboat to Wyandotte in eastern Kansas. These were poor people, dressed in patched, tattered clothes, with little money, a few of them sick and unable to go to work immediately. By that fall, they had been joined by fifteen thousand others, and the Kansas governor promised a delegation of one hundred that they would receive justice and aid.[34]

Former abolitionists established a **Freedman's Relief Association** to provide food and medical supplies, and white people in Kansas seemed willing to provide jobs and homes. Other aid came from as far away as Chicago and New England. Many Black women found jobs cooking and doing laundry in town, while the men secured homesteads outside of town and built homes. Men who could not secure land found jobs on farms, in coal mines, or on the railroad. Within a few years, Black Americans had purchased more than twenty thousand acres of land and built the new Black towns of Dunlap, Singleton, and Nicodemus. Unable to build homes during harsh weather, settlers spent their first winter in dugout shelters. Although Nicodemus is the only one of these formerly all-Black towns still in existence, for a time they were home to hundreds of settlers. Eventually crop failures, lack of water, and damage from winds so strong that they blew away seeds and full-grown plants forced

A handbill from Lexington, Kentucky, urges Black people to migrate to Kansas, 1877.

Nat Love, the black cowboy also known as "Deadwood Dick."

many to move to urban Black communities in Kansas City and Topeka. Although life in the West was generally better than in the South, there was also discrimination, and Black people's precarious lives depended on the ebb and flow of white fears and tolerance. Denver residents refused to rent to Black Americans or to give them jobs, and some communities like Lincoln, Nebraska, expelled Black migrants.[35]

Hundreds of African Americans went West with the cattle drives from Texas to the new settlements of the region. Britton Johnson, a freedman, became a Black cowboy and made his reputation by fighting Native Americans on the Texas frontier. The cowboy Nat Love was said to have won the title "Deadwood Dick" in a roping contest. Stagecoach Mary Fields, born in slavery in Tennessee, became famous driving freight wagons in Montana. James Beckwourth, one of the best-known Black fur trappers and mountain men, was, for a time, a tribal leader of the Crow Indians. Beckwourth opened a pass through the mountains into California that bears his name to this day. Black gunfighters and outlaws, such as Babe Fisher and Isom Dart, called The Black Fox, disrupted town life, while the Black troops of the U.S. Ninth and Tenth Cavalries, whom Native Americans respectfully called **Buffalo Soldiers**, attempted to keep the peace. On both sides of the law, Black westerners exercised a power that challenged assumptions about white supremacy. In an effort to preserve the lives of its citizens, one frontier town passed an ordinance making it a crime to insult or otherwise assault Cherokee Bill, a Black gunfighter known to confront and kill those who molested him. Bill, whose skill with a weapon was notorious, was eventually hanged for murder. On the western frontier, race was sometimes subordinated to the need for cooperation and comradeship. On cattle drives, among the mountain men, and even in some of frontier towns, Black and white people often found an easy association generally not possible in the South or the East.[36]

Legalized Racial Control

The end of slavery, legislative advances in Black rights, expanding education, and the election of African American politicians had promised the realization of the long-hoped-for Black citizenship, but southern Democratic politicians built a new structure of racial control to replace slavery. In the state legislatures and the courts, southern conservatives set about abrogating Black political rights and reversing the social and economic progress made during Reconstruction. By the early 1880s Supreme Court decisions that declared federal civil rights laws unconstitutional left the responsibility for protecting African American rights to the states. This effectively thwarted many of the hard-won rights gained after the Civil War, as Southern states refused to recognize Black civil rights. A new state constitution for Mississippi, adopted in 1890, contained complicated restrictions, including a poll tax and a literacy test, specifically designed to limit or eliminate African American voting. So as not to deprive illiterate white Americans of the vote, the law provided that those who could not pass the literacy test might still vote if their grandfather had voted before 1866. This "grandfather clause" effectively denied Black Americans—most of whom had been enslaved before that time—the voting rights that the Fifteenth Amendment was designed to guarantee.

In the 1896 case of ***Plessy v. Ferguson***, the U.S. Supreme Court's approval of "separate but equal" institutions helped shape social and economic inequality in the postwar South by supporting laws that sustained a far-reaching system of racial **segregation**. Justice John Marshall Harlan, the lone dissenting voice on the Court, observed, "[T]he judgment rendered this day will, in time, prove to be quite as pernicious as the decision made by the tribunal in the Dred Scott case." Gradually other southern states adopted the Mississippi plan for disenfranchising Black Americans and instituted racially discriminatory laws. These were referred to as **Jim Crow** laws, taking their name from the mid-nineteenth century minstrel character performed in blackface by Thomas "Daddy" Rice, a white comedian who portrayed a stereotypical ignorant, helpless African American. These state and local laws separated the races in public transportation and accommodations, public education, and virtually every aspect of public life. Some of the old pre–Civil War patterns remained, as African Americans still performed intimate services for the white middle class and elites, cooking their food, cleaning their houses, and caring for their children. Black men and women often lived conveniently near white people, and they did much of the manual labor in fields and factories owned and operated by white people. But Jim Crow laws enforced inequality and demanded greater racial separation than had generally existed during slavery. Eventually all southern drinking fountains, public parks, swimming pools, hospitals, restaurants, movie theaters, and phone booths were segregated by race. Courtrooms even had separate Bibles for swearing in members of different races. Segregationists drew on so-called experts in the biological sciences to lend support to the theories of Black inferiority concretized in the laws. By the early twentieth century racial discrimination and segregation were the law of the South.[37]

Reconstruction, begun with such promise for African Americans, ended in disappointment as opportunities for Black people in the South constricted, Republican power waned, and Constitutional guarantees vanished under the power of Supreme Court rulings. Debt bound many sharecroppers to the land almost as tightly as slavery had gripped enslaved people before the war. A few Black politicians remained in office, even in the United States Congress, into the twentieth century, but by the 1890s, the reversal of interracial progress was clear. As the nation turned its attention to the more northern concerns of industrialization,

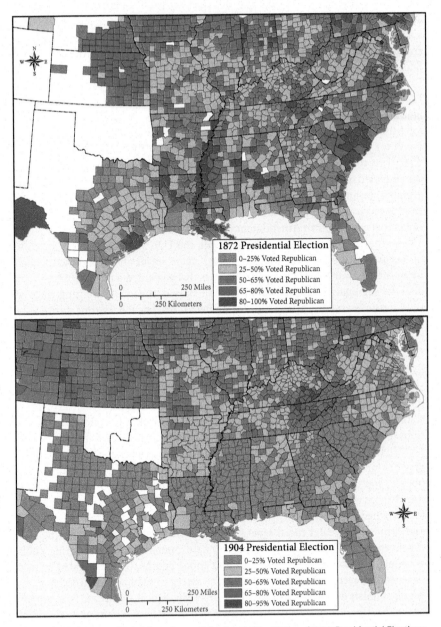

Map 8.3 The Waning of Republican Power in the South: The 1872 and 1904 Presidential Elections Compared

urbanization, and European immigration, the South was increasingly free to develop its own policies on race, and southern Black people found themselves isolated in poverty and oppression. For most African Americans freedom remained—in the words of poet Langston Hughes a generation later—"a dream deferred."

Who, What, Where

Review Questions

8.1 How did Lincoln's changing views of race and equality impact Black Americans?

8.2 What types of aid did freed people receive after the war? How effective were these measures?

8.3 How did Black voters alter the political landscape of the South during Radical Reconstruction? What are some of the lasting accomplishments achieved during this period?

8.4 What were the intentions and motives of white terrorist organizations?

8.5 Why did newly freed Black people choose to emigrate? Who were the Exodusters?

8.6 How did the resurgence of Democratic control in the South lead to racial discrimination and segregation? What were the consequences of *Plessy v. Ferguson*?

For additional digital learning resources please go to **https://www.oup.com/he/horton1e**

Appendix A

Declaration of Independence
Constitution and Amendments
The Emancipation Proclamation
Key Provisions of the Civil Rights Act of 1964
Key Provisions of the Voting Rights Act of 1965

The Declaration of Independence

When in the course of human events, it becomes necessary for one people to dissolve the political bands which have connected them with another, and to assume, among the powers of the earth, the separate and equal station to which the Laws of Nature and of Nature's God entitle them, a decent respect to the opinions of mankind requires that they should declare the causes which impel them to the separation.

We hold these truths to be self-evident, that all men are created equal, that they are endowed by their Creator with certain unalienable Rights, that among these are life, liberty and the pursuit of happiness. That to secure these rights, governments are instituted among men, deriving their just powers from the consent of the governed; that whenever any form of government becomes destructive of these ends, it is the right of the people to alter or to abolish it, and to institute new Government, laying its foundation on such principles and organizing its powers in such form, as to them shall seem most likely to effect their safety and happiness. Prudence, indeed, will dictate that Governments long established should not be changed for light and transient causes; and, accordingly, all experience hath shown, that mankind are more disposed to suffer, while evils are sufferable, than to right themselves by abolishing the forms to which they are accustomed. But when a long train of abuses and usurpations, pursuing invariably the same object evinces a design to reduce them under absolute despotism, it is their right, it is their duty, to throw off such government, and to provide new guards for their future security. Such has been the patient sufferance of these colonies; and such is now the necessity which constrains them to alter their former systems of government. The history of the present King of Great Britain is a history of repeated injuries and usurpations, all having in direct object the establishment of an absolute tyranny over these States. To prove this, let facts be submitted to a candid world:

He has refused his assent to laws, the most wholesome and necessary for the public good.

He has forbidden his governors to pass laws of immediate and pressing importance, unless suspended in their operation till his assent should be obtained; and, when so suspended, he has utterly neglected to attend to them.

He has refused to pass other laws for the accommodation of large districts of people, unless those people would relinquish the right of representation in the legislature, a right inestimable to them and formidable to tyrants only.

He has called together legislative bodies at places unusual, uncomfortable, and distant from the depository of their public records, for the sole purpose of fatiguing them into compliance with his measures.

He has dissolved representative houses repeatedly, for opposing with manly firmness his invasions on the rights of the people.

He has refused for a long time, after such dissolutions, to cause others to be elected; whereby the legislative powers, incapable of annihilation, have returned to the People at large for their exercise; the State remaining in the mean time exposed to all the dangers of invasion from without, and convulsions within.

He has endeavored to prevent the population of these States; for that purpose obstructing the laws for naturalization of foreigners; refusing to pass others to encourage their migrations hither, and raising the conditions of new appropriations of lands.

He has obstructed the administration of justice, by refusing his assent to laws for establishing judiciary powers.

He has made judges dependent on his will alone, for the tenure of their offices, and the amount and payment of their salaries.

He has erected a multitude of new offices, and sent hither swarms of officers to harass our people, and eat out their substance.

He has kept among us, in times of peace, standing armies without the consent of our legislatures.

He has affected to render the Military independent of, and superior to, the civil power.

He has combined with others to subject us to a jurisdiction foreign to our constitution and unacknowledged by our laws; giving his assent to their acts of pretended legislation:

For quartering large bodies of armed troops among us;

For protecting them, by a mock trial, from punishment for any murders which they should commit on the inhabitants of these States;

For cutting off our trade with all parts of the world;

For imposing taxes on us without our Consent;

For depriving us, in many cases, of the benefits of Trial by Jury;

For transporting us beyond Seas to be tried for pretended offences;

For abolishing the free System of English Laws in a neighbouring Province, establishing therein an Arbitrary government, and enlarging its Boundaries so as to render it at once an example and fit instrument for introducing the same absolute rule into these colonies;

For taking away our charters, abolishing our most valuable laws, and altering fundamentally the forms of our governments;

For suspending our own legislatures, and declaring themselves invested with power to legislate for us in all cases whatsoever.

He has abdicated government here, by declaring us out of his protection and waging war against us.

He has plundered our seas, ravaged our coasts, burnt our towns, and destroyed the lives of our people.

He is at this time transporting large armies of foreign mercenaries to complete the works of death, desolation and tyranny, already begun with circumstances of cruelty and perfidy scarcely paralleled in the most barbarous ages, and totally unworthy the head of a civilized nation.

He has constrained our fellow citizens taken captive on the high seas to bear arms against their country, to become the executioners of their friends and brethren, or to fall themselves by their hands.

He has excited domestic insurrections amongst us, and has endeavored to bring on the inhabitants of our frontiers, the merciless Indian savages, whose known rule of warfare, is an undistinguished destruction of all ages, sexes and conditions.

In every stage of these oppressions we have petitioned for redress in the most humble terms; our repeated petitions have been answered only by repeated injury. A prince whose character is thus marked by every act which may define a tyrant, is unfit to be the ruler of a free people.

Nor have we been wanting in attentions to our British brethren. We have warned them from time to time of attempts by their legislature to extend an unwarrantable jurisdiction over us. We have reminded them of the circumstances of our emigration and settlement here. We have appealed to their native justice and magnanimity, and we have conjured them by the ties of our common kindred to disavow these usurpations, which, would inevitably interrupt our connections and correspondence. They, too, have been deaf to the voice of justice and of consanguinity. We must, therefore, acquiesce in the necessity, which denounces our separation, and hold them, as we hold the rest of mankind, enemies in war, in peace friends.

We, therefore, the representatives of the United States of America, in general Congress, assembled, appealing to the Supreme Judge of the world for the rectitude of our intentions, do, in the name, and by the authority of the good people of these colonies, solemnly publish and declare, that these united colonies are, and of right ought to be free and independent states; that they are absolved from all allegiance to the British Crown, and that all political connection between them and the state of Great Britain, is and ought to be totally dissolved; and that, as free and independent states, they have full power to levy war, conclude peace, contract alliances, establish commerce, and to do all other acts and things which independent states may of right do. And for the support of this declaration, with a firm reliance on the protection of Divine Providence, we mutually pledge to each other our lives, our fortunes and our sacred honor.

The Constitution of the United States of America

We the People of the United States, in Order to form a more perfect Union, establish Justice, insure domestic Tranquility, provide for the common defence, promote the general Welfare, and secure the Blessings of Liberty to ourselves and our Posterity, do ordain and establish this Constitution for the United States of America.

Article I

Section 1

All legislative Powers herein granted shall be vested in a Congress of the United States, which shall consist of a Senate and House of Representatives.

Section 2

The House of Representatives shall be composed of Members chosen every second Year by the People of the several States, and the Electors in each State shall have the Qualifications requisite for Electors of the most numerous Branch of the State Legislature.

No Person shall be a Representative who shall not have attained to the Age of twenty five Years, and been seven Years a Citizen of the United States, and who shall not, when elected, be an Inhabitant of that State in which he shall be chosen.

Representatives and direct Taxes shall be apportioned among the several States which may be included within this Union, according to their respective Numbers, which shall be determined by adding to the whole Number of free Persons, including those bound to Service for a Term of Years, and excluding Indians not taxed, three fifths of all other Persons. The actual Enumeration shall be made within three Years after the first Meeting of the Congress of the United States, and within every subsequent Term of ten Years, in such Manner as they shall by Law direct. The Number of Representatives shall not exceed one for every thirty Thousand, but each State shall have at Least one Representative; and until such enumeration shall be made, the State of New Hampshire shall be entitled to choose three, Massachusetts eight, Rhode Island and Providence Plantations one, Connecticut five, New York six, New Jersey four, Pennsylvania eight, Delaware one, Maryland six, Virginia ten, North Carolina five, South Carolina five, and Georgia three.

When vacancies happen in the Representation from any State, the Executive Authority thereof shall issue Writs of Election to fill such Vacancies.

The House of Representatives shall choose their Speaker and other Officers; and shall have the sole Power of Impeachment.

Section 3

The Senate of the United States shall be composed of two Senators from each State, chosen by the Legislature thereof for six Years; and each Senator shall have one Vote.

Immediately after they shall be assembled in Consequence of the first Election, they shall be divided as equally as may be into three Classes. The Seats of the Senators of the first Class shall be vacated at the Expiration of the second Year, of the second Class at the Expiration of the fourth Year, and of the third Class at the Expiration of the sixth Year, so that one third may be chosen every second Year; and if Vacancies happen by Resignation, or otherwise, during the Recess of the Legislature of any State, the Executive thereof may make temporary Appointments until the next Meeting of the Legislature, which shall then fill such Vacancies.

No Person shall be a Senator who shall not have attained to the Age of thirty Years, and been nine Years a Citizen of the United States, and who shall not, when elected, be an Inhabitant of that State for which he shall be chosen.

The Vice President of the United States shall be President of the Senate, but shall have no Vote, unless they be equally divided.

The Senate shall choose their other Officers, and also a President pro tempore, in the Absence of the Vice President, or when he shall exercise the Office of President of the United States.

The Senate shall have the sole Power to try all Impeachments. When sitting for that Purpose, they shall be on Oath or Affirmation. When the President of the United States is tried, the Chief Justice shall preside: And no Person shall be convicted without the Concurrence of two thirds of the Members present.

Judgment in Cases of Impeachment shall not extend further than to removal from Office, and disqualification to hold and enjoy any Office of honor, Trust or Profit under the United States: but the Party convicted shall nevertheless be liable and subject to Indictment, Trial, Judgment and Punishment, according to Law.

Section 4

The Times, Places and Manner of holding Elections for Senators and Representatives, shall be prescribed in each State by the Legislature thereof; but the Congress may at any time by Law make or alter such Regulations, except as to the Places of chusing Senators.

The Congress shall assemble at least once in every Year, and such Meeting shall be on the first Monday in December, unless they shall by Law appoint a different Day.

Section 5

Each House shall be the Judge of the Elections, Returns and Qualifications of its own Members, and a Majority of each shall constitute a Quorum to do Business; but a smaller Number may adjourn from day to day, and may be authorized to compel the Attendance of absent Members, in such Manner, and under such Penalties as each House may provide.

Each House may determine the Rules of its Proceedings, punish its Members for disorderly Behaviour, and, with the Concurrence of two thirds, expel a Member.

Each House shall keep a Journal of its Proceedings, and from time to time publish the same, excepting such Parts as may in their Judgment require Secrecy; and the Yeas and Nays of the Members of either House on any question shall, at the Desire of one fifth of those Present, be entered on the Journal.

Neither House, during the Session of Congress, shall, without the Consent of the other, adjourn for more than three days, nor to any other Place than that in which the two Houses shall be sitting.

Section 6

The Senators and Representatives shall receive a Compensation for their Services, to be ascertained by Law, and paid out of the Treasury of the United States. They shall in all Cases, except Treason, Felony and Breach of the Peace, be privileged from Arrest during their Attendance at the Session of their respective Houses, and in going to and returning from the same; and for any Speech or Debate in either House, they shall not be questioned in any other Place.

No Senator or Representative shall, during the Time for which he was elected, be appointed to any civil Office under the Authority of the United States, which shall have been created, or the Emoluments whereof shall have been increased during such time; and no Person holding any Office under the United States, shall be a Member of either House during his Continuance in Office.

Section 7

All Bills for raising Revenue shall originate in the House of Representatives; but the Senate may propose or concur with Amendments as on other Bills.

Every Bill which shall have passed the House of Representatives and the Senate, shall, before it become a Law, be presented to the President of the United States: If he approve he shall sign it, but if not he shall return it, with his Objections to that House in which it shall have originated, who shall enter the Objections at large on their Journal, and proceed to reconsider it. If after such Reconsideration two thirds of that House shall agree to pass the Bill, it shall be sent, together with the Objections, to the other House, by which it shall likewise be reconsidered, and if approved by two thirds of that House, it shall become a Law. But in all such Cases the Votes of both Houses shall be determined by yeas and Nays, and the Names of the Persons voting for and against the Bill shall be entered on the Journal of each House respectively. If any Bill shall not be returned by the President within ten Days (Sundays excepted) after it shall have been presented to him, the Same shall be a Law, in like Manner as if he had signed it, unless the Congress by their Adjournment prevent its Return, in which Case it shall not be a Law.

Every Order, Resolution, or Vote to which the Concurrence of the Senate and House of Representatives may be necessary (except on a question of Adjournment) shall be presented to the President of the United States; and before the Same shall take Effect, shall be approved by him, or being disapproved by him, shall be repassed by two thirds of the Senate and House of Representatives, according to the Rules and Limitations prescribed in the Case of a Bill.

Section 8

The Congress shall have Power

To lay and collect Taxes, Duties, Imposts and Excises, to pay the Debts and provide for the common Defence and general Welfare of the United States; but all Duties, Imposts and Excises shall be uniform throughout the United States;

To borrow Money on the credit of the United States;

To regulate Commerce with foreign Nations, and among the several States, and with the Indian Tribes;

To establish an uniform Rule of Naturalization, and uniform Laws on the subject of Bankruptcies throughout the United States;

To coin Money, regulate the Value thereof, and of foreign Coin, and fix the Standard of Weights and Measures;

To provide for the Punishment of counterfeiting the Securities and current Coin of the United States;

To establish Post Offices and post Roads;

To promote the Progress of Science and useful Arts, by securing for limited Times to Authors and Inventors the exclusive Right to their respective Writings and Discoveries;

To constitute Tribunals inferior to the supreme Court;

To define and punish Piracies and Felonies committed on the high Seas, and Offences against the Law of Nations;

To declare War, grant Letters of Marque and Reprisal, and make Rules concerning Captures on Land and Water;

To raise and support Armies, but no Appropriation of Money to that Use shall be for a longer Term than two Years;

To provide and maintain a Navy;

To make Rules for the Government and Regulation of the land and naval Forces;

To provide for calling forth the Militia to execute the Laws of the Union, suppress Insurrections and repel Invasions;

To provide for organizing, arming, and disciplining the Militia, and for governing such Part of them as may be employed in the Service of the United States, reserving to the States respectively, the Appointment of the Officers, and the Authority of training the Militia according to the discipline prescribed by Congress;

To exercise exclusive Legislation in all Cases whatsoever, over such District (not exceeding ten Miles square) as may, by Cession of particular States, and the Acceptance of Congress, become the Seat of the Government of the United States, and to exercise like Authority over all Places purchased by the Consent of the Legislature of the State in which the Same shall be, for the Erection of Forts, Magazines, Arsenals, dock Yards, and other needful Buildings;—And

To make all Laws which shall be necessary and proper for carrying into Execution the foregoing Powers, and all other Powers vested by this Constitution in the Government of the United States, or in any Department or Officer thereof.

Section 9

The Migration or Importation of such Persons as any of the States now existing shall think proper to admit, shall not be prohibited by the Congress prior to the Year one thousand eight hundred and eight, but a Tax or duty may be imposed on such Importation, not exceeding ten dollars for each Person.

The Privilege of the Writ of Habeas Corpus shall not be suspended, unless when in Cases of Rebellion or Invasion the public Safety may require it.

No Bill of Attainder or ex post facto Law shall be passed.

No Capitation, or other direct, Tax shall be laid, unless in Proportion to the Census or enumeration herein before directed to be taken.

No Tax or Duty shall be laid on Articles exported from any State.

No Preference shall be given by any Regulation of Commerce or Revenue to the Ports of one State over those of another; nor shall Vessels bound to, or from, one State, be obliged to enter, clear, or pay Duties in another.

No Money shall be drawn from the Treasury, but in Consequence of Appropriations made by Law; and a regular Statement and Account of the Receipts and Expenditures of all public Money shall be published from time to time.

No Title of Nobility shall be granted by the United States: And no Person holding any Office of Profit or Trust under them, shall, without the Consent of the Congress, accept of any present, Emolument, Office, or Title, of any kind whatever, from any King, Prince, or foreign State.

Section 10

No State shall enter into any Treaty, Alliance, or Confederation; grant Letters of Marque and Reprisal; coin Money; emit Bills of Credit; make any Thing but gold and silver Coin a Tender in Payment of Debts; pass any Bill of Attainder, ex post facto Law, or Law impairing the Obligation of Contracts, or grant any Title of Nobility.

No State shall, without the Consent of the Congress, lay any Imposts or Duties on Imports or Exports, except what may be absolutely necessary for executing it's inspection Laws: and the net Produce of all Duties and Imposts, laid by any State on Imports or Exports, shall be for the Use of the Treasury of the United States; and all such Laws shall be subject to the Revision and Control of the Congress.

No State shall, without the Consent of Congress, lay any Duty of Tonnage, keep Troops, or Ships of War in time of Peace, enter into any Agreement or Compact with another State, or with a foreign Power, or engage in War, unless actually invaded, or in such imminent Danger as will not admit of delay.

Article II

Section 1

The executive Power shall be vested in a President of the United States of America. He shall hold his Office during the Term of four Years, and, together with the Vice President, chosen for the same Term, be elected, as follows:

Each State shall appoint, in such Manner as the Legislature thereof may direct, a Number of Electors, equal to the whole Number of Senators and Representatives to which the State may be entitled in the Congress: but no Senator or Representative, or Person holding an Office of Trust or Profit under the United States, shall be appointed an Elector.

The Electors shall meet in their respective States, and vote by Ballot for two Persons, of whom one at least shall not be an Inhabitant of the same State with themselves. And they shall make a List of all the Persons voted for, and of the Number of Votes for each; which List they shall sign and certify, and transmit sealed to the Seat of the Government of the United States, directed to the President of the Senate. The President of the Senate shall, in the Presence of the Senate and House of Representatives, open all the Certificates, and the Votes shall then be counted. The Person having the greatest Number of Votes shall be the President, if such Number be a Majority of the whole Number of Electors appointed; and if there be more than one who have such Majority, and have an equal Number of Votes, then the House of Representatives shall immediately choose by Ballot one of them for President; and if no Person have a Majority, then from the five highest on the List the said House shall in like Manner choose the President. But in choosing the President, the Votes shall be taken by States, the Representation from each State having one Vote; A quorum for this purpose shall consist of a Member or Members from two thirds of the States, and a Majority of all the States shall be necessary to a Choice. In every Case, after the Choice of the President, the Person having the greatest Number of Votes of the Electors shall be the Vice President. But if there should remain two or more who have equal Votes, the Senate shall choose from them by Ballot the Vice President.

The Congress may determine the Time of choosing the Electors, and the Day on which they shall give their Votes; which Day shall be the same throughout the United States.

No Person except a natural born Citizen, or a Citizen of the United States, at the time of the Adoption of this Constitution, shall be eligible to the Office of President; neither shall any Person be eligible to that Office who shall not have attained to the Age of thirty five Years, and been fourteen Years a Resident within the United States.

In Case of the Removal of the President from Office, or of his Death, Resignation, or Inability to discharge the Powers and Duties of the said Office, the Same shall devolve on the Vice President, and the Congress may by Law provide for the Case of Removal, Death, Resignation or Inability, both of the President and Vice President, declaring what Officer shall then act as President, and such Officer shall act accordingly, until the Disability be removed, or a President shall be elected.

The President shall, at stated Times, receive for his Services, a Compensation, which shall neither be increased nor diminished during the Period for which he shall have been elected, and he shall not receive within that Period any other Emolument from the United States, or any of them.

Before he enter on the Execution of his Office, he shall take the following Oath or Affirmation:—"I do solemnly swear (or affirm) that I will faithfully execute the Office of President of the United States, and will to the best of my Ability, preserve, protect and defend the Constitution of the United States."

Section 2

The President shall be Commander in Chief of the Army and Navy of the United States, and of the Militia of the several States, when called into the actual Service of the United States; he may require the Opinion, in writing, of the principal Officer in each of the executive Departments, upon any Subject relating to the Duties of their respective Offices, and he shall have Power to grant Reprieves and Pardons for Offences against the United States, except in Cases of Impeachment.

He shall have Power, by and with the Advice and Consent of the Senate, to make Treaties, provided two thirds of the Senators present concur; and he shall nominate, and by and with the Advice and Consent of the Senate, shall appoint Ambassadors, other public Ministers and Consuls, Judges of the supreme Court, and all other Officers of the United States, whose Appointments are not herein otherwise provided for, and which shall be established by Law: but the Congress may by Law vest the Appointment of such inferior Officers, as they think proper, in the President alone, in the Courts of Law, or in the Heads of Departments.

The President shall have Power to fill up all Vacancies that may happen during the Recess of the Senate, by granting Commissions which shall expire at the End of their next Session.

Section 3

He shall from time to time give to the Congress Information of the State of the Union, and recommend to their Consideration such Measures as he shall judge necessary and expedient; he may, on extraordinary Occasions, convene both Houses, or either of them, and in Case of Disagreement between them, with Respect to the Time of Adjournment, he may adjourn them to such Time as he shall think proper; he shall receive Ambassadors and other public Ministers; he shall take Care that the Laws be faithfully executed, and shall Commission all the Officers of the United States.

Section 4

The President, Vice President and all civil Officers of the United States, shall be removed from Office on Impeachment for, and Conviction of, Treason, Bribery, or other high Crimes and Misdemeanors.

Article III

Section 1

The judicial Power of the United States shall be vested in one supreme Court, and in such inferior Courts as the Congress may from time to time ordain and establish. The Judges, both of the supreme and inferior Courts, shall hold their Offices during good Behaviour, and shall, at stated Times, receive for their Services a Compensation, which shall not be diminished during their Continuance in Office.

Section 2

The judicial Power shall extend to all Cases, in Law and Equity, arising under this Constitution, the Laws of the United States, and Treaties made, or which shall be made, under their Authority;—to all Cases affecting Ambassadors, other public Ministers and Consuls;—to all Cases of admiralty and maritime Jurisdiction;—to Controversies to which the United States shall be a Party;—to Controversies between two or more States;—between a State and Citizens of another State;—between Citizens of different States;—between Citizens of the same State claiming Lands under Grants of different States, and between a State, or the Citizens thereof, and foreign States, Citizens or Subjects.

In all Cases affecting Ambassadors, other public Ministers and Consuls, and those in which a State shall be Party, the supreme Court shall have original Jurisdiction. In all the other Cases before mentioned, the supreme Court shall have appellate Jurisdiction, both as to Law and Fact, with such Exceptions, and under such Regulations as the Congress shall make.

The Trial of all Crimes, except in Cases of Impeachment, shall be by Jury; and such Trial shall be held in the State where the said Crimes shall have been committed; but when not committed within any State, the Trial shall be at such Place or Places as the Congress may by Law have directed.

Section 3

Treason against the United States, shall consist only in levying War against them, or in adhering to their Enemies, giving them Aid and Comfort. No Person shall be convicted of Treason unless on the Testimony of two Witnesses to the same overt Act, or on Confession in open Court.

The Congress shall have Power to declare the Punishment of Treason, but no Attainder of Treason shall work Corruption of Blood, or Forfeiture except during the Life of the Person attainted.

Article IV

Section 1

Full Faith and Credit shall be given in each State to the public Acts, Records, and judicial Proceedings of every other State. And the Congress may by general Laws prescribe the Manner in which such Acts, Records and Proceedings shall be proved, and the Effect thereof.

Section 2

The Citizens of each State shall be entitled to all Privileges and Immunities of Citizens in the several States.

A Person charged in any State with Treason, Felony, or other Crime, who shall flee from Justice, and be found in another State, shall on Demand of the executive Authority of the State from which he fled, be delivered up, to be removed to the State having Jurisdiction of the Crime.

No Person held to Service or Labour in one State, under the Laws thereof, escaping into another, shall, in Consequence of any Law or Regulation therein, be discharged from such Service or Labour, but shall be delivered up on Claim of the Party to whom such Service or Labour may be due.

Section 3

New States may be admitted by the Congress into this Union; but no new State shall be formed or erected within the Jurisdiction of any other State; nor any State be formed by the Junction of two or more States, or Parts of States, without the Consent of the Legislatures of the States concerned as well as of the Congress.

The Congress shall have Power to dispose of and make all needful Rules and Regulations respecting the Territory or other Property belonging to the United States; and nothing in this Constitution shall be so construed as to Prejudice any Claims of the United States, or of any particular State.

Section 4

The United States shall guarantee to every State in this Union a Republican Form of Government, and shall protect each of them against Invasion; and on Application of the Legislature, or of the Executive (when the Legislature cannot be convened), against domestic Violence.

Article V

The Congress, whenever two thirds of both Houses shall deem it necessary, shall propose Amendments to this Constitution, or, on the Application of the

Legislatures of two thirds of the several States, shall call a Convention for proposing Amendments, which, in either Case, shall be valid to all Intents and Purposes, as Part of this Constitution, when ratified by the Legislatures of three fourths of the several States, or by Conventions in three fourths thereof, as the one or the other Mode of Ratification may be proposed by the Congress; Provided that no Amendment which may be made prior to the Year One thousand eight hundred and eight shall in any Manner affect the first and fourth Clauses in the Ninth Section of the first Article; and that no State, without its Consent, shall be deprived of its equal Suffrage in the Senate.

Article VI

All Debts contracted and Engagements entered into, before the Adoption of this Constitution, shall be as valid against the United States under this Constitution, as under the Confederation.

This Constitution, and the Laws of the United States which shall be made in Pursuance thereof; and all Treaties made, or which shall be made, under the Authority of the United States, shall be the supreme Law of the Land; and the Judges in every State shall be bound thereby, any Thing in the Constitution or Laws of any State to the Contrary notwithstanding.

The Senators and Representatives before mentioned, and the Members of the several State Legislatures, and all executive and judicial Officers, both of the United States and of the several States, shall be bound by Oath or Affirmation, to support this Constitution; but no religious Test shall ever be required as a Qualification to any Office or public Trust under the United States.

Article VII

The Ratification of the Conventions of nine States, shall be sufficient for the Establishment of this Constitution between the States so ratifying the Same.

The Word, "the," being interlined between the seventh and eighth Lines of the first Page, the Word "Thirty" being partly written on an Erazure in the fifteenth Line of the first Page, The Words "is tried" being interlined between the thirty second and thirty third Lines of the first Page and the Word "the" being interlined between the forty third and forty fourth Lines of the second Page.

Attest William Jackson Secretary

Done in Convention by the Unanimous Consent of the States present the Seventeenth Day of September in the Year of our Lord one thousand seven hundred and Eighty seven and of the Independence of the United States of America the Twelfth In witness whereof We have hereunto subscribed our Names,

G°. Washington
Presidt and deputy from Virginia
Delaware
Geo: Read
Gunning Bedford jun
John Dickinson

Richard Bassett
Jaco: Broom
Maryland
James McHenry
Dan of St Thos. Jenifer
Danl. Carroll
Virginia
John Blair
James Madison Jr.
North Carolina
Wm. Blount
Richd. Dobbs Spaight
Hu Williamson
South Carolina
J. Rutledge
Charles Cotesworth Pinckney
Charles Pinckney
Pierce Butler
Georgia
William Few
Abr Baldwin
New Hampshire
John Langdon
Nicholas Gilman
Massachusetts
Nathaniel Gorham
Rufus King
Connecticut
Wm. Saml. Johnson
Roger Sherman
New York
Alexander Hamilton
New Jersey
Wil: Livingston
David Brearley
Wm. Paterson
Jona: Dayton
Pennsylvania
B Franklin
Thomas Mifflin
Robt. Morris
Geo. Clymer
Thos. FitzSimons
Jared Ingersoll
James Wilson
Gouv Morris

Articles

In addition to, and Amendment of the Constitution of the United States of America, proposed by Congress, and ratified by the Legislatures of the several States, pursuant to the fifth Article of the original Constitution.

(The first ten amendments to the U.S. Constitution were ratified December 15, 1791, and form what is known as the "Bill of Rights.")

AMENDMENT I

Congress shall make no law respecting an establishment of religion, or prohibiting the free exercise thereof; or abridging the freedom of speech, or of the press; or the right of the people peaceably to assemble, and to petition the Government for a redress of grievances.

AMENDMENT II

A well regulated Militia, being necessary to the security of a free State, the right of the people to keep and bear Arms, shall not be infringed.

AMENDMENT III

No Soldier shall, in time of peace be quartered in any house, without the consent of the Owner, nor in time of war, but in a manner to be prescribed by law.

AMENDMENT IV

The right of the people to be secure in their persons, houses, papers, and effects, against unreasonable searches and seizures, shall not be violated, and no Warrants shall issue, but upon probable cause, supported by Oath or affirmation, and particularly describing the place to be searched, and the persons or things to be seized.

AMENDMENT V

No person shall be held to answer for a capital, or otherwise infamous crime, unless on a presentment or indictment of a Grand Jury, except in cases arising in the land or naval forces, or in the Militia, when in actual service in time of War or public danger; nor shall any person be subject for the same offence to be twice put in jeopardy of life or limb; nor shall be compelled in any criminal case to be a witness against himself, nor be deprived of life, liberty, or property, without due process of law; nor shall private property be taken for public use, without just compensation.

AMENDMENT VI

In all criminal prosecutions, the accused shall enjoy the right to a speedy and public trial, by an impartial jury of the State and district wherein the crime shall have been committed, which district shall have been previously ascertained by law, and to be informed of the nature and cause of the accusation; to be confronted with the witnesses against him; to have compulsory process for obtaining witnesses in his favor, and to have the Assistance of Counsel for his defence.

AMENDMENT VII

In Suits at common law, where the value in controversy shall exceed twenty dollars, the right of trial by jury shall be preserved, and no fact tried by a jury, shall be otherwise re-examined in any Court of the United States, than according to the rules of the common law.

AMENDMENT VIII

Excessive bail shall not be required, nor excessive fines imposed, nor cruel and unusual punishments inflicted.

AMENDMENT IX

The enumeration in the Constitution, of certain rights, shall not be construed to deny or disparage others retained by the people.

AMENDMENT X

The powers not delegated to the United States by the Constitution, nor prohibited by it to the States, are reserved to the States respectively, or to the people.

AMENDMENT XI

Passed by Congress March 4, 1794. Ratified February 7, 1795.

Note: Article III, Section 2, of the Constitution was modified by Amendment XI.

The Judicial power of the United States shall not be construed to extend to any suit in law or equity, commenced or prosecuted against one of the United States by Citizens of another State, or by Citizens or Subjects of any Foreign State.

AMENDMENT XII

Passed by Congress December 9, 1803. Ratified June 15, 1804.

Note: A portion of Article II, Section 1, of the Constitution was superseded by the Twelfth Amendment.

The Electors shall meet in their respective states and vote by ballot for President and Vice-President, one of whom, at least, shall not be an inhabitant of the same state with themselves; they shall name in their ballots the person voted for as President, and in distinct ballots the person voted for as Vice-President, and they shall make distinct lists of all persons voted for as President, and of all persons voted for as Vice-President, and of the number of votes for each, which lists they shall sign and certify, and transmit sealed to the seat of the government of the United States, directed to the President of the Senate;—the President of the Senate shall, in the presence of the Senate and House of Representatives, open all the certificates and the votes shall then be counted;—The person having the greatest number of votes for President, shall be the President, if such number be a majority of the whole number of Electors appointed; and if no person have such majority, then from the persons having the highest numbers not exceeding three on the list of those voted for as President, the House of Representatives shall choose immediately, by ballot, the President. But in choosing the President, the votes shall be taken by states, the representation from each state having one vote; a quorum for this purpose shall consist of a member or members from two-thirds of the states, and a majority of all the states shall be necessary to a choice. [And if the House of Representatives shall not choose a President whenever the right of choice shall devolve upon them, before the fourth day of March next following, then the Vice-President shall act as President, as in case of the death or other constitutional disability of the President.—]* The person having the greatest number of votes as Vice-President, shall be the Vice-President, if such number be a majority of the whole number of Electors appointed, and if no person have a majority, then from the two highest numbers on the list, the Senate shall choose the Vice-President; a quorum for the purpose shall consist of two-thirds of the whole number of Senators, and a majority of the whole number shall be necessary to a choice. But no person constitutionally ineligible to the office of President shall be eligible to that of Vice-President of the United States.

*Superseded by Section 3 of the Twentieth Amendment.

AMENDMENT XIII

Passed by Congress January 31, 1865. Ratified December 6, 1865.

Note: A portion of Article IV, Section 2, of the Constitution was superseded by the Thirteenth Amendment.

SECTION 1

Neither slavery nor involuntary servitude, except as a punishment for crime whereof the party shall have been duly convicted, shall exist within the United States, or any place subject to their jurisdiction.

SECTION 2

Congress shall have power to enforce this article by appropriate legislation.

AMENDMENT XIV

Passed by Congress June 13, 1866. Ratified July 9, 1868.

Note: Article I, Section 2, of the Constitution was modified by Section 2 of the Fourteenth Amendment.

SECTION 1

All persons born or naturalized in the United States, and subject to the jurisdiction thereof, are citizens of the United States and of the State wherein they reside. No State shall make or enforce any law which shall abridge the privileges or immunities of citizens of the United States; nor shall any State deprive any person of life, liberty, or property, without due process of law; nor deny to any person within its jurisdiction the equal protection of the laws.

SECTION 2

Representatives shall be apportioned among the several States according to their respective numbers, counting the whole number of persons in each State, excluding Indians not taxed. But when the right to vote at any election for the choice of electors for President and Vice-President of the United States, Representatives in Congress, the Executive and Judicial officers of a State, or the members of the Legislature thereof, is denied to any of the male inhabitants of such State, being twenty-one years of age,* and citizens of the United States, or in any way abridged, except for participation in rebellion, or other crime, the basis of representation therein shall be reduced in the proportion which the number of such male citizens shall bear to the whole number of male citizens twenty-one years of age in such State.

SECTION 3

No person shall be a Senator or Representative in Congress, or elector of President and Vice-President, or hold any office, civil or military, under the United States, or under any State, who, having previously taken an oath, as a member of Congress, or as an officer of the United States, or as a member of any State legislature, or as an executive or judicial officer of any State, to support the Constitution of the United States, shall have engaged in insurrection or rebellion against the same, or given aid or comfort to the enemies thereof. But Congress may by a vote of two-thirds of each House, remove such disability.

SECTION 4

The validity of the public debt of the United States, authorized by law, including debts incurred for payment of pensions and bounties for services in suppressing insurrection or rebellion, shall not be questioned. But neither the United States nor any State shall assume or pay any debt or obligation incurred in aid of insurrection or rebellion against the United States, or any claim for the loss or emancipation of any slave; but all such debts, obligations and claims shall be held illegal and void.

SECTION 5

The Congress shall have the power to enforce, by appropriate legislation, the provisions of this article.

 *Changed by Section 1 of the Twenty-sixth Amendment.

AMENDMENT XV

Passed by Congress February 26, 1869. Ratified February 3, 1870.

SECTION 1

The right of citizens of the United States to vote shall not be denied or abridged by the United States or by any State on account of race, color, or previous condition of servitude.

SECTION 2

The Congress shall have the power to enforce this article by appropriate legislation.

AMENDMENT XVI

Passed by Congress July 2, 1909. Ratified February 3, 1913.

 Note: Article I, Section 9, of the Constitution was modified by Amendment XVI.

 The Congress shall have power to lay and collect taxes on incomes, from whatever source derived, without apportionment among the several States, and without regard to any census or enumeration.

AMENDMENT XVII

Passed by Congress May 13, 1912. Ratified April 8, 1913.

 Note: Article I, Section 3, of the Constitution was modified by the Seventeenth Amendment.

The Senate of the United States shall be composed of two Senators from each State, elected by the people thereof, for six years; and each Senator shall have one vote. The electors in each State shall have the qualifications requisite for electors of the most numerous branch of the State legislatures.

When vacancies happen in the representation of any State in the Senate, the executive authority of such State shall issue writs of election to fill such vacancies: Provided, That the legislature of any State may empower the executive thereof to make temporary appointments until the people fill the vacancies by election as the legislature may direct.

This amendment shall not be so construed as to affect the election or term of any Senator chosen before it becomes valid as part of the Constitution.

AMENDMENT XVIII
Passed by Congress December 18, 1917. Ratified January 16, 1919. Repealed by Amendment XXI.

SECTION 1
After one year from the ratification of this article the manufacture, sale, or transportation of intoxicating liquors within, the importation thereof into, or the exportation thereof from the United States and all territory subject to the jurisdiction thereof for beverage purposes is hereby prohibited.

SECTION 2
The Congress and the several States shall have concurrent power to enforce this article by appropriate legislation.

SECTION 3
This article shall be inoperative unless it shall have been ratified as an amendment to the Constitution by the legislatures of the several States, as provided in the Constitution, within seven years from the date of the submission hereof to the States by the Congress.

AMENDMENT XIX
Passed by Congress June 4, 1919. Ratified August 18, 1920.

The right of citizens of the United States to vote shall not be denied or abridged by the United States or by any State on account of sex.

Congress shall have power to enforce this article by appropriate legislation.

AMENDMENT XX
Passed by Congress March 2, 1932. Ratified January 23, 1933.

Note: Article I, Section 4, of the Constitution was modified by Section 2 of this amendment. In addition, a portion of the Twelfth Amendment was superseded by Section 3.

SECTION 1
The terms of the President and the Vice President shall end at noon on the 20th day of January, and the terms of Senators and Representatives at noon on the 3d day of January, of the years in which such terms would have ended if this article had not been ratified; and the terms of their successors shall then begin.

SECTION 2
The Congress shall assemble at least once in every year, and such meeting shall begin at noon on the 3d day of January, unless they shall by law appoint a different day.

SECTION 3
If, at the time fixed for the beginning of the term of the President, the President elect shall have died, the Vice President elect shall become President. If a President shall not have been chosen before the time fixed for the beginning of his term, or if the President elect shall have failed to qualify, then the Vice President elect shall act as President until a President shall have qualified; and the Congress may by law provide for the case wherein neither a President elect nor a Vice President shall have qualified, declaring who shall then act as President, or the manner in which one who is to act shall be selected, and such person shall act accordingly until a President or Vice President shall have qualified.

SECTION 4
The Congress may by law provide for the case of the death of any of the persons from whom the House of Representatives may choose a President whenever the right of choice shall have devolved upon them, and for the case of the death of any of the persons from whom the Senate may choose a Vice President whenever the right of choice shall have devolved upon them.

SECTION 5
Sections 1 and 2 shall take effect on the 15th day of October following the ratification of this article.

SECTION 6
This article shall be inoperative unless it shall have been ratified as an amendment to the Constitution by the legislatures of three-fourths of the several States within seven years from the date of its submission.

AMENDMENT XXI
Passed by Congress February 20, 1933. Ratified December 5, 1933.

SECTION 1
The eighteenth article of amendment to the Constitution of the United States is hereby repealed.

SECTION 2
The transportation or importation into any State, Territory, or Possession of the United States for delivery or use therein of intoxicating liquors, in violation of the laws thereof, is hereby prohibited.

SECTION 3
This article shall be inoperative unless it shall have been ratified as an amendment to the Constitution by conventions in the several States, as provided in the Constitution, within seven years from the date of the submission hereof to the States by the Congress.

AMENDMENT XXII
Passed by Congress March 21, 1947. Ratified February 27, 1951.

SECTION 1
No person shall be elected to the office of the President more than twice, and no person who has held the office of President, or acted as President, for more than two years of a term to which some other person was elected President shall be elected to the office of President more than once. But this Article shall not apply to any person holding the office of President when this Article was proposed by Congress, and shall not prevent any person who may be holding the office of President, or acting as President, during the term within which this Article becomes operative from holding the office of President or acting as President during the remainder of such term.

SECTION 2
This article shall be inoperative unless it shall have been ratified as an amendment to the Constitution by the legislatures of three-fourths of the several States within seven years from the date of its submission to the States by the Congress.

AMENDMENT XXIII
Passed by Congress June 16, 1960. Ratified March 29, 1961.

SECTION 1
The District constituting the seat of Government of the United States shall appoint in such manner as Congress may direct:

A number of electors of President and Vice President equal to the whole number of Senators and Representatives in Congress to which the District would be entitled if it were a State, but in no event more than the least populous State; they shall be in addition to those appointed by the States, but they shall be considered, for the purposes of the election of President and Vice President, to be electors appointed by a State; and they shall meet in the District and perform such duties as provided by the twelfth article of amendment.

SECTION 2
The Congress shall have power to enforce this article by appropriate legislation.

AMENDMENT XXIV
Passed by Congress August 27, 1962. Ratified January 23, 1964.

SECTION 1
The right of citizens of the United States to vote in any primary or other election for President or Vice President, for electors for President or Vice President, or for Senator or Representative in Congress, shall not be denied or abridged by the United States or any State by reason of failure to pay poll tax or other tax.

SECTION 2
The Congress shall have power to enforce this article by appropriate legislation.

AMENDMENT XXV
Passed by Congress July 6, 1965. Ratified February 10, 1967.

Note: Article II, Section 1, of the Constitution was affected by the Twenty-fifth Amendment.

SECTION 1
In case of the removal of the President from office or of his death or resignation, the Vice President shall become President.

SECTION 2
Whenever there is a vacancy in the office of the Vice President, the President shall nominate a Vice President who shall take office upon confirmation by a majority vote of both Houses of Congress.

SECTION 3
Whenever the President transmits to the President pro tempore of the Senate and the Speaker of the House of Representatives his written declaration that he is unable to discharge the powers and duties of his office, and until he transmits to them a written declaration to the contrary, such powers and duties shall be discharged by the Vice President as Acting President.

SECTION 4
Whenever the Vice President and a majority of either the principal officers of the executive departments or of such other body as Congress may by law provide, transmit to the President pro tempore of the Senate and the Speaker of the House of Representatives their written declaration that the President is unable to discharge the powers and duties of his office, the Vice President shall immediately assume the powers and duties of the office as Acting President.

Thereafter, when the President transmits to the President pro tempore of the Senate and the Speaker of the House of Representatives his written declaration that no inability exists, he shall resume the powers and duties of his office unless the Vice President and a majority of either the principal officers of the executive department or of such other body as Congress may by law provide, transmit within four days to the President pro tempore of the Senate and the Speaker of the House of Representatives their written declaration that the President is unable to discharge the powers and duties of his office. Thereupon Congress shall decide the issue, assembling within forty-eight hours for that purpose if not in session. If the Congress, within twenty-one days after receipt of the latter written declaration, or, if Congress is not in session, within twenty-one days after Congress is required to assemble, determines by two-thirds vote of both Houses that the President is unable to discharge the powers and duties of his office, the Vice President shall continue to discharge the same as Acting President; otherwise, the President shall resume the powers and duties of his office.

AMENDMENT XXVI
Passed by Congress March 23, 1971. Ratified July 1, 1971.

Note: Amendment XIV, Section 2, of the Constitution was modified by Section 1 of the Twenty-sixth Amendment.

SECTION 1

The right of citizens of the United States, who are eighteen years of age or older, to vote shall not be denied or abridged by the United States or by any State on account of age.

SECTION 2

The Congress shall have power to enforce this article by appropriate legislation.

AMENDMENT XXVII

Originally proposed Sept. 25, 1789. Ratified May 7, 1992.

No law, varying the compensation for the services of the Senators and Representatives, shall take effect, until an election of representatives shall have intervened.

Lincoln's Gettysburg Address

Four score and seven years ago our fathers brought forth on this continent, a new nation, conceived in Liberty, and dedicated to the proposition that all men are created equal.

Now we are engaged in a great civil war, testing whether that nation, or any nation so conceived and so dedicated, can long endure. We are met on a great battle-field of that war. We have come to dedicate a portion of that field, as a final resting place for those who here gave their lives that that nation might live. It is altogether fitting and proper that we should do this.

But, in a larger sense, we can not dedicate—we can not consecrate—we can not hallow—this ground. The brave men, living and dead, who struggled here, have consecrated it, far above our poor power to add or detract. The world will little note, nor long remember what we say here, but it can never forget what they did here. It is for us the living, rather, to be dedicated here to the unfinished work which they who fought here have thus far so nobly advanced. It is rather for us to be here dedicated to the great task remaining before us—that from these honored dead we take increased devotion to that cause for which they gave the last full measure of devotion—that we here highly resolve that these dead shall not have died in vain—that this nation, under God, shall have a new birth of freedom—and that government of the people, by the people, for the people, shall not perish from the earth.

Emancipation Proclamation

By the President of the United States of America: A Proclamation.

Whereas, on the twenty-second day of September, in the year of our Lord one thousand eight hundred and sixty-two, a proclamation was issued by the President of the United States, containing, among other things, the following, to wit:

"That on the first day of January, in the year of our Lord one thousand eight hundred and sixty-three, all persons held as slaves within any State or designated part of a State, the people whereof shall then be in rebellion against the United States, shall be then, thenceforward, and forever free; and the Executive

Government of the United States, including the military and naval authority thereof, will recognize and maintain the freedom of such persons, and will do no act or acts to repress such persons, or any of them, in any efforts they may make for their actual freedom.

"That the Executive will, on the first day of January aforesaid, by proclamation, designate the States and parts of States, if any, in which the people thereof, respectively, shall then be in rebellion against the United States; and the fact that any State, or the people thereof, shall on that day be, in good faith, represented in the Congress of the United States by members chosen thereto at elections wherein a majority of the qualified voters of such State shall have participated, shall, in the absence of strong countervailing testimony, be deemed conclusive evidence that such State, and the people thereof, are not then in rebellion against the United States."

Now, therefore I, Abraham Lincoln, President of the United States, by virtue of the power in me vested as Commander-in-Chief, of the Army and Navy of the United States in time of actual armed rebellion against the authority and government of the United States, and as a fit and necessary war measure for suppressing said rebellion, do, on this first day of January, in the year of our Lord one thousand eight hundred and sixty-three, and in accordance with my purpose so to do publicly proclaimed for the full period of one hundred days, from the day first above mentioned, order and designate as the States and parts of States wherein the people thereof respectively, are this day in rebellion against the United States, the following, to wit:

Arkansas, Texas, Louisiana, (except the Parishes of St. Bernard, Plaquemines, Jefferson, St. John, St. Charles, St. James Ascension, Assumption, Terrebonne, Lafourche, St. Mary, St. Martin, and Orleans, including the City of New Orleans) Mississippi, Alabama, Florida, Georgia, South Carolina, North Carolina, and Virginia, (except the forty-eight counties designated as West Virginia, and also the counties of Berkley, Accomac, Northampton, Elizabeth City, York, Princess Ann, and Norfolk, including the cities of Norfolk and Portsmouth[)], and which excepted parts, are for the present, left precisely as if this proclamation were not issued.

And by virtue of the power, and for the purpose aforesaid, I do order and declare that all persons held as slaves within said designated States, and parts of States, are, and henceforward shall be free; and that the Executive government of the United States, including the military and naval authorities thereof, will recognize and maintain the freedom of said persons.

And I hereby enjoin upon the people so declared to be free to abstain from all violence, unless in necessary self-defence; and I recommend to them that, in all cases when allowed, they labor faithfully for reasonable wages.

And I further declare and make known, that such persons of suitable condition, will be received into the armed service of the United States to garrison forts, positions, stations, and other places, and to man vessels of all sorts in said service.

And upon this act, sincerely believed to be an act of justice, warranted by the Constitution, upon military necessity, I invoke the considerate judgment of mankind, and the gracious favor of Almighty God.

In witness whereof, I have hereunto set my hand and caused the seal of the United States to be affixed.

Done at the City of Washington, this first day of January, in the year of our Lord one thousand eight hundred and sixty three, and of the Independence of the United States of America the eighty-seventh.

By the President: ABRAHAM LINCOLN
WILLIAM H. SEWARD, Secretary of State.

Key Provisions of the Civil Rights Act of 1964

An Act

To enforce the constitutional right to vote, to confer jurisdiction upon the district courts of the United States to provide injunctive relief against discrimination in public accommodations, to authorize the Attorney General to institute suits to protect constitutional rights in public facilities and public education, to extend the Commission on Civil Rights, to prevent discrimination in federally assisted programs, to establish a Commission on Equal Employment Opportunity, and for other purposes.

Be it enacted by the Senate and House of Representatives of the United States of America in Congress assembled, That this Act may be cited as the "Civil Rights Act of 1964."

TITLE I—VOTING RIGHTS

SEC. 101. Section 2004 of the Revised Statutes (42 U.S.C. 1971), as amended by section 131 of the Civil Rights Act of 1957 (71 Stat. 637), and as further amended by section 601 of the Civil Rights Act of 1960 (74 Stat. 90), is further amended as follows:

(a) Insert "1" after "(a)" in subsection (a) and add at the end of subsection (a) the following new paragraphs:

"(2) No person acting under color of law shall—

"(A) in determining whether any individual is qualified under State law or laws to vote in any Federal election, apply any standard, practice, or procedure different from the standards, practices, or procedures applied under such law or laws to other individuals within the same county, parish, or similar political subdivision who have been found by State officials to be qualified to vote;

"(B) deny the right of any individual to vote in any Federal election because of an error or omission on any record or paper relating to any application, registration, or other act requisite to voting, if such error or omission is not material in determining whether such individual is qualified under State law to vote in such election; or

"(C) employ any literacy test as a qualification for voting in any Federal election unless (i) such test is administered to each individual and is conducted wholly in writing, and (ii) a certified copy of the test and of the answers given by the individual is furnished to him within twenty-five days of the submission of his request made within the period of time during which records and papers are required to be retained and preserved pursuant to title III of the Civil Rights Act of 1960 (42 U.S.C. 1974—74e; 74 Stat. 88): Provided, however, That the Attorney General may enter into agreements with appropriate State or local authorities that preparation, conduct, and maintenance of such tests in accordance with the provisions of applicable State or local law, including such special provisions as are necessary in the preparation, conduct, and maintenance of such tests for persons who are blind or otherwise physically handicapped, meet the purposes of this subparagraph and constitute compliance therewith.

"(3) For purposes of this subsection—

"(A) the term 'vote' shall have the same meaning as in subsection (e) of this section;

"(B) the phrase 'literacy test' includes any test of the ability to read, write, understand, or interpret any matter."

(b) Insert immediately following the period at the end of the first sentence of subsection (c) the following new sentence: "If in any such proceeding literacy is a relevant fact there shall be a rebuttable presumption that any person who has not been adjudged an incompetent and who has completed the sixth grade in a public school in, or a private school accredited by, any State or territory, the District of Columbia, or the Commonwealth of Puerto Rico where instruction is carried on predominantly in the English language, possesses sufficient literacy, comprehension, and intelligence to vote in any Federal election."

(c) Add the following subsection "(f)" and designate the present subsection "(f)" as subsection "(g)": "(f) When used in subsection (a) or (c) of this section, the words 'Federal election' shall mean any general, special, or primary election held solely or in part for the purpose of electing or selecting any candidate for the office of President, Vice President, presidential elector, Member of the Senate, or Member of the House of Representatives."

(d) Add the following subsection "(h)":

"(h) In any proceeding instituted by the United States in any district court of the United States under this section in which the Attorney General requests a finding of a pattern or practice of discrimination pursuant to subsection (e) of this section the Attorney General, at the time he files the complaint, or any defendant in the proceeding, within twenty days after service upon him of the complaint, may file with the clerk of such court a request that a court of three judges be convened to hear and determine the entire case. A copy of the request for a three-judge court shall be immediately furnished by such clerk to the chief judge of the circuit (or in his absence, the presiding circuit judge of the circuit) in which the case is pending. Upon receipt of the copy of such request it shall be the duty of the chief justice of the circuit or the presiding circuit judge, as the case may be, to designate immediately three judges in such circuit, of whom at least one shall be a circuit judge and another of whom shall be a district judge of the court in which the proceeding was instituted, to hear and determine such case, and it shall be the duty of the judges so designated to assign the case for hearing at the earliest practicable date, to participate in the hearing and determination thereof, and to cause the case to be in every way expedited.

An appeal from the final judgment of such court will lie to the Supreme Court.

"In any proceeding brought under subsection (c) of this section to enforce subsection (b) of this section, or in the event neither the Attorney General nor any defendant files a request for a three-judge court in any proceeding authorized by this subsection, it shall be the duty of the chief judge of the district (or in his absence, the acting chief judge) in which the case is pending immediately to designate a judge in such district to hear and determine the case. In the event that no judge in the district is available to hear and determine the case, the chief judge of the district, or the acting chief judge, as the case may be, shall certify this fact to the chief judge of the circuit (or, in his absence, the acting chief judge) who shall then designate a district or circuit judge of the circuit to hear and determine the case.

"It shall be the duty of the judge designated pursuant to this section to assign the case for hearing at the earliest practicable date and to cause the case to be in every way expedited."

TITLE II—INJUNCTIVE RELIEF AGAINST DISCRIMINATION IN PLACES OF PUBLIC ACCOMMODATION

SEC. 201. (a) All persons shall be entitled to the full and equal enjoyment of the goods, services, facilities, and privileges, advantages, and accommodations of any place of public accommodation, as defined in this section, without discrimination or segregation on the ground of race, color, religion, or national origin.

(b) Each of the following establishments which serves the public is a place of public accommodation within the meaning of this title if its operations affect commerce, or if discrimination or segregation by it is supported by State action:

(1) any inn, hotel, motel, or other establishment which provides lodging to transient guests, other than an establishment located within a building which contains not more than five rooms for rent or hire and which is actually occupied by the proprietor of such establishment as his residence;

(2) any restaurant, cafeteria, lunchroom, lunch counter, soda fountain, or other facility principally engaged in selling food for consumption on

the premises, including, but not limited to, any such facility located on the premises of any retail establishment; or any gasoline station;

(3) any motion picture house, theater, concert hall, sports arena, stadium or other place of exhibition or entertainment; and

(4) any establishment (A)(i) which is physically located within the premises of any establishment otherwise covered by this subsection, or (ii) within the premises of which is physically located any such covered establishment, and (B) which holds itself out as serving patrons of such covered establishment.

(c) The operations of an establishment affect commerce within the meaning of this title if (1) it is one of the establishments described in paragraph (1) of subsection (b); (2) in the case of an establishment described in paragraph (2) of subsection (b), it serves or offers to serve interstate travelers or a substantial portion of the food which it serves, or gasoline or other products which it sells, has moved in commerce; (3) in the case of an establishment described in paragraph (3) of subsection (b), it customarily presents films, performances, athletic teams, exhibitions, or other sources of entertainment which move in commerce; and (4) in the case of an establishment described in paragraph (4) of subsection (b), it is physically located within the premises of, or there is physically located within its premises, an establishment the operations of which affect commerce within the meaning of this subsection. For purposes of this section, "commerce" means travel, trade, traffic, commerce, transportation, or communication among the several States, or between the District of Columbia and any State, or between any foreign country or any territory or possession and any State or the District of Columbia, or between points in the same State but through any other State or the District of Columbia or a foreign country.

(d) Discrimination or segregation by an establishment is supported by State action within the meaning of this title if such discrimination or segregation (1) is carried on under color of any law, statute, ordinance, or regulation; or (2) is carried on under color of any custom or usage required or enforced by officials of the State or political subdivision thereof; or (3) is required by action of the State or political subdivision thereof.

(e) The provisions of this title shall not apply to a private club or other establishment not in fact open to the public, except to the extent that the facilities of such establishment are made available to the customers or patrons of an establishment within the scope of subsection (b).

SEC. 202. All persons shall be entitled to be free, at any establishment or place, from discrimination or segregation of any kind on the ground of race, color, religion, or national origin, if such discrimination or segregation is or purports to be required by any law, statute, ordinance, regulation, rule, or order of a State or any agency or political subdivision thereof.

SEC. 203. No person shall (a) withhold, deny, or attempt to withhold or deny, or deprive or attempt to deprive, any person of any right or privilege secured by section 201 or 202, or (b) intimidate, threaten, or coerce, or attempt to intimidate, threaten, or coerce any person with the purpose of interfering with any right or privilege secured by section 201 or 202, or (c) punish or attempt to punish any person for exercising or attempting to exercise any right or privilege secured by section 201 or 202.

SEC. 204. (a) Whenever any person has engaged or there are reasonable grounds to believe that any person is about to engage in any act or practice prohibited by section 203, a civil action for preventive relief, including an application for a permanent or temporary injunction, restraining order, or other order, may be instituted by the person aggrieved and, upon timely application, the court may, in its discretion, permit the Attorney General to intervene in such civil action if he certifies that the case is of general public importance. Upon application by the complainant and in such circumstances as the court may deem just, the court may appoint an attorney for such complainant and may authorize the commencement of the civil action without the payment of fees, costs, or security.

(b) In any action commenced pursuant to this title, the court, in its discretion, may allow the prevailing party, other than the United States, a reasonable attorney's fee as part of the costs, and the United States shall be liable for costs the same as a private person.

(c) In the case of an alleged act or practice prohibited by this title which occurs in a State, or political subdivision of a State, which has a State or local law prohibiting such act or practice and establishing or authorizing a State or local authority to grant or seek relief from such practice or to institute criminal proceedings with respect thereto upon receiving notice thereof, no civil action may be brought under subsection (a) before the expiration of thirty days after written notice of such alleged act or practice has been given to the appropriate State or local authority by registered mail or in person, provided that the court may stay proceedings in such civil action pending the termination of State or local enforcement proceedings.

(d) In the case of an alleged act or practice prohibited by this title which occurs in a State, or political subdivision of a State, which has no State or local law prohibiting such act or practice, a civil action may be brought under subsection (a): Provided, That the court may refer the matter to the Community Relations Service established by title X of this Act for as long as the court believes there is a reasonable possibility of obtaining voluntary compliance, but for not more than sixty days: Provided further, That upon expiration of such sixty-day period, the court may extend such period for an additional period, not to exceed a cumulative total of one hundred and twenty days, if it believes there then exists a reasonable possibility of securing voluntary compliance.

SEC. 205. The Service is authorized to make a full investigation of any complaint referred to it by the court under section 204(d) and may hold such hearings with respect thereto as may be necessary. The Service shall conduct any hearings with respect to any such complaint in executive session, and shall not release any testimony given therein except by agreement of all parties involved in the complaint with the permission of the court, and the Service shall endeavor to bring about a voluntary settlement between the parties.

SEC. 206. (a) Whenever the Attorney General has reasonable cause to believe that any person or group of persons is engaged in a pattern or practice of resistance to the full enjoyment of any of the rights secured by this title, and that the pattern or practice is of such a nature and is intended to deny the full exercise of the rights herein described, the Attorney General may bring a civil action in the appropriate district court of the United States by filing with it a complaint (1) signed by him (or in his absence the Acting Attorney General), (2) setting forth facts pertaining to such pattern or practice, and (3) requesting such preventive relief, including an application for a permanent or temporary injunction, restraining order or other order against the person or persons responsible for such pattern or practice, as he deems necessary to insure the full enjoyment of the rights herein described.

(b) In any such proceeding the Attorney General may file with the clerk of such court a request that a court of three judges be convened to hear and determine the case. Such request by the Attorney General shall be accompanied by a certificate that, in his opinion, the case is of general public importance. A copy of the certificate and request for a three-judge court shall be immediately furnished by such clerk to the chief judge of the circuit (or in his absence, the presiding circuit judge of the circuit) in which the case is pending. Upon receipt of the copy of such request it shall be the duty of the chief judge of the circuit or the presiding circuit judge, as the case may be, to designate immediately three judges in such circuit, of whom at least one shall be a circuit judge and another of whom shall be a district judge of the court in which the proceeding was instituted, to hear and determine such case, and it shall be the duty of the judges so designated to assign the case for hearing at the earliest practicable date, to participate in the hearing and determination thereof, and to cause the case to be in every way expedited. An appeal from the final judgment of such court will lie to the Supreme Court.

In the event the Attorney General fails to file such a request in any such proceeding, it shall be the duty of the chief judge of the district (or in his absence, the acting chief judge) in which the case is pending immediately to designate a judge in such district to hear and determine the case. In the event that no judge in the district is available to hear and determine the case, the chief judge of the district, or the acting chief judge, as the case may be, shall certify this fact to the chief judge of the circuit (or in his absence, the acting chief judge) who shall then designate a district or circuit judge of the circuit to hear and determine the case.

It shall be the duty of the judge designated pursuant to this section to assign the case for hearing at the earliest practicable date and to cause the case to be in every way expedited.

SEC. 207. (a) The district courts of the United States shall have jurisdiction of proceedings instituted pursuant to this title and shall exercise the same without regard to whether the aggrieved party shall have exhausted any administrative or other remedies that may be provided by law.

(b) The remedies provided in this title shall be the exclusive means of enforcing the rights based on this title, but nothing in this title shall preclude any individual or any State or local agency from asserting any right based on any other Federal or State law not inconsistent with this title, including any statute or ordinance requiring nondiscrimination in public establishments or accommodations, or from pursuing any remedy, civil or criminal, which may be available for the vindication or enforcement of such right.

TITLE III–DESEGREGATION OF PUBLIC FACILITIES

SEC. 301. (a) Whenever the Attorney General receives a complaint in writing signed by an individual to the effect that he is being deprived of or threatened with the loss of his right to the equal protection of the laws, on account of his race, color, religion, or national origin, by being denied equal utilization of any public facility which is owned, operated, or managed by or on behalf of any State or subdivision thereof, other than a public school or public college as defined in section 401 of title IV hereof, and the Attorney General believes the complaint is meritorious and certifies that the signer or signers of such complaint are unable, in his judgment, to initiate and maintain appropriate legal proceedings for relief and that the institution of an action will materially further the orderly progress of desegregation in public facilities, the Attorney General is authorized to institute for or in the name of the United States a civil action in any appropriate district court of the United States against such parties and for such relief as may be appropriate, and such court shall have and shall exercise jurisdiction of proceedings instituted pursuant to this section. The Attorney General may implead as defendants such additional parties as are or become necessary to the grant of effective relief hereunder.

(b) The Attorney General may deem a person or persons unable to initiate and maintain appropriate legal proceedings within the meaning of subsection

(a) of this section when such person or persons are unable, either directly or through other interested persons or organizations, to bear the expense of the litigation or to obtain effective legal representation; or whenever he is satisfied that the institution of such litigation would jeopardize the personal safety, employment, or economic standing of such person or persons, their families, or their property.

SEC. 302. In any action or proceeding under this title the United States shall be liable for costs, including a reasonable attorney's fee, the same as a private person.

SEC. 303. Nothing in this title shall affect adversely the right of any person to sue for or obtain relief in any court against discrimination in any facility covered by this title.

SEC. 304. A complaint as used in this title is a writing or document within the meaning of section 1001, title 18, United States Code.

TITLE IV–DESEGREGATION OF PUBLIC EDUCATION DEFINITIONS

SEC. 401. As used in this title—

(a) "Commissioner" means the Commissioner of Education.

(b) "Desegregation" means the assignment of students to public schools and within such schools without regard to their race, color, religion, or national origin, but "desegregation" shall not mean the assignment of students to public schools in order to overcome racial imbalance.

(c) "Public school" means any elementary or secondary educational institution, and "public college" means any institution of higher education or any technical or vocational school above the secondary school level, provided that such public school or public college is operated by a State, subdivision of a State, or governmental agency within a State, or operated wholly or predominantly from or through the use of governmental funds or property, or funds or property derived from a governmental source.

(d) "School board" means any agency or agencies which administer a system of one or more public schools and any other agency which is responsible for the assignment of students to or within such system.

SURVEY AND REPORT OF EDUCATIONAL OPPORTUNITIES

SEC. 402. The Commissioner shall conduct a survey and make a report to the President and the Congress, within two years of the enactment of this title, concerning the lack of availability of equal educational opportunities for individuals by reason of race, color, religion, or national origin in public educational institutions at all levels in the United States, its territories and possessions, and the District of Columbia.

TECHNICAL ASSISTANCE

SEC. 403. The Commissioner is authorized, upon the application of any school board, State, municipality, school district, or other governmental unit legally responsible for operating a public school or schools, to render technical assistance to such applicant in the preparation, adoption, and implementation of plans for the desegregation of public schools. Such technical assistance may, among other activities, include making available to such agencies information regarding effective methods of coping with special educational problems occasioned by desegregation, and making available to such agencies personnel of the Office of Education or other persons specially equipped to advise and assist them in coping with such problems.

TRAINING INSTITUTES

SEC. 404. The Commissioner is authorized to arrange, through grants or contracts, with institutions of higher education for the operation of short-term or regular session institutes for special training designed to improve the ability of teachers, supervisors, counselors, and other elementary or secondary school personnel to deal effectively with special educational problems occasioned by desegregation. Individuals who attend such an institute on a full-time basis may be paid stipends for the period of their attendance at such institute in amounts specified by the Commissioner in regulations, including allowances for travel to attend such institute.

GRANTS

SEC. 405. (a) The Commissioner is authorized, upon application of a school board, to make grants to such board to pay, in whole or in part, the cost of—

    (1) giving to teachers and other school personnel inservice training in dealing with problems incident to desegregation, and

    (2) employing specialists to advise in problems incident to desegregation.

  (b) In determining whether to make a grant, and in fixing the amount thereof and the terms and conditions on which it will be made, the Commissioner shall take into consideration the amount available for grants under this section and the other applications which are pending before him; the financial condition of the applicant and the other resources available to it; the nature, extent, and gravity of its problems incident to desegregation; and such other factors as he finds relevant.

PAYMENTS

SEC. 406. Payments pursuant to a grant or contract under this title may be made (after necessary adjustments on account of previously made overpayments or underpayments) in advance or by way of reimbursement, and in such installments, as the Commissioner may determine.

SUITS BY THE ATTORNEY GENERAL

SEC. 407. (a) Whenever the Attorney General receives a complaint in writing—

    (1) signed by a parent or group of parents to the effect that his or their minor children, as members of a class of persons similarly situated, are being deprived by a school board of the equal protection of the laws, or

    (2) signed by an individual, or his parent, to the effect that he has been denied admission to or not permitted to continue in attendance at a public college by reason of race, color, religion, or national origin, and the Attorney General believes the complaint is meritorious and certifies that the signer or signers of such complaint are unable, in his judgment, to initiate and maintain appropriate legal proceedings for relief and that the institution of an action will materially further the orderly achievement of desegregation in public education, the Attorney General is authorized, after giving notice of such complaint to the appropriate school board or college authority and after certifying that he is satisfied that such board or authority has had a reasonable time to adjust the conditions alleged in such complaint, to institute for or in the name of the United States a civil action in any appropriate

district court of the United States against such parties and for such relief as may be appropriate, and such court shall have and shall exercise jurisdiction of proceedings instituted pursuant to this section, provided that nothing herein shall empower any official or court of the United States to issue any order seeking to achieve a racial balance in any school by requiring the transportation of pupils or students from one school to another or one school district to another in order to achieve such racial balance, or otherwise enlarge the existing power of the court to insure compliance with constitutional standards. The Attorney General may implead as defendants such additional parties as are or become necessary to the grant of effective relief hereunder.

(b) The Attorney General may deem a person or persons unable to initiate and maintain appropriate legal proceedings within the meaning of subsection

(a) of this section when such person or persons are unable, either directly or through other interested persons or organizations, to bear the expense of the litigation or to obtain effective legal representation; or whenever he is satisfied that the institution of such litigation would jeopardize the personal safety, employment, or economic standing of such person or persons, their families, or their property.

(c) The term "parent" as used in this section includes any person standing in loco parentis. A "complaint" as used in this section is a writing or document within the meaning of section 1001, title 18, United States Code.

SEC. 408. In any action or proceeding under this title the United States shall be liable for costs the same as a private person.

SEC. 409. Nothing in this title shall affect adversely the right of any person to sue for or obtain relief in any court against discrimination in public education.

SEC. 410. Nothing in this title shall prohibit classification and assignment for reasons other than race, color, religion, or national origin.

TITLE V—COMMISSION ON CIVIL RIGHTS

SEC. 501. Section 102 of the Civil Rights Act of 1957 (42 U.S.C. 1975a; 71 Stat. 634) is amended to read as follows:

"RULES OF PROCEDURE OF THE COMMISSION HEARINGS

"SEC. 102.

(a) At least thirty days prior to the commencement of any hearing, the Commission shall cause to be published in the Federal Register notice of the date on which such hearing is to commence, the place at which it is to be held and the subject of the hearing. The Chairman, or one designated by him to act as Chairman at a hearing of the Commission, shall announce in an opening statement the subject of the hearing.

"(b) A copy of the Commission's rules shall be made available to any witness before the Commission, and a witness compelled to appear before the Commission or required to produce written or other matter shall be served with a copy of the Commission's rules at the time of service of the subpoena.

"(c) Any person compelled to appear in person before the Commission shall be accorded the right to be accompanied and advised by counsel, who shall have the right to subject his client to reasonable examination, and to make objections on the record and to argue briefly the basis for such objections. The Commission shall proceed with reasonable dispatch to conclude any hearing in which it is engaged. Due regard shall be had for the convenience and necessity of witnesses.

"(d) The Chairman or Acting Chairman may punish breaches of order and decorum by censure and exclusion from the hearings.

"(e) If the Commission determines that evidence or testimony at any hearing may tend to defame, degrade, or incriminate any person, it shall receive such evidence or testimony or summary of such evidence o testimony in executive session. The Commission shall afford any person defamed, degraded, or incriminated by such evidence or testimony an opportunity to appear and be heard in executive session, with a reasonable number of additional witnesses requested by him, before deciding to use such evidence or testimony. In the event the Commission determines to release or use such evidence or testimony in such manner as to reveal publicly the identity of the person defamed, degraded, or incriminated, such evidence or testimony, prior to such public release or use, shall be given at a public session, and the Commission shall afford such person an opportunity to appear as a voluntary witness or to file a sworn statement in his behalf and to submit brief and pertinent sworn statements of others. The Commission shall receive and dispose of requests from such person to subpoena additional witnesses.

"(f) Except as provided in sections 102 and 105 (f) of this Act, the Chairman shall receive and the Commission shall dispose of requests to subpoena additional witnesses.

"(g) No evidence or testimony or summary of evidence or testimony taken in executive session may be released or used in public sessions without the consent of the Commission. Whoever releases or uses in public without the consent of the Commission such evidence or testimony taken in executive session shall be fined not more than $1,000, or imprisoned for not more than one year.

"(h) In the discretion of the Commission, witnesses may submit brief and pertinent sworn statements in writing for inclusion in the record. The Commission shall determine the pertinency of testimony and evidence adduced at its hearings.

"(i) Every person who submits data or evidence shall be entitled to retain or, on payment of lawfully prescribed costs, procure a copy or transcript thereof, except that a witness in a hearing held in executive session may for good cause be limited to inspection of the official transcript of his testimony. Transcript copies of public sessions may be obtained by the public upon the payment of the cost thereof. An accurate transcript shall be made of the testimony of all witnesses at all hearings, either public or executive sessions, of the Commission or of any subcommittee thereof.

"(j)   A witness attending any session of the Commission shall receive $6 for each day's attendance and for the time necessarily occupied in going to and returning from the same, and 10 cents per mile for going from and returning to his place of residence. Witnesses who attend at points so far removed from their respective residences as to prohibit return thereto from day to day shall be entitled to an additional allowance of $10 per day for expenses of subsistence including the time necessarily occupied in going to and returning from the place of attendance. Mileage payments shall be tendered to the witness upon service of a subpoena issued on behalf of the Commission or any subcommittee thereof.

"(k)   The Commission shall not issue any subpoena for the attendance and testimony of witnesses or for the production of written or other matter which would require the presence of the party subpoenaed at a hearing to be held outside of the State wherein the witness is found or resides or is domiciled or transacts business, or has appointed an agent for receipt of service of process except that, in any event, the Commission may issue subpoenas for the attendance and testimony of witnesses and the production of written or other matter at a hearing held within fifty miles of the place where the witness is found or resides or is domiciled or transacts business or has appointed an agent for receipt of service of process.

"(l)   The Commission shall separately state and currently publish in the Federal Register (1) descriptions of its central and field organization including the established places at which, and methods whereby, the public may secure information or make requests; (2) statements of the general course and method by which its functions are channeled and determined, and (3) rules adopted as authorized by law. No person shall in any manner be subject to or required to resort to rules, organization, or procedure not so published."

SEC. 502. Section 103(a) of the Civil Rights Act of 1957 (42 U.S.C. 1975b (a); 71 Stat. 634) is amended to read as follows:

"SEC. 103. (a) Each member of the Commission who is not otherwise in the service of the Government of the United States shall receive the sum of $75 per day for each day spent in the work of the Commission, shall be paid actual travel expenses, and per diem in lieu of subsistence expenses when away from his usual place of residence, in accordance with section 5 of the Administrative Expenses Act of 1946, as amended (5 U.S.C 73b-2; 60 Stat. 808)."

SEC. 503. Section 103(b) of the Civil Rights Act of 1957 (42 U.S.C. 1975(b); 71 Stat. 634) is amended to read as follows:

"(b)   Each member of the Commission who is otherwise in the service of the Government of the United States shall serve without compensation in addition to that received for such other service, but while engaged in the work of the Commission shall be paid actual travel expenses, and per diem in lieu of subsistence expenses when away from his usual place of residence, in accordance with the provisions of the Travel Expenses Act of 1949, as amended

(5 U.S.C. 835—42; 63 Stat. 166)."

SEC. 504. (a) Section 104(a) of the Civil Rights Act of 1957 (42 U.S.C. 1975c(a); 71 Stat. 635), as amended, is further amended to read as follows:

"DUTIES OF THE COMMISSION

"SEC. 104. (a) The Commission shall—

"(1) investigate allegations in writing under oath or affirmation that certain citizens of the United States are being deprived of their right to vote and have that vote counted by reason of their color, race, religion, or national origin; which writing, under oath or affirmation, shall set forth the facts upon which such belief or beliefs are based;

"(2) study and collect information concerning legal developments constituting a denial of equal protection of the laws under the Constitution because of race, color, religion or national origin or in the administration of justice;

"(3) appraise the laws and policies of the Federal Government with respect to denials of equal protection of the laws under the Constitution because of race, color, religion or national origin or in the administration of justice;

"(4) serve as a national clearinghouse for information in respect to denials of equal protection of the laws because of race, color, religion or national origin, including but not limited to the fields of voting, education, housing, employment, the use of public facilities, and transportation, or in the administration of justice;

"(5) investigate allegations, made in writing and under oath or affirmation, that citizens of the United States are unlawfully being accorded or denied the right to vote, or to have their votes properly counted, in any election of presidential electors, Members of the United States Senate, or of the House of Representatives, as a result of any patterns or practice of fraud or discrimination in the conduct of such election; and

"(6) Nothing in this or any other Act shall be construed as authorizing the Commission, its Advisory Committees, or any person under its supervision or control to inquire into or investigate any membership practices or internal operations of any fraternal organization, any college or university fraternity or sorority, any private club or any religious organization."

(b) Section 104(b) of the Civil Rights Act of 1957 (42 U.S.C. 1975c(b); 71 Stat. 635), as amended, is further amended by striking out the present subsection "(b)" and by substituting therefor:

"(b) The Commission shall submit interim reports to the President and to the Congress at such times as the Commission, the Congress or the President shall deem desirable, and shall submit to the President and to the Congress a final report of its activities, findings, and recommendations not later than January 31, 1968."

SEC. 505. Section 105(a) of the Civil Rights Act of 1957 (42 U.S.C. 1975d(a); 71 Stat. 636) is amended by striking out in the last sentence thereof "$50 per diem" and inserting in lieu thereof "$75 per diem."

SEC. 506. Section 105(f) and section 105(g) of the Civil Rights Act of 1957 (42 U.S.C. 1975d (f) and (g); 71 Stat. 636) are amended to read as follows:

"(f) The Commission, or on the authorization of the Commission any subcommittee of two or more members, at least one of whom shall be of each major political party, may, for the purpose of carrying out the provisions of this Act, hold such hearings and act at such times and places as the Commission or such authorized subcommittee may deem advisable. Subpoenas for the attendance and testimony of witnesses or the production of written or other matter may be issued in accordance with the rules of the Commission as contained in section 102 (j) and (k) of this Act, over the signature of the Chairman of the Commission or of such subcommittee, and may be served by any person designated by such Chairman. The holding of hearings by the Commission, or the appointment of a subcommittee to hold hearings pursuant to this subparagraph, must be approved by a majority of the Commission, or by a majority of the members present at a meeting at which at least a quorum of four members is present.

"(g) In case of contumacy or refusal to obey a subpoena, any district court of the United States or the United States court of any territory or possession, or the District Court of the United States for the District of Columbia, within the jurisdiction of which the inquiry is carried on or within the jurisdiction of which said person guilty of contumacy or refusal to obey is found or resides or is domiciled or transacts business, or has appointed an agent for receipt of service of process, upon application by the Attorney General of the United States shall have jurisdiction to issue to such person an order requiring such person to appear before the Commission or a subcommittee thereof, there to produce pertinent, relevant and nonprivileged evidence if so ordered, or there to give testimony touching the matter under investigation; and any failure to obey such order of the court may be punished by said court as a contempt thereof."

SEC. 507. Section 105 of the Civil Rights Act of 1957 (42 U.S.C. 1975d; 71 Stat. 636), as amended by section 401 of the Civil Rights Act of 1960 (42 U.S.C. 1975d(h); 74 Stat. 89), is further amended by adding a new subsection at the end to read as follows:

"(i) The Commission shall have the power to make such rules and regulations as are necessary to carry out the purposes of this Act."

TITLE VI—NONDISCRIMINATION IN FEDERALLY ASSISTED PROGRAMS

SEC. 601. No person in the United States shall, on the ground of race, color, or national origin, be excluded from participation in, be denied the benefits of, or be subjected to discrimination under any program or activity receiving Federal financial assistance.

SEC. 602. Each Federal department and agency which is empowered to extend Federal financial assistance to any program or activity, by way of grant, loan, or contract other than a contract of insurance or guaranty, is authorized and directed to effectuate the provisions of section 601 with respect to such program or activity by issuing rules, regulations, or orders of general applicability which shall be consistent with achievement of the objectives of the statute authorizing the financial assistance in connection with which the action is taken. No such rule, regulation, or order shall become effective unless and until approved by the President. Compliance with any requirement adopted pursuant to this section may be effected (1) by the termination of or refusal to grant or to continue assistance under such program or activity to any recipient as to whom there has been an express finding on the record, after opportunity for hearing, of a failure to comply with such requirement, but such termination or refusal shall be limited to the particular political entity, or part thereof, or other recipient as to whom such a finding has been made and, shall be limited in its effect to the particular program, or part thereof, in which such non-compliance has been so found, or (2) by any other means authorized by law: Provided, however, That no such action shall be taken until the department or agency concerned has advised the appropriate person or persons of the failure to comply with the requirement and has determined that compliance cannot be secured by voluntary means. In the case of any action terminating, or refusing to grant or continue, assistance because of failure to comply with a requirement imposed pursuant to this section, the head of the federal department or agency shall file with the committees of the House and Senate having legislative jurisdiction over the program or activity involved a full written report of the circumstances and the grounds for such action. No such action shall become effective until thirty days have elapsed after the filing of such report.

SEC. 603. Any department or agency action taken pursuant to section 602 shall be subject to such judicial review as may otherwise be provided by law for similar action taken by such department or agency on other grounds. In the case of action, not otherwise subject to judicial review, terminating or refusing to grant or to continue financial assistance upon a finding of failure to comply with any requirement imposed pursuant to section 602, any person aggrieved (including any State or political subdivision thereof and any agency of either) may obtain judicial review of such action in accordance with section 10 of the Administrative Procedure Act, and such action shall not be deemed committed to unreviewable agency discretion within the meaning of that section.

SEC. 604. Nothing contained in this title shall be construed to authorize action under this title by any department or agency with respect to any employment practice of any employer, employment agency, or labor organization except where a primary objective of the Federal financial assistance is to provide employment.

SEC. 605. Nothing in this title shall add to or detract from any existing authority with respect to any program or activity under which Federal financial assistance is extended by way of a contract of insurance or guaranty.

TITLE VII—EQUAL EMPLOYMENT OPPORTUNITY DEFINITIONS

SEC. 701. For the purposes of this title—

(a) The term "person" includes one or more individuals, labor unions, partnerships, associations, corporations, legal representatives, mutual companies, joint-stock companies, trusts, unincorporated organizations, trustees, trustees in bankruptcy, or receivers.

(b) The term "employer" means a person engaged in an industry affecting commerce who has twenty-five or more employees for each working day in each of twenty or more calendar weeks in the current or preceding calendar year, and any agent of such a person, but such term does not include (1) the United States, a corporation wholly owned by the Government of the United States, an Indian tribe, or a State or political subdivision thereof, (2) a bona fide private membership club (other than a labor organization) which is exempt from taxation under section 501(c) of the Internal Revenue Code of 1954: Provided, That during the first year after the effective date prescribed in subsection (a) of section 716, persons having fewer than one hundred employees (and their agents) shall not be considered employers, and, during the second year after such date, persons having fewer than seventy-five employees (and their agents) shall not be considered employers, and, during the third year after such date, persons having fewer than fifty employees (and their agents) shall not be considered employers: Provided further, That it shall be the policy of the United States to insure equal employment opportunities for Federal employees without discrimination because of race, color, religion, sex or national origin and the President shall utilize his existing authority to effectuate this policy.

(c) The term "employment agency" means any person regularly undertaking with or without compensation to procure employees for an employer or to procure for employees opportunities to work for an employer and includes an agent of such a person; but shall not include an agency of the United States, or an agency of a State or political subdivision of a State, except that such term shall include the United States Employment Service and the system of State and local employment services receiving Federal assistance.

(d) The term "labor organization" means a labor organization engaged in an industry affecting commerce, and any agent of such an organization, and includes any organization of any kind, any agency, or employee representation committee, group, association, or plan so engaged in which employees participate and which exists for the purpose, in whole or in part, of dealing with employers concerning grievances, labor disputes, wages, rates of pay, hours, or other terms or conditions of employment, and any conference, general committee, joint or system board, or joint council so engaged which is subordinate to a national or international labor organization.

(e) A labor organization shall be deemed to be engaged in an industry affecting commerce if (1) it maintains or operates a hiring hall or hiring office which procures employees for an employer or procures for employees opportunities to work for an employer, or (2) the number of its members (or, where it is a labor organization composed of other labor organizations or their representatives, if the aggregate number of the members of such other labor organization) is (A) one hundred or more during the first year after the effective date prescribed in subsection (a) of section 716, (B) seventy-five or more during the second year after such date or fifty or more during the third year, or (C) twenty-five or more thereafter, and such labor organization—

(1) is the certified representative of employees under the provisions of the National Labor Relations Act, as amended, or the Railway Labor Act, as amended;

(2) although not certified, is a national or international labor organization or a local labor organization recognized or acting as the representative of employees of an employer or employers engaged in an industry affecting commerce; or

(3) has chartered a local labor organization or subsidiary body which is representing or actively seeking to represent employees of employers within the meaning of paragraph (1) or (2); or

(4) has been chartered by a labor organization representing or actively seeking to represent employees within the meaning of paragraph (1) or (2) as the local or subordinate body through which such employees may enjoy membership or become affiliated with such labor organization; or

(5) is a conference, general committee, joint or system board, or joint council subordinate to a national or international labor organization, which includes a labor organization engaged in an industry affecting commerce within the meaning of any of the preceding paragraphs of this subsection.

(f) The term "employee" means an individual employed by an employer.

(g) The term "commerce" means trade, traffic, commerce, transportation, transmission, or communication among the several States; or between a State and any place outside thereof; or within the District of Columbia, or a possession of the United States; or between points in the same State but through a point outside thereof.

(h) The term "industry affecting commerce" means any activity, business, or industry in commerce or in which a labor dispute would hinder or obstruct commerce or the free flow of commerce and includes any activity or industry "affecting commerce" within the meaning of the Labor-Management Reporting and Disclosure Act of 1959.

(i)   The term "State" includes a State of the United States, the District of Columbia, Puerto Rico, the Virgin Islands, American Samoa, Guam, Wake Island, The Canal Zone, and Outer Continental Shelf lands defined in the Outer Continental Shelf Lands Act.

EXEMPTION

SEC. 702. This title shall not apply to an employer with respect to the employment of aliens outside any State, or to a religious corporation, association, or society with respect to the employment of individuals of a particular religion to perform work connected with the carrying on by such corporation, association, or society of its religious activities or to an educational institution with respect to the employment of individuals to perform work connected with the educational activities of such institution.

DISCRIMINATION BECAUSE OF RACE, COLOR, RELIGION, SEX, OR NATIONAL ORIGIN

SEC. 703. (a) It shall be an unlawful employment practice for an employer—

(1)   to fail or refuse to hire or to discharge any individual, or otherwise to discriminate against any individual with respect to his compensation, terms, conditions, or privileges of employment, because of such individual's race, color, religion, sex, or national origin; or

(2)   to limit, segregate, or classify his employees in any way which would deprive or tend to deprive any individual of employment opportunities or otherwise adversely affect his status as an employee, because of such individual's race, color, religion, sex, or national origin.

(b)   It shall be an unlawful employment practice for an employment agency to fail or refuse to refer for employment, or otherwise to discriminate against, any individual because of his race, color, religion, sex, or national origin, or to classify or refer for employment any individual on the basis of his race, color, religion, sex, or national origin.

(c)   It shall be an unlawful employment practice for a labor organization—

(1)   to exclude or to expel from its membership, or otherwise to discriminate against, any individual because of his race, color, religion, sex, or national origin;

(2)   to limit, segregate, or classify its membership, or to classify or fail or refuse to refer for employment any individual, in any way which would deprive or tend to deprive any individual of employment opportunities, or would limit such employment opportunities or otherwise adversely affect his status as an employee or as an applicant for employment, because of such individual's race, color, religion, sex, or national origin; or

(3)   to cause or attempt to cause an employer to discriminate against an individual in violation of this section.

(d) It shall be an unlawful employment practice for any employer, labor organization, or joint labor-management committee controlling apprenticeship or other training or retraining, including on-the-job training programs to discriminate against any individual because of his race, color, religion, sex, or national origin in admission to, or employment in, any program established to provide apprenticeship or other training.

(e) Notwithstanding any other provision of this title, (1) it shall not be an unlawful employment practice for an employer to hire and employ employees, for an employment agency to classify, or refer for employment any individual, for a labor organization to classify its membership or to classify or refer for employment any individual, or for an employer, labor organization, or joint labor-management committee controlling apprenticeship or other training or retraining programs to admit or employ any individual in any such program, on the basis of his religion, sex, or national origin in those certain instances where religion, sex, or national origin is a bona fide occupational qualification reasonably necessary to the normal operation of that particular business or enterprise, and (2) it shall not be an unlawful employment practice for a school, college, university, or other educational institution or institution of learning to hire and employ employees of a particular religion if such school, college, university, or other educational institution or institution of learning is, in whole or in substantial part, owned, supported, controlled, or managed by a particular religion or by a particular religious corporation, association, or society, or if the curriculum of such school, college, university, or other educational institution or institution of learning is directed toward the propagation of a particular religion.

(f) As used in this title, the phrase "unlawful employment practice" shall not be deemed to include any action or measure taken by an employer, labor organization, joint labor-management committee, or employment agency with respect to an individual who is a member of the Communist Party of the United States or of any other organization required to register as a Communist-action or Communist-front organization by final order of the Subversive Activities Control Board pursuant to the Subversive Activities Control Act of 1950.

(g) Notwithstanding any other provision of this title, it shall not be an unlawful employment practice for an employer to fail or refuse to hire and employ any individual for any position, for an employer to discharge any individual from any position, or for an employment agency to fail or refuse to refer any individual for employment in any position, or for a labor organization to fail or refuse to refer any individual for employment in any position, if—

    (1) the occupancy of such position, or access to the premises in or upon which any part of the duties of such position is performed or is to be performed, is subject to any requirement imposed in the interest of the national security of the United States under any security program in effect pursuant to or administered under any statute of the United States or any Executive order of the President; and

(2) such individual has not fulfilled or has ceased to fulfill that requirement.

(h) Notwithstanding any other provision of this title, it shall not be an unlawful employment practice for an employer to apply different standards of compensation, or different terms, conditions, or privileges of employment pursuant to a bona fide seniority or merit system, or a system which measures earnings by quantity or quality of production or to employees who work in different locations, provided that such differences are not the result of an intention to discriminate because of race, color, religion, sex, or national origin, nor shall it be an unlawful employment practice for an employer to give and to act upon the results of any professionally developed ability test provided that such test, its administration or action upon the results is not designed, intended or used to discriminate because of race, color, religion, sex or national origin. It shall not be an unlawful employment practice under this title for any employer to differentiate upon the basis of sex in determining the amount of the wages or compensation paid or to be paid to employees of such employer if such differentiation is authorized by the provisions of section 6(d) of the Fair Labor Standards Act of 1938, as amended (29 U.S.C. 206(d)).

(i) Nothing contained in this title shall apply to any business or enterprise on or near an Indian reservation with respect to any publicly announced employment practice of such business or enterprise under which a preferential treatment is given to any individual because he is an Indian living on or near a reservation.

(j) Nothing contained in this title shall be interpreted to require any employer, employment agency, labor organization, or joint labor-management committee subject to this title to grant preferential treatment to any individual or to any group because of the race, color, religion, sex, or national origin of such individual or group on account of an imbalance which may exist with respect to the total number or percentage of persons of any race, color, religion, sex, or national origin employed by any employer, referred or classified for employment by any employment agency or labor organization, admitted to membership or classified by any labor organization, or admitted to, or employed in, any apprenticeship or other training program, in comparison with the total number or percentage of persons of such race, color, religion, sex, or national origin in any community, State, section, or other area, or in the available work force in any community, State, section, or other area.

OTHER UNLAWFUL EMPLOYMENT PRACTICES

SEC. 704. (a) It shall be an unlawful employment practice for an employer to discriminate against any of his employees or applicants for employment, for an employment agency to discriminate against any individual, or for a labor organization to discriminate against any member thereof or applicant for membership, because he has opposed, any practice made an unlawful employment practice by this title, or because he has made a charge, testified, assisted, or participated in any manner in an investigation, proceeding, or hearing under this title.

(b) It shall be an unlawful employment practice for an employer, labor organization, or employment agency to print or publish or cause to be printed or published any notice or advertisement relating to employment by such an employer or membership in or any classification or referral for employment by such a labor organization, or relating to any classification or referral for employment by such an employment agency, indicating any preference, limitation, specification, or discrimination, based on race, color, religion, sex, or national origin, except that such a notice or advertisement may indicate a preference, limitation, specification, or discrimination based on religion, sex, or national origin when religion, sex, or national origin is a bona fide occupational qualification for employment.

EQUAL EMPLOYMENT OPPORTUNITY COMMISSION

SEC. 705. (a) There is hereby created a Commission to be known as the Equal Employment Opportunity Commission, which shall be composed of five members, not more than three of whom shall be members of the same political party, who shall be appointed by the President by and with the advice and consent of the Senate. One of the original members shall be appointed for a term of one year, one for a term of two years, one for a term of three years, one for a term of four years, and one for a term of five years, beginning from the date of enactment of this title, but their successors shall be appointed for terms of five years each, except that any individual chosen to fill a vacancy shall be appointed only for the unexpired term of the member whom he shall succeed. The President shall designate one member to serve as Chairman of the Commission, and one member to serve as Vice Chairman. The Chairman shall be responsible on behalf of the Commission for the administrative operations of the Commission, and shall appoint, in accordance with the civil service laws, such officers, agents, attorneys, and employees as it deems necessary to assist it in the performance of its functions and to fix their compensation in accordance with the Classification Act of 1949, as amended. The Vice Chairman shall act as Chairman in the absence or disability of the Chairman or in the event of a vacancy in that office.

(b) A vacancy in the Commission shall not impair the right of the remaining members to exercise all the powers of the Commission and three members thereof shall constitute a quorum.

(c) The Commission shall have an official seal which shall be judicially noticed.

(d) The Commission shall at the close of each fiscal year report to the Congress and to the President concerning the action it has taken; the names, salaries, and duties of all individuals in its employ and the moneys it has disbursed; and shall make such further reports on the cause of and means of eliminating discrimination and such recommendations for further legislation as may appear desirable.

(e) The Federal Executive Pay Act of 1956, as amended (5 U.S.C. 2201-2209), is further amended—
     (1) by adding to section 105 thereof (5 U.S.C. 2204) the following clause: "(32) Chairman, Equal Employment Opportunity Commission"; and
     (2) by adding to clause (45) of section 106(a) thereof (5 U.S.C. 2205(a)) the following: "Equal Employment Opportunity Commission (4)."

(f) The principal office of the Commission shall be in or near the District of Columbia, but it may meet or exercise any or all its powers at any other place. The Commission may establish such regional or State offices as it deems necessary to accomplish the purpose of this title.

(g) The Commission shall have power—
     (1) to cooperate with and, with their consent, utilize regional, State, local, and other agencies, both public and private, and individuals;
     (2) to pay to witnesses whose depositions are taken or who are summoned before the Commission or any of its agents the same witness and mileage fees as are paid to witnesses in the courts of the United States;
     (3) to furnish to persons subject to this title such technical assistance as they may request to further their compliance with this title or an order issued thereunder;
     (4) upon the request of (i) any employer, whose employees or some of them, or (ii) any labor organization, whose members or some of them, refuse or threaten to refuse to cooperate in effectuating the provisions of this title, to assist in such effectuation by conciliation or such other remedial action as is provided by this title;
     (5) to make such technical studies as are appropriate to effectuate the purposes and policies of this title and to make the results of such studies available to the public;
     (6) to refer matters to the Attorney General with recommendations for intervention in a civil action brought by an aggrieved party under section 706, or for the institution of a civil action by the Attorney General under section 707, and to advise, consult, and assist the Attorney General on such matters.

(h) Attorneys appointed under this section may, at the direction of the Commission, appear for and represent the Commission in any case in court.

(i) The Commission shall, in any of its educational or promotional activities, cooperate with other departments and agencies in the performance of such educational and promotional activities.

(j) All officers, agents, attorneys, and employees of the Commission shall be subject to the provisions of section 9 of the Act of August 2, 1939, as amended (the Hatch Act), notwithstanding any exemption contained in such section.

PREVENTION OF UNLAWFUL EMPLOYMENT PRACTICES

SEC. 706. (a) Whenever it is charged in writing under oath by a person claiming to be aggrieved, or a written charge has been filed by a member of the Commission where he has reasonable cause to believe a violation of this title has occurred (and such charge sets forth the facts upon which it is based) that an employer, employment agency, or labor organization has engaged in an unlawful employment practice, the Commission shall furnish such employer, employment agency, or labor organization (hereinafter referred to as the "respondent") with a copy of such charge and shall make an investigation of such charge, provided that such charge shall not be made public by the Commission. If the Commission shall determine, after such investigation, that there is reasonable cause to believe that the charge is true, the Commission shall endeavor to eliminate any such alleged unlawful employment practice by informal methods of conference, conciliation, and persuasion. Nothing said or done during and as a part of such endeavors may be made public by the Commission without the written consent of the parties, or used as evidence in a subsequent proceeding. Any officer or employee of the Commission, who shall make public in any manner whatever any information in violation of this subsection shall be deemed guilty of a misdemeanor and upon conviction thereof shall be fined not more than $1,000 or imprisoned not more than one year.

(b) In the case of an alleged unlawful employment practice occurring in a State, or political subdivision of a State, which has a State or local law prohibiting the unlawful employment practice alleged and establishing or authorizing a State or local authority to grant or seek relief from such practice or to institute criminal proceedings with respect thereto upon receiving notice thereof, no charge may be filed under subsection (a) by the person aggrieved before the expiration of sixty days after proceedings have been commenced under the State or local law, unless such proceedings have been earlier terminated, provided that such sixty-day period shall be extended to one hundred and twenty days during the first year after the effective date of such State or local law. If any requirement for the commencement of such proceedings is imposed by a State or local authority other than a requirement of the filing of a written and signed statement of the facts upon which the proceeding is based, the proceeding shall be deemed to have been commenced for the purposes of this subsection at the time such statement is sent by registered mail to the appropriate State or local authority.

(c) In the case of any charge filed by a member of the Commission alleging an unlawful employment practice occurring in a State or political subdivision of a State, which has a State or local law prohibiting the practice alleged and establishing or authorizing a State or local authority to grant or seek relief from such practice or to institute criminal proceedings with respect thereto upon receiving notice thereof, the Commission shall, before taking any action with respect to such charge, notify the appropriate State or local officials and, upon request, afford them a reasonable time, but not less than sixty days (provided that such sixty-day period shall be extended to one hundred and twenty days during the first year after the effective day of such State or local law), unless a shorter period is requested, to act under such State or local law to remedy the practice alleged.

(d) A charge under subsection (a) shall be filed within ninety days after the alleged unlawful employment practice occurred, except that in the case of an unlawful employment practice with respect to which the person aggrieved has followed the procedure set out in subsection (b), such charge shall be filed by the person aggrieved within two hundred and ten days after the alleged unlawful employment practice occurred, or within thirty days after receiving notice that the State or local agency has terminated the proceedings under the State or local, law, whichever is earlier, and a copy of such charge shall be filed by the Commission with the State or local agency.

(e) If within thirty days after a charge is filed with the Commission or within thirty days after expiration of any period of reference under subsection (c) (except that in either case such period may be extended to not more than sixty days upon a determination by the Commission that further efforts to secure voluntary compliance are warranted), the Commission has been unable to obtain voluntary compliance with this title, the Commission shall so notify the person aggrieved and a civil action may, within thirty days thereafter, be brought against the respondent named in the charge (1) by the person claiming to be aggrieved, or (2) if such charge was filed by a member of the Commission, by any person whom the charge alleges was aggrieved by the alleged unlawful employment practice. Upon application by the complainant and in such circumstances as the court may deem just, the court may appoint an attorney for such complainant and may authorize the commencement of the action without the payment of fees, costs, or security. Upon timely application, the court may, in its discretion, permit the Attorney General to intervene in such civil action if he certifies that the case is of general public importance. Upon request, the court may, in its discretion, stay further proceedings for not more than sixty days pending the termination of State or local proceedings described in subsection (b) or the efforts of the Commission to obtain voluntary compliance.

(f) Each United States district court and each United States court of a place subject to the jurisdiction of the United States shall have jurisdiction of actions brought under this title. Such an action may be brought in any judicial district in the State in which the unlawful employment practice is alleged to have been committed, in the judicial district in which the employment records relevant to such practice are maintained and administered, or in the judicial district in which the plaintiff would have worked but for the alleged unlawful employment practice, but if the respondent is not found within any such district, such an action may be brought within the judicial district in which the respondent has his principal office. For purposes of sections 1404 and 1406 of title 28 of the United States Code, the judicial district in which the respondent has his principal office shall in all cases be considered a district in which the action might have been brought.

(g) If the court finds that the respondent has intentionally engaged in or is intentionally engaging in an unlawful employment practice charged in the complaint, the court may enjoin the respondent from engaging in such unlawful employment practice, and order such affirmative action as may be appropriate, which may include reinstatement or hiring of employees, with or without back pay (payable by the employer, employment agency, or labor organization, as the case may be, responsible for the unlawful employment practice). Interim earnings or amounts earnable with reasonable diligence by the person or persons discriminated against shall operate to reduce the back pay otherwise allowable. No order of the court shall require the admission or reinstatement of an individual as a member of a union or the hiring, reinstatement, or promotion of an individual as an employee, or the payment to him of any back pay, if such individual was refused admission, suspended, or expelled or was refused employment or advancement or was suspended or discharged for any reason other than discrimination on account of race, color, religion, sex or national origin or in violation of section 704(a).

(h) The provisions of the Act entitled "An Act to amend the Judicial Code and to define and limit the jurisdiction of courts sitting in equity, and for other purposes," approved March 23, 1932 (29 U.S.C. 101-115), shall not apply with respect to civil actions brought under this section.

(i) In any case in which an employer, employment agency, or labor organization fails to comply with an order of a court issued in a civil action brought under subsection (e), the Commission may commence proceedings to compel compliance with such order.

(j) Any civil action brought under subsection (e) and any proceedings brought under subsection (i) shall be subject to appeal as provided in sections 1291 and 1292, title 28, United States Code.

(k) In any action or proceeding under this title the court, in its discretion, may allow the prevailing party, other than the Commission or the United States, a reasonable attorney's fee as part of the costs, and the Commission and the United States shall be liable for costs the same as a private person.

SEC. 707. (a) Whenever the Attorney General has reasonable cause to believe that any person or group of persons is engaged in a pattern or practice of resistance to the full enjoyment of any of the rights secured by this title, and that the pattern or practice is of such a nature and is intended to deny the full exercise of the rights herein described, the Attorney General may bring a civil action in the appropriate district court of the United States by filing with it a complaint (1) signed by him (or in his absence the Acting Attorney General), (2) setting forth facts pertaining to such pattern or practice, and (3) requesting such relief, including an application for a permanent or temporary injunction, restraining order or other order against the person or persons responsible for such pattern or practice, as he deems necessary to insure the full enjoyment of the rights herein described.

(b) The district courts of the United States shall have and shall exercise jurisdiction of proceedings instituted pursuant to this section, and in any such proceeding the Attorney General may file with the clerk of such court a request that a court of three judges be convened to hear and determine the case. Such request by the Attorney General shall be accompanied by a certificate that, in his opinion, the case is of general public importance. A copy of the certificate and request for a three-judge court shall be immediately furnished by such clerk to the chief judge of the circuit (or in his absence, the presiding circuit judge of the circuit) in which the case is pending. Upon receipt of such request it shall be the duty of the chief judge of the circuit or the presiding circuit judge, as the case may be, to designate immediately three judges in such circuit, of whom at least one shall be a circuit judge and another of whom shall be a district judge of the court in which the proceeding was instituted, to hear and determine such case, and it shall be the duty of the judges so designated to assign the case for hearing at the earliest practicable date, to participate in the hearing and determination thereof, and to cause the case to be in every way expedited. An appeal from the final judgment of such court will lie to the Supreme Court.

In the event the Attorney General fails to file such a request in any such proceeding, it shall be the duty of the chief judge of the district (or in his absence, the acting chief judge) in which the case is pending immediately to designate a judge in such district to hear and determine the case. In the event that no judge in the district is available to hear and determine the case, the chief judge of the district, or the acting chief judge, as the case may be, shall certify this fact to the chief judge of the circuit (or in his absence, the acting chief judge) who shall then designate a district or circuit judge of the circuit to hear and determine the case.

It shall be the duty of the judge designated pursuant to this section to assign the case for hearing at the earliest practicable date and to cause the case to be in every way expedited.

EFFECT ON STATE LAWS

SEC. 708. Nothing in this title shall be deemed to exempt or relieve any person from any liability, duty, penalty, or punishment provided by any present or future law of any State or political subdivision of a State, other than any such law which purports to require or permit the doing of any act which would be an unlawful employment practice under this title.

INVESTIGATIONS, INSPECTIONS, RECORDS, STATE AGENCIES

SEC. 709. (a) In connection with any investigation of a charge filed under section 706, the Commission or its designated representative shall at all reasonable times have access to, for the purposes of examination, and the right to copy any evidence of any person being investigated or proceeded against that relates to unlawful employment practices covered by this title and is relevant to the charge under investigation.

(b) The Commission may cooperate with State and local agencies charged with the administration of State fair employment practices laws and, with the consent of such agencies, may for the purpose of carrying out its functions and duties under this title and within the limitation of funds appropriated specifically for such purpose, utilize the services of such agencies and their employees and, notwithstanding any other provision of law, may reimburse such agencies and their employees for services rendered to assist the Commission in carrying out this title. In furtherance of such cooperative efforts, the Commission may enter into written agreements with such State or local agencies and such agreements may include provisions under which the Commission shall refrain from processing a charge in any cases or class of cases specified in such agreements and under which no person may bring a civil action under section 706 in any cases or class of cases so specified, or under which the Commission shall relieve any person or class of persons in such State or locality from requirements imposed under this section. The Commission shall rescind any such agreement whenever it determines that the agreement no longer serves the interest of effective enforcement of this title.

(c) Except as provided in subsection (d), every employer, employment agency, and labor organization subject to this title shall (1) make and keep such records relevant to the determinations of whether unlawful employment practices have been or are being committed, (2) preserve such records for such periods, and (3) make such reports therefrom, as the Commission shall prescribe by regulation or order, after public hearing, as reasonable, necessary, or appropriate for the enforcement of this title or the regulations or orders thereunder. The Commission shall, by regulation, require each employer, labor organization, and joint labor-management committee subject to this title which controls an apprenticeship or other training program to maintain such records as are reasonably necessary to carry out the purpose of this title, including, but not limited to, a list of applicants who wish to participate in such program, including the chronological order in which such applications were received, and shall furnish to the Commission, upon request, a detailed description of the manner in which persons are selected to participate in the apprenticeship or other training program. Any employer, employment agency, labor organization, or joint labor-management committee which believes that the application to it of any regulation or order issued under this section would result in undue hardship may (1) apply to the Commission for an exemption from the application of such regulation or order, or (2) bring a civil action in the United States district court for the district where such records are kept. If the Commission or the court, as the case may be, finds that the application of the regulation or order to the employer, employment agency, or labor organization in question would impose an undue hardship, the Commission or the court, as the case may be, may grant appropriate relief.

(d) The provisions of subsection (c) shall not apply to any employer, employment agency, labor organization, or joint labor-management committee with respect to matters occurring in any State or political subdivision thereof which has a fair employment practice law during any period in which such employer, employment agency, labor organization, or joint labor-management committee is subject to such law, except that the

Commission may require such notations on records which such employer, employment agency, labor organization, or joint labor-management committee keeps or is required to keep as are necessary because of differences in coverage or methods of enforcement between the State or local law and the provisions of this title. Where an employer is required by Executive Order 10925, issued March 6, 1961, or by any other Executive order prescribing fair employment practices for Government contractors and subcontractors, or by rules or regulations issued thereunder, to file reports relating to his employment practices with any Federal agency or committee, and he is substantially in compliance with such requirements, the Commission shall not require him to file additional reports pursuant to subsection (c) of this section.

(e) It shall be unlawful for any officer or employee of the Commission to make public in any manner whatever any information obtained by the Commission pursuant to its authority under this section prior to the institution of any proceeding under this title involving such information. Any officer or employee of the Commission who shall make public in any manner whatever any information in violation of this subsection shall be guilty of a misdemeanor and upon conviction thereof, shall be fined not more than $1,000, or imprisoned not more than one year.

INVESTIGATORY POWERS

SEC. 710. (a) For the purposes of any investigation of a charge filed under the authority contained in section 706, the Commission shall have authority to examine witnesses under oath and to require the production of documentary evidence relevant or material to the charge under investigation.

(b) If the respondent named in a charge filed under section 706 fails or refuses to comply with a demand of the Commission for permission to examine or to copy evidence in conformity with the provisions of section 709(a), or if any person required to comply with the provisions of section 709 (c) or (d) fails or refuses to do so, or if any person fails or refuses to comply with a demand by the Commission to give testimony under oath, the United States district court for the district in which such person is found, resides, or transacts business, shall, upon application of the Commission, have jurisdiction to issue to such person an order requiring him to comply with the provisions of section 709 (c) or (d) or to comply with the demand of the Commission, but the attendance of a witness may not be required outside the State where he is found, resides, or transacts business and the production of evidence may not be required outside the State where such evidence is kept.

(c) Within twenty days after the service upon any person charged under section 706 of a demand by the Commission for the production of documentary evidence or for permission to examine or to copy evidence in conformity with the provisions of section 709(a), such person may file in the district court of the United States for the judicial district in which he resides, is found, or transacts business, and serve upon the Commission a petition for an order of such court modifying or setting aside such demand. The time allowed for compliance with the demand in whole or in part as deemed proper and ordered by the court shall not run during the pendency of such petition in the court. Such petition shall specify each ground upon which the petitioner relies in seeking such relief, and may be based upon any failure of such demand to comply with the provisions of this title or with the limitations generally applicable to compulsory process or upon any constitutional or other legal right or privilege of such person. No objection which is not raised by such a petition may be urged in the defense to a proceeding initiated by the Commission under subsection (b) for enforcement of such a demand unless such proceeding is commenced by the Commission prior to the expiration of the twenty-day period, or unless the court determines that the defendant could not reasonably have been aware of the availability of such ground of objection.

(d) In any proceeding brought by the Commission under subsection (b), except as provided in subsection (c) of this section, the defendant may petition the court for an order modifying or setting aside the demand of the Commission.

SEC. 711. (a) Every employer, employment agency, and labor organization, as the case may be, shall post and keep posted in conspicuous places upon its premises where notices to employees, applicants for employment, and members are customarily posted a notice to be prepared or approved by the Commission setting forth excerpts from or, summaries of, the pertinent provisions of this title and information pertinent to the filing of a complaint.

(b) A willful violation of this section shall be punishable by a fine of not more than $100 for each separate offense.

VETERANS' PREFERENCE

SEC. 712. Nothing contained in this title shall be construed to repeal or modify any Federal, State, territorial, or local law creating special rights or preference for veterans.

RULES AND REGULATIONS

SEC. 713. (a) The Commission shall have authority from time to time to issue, amend, or rescind suitable procedural regulations to carry out the provisions of this title. Regulations issued under this section shall be in conformity with the standards and limitations of the Administrative Procedure Act.

(b) In any action or proceeding based on any alleged unlawful employment practice, no person shall be subject to any liability or punishment for or on account of (1) the commission by such person of an unlawful employment practice if he pleads and proves that the act or omission complained of was in good faith, in conformity with, and in reliance on any written interpretation or opinion of the Commission, or (2) the failure of such person to publish and file any information required by any provision of this title if he pleads and proves that he failed to publish and file such information in good faith, in conformity with the instructions of the Commission issued under this title regarding the filing of such information. Such a defense, if established, shall be a bar to the action or proceeding, notwithstanding that (A) after such act or omission, such interpretation or opinion is modified or rescinded or is determined by judicial authority to be invalid or of no legal effect, or (B) after publishing or filing the description and annual reports, such publication or filing is determined by judicial authority not to be in conformity with the requirements of this title.

FORCIBLY RESISTING THE COMMISSION OR ITS REPRESENTATIVES

SEC. 714. The provisions of section 111, title 18, United States Code, shall apply to officers, agents, and employees of the Commission in the performance of their official duties.

SPECIAL STUDY BY SECRETARY OF LABOR

SEC. 715. The Secretary of Labor shall make a full and complete study of the factors which might tend to result in discrimination in employment because of age and of the consequences of such discrimination on the economy and individuals affected. The Secretary of Labor shall make a report to the Congress not later than June 30, 1965, containing the results of such study and shall include in such report such recommendations for legislation to prevent arbitrary discrimination in employment because of age as he determines advisable.

EFFECTIVE DATE

SEC. 716. (a) This title shall become effective one year after the date of its enactment.

(b) Notwithstanding subsection (a), sections of this title other than sections 703, 704, 706, and 707 shall become effective immediately.

(c) The President shall, as soon as feasible after the enactment of this title, convene one or more conferences for the purpose of enabling the leaders of groups whose members will be affected by this title to become familiar with the rights afforded and obligations imposed by its provisions, and for the purpose of making plans which will result in the fair and effective administration of this title when all of its provisions become effective. The President shall invite the participation in such conference or conferences of (1) the members of the President's Committee on Equal Employment Opportunity, (2) the members of the Commission on Civil Rights, (3) representatives of State and local agencies engaged in furthering equal employment opportunity, (4) representatives of private agencies engaged in furthering equal employment opportunity, and (5) representatives of employers, labor organizations, and employment agencies who will be subject to this title.

TITLE VIII—REGISTRATION AND VOTING STATISTICS

SEC. 801. The Secretary of Commerce shall promptly conduct a survey to compile registration and voting statistics in such geographic areas as may be recommended by the Commission on Civil Rights. Such a survey and compilation shall, to the extent recommended by the Commission on Civil Rights, only include a count of persons of voting age by race, color, and national origin, and determination of the extent to which such persons are registered to vote, and have voted in any statewide primary or general election in which the Members of the United States House of Representatives are nominated or elected, since January 1, 1960. Such information shall also be collected and compiled in connection with the Nineteenth Decennial Census, and at such other times as the Congress may prescribe. The provisions of section 9 and chapter 7 of title 13, United States Code, shall apply to any survey, collection, or compilation of registration and voting statistics carried out under this title: Provided, however, That no person shall be compelled to disclose his race, color, national origin, or questioned about his political party affiliation, how he voted, or the reasons therefore, nor shall any penalty be imposed for his failure or refusal to make such disclosure. Every person interrogated orally, by written survey or questionnaire or by any other means with respect to such information shall be fully advised with respect to his right to fail or refuse to furnish such information.

Key Provisions of the Voting Rights Act of 1965

AN ACT To enforce the fifteenth amendment to the Constitution of the United States, and for other purposes.

Be it enacted by the Senate and House of Representatives of the United States of America in Congress assembled, That this Act shall be known as the "Voting Rights Act of 1965."

SEC. 2. No voting qualification or prerequisite to voting, or standard, practice, or procedure shall be imposed or applied by any State or political subdivision to deny or abridge the right of any citizen of the United States to vote on account of race or color.

SEC. 3. (a) Whenever the Attorney General institutes a proceeding under any statute to enforce the guarantees of the fifteenth amendment in any State or political subdivision the court shall authorize the appointment of Federal examiners by the United States Civil Service Commission in accordance with section 6 to serve for such period of time and for such political subdivisions as the court shall determine is appropriate to enforce the guarantees of the fifteenth amendment (1) as part of any interlocutory order if the court determines that the appointment of such examiners is necessary to enforce such guarantees or (2) as part of any final judgment if the court finds that violations of the fifteenth amendment justifying equitable relief have occurred in such State or subdivision: Provided, That the court need not authorize the appointment of examiners if any incidents of denial or abridgement of the right to vote on account of race or color (1) have been few in number and have been promptly and effectively corrected by State or local action, (2) the continuing effect of such incidents has been eliminated, and (3) there is no reasonable probability of their recurrence in the future.

(b) If in a proceeding instituted by the Attorney General under any statute to enforce the guarantees of the fifteenth amendment in any State or political subdivision the court finds that a test or device has been used for the purpose or with the effect of denying or abridging the right of any citizen of the United States to vote on account of race or color, it shall suspend the use of tests and devices in such State or political subdivisions as the court shall determine is appropriate and for such period as it deems necessary.

(c) If in any proceeding instituted by the Attorney General under any statute to enforce the guarantees of the fifteenth amendment in any State or political subdivision the court finds that violations of the fifteenth amendment justifying equitable relief have occurred within the territory of such State or political subdivision, the court, in addition to such relief as it may grant, shall retain jurisdiction for such period as it may deem appropriate and during such period no voting qualification or prerequisite to voting, or standard, practice, or procedure with respect to voting different from that in force or effect at the time the proceeding was commenced shall be enforced unless and until the court finds that such qualification, prerequisite, standard, practice, or procedure does not have the purpose and will not have the effect of denying or abridging the right to vote on account of race or color: Provided, That such qualification, prerequisite, standard, practice, or procedure may be enforced if the qualification, prerequisite, standard, practice, or procedure has been submitted by the chief legal officer or other appropriate official of such State or subdivision to the Attorney General and the Attorney General has not interposed an objection within sixty days after such submission, except that neither the court's finding nor the Attorney General's failure to object shall bar a subsequent action to enjoin enforcement of such qualification, prerequisite, standard, practice, or procedure.

SEC. 4. (a) To assure that the right of citizens of the United States to vote is not denied or abridged on account of race or color, no citizen shall be denied the right to vote in any Federal, State, or local election because of his failure to comply with any test or device in any State with respect to which the determinations have been made under subsection (b) or in any political subdivision with respect to which such determinations have been made as a separate unit, unless the United States District Court for the District of Columbia in an action for a declaratory judgment brought by such State or subdivision against the United States has determined that no such test or device has been used during the five years preceding the filing of the action for the purpose or with the effect of denying or abridging the right to vote on account of race or color: Provided, That no such declaratory judgment shall issue with respect to any plaintiff for a period of five years after the entry of a final judgment of any court of the United States, other than the denial of a declaratory judgment under this section, whether entered prior to or after the enactment of this Act, determining that denials or abridgments of the right to vote on account of race or color through the use of such tests or devices have occurred anywhere in the territory of such plaintiff. An action pursuant to this subsection shall be heard and determined by a court of three judges in accordance with the provisions of section 2284 of title 28 of the United States Code and any appeal shall lie to the Supreme Court. The court shall retain jurisdiction of any action pursuant to this subsection for five years after judgment and shall reopen the action upon motion of the Attorney General alleging that a test or device has been used for the purpose or with the effect of denying or abridging the right to vote on account of race or color.

If the Attorney General determines that he has no reason to believe that any such test or device has been used during the five years preceding the filing of the action for the purpose or with the effect of denying or abridging the right to vote on account of race or color, he shall consent to the entry of such judgment

(b) The provisions of subsection (a) shall apply in any State or in any political subdivision of a state which (1) the Attorney General determines maintained on November 1, 1964, any test or device, and with respect to which (2) the Director of the Census determines that less than 50 percentum of the persons of voting age residing therein were registered on November 1, 1964, or that less than 50 percentum of such persons voted in the presidential election of November 1964.

A determination or certification of the Attorney General or of the Director of the Census under this section or under section 6 or section 13 shall not be reviewable in any court and shall be effective upon publication in the Federal Register.

(c) The phrase "test or device" shall mean any requirement that a person as a prerequisite for voting or registration for voting (1) demonstrate the ability to read, write, understand, or interpret any matter, (2) demonstrate any educational achievement or his knowledge of any particular subject, (3) possess good moral character, or (4) prove his qualifications by the voucher of registered voters or members of any other class.

(d) For purposes of this section no State or political subdivision shall be determined to have engaged in the use of tests or devices for the purpose or with the effect of denying or abridging the right to vote on account of race or color if (1) incidents of such use have been few in number and have been promptly and effectively corrected by State or local action, (2) the continuing effect of such incidents has been eliminated, and (3) there is no reasonable probability of their recurrence in the future.

(e)

(1) Congress hereby declares that to secure the rights under the fourteenth amendment of persons educated in American-flag schools in which the predominant classroom language was other than English, it is necessary to prohibit the States from conditioning the right to vote of such persons on ability to read, write, understand, or interpret any matter in the English language.

(2) No person who demonstrates that he has successfully completed the sixth primary grade in a public school in, or a private school accredited by, any State or territory, the District of Columbia, or the Commonwealth of Puerto Rico in which the predominant classroom language was other than English, shall be denied the right to vote in any Federal, State, or local election because of his inability to read, write, understand, or interpret any matter in the English language, except that, in States in which State law provides that a different level of education is presumptive of literacy, he shall demonstrate that he has successfully completed an equivalent level of education in a public school in, or a private school accredited by, any State or territory, the District of Columbia, or the Commonwealth of Puerto Rico in which the predominant classroom language was other than English.

SEC. 5. Whenever a State or political subdivision with respect to which the prohibitions set forth in section 4(a) are in effect shall enact or seek to administer any voting qualification or prerequisite to voting, or standard, practice, or procedure with respect to voting different from that in force or effect on November 1, 1964, such State or subdivision may institute an action in the United States District Court for the District of Columbia for a declaratory judgment that such qualification, prerequisite, standard, practice, or procedure does not have the purpose and will not have the effect of denying or abridging the right to vote on account of race or color, and unless and until the court enters such judgment no person shall be denied the right to vote for failure to comply with such qualification, prerequisite, standard, practice, or procedure: Provided, That such qualification, prerequisite, standard, practice, or procedure may be enforced without such proceeding if the qualification, prerequisite, standard, practice, or procedure has been submitted by the chief legal officer or other appropriate official of such State or subdivision to the Attorney General and the Attorney General has not interposed an objection within sixty days after such submission, except that neither the Attorney General's failure to object nor a declaratory judgment entered under this section shall bar a subsequent action to enjoin enforcement of such qualification, prerequisite, standard, practice, or procedure. Any action under this section shall be heard and determined by a court of three judges in accordance with the provisions of section 2284 of title 28 of the United States Code and any appeal shall lie to the Supreme Court.

SEC. 6. Whenever (a) a court has authorized the appointment of examiners pursuant to the provisions of section 3(a), or (b) unless a declaratory judgment has been rendered under section 4(a), the Attorney General certifies with respect to any political subdivision named in, or included within the scope of, determinations made under section 4(b) that (1) he has received complaints in writing from twenty or more residents of such political subdivision alleging that they have been denied the right to vote under color of law on account of race or color, and that he believes such complaints to be meritorious, or (2) that, in his judgment (considering, among other factors, whether the ratio of nonwhite persons to white persons registered to vote within such subdivision appears to him to be reasonably attributable to violations of the fifteenth amendment or whether substantial evidence exists that bona fide efforts are being made within such subdivision to comply with the fifteenth amendment), the appointment of examiners is otherwise necessary to enforce the guarantees of the fifteenth amendment, the Civil Service Commission shall appoint as many examiners for such subdivision as it may deem appropriate to prepare and maintain lists of persons eligible to vote in Federal, State, and local elections. Such examiners, hearing officers provided for in section 9(a), and other persons deemed necessary by the Commission to carry out the provisions and purposes of this Act shall be appointed, compensated, and separated without regard to the provisions of any statute administered by the Civil Service Commission, and service under this Act shall not be considered employment for the purposes of any statute administered by the Civil Service Commission, except the provisions of section 9 of the Act of August 2, 1939, as amended (5 U.S.C. 118i), prohibiting partisan political activity: Provided, That the Commission is authorized, after consulting the head of the appropriate department or agency, to designate suitable persons in the official service of the United States, with their consent, to serve in these positions. Examiners and hearing officers shall have the power to administer oaths.

Glossary

1619   The year that the first Africans arrived in the Virginia colony.

African Colonization Society   Promoted the settlement of formerly enslaved people in the American colony of Liberia, in West Africa.

American Anti-Slavery Society   An abolitionist society organized by William Lloyd Garrison in 1833 with immediate abolition as its core objective.

American Colonization Society   A society of white people, founded in 1817, which advocated freeing some enslaved Americans and settling them in Africa.

Anthony Burns   (1834–1862) A fugitive from Georgia who was arrested in Boston in 1854. Several hundred abolitionists stormed the jail in a failed attempt to rescue him.

Atlantic slave trade   The trade in captured or kidnapped enslaved Africans to Europe and the Americas, begun by the Portuguese in the early 1440s, was an essential part of global commercial relationships.

Bacon's Rebellion   An uprising of poor white men, free Black men, and some enslaved people led by Nathaniel Bacon, that temporarily drove the colonial governor William Berkeley from Jamestown.

Banditti   Loyalist groups of guerrilla fighters, composed of fugitives from slavery, indentured servants, Native Americans, and poor white farmers, who worked independently and with British forces.

Barbados   A British colony in the West Indies. The majority of the settlers of the Carolina colony came from Barbados. The enslaved West Africans who came with them had knowledge of rice cultivation, which contributed to its emergence as the first commodity crop in the Carolinas.

Benin   A kingdom in what is now southern Nigeria. It was founded during the eleventh century and existed until it was annexed by the British Empire in 1897. It was known for its art, particularly carvings in bronze, iron, and ivory.

Bill of Rights   The first ten amendments to the United States Constitution, ratified by the states in 1791.

Black Belt   The prime cotton-growing region, known for its rich black soil.

Blackface minstrel shows   Stereotypical caricatures of Black music, dance, and humor performed by white men with faces painted black. Blackface minstrel shows were popular in the North, particularly among the white working class, in the years before the Civil War.

Blackness   When the English encountered Africans in the context of the slave trade in seventeenth-century Africa, the exaggerated differences they perceived between British and African societies extended to skin color. Given its negative connotations in the English language, blackness seemed to the English to mark Africans as "natural slaves."

Bleeding Kansas   Conflict between Free-Soil and pro-slavery forces in Kansas sparked by the popular sovereignty position of the Kansas-Nebraska Act.

Boston Massacre   An altercation between occupying British troops and a Boston mob, resulting in the death of five colonists. This was a significant incident in the buildup of tensions between Britain and the colonies in the years leading up to the American Revolution.

Buffalo Soldiers   Native American name for the Black soldiers of the U.S. 9th and 10th Cavalry units. They served in the western territories and attempted to keep the peace between Native Americans and white settlers.

Canada   As part of the British Empire, slavery was illegal in Canada after the 1830s. Many enslaved people fled there to find a refuge from their former owners, and some free African Americans emigrated to Canada as well.

Carolina   The first North American colony founded with enslaved labor as the base of its economy. Because of the success of commodity crops there, Charleston became the major port of entry for Africans brought to North America from Africa and the Caribbean.

Chesapeake   The colonies founded along the Chesapeake Bay used enslaved and indentured laborers to grow tobacco as a commodity crop. A growing scarcity of British indentured laborers led to an increased reliance on enslaved African laborers.

Closed society   A police state wherein the state barred dissent. The South was a closed society by the 1850s—social acceptance and individual safety there required acceptance of the legitimacy of slavery.

Communalism   The basic social structure of traditional African societies, wherein an individual's identity is derived from the family, and therefore primary responsibility is to the family. Community is viewed as simply an extension of the family.

Confederate States of America   The political structure adopted by the Southern states that seceded from the United States in 1860–61.

Constitutional Convention   Meetings of representatives from each state of the newly-established United States to decide what powers the national government should be given.

Contraband   Legal term denoting war materials that can be seized from an enemy during wartime. During the Civil War, Northern leaders used the term to refer to enslaved people who fled to Union lines seeking freedom.

Cotton gin   A mechanical device that removed seeds from cotton far faster than could be done by hand. The cotton gin made the production of short-staple cotton, which could be grown inland, economically feasible for the first time.

Cotton Kingdom   The Black Belt of Mississippi, Alabama, and Arkansas, and western Georgia, which became the nation's prime cotton-growing region thanks to both the removal of Native American residents and the invention of the cotton gin.

Creole languages   Languages that develop from mixing several different languages into one language in a relatively brief period of time. Gullah and Geechee, for example, are both creole languages spoken by African Americans living on the sea islands of the Lowcountry of South Carolina and Georgia and are a mix of English with several West and Central African languages.

Crispus Attucks (c. 1723–1770) Formerly enslaved Bostonian who led some of his fellow workingmen in harassment of British soldiers that resulted in the Boston Massacre. He was one of four men killed in that incident, and was mythologized as a martyr to the Patriot cause.

Dahomey An African kingdom located within the current nation of Benin. It was founded around 1600 and lasted until it was annexed by the French Empire in 1904. Dahomey was a key regional state with an economy built on slave labor and the slave trade with European states.

David Walker An African American abolitionist, famous for his call to resist slavery in an appeal to the Coloured Citizens of the World.

Deep South Mississippi, Alabama, Arkansas, and Georgia.

Democratic-Republicans One of the two parties to make up the first American party system. Following the fiscal and political views of Jefferson and Madison, Democratic Republicans generally advocated a weak federal government and opposed federal intervention in the economy of the nation.

Denmark Vesey (1767–1822) A formerly enslaved carpenter from Charleston, South Carolina, who devised one of the most extensive slave plots in American history. His plan was betrayed by an enslaved co-conspirator, and he was executed.

Dred Scott (c.1799–1858) An enslaved man who sued his owner for his freedom in 1857, based on having resided with him in the free territories of Wisconsin and Illinois for several years. He lost the case in the the the Supreme Court, and the chief justice's opinion announcing that loss declared that African Americans were not U.S. citizens and therefore had no rights under the Constitution.

Dutch West India Company A corporation founded by merchants and chartered by the Netherlands to counter trade competition from Spain and Portugal. For a time, it held monopolistic control over the slave trade between West Africa and Dutch colonies in North and South America and the Caribbean.

Elmina One of the first large castles, walled settlements providing accommodations and offices for European traders, storage facilities for supplies, and holding pens for enslaved people. Elmina was built by the Portuguese on the Gold Coast in present-day Ghana in 1482.

Emancipation Proclamation Proclamation by Abraham Lincoln that declared freedom for enslaved people living in areas under Confederate control on January 1, 1863.

Estevanico (c. 1500–1539) A Moroccan explorer who became the first African to explore North America. As an enslaved man he served as a guide for Cortés, and later for Spanish troops searching for cities of gold in the American Southwest.

Exodusters African Americans who fled the South in search of better opportunities and treatment in the West after the Civil War.

Federalists One of the two political parties to make up the first American party system. Following the fiscal and political policies proposed by Alexander Hamilton, Federalists generally advocated the importance of a strong federal government, including federal intervention in the economy of the new nation.

Fifteenth Amendment   An 1870 constitutional amendment forbidding discrimination in voting on the basis of race, color, or previous condition of servitude.

First Great Awakening   A time of religious fervor that began in England in the 1720s and spread to the American colonies by the 1750s. The movement consisted of revivals with fervent, emotion-laden preaching and an increased emphasis on believers' ability to communicate directly with God. Revivalists typically rejected formal church hierarchy.

Fisk University   A university located in Nashville, Tennessee, founded in 1866 to offer higher education to African American students.

Fort Pillow   A massacre of captured U.S. troops, half of whom were Black, ordered by General Nathan Bedford Forrest when Fort Pillow fell to Confederate troops in the spring of 1864.

Fourteenth Amendment   An 1868 constitutional amendment removing racial restrictions on citizenship and mandating equal justice before the law.

Frederick Douglass   A man who escaped slavery and became the most famous American abolitionist, well known for both his writing and speaking abilities.

Freedman's Relief Association   Organizations established by former abolitionists to aid formerly enslaved people, one of which provide food and medical supplies to the Exodusters in Kansas.

Freedmen's Bureau   The Bureau of Refugees, Freedman, and Abandoned Lands, a government agency formed in 1865 and administered by the army in the area of the former Confederacy. It afforded aid and protection to freed people and assistance to poor white southerners.

Free-Soilers   Immigrants to Kansas who were determined to have it admitted to the Union as a free state after the passage of the Kansas-Nebraska Act with its provision for popular sovereignty. The Free Soil Party, formed in 1848, succeeded the Liberty Party and aimed to prevent the expansion of slavery to the West. Its members became part of the new Republican Party.

Gabriel   (1776–1800) A skilled blacksmith who was enslaved in Virginia, he helped plan an uprising in 1800 that attempted to overthrow Virginia slave society.

Ghana   A West African empire, it was founded in the fourth century and began to decline after 1100, until it became a vassal of the Empire of Mali in the thirteenth century. The introduction of the camel into the Western Sahara during the third century allowed Ghana to develop an economy based on trans-Saharan trade, primarily in gold and salt.

Gold Coast   The name for a region on the Gulf of Guinea in West Africa that was rich in gold. The slave trade was centered here, in a series of forts and castles built by Europeans. After gaining its independence from colonial rule in 1957, the newly independent country took the name of Ghana.

Gradual emancipation   Strategies for abolishing slavery that freed people gradually over time and were less economically and socially disruptive for slaveowners than immediate emancipation. They freed only those people born after the passage of the law, and only when they had reached a certain age.

Great Dismal Swamp   A swamp along the border of North Carolina and Virginia that may have originally covered over a million acres. Before the Civil

War it sheltered a self-sustaining community of maroons, made up primarily of people who ran away from slavery, their families, and their descendants.

Haitian Revolution   The Revolution that overthrew French rule in Haiti and founded the first Black-led nation in the Western Hemisphere.

Half freedom   A system practiced by the Dutch West India Company wherein enslaved Africans were allowed to live independently in exchange for their agreement to pay a yearly tax and provide labor for the company when needed.

Harpers Ferry   Town in Virginia where abolitionist John Brown led a failed raid on a U.S. arsenal. Brown's capture and execution led to greater regional tensions leading up to the Civil War.

Harriet Beecher Stowe   (1811–1896) A white writer and abolitionist, she was the author of Uncle Tom's Cabin. Its depiction of the horrors of slavery and the plight of fugitives made it the most influential piece of antislavery literature of the nineteenth century.

Harriet Jacobs   (c.1813–1897) An enslaved woman who wrote her autobiography, Incidents in the Life of a Slave Girl, detailing the horrors of slavery from a woman's point of view.

Harriet Tubman   (c.1822–1913) The most famous conductor of the Underground Railroad, she was born into slavery on the Eastern Shore of Maryland. Tubman escaped before she could be sold into the Deep South, and returned continually to help other enslaved people escape until the end of the Civil War.

Henry Highland Garnet   An abolitionist who supported all means, including the use of violent action, to end slavery, including slave revolts and uprisings.

Immediate emancipation   An act ending slavery for all enslaved people at once, as opposed to gradually. Vermont and Massachusetts had immediate emancipation after the Revolution, and New York changed from gradual to immediate in the 1820s.

Impressment   The practice of drafting young men into British naval service by press gang, in a fashion that was virtual kidnapping.

Indentured servants   People contracted to work for a term of years (usually between two and seven) in exchange for passage to the New World.

Internal slave trade   Trade in enslaved people from the states of the Upper South to the Deep South, where expanding cotton and sugarcane plantations had higher mortality rates and demanded a constant influx of enslaved labor. This trade flourished after the trans-Atlantic slave trade was banned in 1808.

Jim Crow   Statutes discriminating against nonwhite Americans, particularly in the South. The term specifically refers to regulations enforcing racial segregation.

John Brown   An evangelical abolitionist who attacked proslavery men in Kansas and later led a failed raid on the federal armory in Harpers Ferry.

Joseph Cinque   (c.1814–c.1879) Leader of the group of kidnapped Africans who arrived in the United States on board the Spanish ship Amistad.

Juneteenth   A holiday celebrating the emancipation of the enslaved, it is celebrated on June 19, the day that the Union Army announced freedom from slavery in Texas. These were the last enslaved people in the United States to learn of their freedom.

Kansas-Nebraska Act   Congressional act that effectively repealed the Missouri Compromise. The bill's new policy of "popular sovereignty," intended to allow settlers in a territory to decide the status of slavery, inflamed the debate about the future of slavery in the western territories.

Ku Klux Klan   One of many white terrorist organizations associated with the bitterest and most violent opponents of Reconstruction and Black freedom. Formed in Pulaski, Tennessee, in late 1865, Klan members devoted themselves to denying African Americans any legitimate role in the public sphere, stressing the superiority of white, Protestant, Anglo-Saxon citizens.

League of Gileadites   A guerrilla force organized in Springfield, Massachusetts, by John Brown. This armed group's avowed purpose was to defend fugitives and attack slavery.

Liberia   A colony founded in West Africa by the American Colonization Society, it was intended to be a home for formerly enslaved Americans.

Liberty Party   A political party organized by abolitionists from New York. The party ran antislavery candidates for local and national offices, including James G. Birney for president, in 1840.

Louisiana Purchase   Thomas Jefferson's purchase from France of a large swath of western territory, stretching from Louisiana north to the Canadian border and from the Mississippi River to the Rocky Mountains.

Low Country   The marshy lowlands extending along the coast of the Carolina and Georgia colonies; the landscape proved to be beneficial for rice cultivation.

Lower South   South Carolina and Georgia, where planters with vast plantations held political and economic power and the Black population was large.

Loyalist   Those who remained devoted to the British monarchical government during the Revolutionary War.

Mali   The successor state to Ghana in West Africa, it was founded by the ruler Sundiata in 1235 and lasted until 1670. The Empire of Mali was a center of Islamic learning and was well known for the wealth of its rulers, which was based on both gold and taxes on trade.

Mansa Musa   (c. 1280–c. 1337) One of the most famous rulers of Mali, he is known for his hajj, or pilgrimage, to Mecca in the early fourteenth century. Sources record the vast wealth he brought with him into the Arab world.

Manumission   The freeing of enslaved people by their owners.

Margaret Garner   (?–c.1858) A fugitive from Kentucky, when the house she was staying in in Cincinnati was surrounded by slave hunters aided by US Marshals she attempted to kill her three children rather than see them return to slavery.

Maroons   Groups of people who escaped slavery and formed independent communities, usually in inaccessible places. Such communities existed in the Caribbean as well as North and South America.

Mary Ann Shadd   (1823–1893) Prominent Black abolitionist from Philadelphia who emigrated to Canada. She began a school for Black people in Windsor,

Ontario, just across the Canadian border from Detroit. She edited a newspaper there and became one of Canada's most effective and prominent abolitionist speakers.

Masons   A fraternal organization, begun in Britain but popular in the American colonies.

Massachusetts General Colored Association   One of the first Black antislavery organizations, founded in Boston in 1826. David Walker was one of its founders.

Middle Colonies   The colonies north of the Chesapeake and south of New England. There were fewer large plantations in this area, so slaveholdings were generally smaller and Black people were a smaller proportion of the population.

Middle Passage   The Atlantic trade route that transported enslaved Africans to the Americas. The ships that made this trip were well known for crowding and brutal treatment, and the mortality rate among enslaved people sometimes reached 25 to 30 percent.

Missouri Compromise of 1820   A compromise between slaveholding and nonslaveholding states wherein Missouri was admitted to the Union as a slave state while Maine was admitted as a free state and Missouri's southern border became the line between slave and nonslave states.

Mixed-race person   A person of mixed Black and white ancestry.

Nat Turner   An enslaved preacher who planned and launched a slave uprising in Virginia which killed nearly sixty people and sent Virginia, and all southern states, into a panic.

Negro Seaman's Acts   Laws confining Black seamen to their ships when in port in southern states. These laws were intended to prevent the spread of antislavery propaganda among enslaved people in the South.

New England   The northernmost group of British colonies, originally settled by the Puritans. Primarily because these colonies were mostly small farms, the enslaved population was low, and for the most part more integrated into the household.

New England Anti-Slavery Society   An integrated abolitionist organization founded by William Lloyd Garrison. It was dedicated to immediate abolition and opposed to African colonization.

Northwest Ordinance   The 1787 ordinance outlining government in territories north of the Ohio River and outlawing slavery in the Old Northwest.

Olaudah Equiano   (c. 1745–1797) Also known as Gustavus Vassa, Equiano was a writer and abolitionist. He was kidnapped from the kingdom of Benin as a child in the early eighteenth century. He published his autobiography, one of the first books to depict the horrors of slavery in English. Its popularity helped gain passage of the British Slave Trade Act of 1807, which outlawed slavery in the British Empire.

Pacifism   The belief that violence is always wrong. Quakers were pacifists, and this doctrine heavily influenced the abolitionist movement. William Lloyd Garrison was a pacifist and demanded commitment to nonviolence from his followers.

Paul Cuffe (1759–1817) A free Black man and ship's captain who became wealthy through trade after the Revolutionary War. He became committed to the idea of resettling freed people in Africa, and helped found the colony of Liberia.

Plantation A large scale estate which farmed cash crops, generally with laborers including enslaved Africans.

Plessy v. Ferguson U.S. Supreme Court decision that upheld the legality of Jim Crow laws, declaring that segregation based on race was constitutional as long as "separate" facilities were "equal." It soon became clear, however, that facilities for Black Americans, such as schools, railroad cars, and waiting rooms, were rarely, if ever, equal to those provided for white people.

Popular sovereignty A policy established in the mid-nineteenth century that permitted settlers in newly established western territories to decide on the policy of slavery for themselves.

Port Royal Experiment An early social welfare project established on the coast of South Carolina after U.S. troops occupied the sea islands of South Carolina and Georgia early in the war. Medical professionals, teachers, and missionaries came from the North to help freed people in their transition to freedom.

Prince Hall (c.1735–1807) A free Black man in Boston who founded the Black Masons in America, later known as the Prince Hall Masons.

Puritans A group of English Protestants who wanted to reform the Church of England. Many of them emigrated to New England in the seventeenth century and their beliefs created the foundation of modern day Congregationalist churches.

Quakers A Christian religious sect, officially The Religious Society of Friends, that broke from the Church of England in the mid-1600s. It established itself in North America during the seventeenth century, and many Quakers became known for their dedication to their antislavery beliefs.

Radical Abolitionism A pre–Civil War movement devoted to the emancipation of enslaved people and their inclusion in American society as citizens with equal rights.

Radical Reconstruction The period following the Civil War when radical Republicans in Congress took control of Reconstruction policy, enacting legislation to protect the rights of Black citizens, especially the people recently freed from slavery.

Rebellion at the Stono River The largest uprising of enslaved Africans in mainland North America during the eighteenth century, in which eighty or more enslaved men burned South Carolina plantations as they marched toward Spanish Florida.

Republican Party A new political party formed in 1854, consisting of abolitionists, former Liberty Party members, Free-Soilers, and disaffected Whigs. Their slogan was "Free Labor, Free Soil, Free Men," but their platform was containment of slavery in the South, not abolition.

Ring shout A ritual circle dance done by citizens of Dahomey, Kongo, and other West African kingdoms. Many African American communities integrated it into their practice of Christianity.

Royal African Company   An English trading company set up by the British Crown in 1660 to trade along the west coast of Africa. Although originally intended to trade in gold, it quickly developed an interest in the slave trade, primarily shipping enslaved Africans from the Gold Coast to British possessions in the Caribbean.

Seasoning   The process of attempting to break Africans' resistance to enslavement using the harsh system of gang labor common in the West Indian sugar colonies. Enslaved people who had worked for a stint in one of these colonies were then sometimes sold on to the mainland.

Secession   The act of formally withdrawing from an existing union with another political state.

Segregation   The separation of Black and white people into separate racial groups in daily life.

Sharecropping   The practice of a tenant farming the landlord's ground for a share of the crop, sold when the harvest came in. This was the only available form of employment to many formerly enslaved people in the post–Civil War South and became a way of maintaining wealthy white power, ensuring Black indebtedness and dependence on white landowners.

Shays's Rebellion   An armed insurrection by indebted Massachusetts farmers, led by Daniel Shays, to prevent the state government from seizing their property.

Sierra Leone   A British colony in West Africa founded in 1787.

Slave codes   Laws enacted in the colonies to control the behavior of enslaved people and prevent potential slave rebellions.

Society for the Relief of Free Negroes Unlawfully Held in Bondage   The world's first antislavery society, founded in Philadelphia in 1775.

Solomon Northup   (c.1808–c.1857) A free Black musician who lived in New York State, he was kidnapped from Washington, D.C., and sold into slavery in the Deep South. He later wrote his memoir, Twelve Years a Slave.

Songhay   The Songhay Empire dominated the western Sahel in the fifteenth and sixteenth centuries. It was the successor state to the Empire of Mali and its primary cities of Gao, Djenne and Timbuktu were thriving cultural and commercial centers.

St. Domingue   A French-held island in the Caribbean which would become the independent nation of Haiti.

Stamp Act   British parliamentary act that required many forms of colonial printed materials and products to be affixed with revenue stamps, or taxes, paid to the British.

Susie King Taylor   (1848–1912) A formerly enslaved woman from Georgia, she became a teacher for freed people as well as a nurse during the war, and spent time with her husband's all-Black unit.

The American Society of Free Persons of Colour   The first of the Black National Conventions, it first met in Philadelphia after the Cincinnati riots of 1829.

The Fugitive Slave Law of 1850   Federal law supporting the capture and return of fugitives from slavery by allowing federal commissioners to decide cases and requiring the active cooperation of state officers and bystanders.

Thirteenth Amendment   An 1865 constitutional amendment that outlawed slavery in the United States except as a punishment for a crime.

Toussaint L'Ouverture   The formerly enslaved Black military leader of the Haitian Revolution.

Triangular Trade   The name for the trans-Atlantic trade between Europe, Africa, and the Americans in finished goods, commodity crops, and enslaved Africans.

Underground Railroad   Name for the relatively unstructured covert process of helping enslaved people escape to freedom. It consisted of a network of safe houses and guides, or "conductors."

Upper South   Maryland, Virginia, and North Carolina, the colonies that maintained slavery but also encouraged voluntary manumission during the colonial period.

Virginia Company   The corporation that funded the Jamestown colony, the first English colony in North America.

Vodou   Haitian vodou developed on the island of St. Domingue under French rule. It combined aspects of traditional African spiritual practices with French Catholicism. The more generalized western term of voodoo refers to the broad and varied religions that emerged from the mixing of traditional African religions with western religions, especially Christianity.

William Lloyd Garrison   A Quaker, an abolitionist, and the founder of the New England Anti-Slavery Society and the editor of the antislavery newspaper The Liberator.

Notes

CHAPTER 1

1 Olaudah Equiano, *The Interesting Narrative of the Life of Olaudah Equiano, or Gustavus Vassa, the African* (1789), reprinted in *Great Slave Narratives*, ed. Arna Bontemps (Boston: Beacon Press, 1969), 7; The discovery of seemingly contradictory documents has led some scholars to question whether Equiano's description of Africa was based on personal experience or oral history. See Vincent Carratta, "Olaudah Equiano or Gustavas Vasa? New Light on an Eighteenth-Century Question of Identity," *Slavery and Abolition* 20, no. 3 (1999): 96–105.

2 Philip Curtin, Steven Feierman, Leonard Thompson, and Jan Vansina, *African History*, 9th ed. (New York: Longman, 1991); A.J. Arkell, *A History of Sudan from the Earliest Times to 1821* (London: University of London, Athlone Press, 1961).

3 Basil Davidson, *The Search for Africa: History, Culture, Politics* (New York: Random House, 1994), 73; Colin A. Palmer, *Passageways: An Interpretive History of Black America, 1619–1863*, vol. I (Fort Worth, TX: Harcourt Brace College Publishers, 1998), 5. Quotes from Philip Foner, *History of Black Americans*, vol. I (Westport, CT: Greenwood Press, 1975), 40–41. See also Jean Rouch, *Les Songhay* (Paris: Presses Universitaires de France, 1954) and R.E. Bradbury, *The Benin Kingdom and the Edo-speaking Peoples of Southwestern Nigeria* (London: International African Institute, 1957).

4 John Hope Franklin, Alfred P. Moss, Jr., *From Slavery to Freedom: A History of Negro Americans* 6th ed., (New York: Knopf, 1988); Foner, *History of Black Americans*, vol. 1, 43–47.

5 David Brion Davis, *The Problem of Slavery in Western Culture* (Ithaca, NY: Cornell University Press, 1966), 52; David Brion Davis, *Inhuman Bondage: The Rise and Fall of Slavery in the New World* (New York: Oxford University Press, 2006); Ronald Sanders, *Lost Tribes and Promised Lands: The Origins of American Racism* (New York: Harper Perennial, 1992); Curtin et al., *African History*, 183–9.

6 Philip D. Curtin, "Migration in the Tropical World," in *Immigration Reconsidered*, ed. Virginia Yans-McLaughlin (New York: Oxford University Press, 1990), 21–36.

7 Enslaved people in Africa retained an acknowledged humanness, for slavery was a condition of their lives and a social status into which they had fallen. Slavery was not, as it would later become in the United States, a racially defined, permanent state connoting a supposed genetic inferiority.

8 Equiano, in Bontemps, ed., *Narratives*, 11; Donald R. Wright, *African Americans in the Colonial Era: From African Origins Through the American Revolution* (Arlington Heights, IL: Harlan Davidson, Inc., 1990). Dahomey was most transformed by its access to firearms and became committed to the slave trade as the principal foundation of its national economy by the early sixteenth century. The Dutch established trade in Allada, the major trading state in the region, before the end of the century. See I.A. Akinjogbin, *Dahomey and Its Neighbors, 1708–1818* (Cambridge, UK: Cambridge University Press, 1967).

9 Colin Palmer, "African Slave Trade: The Cruelest Commerce," *National Geographic* 182, no. 3 (September 1992): 67–68.

10 Akinjogbin, *Dahomey*; Equiano, in Bontemps, ed., *Narratives*, 27.

11 Sanders, *Lost Tribes*, 17.

12 Davis, *The Problem of Slavery*; Winthrop D. Jordan, *White Over Black: American Attitudes Toward the Negro, 1550–1812* (Chapel Hill, NC: University of North Carolina Press, 1968), 7; Davis, *Inhuman Bondage*, 78, 53.

13 Equiano, in Bontemps, ed., *Narratives*, 28–29.

14 Ibid, 30.

15 Jay Coughtry, *The Notorious Triangle: Rhode Island and the African Slaves Trade, 1700–1807* (Philadelphia: Temple University Press, 1981).

16 Alexander Falconbridge, *An Account of the Slave Trade on the Coast of Africa* (London: J. Phillips, Lombard Street, 1788), 16–22.

17 William Loren Katz, *Eyewitness: The Negro in American History* (Belmont, CA: Fearon Pitman Publishers, Inc., 1974), 6.

18 "Samuel Waldo to Captain Samuel Rhodes, 1734," in *Documents Illustrative of the History of the Slave Trade in America*, vol. 3, ed. Elizabeth Donnan (Washington, D.C.: Carnegie Institution of Washington, 1932), 45; Vincent Harding, *There Is a River: The Black Struggle for Freedom in America* (New York: Harcourt Brace Jovanovich, 1981), 12–13.

19 Ivan Van Sertima, *They Came Before Columbus* (New York: Random House, 1976).

20 William D. Piersen, *From Africa to America: African American History from the Colonial Era to the Early Republic, 1526–1790* (New York: Twayne Publishers, 1996), 37–44.

21 Germany later broadened its slave trading but never became a dominant player, largely because it did not develop substantial American holdings.

22 Estimates for Africans in the Atlantic trade do not include those who died in capture, internment, or the Middle Passage. Paul E. Lovejoy, *Transformations in Slavery: A History of Slavery in Africa*, 3rd ed. (Cambridge, UK: Cambridge University Press, 2012), 19; Wright, *African Americans in the Colonial Era*, 40.

23 Darold Wax, "Preferences for Slaves in Colonial America," *Journal of Negro History* 58, no. 4 (1973): 375–6.

24 Intra=America Trans-Atlantic Slave Trade Database, https://www.slavevoyages.org/american/database#statistics

CHAPTER 2

1 The ship bringing the Africans to Virginia has previously been identified as a Dutch ship, as reported by John Rolfe in Virginia at the time. Recent scholarship, however, has shown that the ship, the *White Lion*, was a British warship sailing out of the Netherlands with a Dutch letter of marque that permitted it to attack Spanish trade. This was one of two British privateers that attacked a Portuguese slave ship from Angola bound for Mexico and confiscated some of its human cargo. "Virginia's First Africans," contributed by Martha McCartney, *Encyclopedia Virginia*, Virginia Humanities and Library of Virginia, https://www.encyclopediavirginia.org/Virginia_s_First_Africans.

2 Winthrop Jordan, *White Over Black: American Attitudes Towards the Negro, 1550–1812* (New York: W. W. Norton, 1977), 75; Darrett B. Rutman and Anita H. Rutman, *A Place in Time: Middlesex County, Virginia, 1650–1750* (New York: Norton Publishing, 1984).

3 Jordan, *White Over Black*, 75, 79, 81; David Brion Davis, *The Problem of Slavery in Western Culture* (Ithaca, NY: Cornell University Press, 1966), 102; James Oliver Horton and Lois E. Horton, *Slavery and the Making of America* (New York: Oxford University Press, 2005), 28–29.

4 *Pennsylvania Gazette*, October 8, 1747; *Journal and Baltimore Advisor*, October 10, 1779.

5 Carl N. Degler, "Slavery and the Genesis of Race Prejudice," *Comparative Studies in Society and History* 2 (1959), 61.

6 Edward Pearson, "From Stono to Vesey: Slavery, Resistance, and Ideology in South Carolina, 1739–1822," PhD diss. (University of Wisconsin, 1991). Pearson provides a detailed account of the establishment of slavery in South Carolina and the transition of the colony's economy from timber producing and herding to rice cultivation. He also offers a fascinating argument on the impact of this transition on the gender conventions of African enslaved people. Donald R. Wright, *African Americans in the Colonial Era: From African Origins through the American Revolution* (Arlington Heights, IL: Harlan Davidson, Inc., 1990); Ira Berlin, *Many Thousands Gone: The First Two Centuries of Slavery in North America* (Cambridge, MA: Harvard University Press, 1998), 149. Slaveholders believed that Africans were immune to malaria. This was not true, but many Africans did display a resistance to the disease that was greater than that of Europeans.

7 Philip D. Morgan, *Slave Counterpoint: Black Culture in the Eighteenth Century Chesapeake & Lowcountry* (Chapel Hill: University of North Carolina Press, 1998), 394, 264–5.

8 William Loren Katz, *Eyewitness: The Negro in American History* (Belmont, CA: Fearon Pitman Publishers, Inc., 1974), 22.

9 Darold Wax, "Georgia and the Negro Before the American Revolution," *Georgia Historical Quarterly* 51 (March 1967), 63–75.

10 Berlin, *Many Thousands Gone*, 369–70.

11 William D. Piersen, *From Africa to America: African American History from the Colonial Era to the Early Republic, 1526–1790* (New York: Twayne Pulishers, 1996), 57–65; Philip S. Foner, *History of Black Americans*, vol. 1 (Westport, CT: Greenwood Press, 1975), 228; Clement Alexander Price, *Freedom Not Far Distant: A Documentary History of Afro-Americans in New Jersey*, (Newark, NJ: New Jersey Historical Society, 1980), 35. Population numbers are estimates, since there was no official Pennsylvania census during the colonial period.

12 Gary Nash, *Forging Freedom: The Formation of Philadelphia's Black Community 1720–1840* (Cambridge, MA: Harvard University Press, 1988); Israel Acrelius, *A History of New Sweden; or The Settlements on the Delaware* (Philadelphia: Historical Society of Pennsylvania, 1874); Katz, *Eyewitness*, 23.

13 Jean R. Soderlund, *Quakers and Slavery: A Divided Spirit* (Princeton, NJ: Princeton University Press, 1985), 15–16.

14 Black persons in New York and New Jersey frequently spoke both English and Dutch because the area was controlled by Holland until the 1660s. *Pennsylvania Gazette*, September 24, 1741; June 6, 1746; July 31, 1740; July 4, 1745; and September 20, 1764; *New York Gazette*, July 31, 1766.

15 A. Leon Higginbotham, *In the Matter of Color: Race and the American Legal Process* (New York: Oxford University Press, 1978); Joyce D. Goodfriend, *Before the Melting Pot: Society and Culture in Colonial New York City, 1664–1730* (Princeton, NJ: Princeton University Press, 1992), 111–32. See also Shane White, *Somewhat More Independent: The End of Slavery in New York City, 1770–1810* (Athens, GA: University of Georgia Press, 1991) and Edgar J. McManus, *Black Bondage in the North* (Syracuse, NY: University of Syracuse Press, 1973).

16 Ira Berlin, "Time, Space, and the Evolution of Afro-American Society," *American Historical Review* 85 (February 1980): 44–78; McManus, *Black Bondage*, 84.

17 McManus, *Black Bondage*, 208–11; White, *Somewhat More Independent*, 3.

18 James Oliver Horton and Lois E. Horton, *In Hope of Liberty: Culture, Community, and Protest among Northern Free Blacks* (New York: Oxford University Press, 1977), 10, 37.

19 Jane G. Austin, *Dr. LeBaron and His Daughters* (Cambridge, MA: Riverside Press; Boston: Houghton, Mifflin & Co., 1892), 55.

20 Austin, *Dr. LeBaron*, 91.

21 Arthur Zilversmit, *The First Emancipation: The Abolition of Slavery in the North* (Chicago: University of Chicago Press, 1967), 33; James A. Henretta, "Economic Development and Social Structure in Colonial Boston," *William and Mary Quarterly* 22 (1965): 75–92; Lorenzo J. Greene, *The Negro in Colonial New England 1620–1766* (New York: Columbia University Press, 1942; New York: Athenaeum Press, 1968), 84; William D. Piersen, *Black Yankees* (Amherst, MA: University of Massachusetts Press, 1988); Nash, *The Urban Crucible*. See also Robert C. Twombly and Robert M. Moore, "Black Puritan: The Negro in Seventeenth Century Massachusetts," *William and Mary Quarterly*, 3rd series, 24 (April 1967): 224–42.

22 Higginbotham, *In the Matter of Color*, 203; Peter Wood, *Black Majority: Negroes in Colonial South Carolina from 1670 Through the Stono Rebellion* (New York: Norton Publishing, 1974), 152. The Stono Rebellion is described in Chapter 3.

23 Free Black people were taxed more heavily than white people and had to pay a poll tax from age twelve. White individuals did not have to pay the poll tax until age sixteen. After 1760 Black persons were required to possess fifty acres of land in order to be eligible to vote. There is reason to believe that some free Black individuals in South Carolina voted. See Higginbotham, *In the Matter of Color*, 204. See examples of conspiratorial free Black men and women in Robert Olwell, "Becoming Free: Manumission and the Genesis of a Free Black Community in South Carolina, 1740–90," in *Against the Odds: Free Blacks in the Slave Societies of the Americas*, ed. Jane Landers (Portland, OR: Frank Cass, 1996), 1–19.

24 *New England Weekly Journal*, May 1, 1732.

25 Katz, *Eyewitness*, 24.

26 James D. Rice, "Bacon's Rebellion in Indian Country," *Journal of American History*, 101, 3 (2014): 726–50; Winthrop Jordan, *White Over Black*, 139; Greene, *The Negro in Colonial New England*; Debra L. Newman, "Black Women in the Era of the American Revolution in Pennsylvania," *Journal of Negro History* LXI, no. 3 (July 1976): 276–89.

27 Horton and Horton, *In Hope of Liberty*, 30–54, 39; Katz, *Eyewitness*, 27.

28 Jack D. Forbes, *Black Africans and Native Americans: Color, Race, Caste in the Evolution of Red-Black Peoples* (New York: Basil Blackwell, 1988).

29 Lamont D. Thomas, *Rise to Be a People: A Biography of Paul Cuffe* (Urbana, IL: University of Illinois Press, 1986); Horton and Horton, *In Hope of Liberty*.

30 Alice Morse Earle, *Colonial Days in Old New York* (New York: C. Scriber's Sons, 1896; New York: Empire Book Company, 1926), 196–200. See also White, *Somewhat More Independent* and Sterling Stuckey, *Slave Culture: Nationalist Theory and the Foundations of Black America* (New York: Oxford University Press, 1987).

31 Albert J. Raboteau, *Slave Religion: The "Invisible Institution" in the Antebellum South* (New York: Oxford University Press, 1978), 15; Berlin, *Many Thousands Gone*.

32 Samuel E. Morrison, "A Poem on Election Day in Massachusetts about 1760," *Proceedings of the Colonial Society of Massachusetts* 18 (February 1915): 54–61; Eileen Southern, ed., *Readings in Black American Music* (New York: W. W. Norton & Co, Inc., 1971), 41.

33 Wood, *Black Majority*. Reports by eighteenth-century European doctors traveling in West Africa and anthropological studies in the twentieth century confirm that inoculation was an ancient practice in West Africa. For an important argument on the impact of African medicine on American medicine see William D. Piersen, *Black Legacy: America's Hidden Heritage* (Amherst, MA: University of Massachusetts Press, 1993), 101–2.

34 Piersen, *Black Legacy*.

CHAPTER 3

1 Robert Olwell, *Masters, Slaves and Subjects: The Culture of Power in the South Carolina Low Country, 1740-1790* (Ithaca, NY: Cornell University Press, 1998), 22–23. These Africans are generally referred to as Angolans, but John Thornton provides a convincing argument that they were most likely to have been from the Kingdom of Kongo in modern Angola. See John K. Thornton, "African Dimensions of the Stono Rebellion," *American Historical Review* 96, no. 4 (October 1991): 1101–14, 1103.

2 Jane G. Landers, "Acquisition and Loss on a Spanish Frontier: The Free Black Homesteaders of Florida, 1784-1821," in *Against the Odds: Free Blacks in the Slave Societies of the Americas*, ed. Jane G. Landers (Portland, OR: Frank Cass, 1996), 85–101, 87.

3 Olwell, *Masters, Slaves and Subjects*, 22, 24; Thornton, "African Dimensions of the Stono Rebellions," 1111.

4 Olwell, *Masters, Slaves and Subjects*, 26–29.

5 Ira Berlin, *Many Thousands Gone: The First Two Centuries of Slavery in North America* (Cambridge, MA: Harvard University Press, 1998), 171–3.

6 Berlin, *Many Thousands Gone*, 171–3.; James Oliver Horton and Lois E. Horton, *In Hope of Liberty: Culture Community and Protest Among Northern Free Blacks, 1700-1860* (New York: Oxford University Press, 1997); Alan Gallay, "Planters and Slaves in the Great Awakening," in *Masters and Slaves in the House of the Lord: Race and Religion in the American South, 1740-1870*, ed. John B. Boles (Lexington, KY: University Press of Kentucky, 1988), 19–36; Nathan O. Hatch, *The Democratization of American Christianity* (New Haven: Yale University Press, 1989).

7 Leonard W. Labaree, "The Conservative Attitude Toward the Great Awakening," *William and Mary Quarterly* 1 (1944), 339, 336.

8 Robert Cottrol, *The Afro-Yankees: Providence's Black Community in the Antebellum Era* (Westport, CT: Greenwood Press, 1982); *New York Weekly Journal*, August 9, 1742; Daniel Horsmanden, *The New York Conspiracy* (Boston: Beacon Press, 1971); Thomas J. Davis, *A Rumor of Revolt: The Great Negro Plot in Colonial New York* (New York: Free Press, 1985).

9 Davis, *Rumor of Revolt*.

10 Gary Nash, "Up From the Bottom in Franklin's Philadelphia," *Past and Present* 77 (1977): 57–83; Eric Foner, *Tom Paine and Revolutionary America* (New York: Oxford University Press, 1976), 48. For a description of the process of the concentration of colonial wealth and political power see James A. Henretta, *The Evolution of American Society, 1700-1815: An Interdisciplinary Analysis* (Lexington, Mass.: D.C. Heath, 1973). Josiah Quincy Jr., *Reports of Cases Argued and Adjudged in the Superior Court of Judicature of*

the Province of Massachusetts Bay, between 1761 and 1772, ed. Samuel M. Quincy (Boston: Little Brown, 1865), 237–8; Gary B. Nash, The Urban Crucible: Social Change, Political Consciousness, and the Origins of the American Revolution (Cambridge, MA: Harvard University Press, 1979), 8. Nash has analyzed the tax records for Boston, New York, and Philadelphia from the late seventeenth to the late eighteenth century and found that in all three cities the rich increased their share of the community's wealth.

11 Benjamin Colman to Mr. Samuel Holden, Boston May 8, 1737, "Colman Papers," unpublished papers, vol. 2, Massachusetts Historical Society.

12 Jesse Lemisch, "Jack Tar in the Streets: Merchant Seamen in the Politics of Revolutionary America," William and Mary Quarterly 25 (1968): 371–407; Howard Zinn, A People's History of the United States (New York: Harper and Row, 1980), 51; Nash, Urban Crucible, 221–23.

13 Roi Ottley and William J. Weatherby, eds., The Negro in New York: An Informal Social History, 1626–1940 (New York: New York Public Library, 1967), 36–37.

14 William C. Nell, "Crispus Attucks Once a Slave in Massachusetts," Liberator, August 5, 1859, 124. See the Boston Gazette and Weekly Journal, October 2, November 13, and November 20, 1750 for the runaway ad for Attucks.

15 Ibid.

16 John Adams, quoted in Howard Zinn, A People's History of the United States (New York: Harper & Row, 1980), 67. See Boston Gazette, March 12, 1770, for an eye-witness account of this event.

17 Benjamin Thatcher, Traits of the Tea Party: Being a Memoir of George R. T. Hewes (New York: Harper & Brothers, 1835), 103–4. See also William Cooper Nell, The Colored Patriots of the American Revolution (Boston: Robert F. Wallcut, 1855; reprint Salem, NH: Ayer Company, 1986). One of those initially wounded died later. Thatcher, Traits of the Tea Party, 123–4.

18 John Adams diary, July, 1773, in Sidney Kaplan, The Black Presence in the Era of the American Revolution, 1770–1800 (Washington, D.C.: Smithsonian Institution Press, 1973), 9. The original diary is housed at the Massachusetts Historical Society, Boston, Massachusetts.

19 Jack P. Greene, ed., The Reinterpretation of the American Revolution (New York: Harper & Row, 1968), 169. There is evidence that Revolutionary leaders such as Sam Adams tended to disqualify African Americans from consideration as persons deserving freedom from British rule, conveniently separating the actual slavery of Black people from the metaphorical slavery of white colonists. See Patricia Bradley, Slavery, Propaganda, and the American Revolution (Jackson, MS: University of Mississippi Press, 1998). Sidney Kaplan, The Black Presence in the Era of the American Revolution, 1770–1800 (Greenwich, NY: New York Graphic Society, 1973), 11–13.

20 James Otis, The Rights of the British Colonies Asserted and Proved (Boston, MA: Edes and Gill, 1764), 37; Abigail Adams to John Adams, September 22, 1774, ed. Lyman H. Butterfield, Adams Family Correspondence (Cambridge, MA: Harvard University Press, 1963), vol. 1, 162, 12–14.

21 The Boston Tea Party in 1773 was part of the protest over England's tax on tea. Revolutionaries dressed as Native Americans boarded a vessel in the port and dumped the ship's cargo of tea overboard. Philip S. Foner, History of Black Americans: From Africa to the Emergence of the Cotton Kingdom, vol. 1 (Westport, Conn.: Greenwood Press, 1975), 307.

22 Benjamin Quarles, The Negro in the American Revolution (Chapel Hill, NC: University of North Carolina Press, 1961).

23 Howard Zinn, People's History, 81; Ellen Gibson Wilson, Loyal Blacks (New York: Capricorn Books, 1976); Pennsylvania Gazette, June 12, 1780; For information about the banditti and quote from the South-Carolina Gazette, June 12, 1784, see Rachel N. Klein, Unification of a Slave State: The Rise of the Planter Class in the South Carolina Backcountry, 1760–1808 (Chapel Hill, NC: University of North Carolina Press, 1990), 95–99, quote on 99.

24 Paul Finkelman, Slavery in the Courtroom: An Annotated Bibliography of American Cases (Washington, D.C.: Library of Congress, 1985); Foner, History of Black Americans, 296–7; Bradley, Slavery, Propaganda, 66–80.

25 Wilson, Loyal Blacks, 21; Franklin and Moss Jr., From Slavery to Freedom, 6th ed. (New York: McGraw-Hill Publishing Company, 1988), 70.

26 Quotes in Foner, *History of Black Americans*, 316. Benjamin Quarles suggested that Washington was also moved by black requests to be included in the American forces and although this undoubtedly did play a role in his decision, we agree with Philip Foner that military considerations were mainly responsible for the change in policy. See Benjamin Quarles, *The Negro in the American Revolution* and Foner, *History of Black Americans*.

27 Revolutionary War Pension Records, Prince Hazeltine, Records of the Veterans' Administration, Record Group #15, National Archives and Record Service, Washington, D.C.

28 Quarles, *Negro in the American Revolution*, ix; Sylvia R. Frey, *Water from the Rock: Black Resistance in a Revolutionary Age* (Princeton, NJ: Princeton University Press, 1991), 121–2.

29 Joanne Melish, "Recovering (from) Slavery: Four Struggles to Tell the Truth," in *Slavery and Public History: The Tough Stuff of American Memory*, eds. James Oliver Horton and Lois E. Horton (New York: The New Press, 2006), 103–33; "The Negro in the Military Service of the United States: A Compilation of Official Records, State Papers, Historical Records, Etc.," National Archives, Washington, D.C., 206–14, 220, cited in Foner, *History of Black Americans*, 333. British slaveholders in the West Indies or those in America who remained loyal to the Crown expressed similar fears about Lord Dunmore's arming enslaved men to fight for the British Empire. Many believed that before the war was over British troops would have to be used to defend against the armed rebellion of their enslaved allies. See "The Negro in the Military Services of the United States: A Compilation of Official Records, State Papers, Historical records, etc.," National Archives, Washington, D.C.

30 Revolutionary War Pension Records, Cato Cuff, Samuel Coombs, Prince Whipple, Oliver Cromwell, and Prince Bent.

31 Wilson, *Loyal Blacks*; Robin W. Winks, *The Blacks in Canada: A History* (Montreal: McGill-Queen's Univ. Press, 1997).

32 Roi Ottley and William J. Weatherby, eds., *The Negro in New York*, 40.

33 Wilson, *Loyal Blacks*, 42, 70–80.

34 John H. Watson, "In Re Vermont Constitution of 1777 … ," *Proceedings of the Vermont Historical Society, 1919-1920*, cited in Foner, *History of Black Americans*, 347; *Negro Population In The United States, 1790-1915* (New York: Arno Press, 1968), 57. In 1857 free Black men and women were also declared to be full citizens of the state of New Hampshire. Herbert Aptheker, ed., *A Documentary History of the Negro People in the United States* (New York: New Citadel Press, 1951), 10–12. See also Isaac W. Hammond, "Slavery in New Hampshire," *Magazine of American History*, 21 (1889), 62–65.

35 Zilversmit, *The First Emancipation*; James Oliver Horton and Lois E. Horton, *In Hope of Liberty: Culture, Community and Protest Among Northern Free Blacks, 1700-1860* (New York: Oxford University Press, 1997).

36 Ira Berlin, *Slaves Without Masters: The Free Negro in the Antebellum South* (New York: Pantheon Books, 1975); *Negro Population in the United States, 1790-1915* (New York: Arno Press, 1968).

37 Paul Finkelman, *An Imperfect Union* (Chapel Hill, NC: University of North Carolina Press, 1981), 80; "Removal to the South, 1818" quoted in Clement Alexander Price, *Freedom Not Far Distant: A Documentary History of Afro Americans in New Jersey* (Newark, NJ: New Jersey Historical Society, 1980), 85–86. For quotes, see Jacqueline Bernard, *Journey Toward Freedom: The Story of Sojourner Truth* (New York: The Feminist Press at The City University of New York, 1990), 71. Also see Bert James Loewenberg and Ruth Bogin, eds., *Black Women in Nineteenth-Century American Life* (University Park, PA: The Pennsylvania State University Press, 1976), 234–42; Harriet Beecher Stowe, "Sojourner Truth, The Libyan Sibyl," *Atlantic Monthly*, April 1863, 473–81.

38 Revolutionary War Pension Records, Cato Howe; James Deetz, *In Small Things Forgotten: The Archeology of Early American Life* (Garden City, NY: Anchor Doubleday, 1977).

CHAPTER 4

1 James Oliver Horton and Lois E. Horton, *In Hope of Liberty: Culture, Community and Protest Among Northern Free Blacks, 1700-1860* (New York: Oxford University Press, 1997), 69–70; Gary Nash, *Forging Freedom: The Formation of Philadelphia's Black Community, 1720-1840* (Cambridge, MA: Harvard University Press, 1988), 52.

2 Gary B. Nash, *Race and Revolution* (Madison, WI: Madison House, 1990), 6.

3 Nash, *Race and Revolution*; David P. Szatmary, *Shays' Rebellion: The Making of*

an Agrarian Insurrection (Amherst, MA: University of Massachusetts Press, 1980); Horton and Horton, *In Hope of Liberty*, 177. The African Americans' petition for funds to transport them to Africa was unsuccessful. In 1787 Shays's followers won control of the Massachusetts legislature and later secured a pardon for their leader.

4 Thomas Jefferson attempted to include the southwestern territories as part of the area in which slavery was outlawed, but his recommendation failed to be adopted by Congress by a single vote. Apparently the New Jersey congressman who would have voted for its inclusion missed the vote because of illness. Had slavery been prohibited from taking root in the southwest as well as the northwest, the course of American history during the nineteenth century and beyond might well have been considerably different. See Staughton Lynd, *Class, Conflict and Slavery, and the United States Constitution* (Indianapolis, IN: Bobbs-Merrill, 1967); Emma Lou Thornbrough, *The Negro in Indiana: A Study of a Minority* (Indianapolis, IN: Bobbs-Merrill, 1957); Paul Finkelman, "Slavery and the Northwest Ordinance: A Study in Ambiguity," *Journal of the Early Republic* 6 (Winter 1986), 343–70; Leon Litwack, *North of Slavery: The Negro in the Free States, 1790–1860* (Chicago: University of Chicago Press, 1961). Indiana's Black population increased from fewer than 300 in 1800 to 1,400 by 1820 to more than 11,000 by 1850. Ohio's Black population, numbering fewer than 400 in 1800, stood above 25,000 by mid-nineteenth century. *Negro Population in the United States, 1790–1915* (Washington, D.C.: Government Printing Office, 1918; New York: Arno Press, 1968), 45.

5 James Walvin, *An African's Life: The Life and Times of Olaudah Equiano, 1745–1797* (New York: Cassell, 1998).

6 Equiano's narrative style influenced the 19th century antislavery autobiographies of formerly enslaved people like Frederick Douglass. See the introduction by Henry Louis Gates, Jr. to *The Classic Slave Narratives* (New York: Penguin Books, 1987), xiii.

7 C.L.R. James, *The Black Jacobins* (London: Secker & Warburg, 1938; New York: Vintage Books, 1963); Donald R. Hickey, "America's Response to the Slave Revolt in Haiti, 1791–1806," *Journal of the Early Republic* 2 (Winter 1982), 361–79.

8 Shane White, *Somewhat More Independent: The End of Slavery in New York City, 1770–1810*

(Athens, GA: University of Georgia Press, 1991); Gary B. Nash and Jean R. Soderlund, *Freedom By Degrees: Emancipation in Pennsylvania and its Aftermath* (New York: Oxford University Press, 1991); Paul A. Gilje, *The Road to Mobocracy* (Chapel Hill, NC: University of North Carolina Press, 1987), 149. Philadelphia was the seat of the national government from 1790 to 1800, when Washington became the capital.

9 Douglas R. Egerton, "Gabriel's Conspiracy and the Election of 1800," *Journal of Southern History* 56 (May 1990): 191–214. See also Egerton's, *Gabriel's Rebellion: The Virginia Slave Conspiracies of 1800 & 1802* (Chapel Hill, NC: University of North Carolina Press, 1993). Egerton speculates that Gabriel favored the Democratic-Republicans in any struggle with the Federalists because he failed to appreciate that the Republican commitment to freedom and liberty did not apply to Black people. This interpretation seems suspect in light of the fact that in Philadelphia, New York, and even in the Upper South, Federalists were those who founded the antislavery societies of the late eighteenth century. If Gabriel was aware of the international tensions between the United States and France, it seems likely that he would have also been aware of the antislavery leanings of many Federalists in Philadelphia and Virginia. See also Gerald W. Mullin, *Flight and Rebellion: Slave Resistance in Eighteenth-Century Virginia* (New York: Oxford University Press, 1972) and Sterling Stuckey, *Slave Culture: Nationalist Theory and the Foundations of Black America* (New York: Oxford University Press, 2013).

10 Donald R. Wright, *African Americans in the Early Republic, 1789–1831* (Arlington Heights, IL: Harlan Davidson, Inc., 1993); Edward W. Phifer, "Slavery in Microcosm: Burke County, North Carolina," in *American Negro Slavery: A Modern Reader*, ed. Allan Weinstein and Frank Otto Gatell (New York: Oxford University Press, 1968), 74–97.

11 Richard B. Morris and Jeffrey B. Morris, eds., *Encyclopedia of American History* (New York: Harper & Row, 1976), 757, 759; Douglas C. North, *The Economic Growth of the United States, 1790–1860* (New York: W. W. Norton & Company, 1966), 75–76.

12 Ann Patton Malone, *Sweet Chariot: Slave Family and Household Structure in*

Nineteenth-Century Louisiana (Chapel Hill, NC: University of North Carolina Press, 1992), 52; Charles Duncan Rice, *The Rise and Fall of Black Slavery* (New York: Harper &Row, 1975), 286–7; Gavin Wright, *The Political Economy of the Cotton South: Households, Markets and Wealth in the Nineteenth Century* (New York: W. W. Norton & Company, Inc., 1978).

13 Sven Beckert and Seth Rockman, eds., *Slavery's Capitalism: A New History of American Economic Development* (Philadelphia: University of Pennsylvania Press, 2016), 14; Edward E. Baptist, "Toward a Political Economy of Slave Labor Hands: Whipping-Machines, and Modern Power," in *Slavery's Capitalism*, ed. Beckert and Rockman, 31–61, 48, 40. See also Edward E. Baptist, *The Half Has Never Been Told: Slavery and the Making of American Capitalism* (New York: Basic Books, 2014).

14 Lewis Clarke, *Narrative of the Sufferings of Lewis Clarke, during a Captivity of More than Twenty-Five Years among the Algerines of Kentucky* (Boston: D.H. Eli, 1845), 121; James Williams, *Narrative of James Williams, An American Slave, Who Was for Several Years a Driver on a Cotton Plantation in Alabama* (New York: American Anti-Slavery Society, 1838; Philadelphia: Historic Publications, 1969), 32; Benjamin Drew, ed., *A North-Side View of Slavery: The Refugee, or the Narratives of Fugitive Slaves in Canada Related by Themselves* (Boston: John P. Jewett, 1856; New York: Negro Universities Press, 1968), 178; Israel Campbell, *Bond and Free; or Yearnings for Freedom, from My Green Briar House; Being the Story of My Life in Bondage and My Life in Freedom* (Philadelphia: by the author, 1861), 18.

15 Michael Tadman, *Speculators and Slaves: Masters, Traders, and Slaves in the Old South* (Madison, WI: University of Wisconsin, 1989); Malone, *Sweet Chariot*, 15, 193.

16 Gary B. Nash, "Forging Freedom: The Emancipation Experience in the Northern Seaport Cities, 1775–1820," in *Slavery and Freedom in the Age of the American Revolution*, ed. Ira Berlin and Ronald Hoffman (Charlottesville, VA: published for the United States Capitol Historical Society by the University Press of Virginia, 1983), 3–48; Leonard P. Curry, *The Free Black in Urban America 1800–1850* (Chicago: University of Chicago Press, 1981), 244–8. In addition to these free Black people, Philadelphia still had about fifty enslaved people and New York City nearly three thousand in 1800.

17 Lamont D. Thomas, *Rise to Be a People: A Biography of Paul Cuffe* (Urbana, IL: University of Illinois Press, 1986).

18 Gary B. Nash, *Forging Freedom* (Cambridge: Harvard University Press, 1988); James B. Browning, "The Beginnings of Insurance Enterprise Among Negroes," *Journal of Negro History* 22, no. 4 (October 1937): 417–32; Robert L. Harris, Jr., "Early Black Benevolent Societies, 1780–1830," *The Massachusetts Review* 20, no. 3 (Autumn 1979): 603–25.

19 Harris, "Early Black Benevolent Societies"; James B. Browning, "The Beginnings of Insurance Enterprise Among Negroes," *Journal of Negro History* 22, no. 4 (October 1937): 417–32; "Colored Population of Philadelphia," *National Enquirer and Constitutional Advocate of Universal Liberty* I, no. 7 (October 22, 1836): 27.

20 James Oliver Horton and Lois E. Horton, *Black Bostonians* (New York: Holmes & Meier, 1979); C. Eric Lincoln and Lawrence H. Mamiya, *The Black Church in the African American Experience* (Durham, NC: Duke University Press, 1990); Edward Smith, *Climbing Jacob's Ladder: The Rise of Black Churches in Eastern American Cities 1740–1877* (Washington, D.C.: Smithsonian Institution Press, 1988).

21 Charles V. Hamilton, *The Black Preacher in America* (New York: William Morrow & Company, Inc., 1972); David E. Swift, *Black Prophets of Justice: Activist Clergy Before the Civil War* (Baton Rouge, LA: Louisiana State University Press, 1989).

22 Ira Berlin, *Slaves Without Masters: The Free Negro in the Antebellum South* (New York: Pantheon Books, 1974).

23 Berlin, *Slaves Without Masters*. Berlin argues that the role of free Black Americans differed from one region of the South to another and over time. Also see Horton and Horton, *In Hope of Liberty* for important distinctions between the roles of free Black people, especially people of mixed race, in the North and in the South.

24 Thomas, *Rise to Be a People*.

25 Philip S. Foner, *History of Black Americans* vol. 1 (Westport, CT: Greenwood Press, 1975), 485.

26 *New York Evening Post*, August 20, 1814, quoted in Shane White, *Somewhat More Independent* (Athens, GA.: University of Georgia Press, 1991), 150. Quoted in Foner, *History of Black Americans,* vol. 1, 486.

27 Foner, *History of Black Americans*, vol. 1, 487; William Cooper Nell, *Colored Patriots of the American Revolution* (Boston: Robert F. Wallcut, 1855; New York: Arno Press, 1968), 190–1. Sailors were commonly called tars.

28 W. Jeffrey Bolster, *Black Jacks: African American Seamen in the Age of Sail* (Cambridge, MA: Harvard University Press, 1997), 127; George Hugh Crichton, "Old Boston and Its Once Familiar Faces" unpublished, Boston, 1881.

29 Donald E. Everett, "Emigres and Militiamen: Free Persons of Color in New Orleans, 1803–1815," *Journal of Negro History* 38, no. 4 (October 1953): 377–402.

30 James Roberts, *The Narrative of James Roberts: Soldier in the Revolutionary War and at the Battle of New Orleans* (Chicago: printed for the author, 1858), 32; Arnett G. Lindsay, "Diplomatic Relations Between the United States and Great Britain Bearing on the Return of Negro Slaves, 1783–1828," *Journal of Negro History* 5 (October 1920), 391–419.

31 William S. McFeely, *Frederick Douglass* (New York: W. W. Norton & Company, Inc., 1991), 318.

CHAPTER 5

1 Peter Kolchin, *American Slavery, 1619–1877* (New York: Hill and Wang, 1993), 242; Solomon Northup, *Twelve Years a Slave* (Auburn, NY: Derby and Miller, 1853; ed. Sue Eakin and Joseph Logsdon, Baton Rouge, LA: Louisiana State University Press, 1968).

2 Walter M. Brasch, *Black English and the Mass Media* (Amherst, MA: University of Massachusetts Press, 1981); Charles Joyner, *Down by the Riverside: A South Carolina Slave Community* (Urbana, IL: University of Illinois Press, 1984).

3 Austin Steward, *Twenty-Two Years a Slave and Forty Years a Freeman* (Rochester, NY: W. Alling, 1857), 33–38. For a description of retribution taken against enslaved people in Virginia after the Nat Turner rebellion, see Harriet A. Jacobs, *Incidents in the Life of a Slave Girl, Written by Herself*, (ed. L. Maria Child,

Boston: published for the author, 1861; ed. Jean Fagan Yellin, Cambridge, MA: Harvard University Press, 1987).

4 William F. Cheek, *Black Resistance Before the Civil War* (Beverly Hills, CA: Glencoe Press, 1970), 99.

5 Norrece T. Jones Jr., *Born a Child of God Yet a Slave: Mechanisms of Control and Strategies of Resistance in Antebellum South Carolina* (Hanover, NH: University Press of New England, 1990).

6 Benjamin Drew, ed., *North-Side View of Slavery, the Refugee: or the Narrative of Fugitive Slaves in Canada. Related by Themselves* (Boston: John P. Jewett, 1856), 223.

7 Bernard E. Powers, *Black Charlestonians: A Social History, 1822–1885* (Fayetteville, AK: University of Arkansas Press, 1994), 31–33; Eric Foner, ed., *Nat Turner* (Englewood Cliffs, NJ: Prentice-Hall, Inc., 1971); Ira Berlin, *Slaves Without Masters: The Free Negro in the Antebellum South* (New York: Pantheon Books, 1974), 188–7, 195; Henry Irving Tragle, *The Southampton Slave Rebellion of 1831: A Compilation of Source Material* (Amherst, MA: University of Massachusetts Press, 1971).

8 John Hope Franklin, *The Militant South, 1800–1860* (Cambridge: Harvard University Press, 1956); Sterling Stuckey, *Slave Culture: Nationalist Theory and the Foundation of Black America* (New York: Oxford University Press, 1987); Eugene D. Genovese, *Roll, Jordan, Roll: The World the Slaves Made* (New York: Pantheon Books, 1974).

9 Bertram Wyatt-Brown, *Southern Honor: Ethics and Behavior in the Old South* (New York: Oxford University Press, 1982), 88, 366. Wyatt-Brown describes the violence in southern society but attributes it to cultural factors imported from ancient Ireland. Although he may be correct, slavery almost certainly necessitated its regular practice and helped to create the atmosphere in which this violence took on a racial dimension. Wyatt-Brown has interesting information comparing northern and southern crime rates generally and concludes that northern society's lower crime rate reflected its less violent culture. One might ask if the early abolition of slavery in the North—an institution which was never as widespread or as significant there as in the South—was not a major factor in this cultural difference.

10 Northup, *Twelve Years a Slave*.

11 Northup, *Twelve Years a Slave*, 61–69.

12 Northup, *Twelve Years a Slave*, 122–44.

13 Quoted in James Oliver Horton and Lois E. Horton, "Black Theology and Historical Necessity," in *Transforming Faith: The Sacred and Secular in Modern America*, ed. Miles L. Bradbury and James B. Gilbert (Westport, CT: Greenwood Press, 1989), 25–37, 28.

14 Melville J. Herskovits, *Dahomey* (New York: Augustin, 1938); Robert Farris Thompson, *The Four Moments of the Sun* (Washington, D.C.: National Gallery of Art, 1981). For an important interpretation of the ring shout and its significance as a link between West African culture and that of American Americans, see Stuckey, *Slave Culture*; James Lindsay Smith, *Autobiography of James Lindsay Smith* (Norwich, CT: Press of the Bulletin Co., 1881), 27.

15 Francis Fedric, *Slave Life in Virginia and Kentucky* (London: Wertheim, MacIntosh, and Hunt, 1863), 5.

16 Joyner, *Down by the Riverside*, quoted in Horton and Horton, "Black Theology and Historical Necessity," 29.

17 Northup, *Twelve Years a Slave*, 172.

18 Ann Patton Malone, *Sweet Chariot: Slave Family and Household Structure in Nineteenth-Century Louisiana* (Chapel Hill, NC: University of North Carolina Press, 1992). See also Herbert Gutman, *The Black Family in Slavery and Freedom* (New York: Pantheon Press, 1976) and Leslie Howard Owens, *This Species of Property: Slave Life and Culture in the Old South* (New York: Oxford University Press, 1976).

19 Owens, *This Species of Property*, 198.

20 Brenda Stevenson, "A Heroine's Heroine: Slave Women Choose" (paper presented at the Intercollegiate Department of Black Studies' Conference, Claremont Colleges, Claremont, California, January, 1994).

21 Gutman, *Black Family*, 191. Elizabeth's father and mother belonged to different owners, and before her father was moved to the West he was able to visit only twice a year.

22 Frederick Douglass, *The Life and Times of Frederick Douglass* (New York: Collier Books, 1962); James W.C. Pennington, *The Fugitive Blacksmith* in Arna Bontemps, ed., *Great Slave Narratives* (Boston: Beacon Press, 1969), 193–267, 207.

23 Jacobs, *Incidents in the Life of a Slave Girl*, 77.

24 Northup, *Twelve Years a Slave*, 151–2.

25 Northup, *Twelve Years a Slave*, 116, 123–5.

26 Ibid.

27 Frederick Law Olmsted, *The Slave States* (1856; reprinted revised and enlarged edition, New York: Capricorn Books, 1959), 203.

28 Edward E. Baptist, *The Half Has Never Been Told: Slavery and the Making of American Capitalism* (New York: Basic Books, 2014); Northup, *Twelve Years a Slave*, 125.

29 Joyner, *Down by the Riverside*, 23–24, 42. See also John Michael Vlach, *The Afro-American Tradition in Decorative Arts* (Athens, GA: University of Georgia Press, 1990).

30 John Brown, *Slave Life in Georgia: A Narrative of the Life, Suffering, and Escape of John Brown, A Fugitive Now in England* (London: W.M. Watts, 1855), 186–7; Joyner, *Down by the Riverside*. Joyner gives a detailed description of the task system and its advantages to enslaved people over the gang system used in cotton cultivation.

31 Charles Joyner, "The World of the Plantation," in *Before Freedom Came*, ed. Edward D.C. Campbell Jr. with Kim S. Rice (Charlottesville and Richmond, VA: University Press of Virginia and The Museum of the Confederacy, 1991), 51–99, 82; Frederick Law Olmsted, *The Slave States: Before the Civil War* (New York: Capricorn Books, 1959), 115; Lawrence W. Levine, *Black Culture and Black Consciousness: Afro-American Folk Thought From Slavery to Freedom* (New York: Oxford University Press, 1977), 5–19; Miles Mark Fisher, *Negro Slave Songs in the United States* (Ithaca, NY: published for the American Historical Association by the Cornell University Press, 1953; New York: Carol Publishing Group, 1990).

32 Northup, *Twelve Years a Slave*, 135–6.

33 Sylviane A. Diouf, *Slavery's Exiles: The Story of the American Maroons* (New York: New York University Press, 2014), 5, 209–10.

34 Henry Clay Bruce, *The New Man: Twenty-Nine Years a Slave, Twenty-Nine Years a Free Man. Recollections of H.C. Bruce* (York, PA: P. Anstadt and Sons, 1895).

35 Booker Taliaferro Washington, *Up From Slavery: An Autobiography* (Garden City, NY: Doubleday & Co., 1900; New York: Dell

Publishing Co. Inc., 1965), 26; James Oliver Horton, *Free People of Color: Inside the African American Community* (Washington, D.C.: Smithsonian Institution Press, 1993).

36 James Oliver Horton, "Links to Bondage," *Free People of Color* (Washington, D.C.: Smithsonian Press, 1993), 53–74.

CHAPTER 6

1 Just before the Civil War, the South Carolina legislature considered a provision that would have deprived all free Black Americans in the state of their freedom. See James Roark and Michael Johnson, *Black Masters: A Free Family of Color in the Old South* (New York: W. W. Norton & Company, Inc., 1984). Gary B. Nash, "Forging Freedom: The Emancipation Experience in the Northern Seaport Cities, 1775–1820," in *Slavery and Freedom in the Age of the American Revolution*, ed. Ira Berlin and Ronald Hoffman (Charlottesville, VA: University Press of Virginia, for the United States Capitol Historical Society, 1983): 3–48, quote 32–33.

2 David Walker, *David Walker's Appeal to the Coloured Citizens of the World* (1829), introduction by Sean Wilentz (New York: Hill and Wang, 1995), 21.

3 *Freedom's Journal,* March 16, 1827; Walker, *David Walker's Appeal;* Peter P. Hinks, *To Awaken My Afflicted Brethren: David Walker and the Problem of Antebellum Slave Resistance* (University Park, PA: Pennsylvania State University Press, 1997).

4 Henry Mayer, *All On Fire: William Lloyd Garrison and the Abolition of Slavery* (New York: St. Martin's Press, 1998), 101; *Liberator,* January 1, 1831.

5 James O. Horton and Lois Horton, *In Hope of Liberty; Culture, Community, and Protest Among Northern Free Blacks* (New York: Oxford University Press, 1997), 213, n. 1; James Oliver Horton and Lois E. Horton, *Black Bostonians: Family Life and Community Struggle in the Antebellum North* (New York: Holmes and Meier Publishers, 1979).

6 Donald M. Jacobs, "David Walker: Boston Race Leader, 1825–1830," *Essex Institute Historical Collection* 107 (January 1971), 94–107; Peter P. Hinks, *To Awaken My Afflicted Brethren* Philip S. Foner, *History of Black Americans,* vol. 2, (Westport, CN: Greenwood Press, 1983), 399, 401.

7 Richard S. Newman, *The Transformation of American Abolitionism: Fighting Slavery in the Early Republic* (Chapel Hill, NC: University of North Carolina Press, 2002), 152.

8 Horton and Horton, *In Hope of Liberty*, 244–5.

9 Horton and Horton, *In Hope of Liberty*, 102–3.

10 Horton and Horton, *In Hope of Liberty*, 208-223.

11 Howard Homan Bell, ed., *Minutes of the Proceedings of the National Negro Conventions 1830-1864* (New York: Arno Press and The New York Times, 1969). For an account of the Cincinnati race riot see Richard Wade, *The Urban Frontier: The Rise of Western Cities, 1790-1830* (Cambridge, MA: Harvard University Press, 1959), 222–9.

12 Horton and Horton, *In Hope of Liberty*, 193–6.

13 Horton and Horton, *In Hope of Liberty*, 262.

14 C. Peter Ripley, Roy E. Finkenbine, Michael F. Hembree and Donald Yacovone, eds., *The Black Abolitionist Papers: Canada, 1830–1865*, vol. 2 (Chapel Hill, NC: University of North Carolina Press, 1991), 109–12.

15 Dorothy Sterling, *Speak Out in Thunder Tones: Letters and Other Writings by Black Northerners 1787–1865* (New York: Da Capo Press, 1998); James Stewart, *William Lloyd Garrison and the Challenge of Emancipation* (Arlington Heights, IL: H. Davison Press, 1992). Formerly enslaved renowned abolitionist speaker Frederick Douglass promoted the manual-labor-school idea for Black Americans, both at conventions and in his newspapers during this later period. See Horton and Horton, *Black Bostonians*, 84.

16 Carlton Mabee, *Black Education in New York State* (Syracuse, NY: Syracuse University Press, 1979), 108–66; Ripley et al., eds., *The Black Abolitionist Papers*, vol. 3, 337n; Nat Brandt, *The Town that Started the Civil War* (Syracuse, NY: Syracuse University Press, 1990), 38.

17 "Report of the Condition of the People of Color in the State of Ohio," April 1835, reprinted in Aptheker, *Documentary History*, 157–8; Horton and Horton, *Black Bostonians*; James Oliver Horton, *Free People of Color: Inside the African American Community* (Washington, D.C.: Smithsonian Institution Press, 1993), 49–50; Christine Stansell, *City of Women* (New York: Alfred A. Knopf, 1982), 63–73; Barbara Meil Hobson, *Uneasy Virtue* (New York: Basic Books, 1987), 51–54.

18 *Colored American*, March 15, 1838.

19 Stewart, *Garrison*, 82; Ripley et al., eds., *The Black Abolitionist Papers*, vol. 3, 482; Horton and Horton, *In Hope of Liberty*, 243.

20 David W. Blight, *Frederick Douglass: Prophet of Freedom* (New York: Simon & Schuster, 2018).

21 Ibid. See also Frederick Douglass, *Narrative of the Life of Frederick Douglass,* edited by David W. Blight (New York: Bedford Books, 1993).

22 John G. Whittier, *Narrative of James Williams an American Slave* (New York: Isaac Knapp, 1838), 97–99.

23 Ibid.

24 Dorothy B. Parker, "David B. Ruggles, An Apostle for Human Freedom," *Journal of Negro History*, (January, 1943), 23–50.

25 Ripley et al., eds., *The Black Abolitionist Papers*, vol. 4, 184–5 n.

26 J.C. Furnas, *Goodby to Uncle Tom* (New York: William Sloane Associates, 1956), 214; Horton and Horton, *Black Bostonians*; Lois E. Horton, *Harriet Tubman and the Fight for Freedom: A Brief History with Documents* (Boston: Bedford/St. Martins, 2013).

27 Horton, *Harriet Tubman*, 27; "James G. Birney to Lewis Tappan, February 27, 1837," in Dwight L. Dumond, ed., *Letters of James Gillespie Birney*, vol. 2 (New York, D. Appleton-Century, 1938), 379; Levi Coffin, *Reminiscences of Levi Coffin* (Cincinnati: Robert Clarke, 1876), 106. Coffin was speaking specifically of Newport, Indiana, but it was also more generally true.

28 Calvin Fairbank, *During Slavery Times* (Chicago, R. R. McCabe 1890), 46–93.

29 Jonathan Walker, *Trial and Imprisonment of Jonathan Walker* (Boston: Anti-slavery Office, 1845; Gainesville: University Presses of Florida, 1974); John W. Blassingame, *The Frederick Douglass Papers 1841–1846*, vol. 1 (New Haven, CT: Yale University Press, 1979), 226.

30 William Jeffrey Bolster, *Black Jacks: African American Seamen in the Age of Sail* (Cambridge, MA: Harvard University Press, 1997); *Richmond Enquirer*, November 15,1850.

31 Horton, *Free People of Color*.

32 "Original Records of the Union Baptist Church, Cincinnati, Ohio, 1834," Cincinnati Historical Society.

33 Brandt, *The Town That Started The Civil War*, 212.

34 *Colored American*, December 9, 1837, September 9, 1837.

35 "Minutes of the National Convention of Colored Citizens, Held in Buffalo, 1843," *Minutes of the Proceedings of the National Negro Conventions, 1830–1864*, ed. Howard Holman Bell (New York: Arno Press and *The New York Times*, 1969), 7; Henry Highland Garnet, *Walker's Appeal, With a Brief Sketch of His Life, and Also Garnet's Address to the Slaves of the United States of America* (New York: J.H. Tobitt, 1848), 90–96.

36 "Minutes of the National Convention ... ," 23.

37 *Colored American*, April 18, 1840, August 29, 1840; "The Poor Man's Party," broadside dated October 17, 1846, Peterboro, NY, Cornell University Archives, Ithaca, NY.
In October 1845 Black Americans from western New York State held a meeting in Geneva, New York, to protest racial restrictions on voting. They alerted the state's Black residents to be ready to act if a convention was called to amend the state constitution. Among those attending were William Wells Brown and Samuel Ringold Ward. See *Ithaca Chronicle*, October 1, 1845. "Gift of Land and Money to Negroes" (undated names list) and "To Gerrit Smith Grantees" (broadside dated October 4, 1854), box 145, Gerrit Smith Papers, George Arents Research Library, Syracuse University, Syracuse, NY.

38 Ripley et al., *The Black Abolitionist Papers*, vol. 3, 409; Foner, *History of Black Americans*, vol. 2, 543; *National Anti-Slavery Standard*, October 15, 1846, 77.

CHAPTER 7

1 Quoted in James Oliver Horton and Lois E. Horton, *Black Bostonians: Family Life and Community Struggle in the Antebellum North*, rev. ed. (New York: Holmes and Meier, 1999), 102; "State Convention of Colored Citizens of Ohio, Columbus," in *Proceedings of the Black State Conventions, 1840–1865*, ed. Philip S. Foner and George W. Walker (Westport, CT: Greenwood Press, 1979), 229; *North Star*, February 9, 1849, quoted in Robert C. Dick, *Black Protest: Issues and Tactics* (Westport, CT: Greenwood Press, 1974), 138.

2 Fillmore is not known for antislavery sentiments, but his past indicated that he had some sympathy for fugitives. When Fillmore was a lawyer in Buffalo during the 1830s, according to William Wells Brown, he served

without charge as defense counsel for a fugitive from slavery. William E. Farrison, "William Wells Brown in Buffalo," *Journal of Negro History* 39, no. 4 (October 1954), 298–314.

3 William Loren Katz, *Eyewitness: The Negro in American History,* 3rd ed. (Belmont, CA: Fearon Pitman Publishers, 1974), 189; James Oliver Horton and Lois E. Horton, "A Federal Assault: African Americans and the Impact of the Fugitive Slave Act of 1850," *Chicago-Kent Law Review* 68, no. 3 (Fall, 1993), 1179–97; Carol Wilson, *Freedom at Risk: The Kidnapping of Free Blacks in America, 1780–1865* (Lexington, KY: University Press of Kentucky, 1994). See also R.J.M. Blackett, *The Captive's Quest for Freedom: Fugitive Slaves, the 1850 Fugitive Slave Act and the Politics of Slavery* (Cambridge, UK: Cambridge University Press, 2018).

4 Olivia Mahoney, "Black Abolitionist," *Chicago History* 20, nos. 1–2 (1991): 22–37; *Liberator,* October 18, 1850, October 25, 1850; Foner and Walker, eds., *Proceedings,* 318; Horton and Horton, *Black Bostonians,* 130–1.

5 Lois E. Horton, "Kidnapping and Resistance: Antislavery Direct Action in the 1850s," in *Passages to Freedom: The Underground Railroad in History and Memory,* ed. David W. Blight (Washington, D.C.: Smithsonian Books, 2004), 149–73; Fred Landon, "The Negro Migration to Canada After the Passing of the Fugitive Slave Act," *Journal of Negro History* 5, no. 1 (January, 1920), 22–36; *Liberator,* October 4, 1850; *Pennsylvania Telegraph,* October 2, 1850; Horton and Horton, *Black Bostonians,* 112; *Liberator,* December 13, 1850; Michael F. Hembree, "The Question of 'Begging': Fugitive Slave Relief in Canada, 1830-1865," *Civil War History* 37, no. 4 (Dec., 1991), 314–27, 315. See also, Mechal Sobel, *Trabelin' On: The Slave Journey to an Afro-Baptist Faith* (Princeton, NJ: Princeton University Press, 1988), 216; *Liberator,* April 25, 1851; James K. Lewis, "Religious Nature of the Early Negro Migration to Canada and the Amherstburg Baptist Association," *Ontario History* 58 (1966), 117–32.

6 "Slave-Hunters in Boston," *Liberator,* November 1, 1850.

7 For a more complete account of the Crafts in Boston see Horton and Horton, *Black Bostonians,* 112–13.

8 Gary Collison, *Shadrach Minkins: From Fugitive Slave to Citizen* (Cambridge, MA: Harvard University Press, 1997); Foner, *History of Black Americans,* vol. 3, 35–36.

9 Foner, *History of Black Americans,* vol. 3, 35–36; Thomas P. Slaughter, *Bloody Dawn: The Christiana Riot and Racial Violence in the Antebellum North* (New York: Oxford University Press, 1991); Horton and Horton, *Black Bostonians,* 120–3; Albert J. Von Frank, *The Trials of Anthony Burns: Freedom and Slavery in Emerson's Boston* (Cambridge, MA: Harvard University Press, 1998).

10 Yanuck, "The Garner Fugitive Slave Case"; Weisenburger, *Modern Medea.*

11 Philip S. Foner, ed., *The Life and Writings of Frederick Douglass,* vol. 4 (New York: International Publishers, 1950), 227.

12 Donald E. Liedel, "The Antislavery Publishing Revolution in the 1850s," *Library Journal* 2 (1972), 67–80.

13 C. Peter Ripley, Roy E. Finkenbine, Michael F. Hembree, and Donald Yacovone, eds., *The Black Abolitionist Papers,* vol. 4, (Chapel Hill: University of North Carolina Press, 1991), 144; James M. McPherson, *Battle Cry of Freedom: The Civil War Era* (New York: Oxford University Press, 1988), 90.

14 Eugene D. Genovese, *The Slaveholders Dilemma* (Columbia, SC: University of South Carolina Press, 1992); Merton L. Dillon, *The Abolitionists: The Growth of a Dissenting Minority* (DeKalb, IL: Northern Illinois University Press, 1974), 86.

15 *Frederick Douglass' Paper,* May 26, 1854.

16 Benjamin Quarles, *Allies for Freedom: Blacks and John Brown* (New York: Oxford University Press, 1974), 32–36.

17 Eric Foner, *Free Labor, Free Soil, Free Men* (New York: Oxford University Press, 1970); Frederick Douglass, "The Unholy Alliance of Negro Hate and Anti-slavery," *Frederick Douglass' Paper,* April 5, 1856.

18 David R. Roediger, *The Wages of Whiteness: Race and the Making of the American Working Class* (New York: Verso, 1991); Eric Lott, *Love and Theft: Blackface Minstrelsy and the American Working Class* (New York: Oxford University Press, 1993).

19 Benjamin Quarles, *Black Abolitionists* (New York: Oxford University Press, 1969), 189; *Liberator,* September 5, 1856, October 1, 1858.

20 Quoted in Foner, *History of Black Americans,* vol. 3, 213; Foner, *Life and Writings of Frederick Douglass,* vol. 2 , 406.

Millard Fillmore, former president, ran on the nativist American Party (Know-Nothing) ticket and got just under nine hundred thousand votes.

21 *Dred Scott v. Sanford* (1857), 19 Howard, 393.

22 Leon F. Litwack, *North of Slavery: The Negro in the Free States, 1790-1860* (Chicago: University of Chicago Press, 1961), 57.

23 Wilson Jeremiah Moses, *The Golden Age of Black Nationalism. 1850-1925* (New York: Oxford University Press, 1978).

24 *Douglass' Paper*, September 7, 1855; *Liberator*, November 27, 1857, August 13, 1858; "Proceedings of the State Convention of Colored Men of the State of Ohio, Held in the City of Columbus, January 21st, 22d & 23d, 1857," in Foner and Walker, *Proceedings*, vol. 1, 320; Ripley, Finkenbine, Hembree, and Yacovone, eds., *Black Abolitionist Papers*, vol. 4, 319.

25 *Liberator*, November 11, 1959.

26 Horton, *Harriet Tubman*; Benjamin Quarles, *Allies for Freedom: Blacks and John Brown*, (New York: Oxford University Press, 1974), 86–87; Quoted in James Oliver Horton and Lois E. Horton, *Slavery and the Making of America* (New York: Oxford University Press, 2005), 165.

27 William S. McFeely, *Frederick Douglass* (New York: W. W. Norton & Company, 1991), 198–203; Quarles, *Allies for Freedom*. After the raid Harriet Newby was sold to a Louisiana slave dealer.

28 *Weekly Anglo-African*, December, 1859; *Liberator*, December, 9, 1859; Benjamin Quarles, ed., *Blacks on John Brown* (Urbana, IL: University of Illinois Press, 1972), 20–21.

29 *Liberator*, March 12, 1858; Broadside, signed by Harvey C. Jackson, Simcoe, Canada West, December 7,1859, in Boyd B. Stutler Collection of the John Brown Papers, MSS 42, Roll 5, Ohio Historical Society; *Weekly Anglo-African*, December, 31, 1859.

30 Quoted in Foner, *History of Black Americans*, vol. 3, 270–1.

31 *Liberator*, January 27, 1860, quoted in James M. McPherson, *The Negro's Civil War: How American Negroes Felt and Acted During the War for the Union* (New York: Vintage Books, 1965), 5, 10; *Anglo-African*, February 4, 1860; *Liberator*, October 19, 1860.

32 Hondon B. Hargrove, *Black Union Soldiers in the Civil War* (Jefferson, NC: McFarland & Co., Inc., Publishers, 1988).

33 Quoted in McPherson, *Negro's Civil War*, 163; *New York Tribune*, February 12, 1862; *Douglass' Monthly*, September 1861.

34 Quoted in McPherson, *Negro's Civil War*, 11, 17–18. See also James O. Horton, "'Making Free': African Americans and the Civil War," in Frances H. Kennedy, ed., *The Civil War Battlefield Guide* (Boston: Houghton Mifflin Co., 1990), 261–3.

35 Horton and Horton, *Slavery and the Making of America*, 175–6; *Pine and Palm*, May 25, 1861, also quoted in McPherson, *Negro's Civil War*, 29.

36 Quoted in McPherson, *Negro's Civil War*, 166–7.

37 R.J.M. Blackett, ed., *Thomas Morris Chester: Black Civil War Correspondent* (Baton Rouge, LA: Louisiana State University Press, 1989); Mitch Kachun, *Festivals of Freedom: Memory and Meaning in African American Emancipation Celebrations, 1808-1915* (Amherst, MA: University of Massachusetts Press, 2003). Other freedom days included Emancipation Day on August 1, commemorating the abolition of slavery in the British Empire in 1834 and celebrated by northern Black communities, and January 1, commemorating the 1863 Emancipation Proclamation. Legally, slavery was abolished in the United States by the ratification of the Thirteenth Amendment to the Constitution on December 6, 1865.

38 Quoted in McPherson, *Negro's Civil War*, 168; *New York Tribune*, March 28, 1863; James M. McPherson, *What They Fought For, 1861-1865* (Baton Rouge, LA: Louisiana State University Press, 1994), 66–67.

39 Blackett, *Thomas Morris Chester*, 33–38. Only when Harrisburg, Pennsylvania, faced Confederate invasion were Black defenders considered. They were quickly rejected after the threat receded.

40 McPherson, *Negro's Civil War*, 178–9.

41 Although in 1864 Congress authorized equal pay for Black men who had been free before the war, until March 1865 it did not include those who had been enslaved at the time of enlistment. At that time, equal pay was made retroactive to their date of enlistment. Ira Berlin, Joseph P. Reidy and Leslie S. Rowland, *Freedom: A Documentary History of Emancipation, 1861-1867* (Cambridge, UK: Cambridge University Press, 1982), series 2, 363, 367–8, 365–6; Virginia M. Adams, ed.,

On the Altar of Freedom: A Black Soldier's Civil War Letters From the Front (Amherst, MA: University of Massachusetts Press, 1991), 83; McPherson, *Negro's Civil War*, 199.

42 Horton, *Harriet Tubman*; Suzie King Taylor, *Reminiscences of My Life in Camp With the 33D United States Colored Troops Late First S.C. Volunteers* (Boston: published by the author, 1902).

43 Joseph T. Glatthaar, *Forged in Battle: The Civil War Alliance of Black Soldiers and White Officers* (New York: Free Press, 1990), 91.

44 Foner, *History of Black Americans*, vol. 3, 374.

45 Ibid, 375; Harriet Tubman, interview by Albert Bushnell Hart, in *Slavery and Abolition, 1831–1841* (New York: Harper & Brothers, 1906), 209.

46 Foner, *History of Black Americans*, vol. 3, 376.

CHAPTER 8

1 R.J.M. Blackett, ed., *Thomas Morris Chester: Black Civil War Correspondent,* (Baton Rouge, LA: Louisiana State University Press, 1989), 5, 10–12.

2 Blackett, *Thomas Morris Chester*, 41.

3 Jack Hurst, *Nathan Bedford Forrest: A Biography* (New York: Alfred A. Knopf, 1993), 172–8, 186; Blackett, *Thomas Morris Chester*, 125.

4 James M. McPherson, *What They Fought For, 1861–1865* (Baton Rouge, LA: Louisiana State University Press, 1994), 67; James M. McPherson, *For Cause and Comrades: Why Men Fought in the Civil War* (New York: Oxford University Press, 1997), 138. Some wives of U.S. troops also sent letters asking their men to return home.

5 McPherson, *For Cause & Comrades*, 172; Ira Berlin, Joseph P. Reidy, and Leslie S. Rowland, eds., *Freedom: A Documentary History of Emancipation, 1861–1867* (New York: Cambridge University Press, 1982), 295; Bruce Levine, "In Search of a Usable Past: Neo-Confederates and Black Confederates," in *Slavery and Public History: The Tough Stuff of American Memory*, ed. James Oliver Horton and Lois E. Horton (New York: The New Press, 2006), 187–211. See also Bruce Levine, *Confederate Emancipation: Southern Plans to Free and Arm Slaves During the Civil War* (New York: Oxford University Press, 2005).

6 *Liberator*, April 7, 1865; Benjamin Quarles, *The Negro in the Civil War* (Boston: Little, Brown and Co., 1969), p. 331; Leon Litwack, *Been in the Storm So Long: The Aftermath of Slavery* (New York: Alfred A. Knopf, 1979), 167–8.

7 David W. Blight, *Race and Reunion: The Civil War in American* Memory (Cambridge, MA: Harvard University Press, 2001), 64; Litwack, *Been in the Storm So Long*, 168–9; Virginia M. Adams, ed., *On the Altar of Freedom: A Black Soldier's Civil War Letters From the Front* (Amherst: University of Massachusetts Press, 1991), 18–19; Mark E. Neely, Jr., *The Last Best Hope on Earth: Abraham Lincoln and the Promise of America* (Springfield, IL: Illinois State Historical Library, 1993).

8 James M. McPherson, *Battle Cry of Freedom: The Civil War Era* (New York: Oxford University Press, 1988), 852.

9 *Rochester Democrat*, April, 17, 1865; Noah Andre Trudeau, *Like Men of War: Black Troops in the Civil War, 1862–1865* (Boston: Little, Brown, 1998), 434. Secretary of State William H. Seward was also attacked and wounded by a knife-wielding conspirator. Booth died during his capture, and subsequently eight conspirators were tried and convicted, four of whom were hanged and four imprisoned.

10 Eric Foner, *Reconstruction: America's Unfinished Revolution, 1863–1877* (New York: Harper & Row, 1989), 49.

11 Willie Lee Rose, *Rehearsal for Reconstruction* (New York: Random House, 1964).

12 Litwack, *Been in the Storm So Long*, 485.

13 Foner, *Reconstruction*.

14 Litwack, *Been in the Storm So Long*, 232.

15 Dorothy Sterling, ed., *Speak Out in Thunder Tones: Letters and Other Writings by Black Northerners, 1787–1865* (Garden City, NY: Doubleday, 1973), 363.

16 Litwack, *Been in the Storm So Long*, 401, 402; Foner, *Reconstruction*, 104; Whitelaw Reid, *After the War: A Tour of the Southern States, 1865–66* (1866; reprint, New York: Harper & Row, 1965), 564–5, quoted in William H. Harris, *The Harder We Run* (New York: Oxford University Press, 1982), 9.

17 Litwack, *Been in the Storm So Long*, 402; "The Mississippi Black Codes (1865)," in *The Civil War and Reconstruction: A Documentary*

Collection, ed. William E. Gienapp (New York: W. W. Norton, 2001), 325–7; Foner, *Reconstruction*.

18 The oldest Black college in the United States was founded in the North in 1854. Ashmun Institute in Pennsylvania, begun by Presbyterians, was renamed Lincoln University after the Civil War.

19 W.E.B. DuBois, *Black Reconstruction in America, 1860–1880* (New York: Atheneum, 1973), 389–9.

20 Philip S. Foner, ed., *The Life and Writings of Frederick Douglass*, vol. 4 (New York: International Publishers, 1955), 46.

21 Du Bois, *Black Reconstruction*, 399.

22 Thomas Holt, *Black Over White: Negro Political Leadership in South Carolina during Reconstruction* (Urbana, IL: University of Illinois Press, 1977), 34–35; *Loyal Georgian*, July 6, 1867, cited in Litwack, *Been in the Storm So Long*, 547; Noralee Frankel, *Freedom's Women: African American Women and Family in Civil War Era Mississippi* (Bloomington, IN: Indiana University Press, 1999); Holt, *Black Over White*, 35.

23 Litwack, *Been in the Storm So Long*, 252.

24 Holt, *Black Over White*, 448; Steven Mintz, ed., *African American Voices: The Life Cycle of Slavery* (St. James, NY: Brandywine Books, 1993), 170.

25 Mintz, *African American* Voices, 166; Ira Berlin, ed., *Freedom: A Documentary History of Emancipation, 1861–1867* (Cambridge, MA: Cambridge University Press, 1982), 754–5; Litwack, *Been in the Storm So Long*, 486.

26 Mintz, *African American Voices*, 169.

27 Du Bois, *Black Reconstruction*, 686, 687.

28 Hurst, *Nathan Bedford Forrest*; Foner, *Reconstruction*.

29 George C. Wright, *Racial Violence in Kentucky, 1865–1940* (Baton Rouge, LA:

Louisiana State University Press, 1990); Litwack, *Been in the Storm So Long*, 269.

30 See, for example, David M. Chalmers, *Hooded Americanism: The History of the Ku Klux Klan* (New York: New Viewpoints, 1981), 13–21; James Oliver Horton and Lois E. Horton, *Slavery and the Making of* America (New York: Oxford University Press, 2005), 217–19.

31 Howard Zinn, *A Peoples History of the United States*, rev. ed. (New York: Harper Perennial, 1995), 199; Wright, *Racial Violence in Kentucky*, 162.

32 Foner, *Reconstruction*, 532. For the Supreme Court cases from the *Slaughter-House Cases* in 1873 to the *Civil Rights Cases* in 1883, see A. Leon Higginbotham, Jr., *Shades of Freedom: Racial Politics and Presumptions of the American Legal Process* (New York: Oxford University Press, 1996).

33 Foner, *Reconstruction*, 599; Edwin S. Redkey, *Black Exodus: Black Nationalist and Back-to-Africa Movements, 1890–1910* (New Haven, CT: Yale University Press, 1969).

34 Franklin, *From Slavery to Freedom*, 278; Henry King, "A Year of the Exodus in Kansas," *Scribner's Monthly*, 8 (June, 1880), 211–15; William Loren Katz, *The Black West: A Documentary and Pictorial History of the African American Westward Expansion of the United States* (New York: Simon & Schuster, 1996); Nell Irvin Painter, *Exodusters: Black Migration to Kansas after Reconstruction* (New York: W. W. Norton, 1976).

35 Painter, *Exodusters*.

36 Philip Durham and Everett L. Jones, *The Negro Cowboys* (Lincoln: University of Nebraska Press, 1965), 173–4.

37 Leslie H. Fishel and Benjamin Quarles, eds., *The Black American: A Documentary History* (Glenview, IL: Scott, Foresman, 1970), 339. See the *Slaughter-House Cases* (1873) and *United States v. Cruikshank* (1876). In 1883 the Supreme Court struck down the Civil Rights Act of 1875.

Credits

Chapter One

- **Chapter One CO Photo:** AP Photo
- **Photo 1.4:** The Metropolitan Museum of Art, Gift of Ernst Anspach, 1999.

Chapter Two

- **Chapter Two CO Photo:** Benjamin Henry Latrobe, Sketchbook, III, 33, Maryland Historical Society, Baltimore
- **Photo 2.2:** Courtesy the Rhode Island Historical Society

Chapter Three

- **Photo 3.1:** The Gilder Lehrman Institute of American History. Collection #: GLC04205.01
- **Photo 3.4:** Everett Collection/Bridgeman Images

Chapter Four

- **Photo 4.1:** Bridgeman Images
- **Photo 4.2:** Science History Images/Alamy Stock Photo
- **Photo 4.3:** Alamy Stock Photo

Chapter Five

- **Photo 5.4:** Saring Images/GRANGER
- **Photo 5.6:** Saring Images/GRANGER
- **Photo 5.8:** Shawshots/Alamy Stock Photo
- **Photo 5.9:** Collection of the Smithsonian National Museum of African American History and Culture
- **Photo 5.10:** Bridgeman Images

Chapter Six

- **Chapter Six CO Photo:** Bequest of Martha C. Karolik for the M. and M. Karolik Collection of American Paintings, 1815–1865
- **Photo 6.2:** Sarin Images/GRANGER
- **Photo 6.3:** Science History Images/Alamy Stock Photo
- **Photo 6.5:** Albert Cook Myers Collection, Chester County Historical Society

Chapter Seven

- **Photo 7.6:** Fotosearch/Getty Images

Chapter Eight

- **Photo 8.8:** Saring Images/GRANGER

Index

A

Abolitionism. *See also* Emancipation; *specific person or organization*
building antislavery movement, 153–157
emergence of, 144–147
Garrisonians, 146–147
growth of, 177–181
integrated abolitionism, 147–149, 155
militant abolitionism, 164–168
National Black Convention, 149–153, 171
pacifism and, 164–165
political power and, 164–168
violence and, 171–172
Abram (slave), 126
Acrelius, Israel, 37
Adams, Abigail, 68
Adams, Henry, 220–221
Adams, John, 67–68
Adams, John Quincy, 121*b*, 148
Adams, Samuel, 65, 67
Africa
Christianity in, 4–5
colonization of African Americans in, 108–109, 111–114
cultural variation in, 12
dance in, 8
geography of, xiv*f*, 4
history of, 3–10
Islam in, 4–6
music in, 8
religion in, 7–8
science in, 7
West African Kingdoms, 7*f*
African American Methodist Episcopal Church, 220
African Americans. *See specific topic*
African Baptist Church (Boston), 106–107
African Benevolent Society (Newport), 105
African Church (Philadelphia), 106
African Civilization Society, 182
African Episcopal Church of St. Thomas (Philadelphia), 106
African Institutions, 112
African Lodge Number One of Boston, 105
African Marine Fund (New York), 105

African Masonic Lodge (Boston), 153
African Meeting House (Boston), 107, 147
African Methodist Episcopal Church, 214*b*
African Methodist Episcopal Zion Church (New Bedford), 156
African Society (Boston), 104–106, 153
African Union Society (Newport), 104
Aiken County, South Carolina, 218
Alabama
African American political power during Reconstruction, 211
brutality of slavery in, 136
cotton and, 99–101
internal slave trade in, 81
secession of, 185
as slave State, 98
Albany, New York, 174
Alcorn Agricultural and Mining College, 214*b*
Alexander, "Pop," 162*f*
Alexandria, Virginia, 100
Allen, Ethan, 74
Allen, Richard, 104, 106, 112, 152
American Anti-Slavery Society, 154*f*, 155–156, 159
American Colonization Society, 112–113, 121*b*, 149–150, 182, 199
American Masonic Order, 105
American Moral Reform Society, 154
American Revolution
banditti, 71
Black soldiers in, 72–76
Boston Massacre and, 65–68, 66*f*
Bunker Hill, Battle of, 69
Committees of Correspondence, 68
Concord, Battle of, 69
Continental Army, 69, 74
Continental Congress, 69
Ethiopian Regiment, 72
guerrilla warfare in, 71
impressment and, 64
"Intolerable Acts" and, 68
Lake Champlain, Battle of, 76
Lexington, Battle of, 69
Loyalists, 71, 77

Minutemen, 69
participation by Blacks in, 68–69, 71
slavery, hypocrisy regarding, 68–69
Stamp Act and, 65
taxes and, 64–65
Trenton, Battle of, 76
Yorktown, Battle of, 56*f*, 75*f*
American Society of Free Persons of Color, 149
Amistad (slave ship), 148, 148*f*
Anderson, Osborne, 183
Andrew, John A., 190
Anglican Church, 35, 61
Anglo-African, 207
Angola, 10, 18, 32*b*
Anthony, Jack, 74
Antietam, Battle of, 188
Appomattox Court House, Virginia, 203
Arizona, migration of African Americans to, 221
Arkansas
cotton and, 99
secession of, 186
as slave State, 98
Armistead, James, 74, 75*f*
Army of the Potomac, 188
Ashante (historical African nation), 10
Atlanta, Georgia, 202
Atlantic slave trade. *See also specific country*
in Caribbean, 16–18, 21, 23
Caribbean and, 33–34
children in, 16, 22
conditions of, 13–16
under Constitution, 88
Constitutional prohibition of, 88, 99, 117
gold and, 21
growth of, 16–18, 20–23, 25
historical background, 10–12
Islam and, 9, 11–12
Middle Passage, 13–16
plantations and, 8, 16–18, 21–23
routes, 18*f*, 24*f*
rum and, 43
seasoning, 29
slave ships, 13–16, 15*f*, 20–21, 70*b*
statistics on, 21–23, 25
sugar and, 16–18, 21–23, 43
Triangular Trade, 42*f*, 43
women in, 16, 22

311